WONDERFUL AND BROKEN

WONDERFUL AND BROKEN

The Complex Reality of Primary Care in the United States

TROYEN A. BRENNAN

JOHNS HOPKINS UNIVERSITY PRESS

© 2025 Johns Hopkins University Press
All rights reserved. Published 2025
Printed in the United States of America on acid-free paper

2 4 6 8 9 7 5 3 1

Johns Hopkins University Press
2715 North Charles Street
Baltimore, Maryland 21218
www.press.jhu.edu

Library of Congress Cataloging-in-Publication Data is available.

A catalog record for this book is available from the British Library.

ISBN 978-1-4214-5219-7 (hardcover)
ISBN 978-1-4214-5220-3 (ebook)

Special discounts are available for bulk purchases of this book. For more information, please contact Special Sales at specialsales@jh.edu.

EU GPSR Authorized Representative
LOGOS EUROPE, 9 rue Nicolas Poussin, 17000, La Rochelle, France
E-mail: Contact@logoseurope.eu

CONTENTS

Preface   vii

1. The Somewhat Recent History of Primary Care   1
2. Signs of a New Deal for Primary Care?   44
3. What Can the Federal Government Do to Promote Primary Care?   91
4. The States' Role in Primary Care Reform   140
5. State-Based Health Insurers' Role in Primary Care   188
6. The National Health Insurers (and Other Corporations)   232
7. The Role of Private Equity   292
8. The Future of Primary Care   343

Notes   397
Index   437

PREFACE

This is a book about the current and potential role of primary care in American health care. Most of my research comes from several years of interviewing primary care clinicians about the profoundly human endeavor of their care for patients. But my lens has been, as in most of my writing, the financial structure of the health care system. Indeed, I find today's primary care to be inextricably entangled with our systems of financing care, and I hope for much better primary care in the future. The case can be succinctly stated.

Health care in the United States has traditionally operated on a simple financial chassis known as fee-for-service. In this system, doctors and hospitals offered their services to patients who paid for each service offered. The profit motive influenced the providers of care to do more—that is, offer more services—to get paid more. The patient's lack of knowledge about the intricacies of medical treatment meant that there was little consumer oversight of value.

The fee-for-service incentives were greatly enhanced and facilitated by the introduction of health insurance. With a distant third party paying for the costs of care, the key first two parties—providers and patients—did not have to be concerned about overutilization and total costs of care. Add to this mix the availability of new technology that could support both diagnostic and therapeutic procedures, as well as an increasingly deep specialization by physicians, and one has the modern American health care system. It is a system that thrives on wasteful but lucrative care, with little focus on population health, preventive care, or cost. As a result, we pay much more for care than other similar economies and have far worse outcomes.[1]

Fee-for-service dominates American medicine today. Yet there has always been an alternative. *Prospective payment* for care—paying a set amount for each person based on their risk of disease—has historically been the stalking horse of retrospective fee-for-service. For more than a hundred years, some clinical organizations have accepted prospective payment for their patients, then cared for them under incentives that are directly opposite those of fee-for-service: doing less and keeping the patient healthy to avoid costs. Best known as health maintenance organizations, these entities have persisted, exemplified by the Kaiser Permanente system.

For many years, the process of scrutinizing patients' needs, promoting health, and avoiding unnecessary care was known as *managing care*. The concept of managing care began to gain negative connotations in the 1990s, with fears and then lawsuits that suggested that doctors operating in a managed care environment might have incentives to undertreat patients and ration care. Professionalism was intended as the antidote to this concern; providers would be just as committed to the patient's well-being in managed care as they would be in fee-for-service. But fear of undertreatment was greater than fear of overtreatment.

As a result, those concerned about the corrosion of fee-for-service had to find an alternative. Over the past nearly twenty years, value-based care has emerged as that alternative. It emphasizes rendering cost-effective services and avoiding less-than-valuable services, services that might nonetheless be lucrative under fee-for-service. Today, reformers call for value-based care when they are trying to move from pure fee-for-service. The concept is so broad that all key constituencies can endorse it: doctors, hospitals, insurance companies, and the government. This is not to say, however, that mere exhortation is having any real impact.

The concept of value-based payment can thus encompass a return to prospective payment, where provision of value-based care, and only value-based care, leads to better outcomes and lower costs. Underlying this concept is *capitation*, a payment that is based on each head/patient. The provider accepts the prospective, capitated payment for the patient and assumes the risk for the costs of care. The provider must be prepared to avoid unnecessary care, and to prevent illness to the greatest extent possible. The incentives are aligned to maintaining better health for the patient.

Such a capitation program requires a few other key provisions. First, the individual patient must be "attributed" to an organization that can take responsibility for arranging the value-based care. Second, the costs of care for that patient must be calculated in advance. Not all patients are created equal: some are sick, others are not. The sicker patient's capitation payment must be higher, adjusted according to their risk. Capitation-centered value-based care requires a complicated infrastructure for both the payers and the providers. But if it eliminates the estimated 20% to 30% of care that is not value based under fee-for-service, then that infrastructure is well worth the cost.

The salvation from fee-for-service excesses promised by value-based care that involves risk for providers is what brings primary care to the front of the health policy stage today. The attribution of a patient fits naturally with the assignment of a patient to a primary care clinician. The ongoing effort to ensure that all care is value-based is possible through a continuous relationship between a patient and her primary care clinician. Good primary care fits hand in glove with prospective payment that relies on value-based care.

The American Academy of Family Physicians states that "primary care is the provision of integrated, accessible health care services by physicians and their health care teams who are accountable for addressing a large majority of personal health care needs, developing a sustained partnership with patients, and practicing in the context of family and community."[2] I think this definition resonates with most people, as a primary care clinician is the person they go to first for a variety of complaints when they are sick. They also expect to have a long-term relationship with this doctor, who knows that individual's medical history. A primary care clinician is a person's point of access to the health care system, the coordinator of care when things get complicated, and a trusted, longtime advisor. Unlike other relationships in our health care system, this one is meant to be continuous, not episodic.

This hand-in-glove relationship between value-based risk and primary care is not new. The original health maintenance organizations were all primary care based, as is the Kaiser Permanente system today. The phenomenon of primary care doctors organized to take capitation payment and full risk for a patient's health care (and its costs) is prevalent in some parts of the country, especially Southern California. In that value-based care is today the only vehicle that most health policy-makers consider to be the alternative to our fractured fee-for-service system, it is not surprising that primary care is at the center of reform. When asked, "Where do we turn for a better health care system?" no policy analyst will respond, "hospitals," or "surgeons," or "insurers." Rather, it is to a primary care–based system that is founded on value-based care.

Primary care envisioned as the salvation for an inefficient and poor performing health care system features long-term continuity between the primary care clinician and the patient, as the clinician guides the patient through care, especially chronic care. The clinician is not isolated but surrounded by and supported by a team of individuals—nurses, care coordinators, and pharmacists—who all have relationships with the patient. The resources required are significant, but they pay off in terms of prevented illnesses, unnecessary visits to the emergency department, or hospitalizations.

This support for the patient through a well-resourced team and emphasis on proactive care is what distinguishes the 2020s value-based primary care from the 1990s managed care. Over that 30-year span, the primary care clinician was often referred to as the "gatekeeper," meaning that she decided what care was necessary. The connotation was rationing through blocking, and many lawsuits sounded in that context. There is no need to block care in value-based primary care; rather, one avoids care that does not have value. The shift here is subtle but real. It follows from the insight that much of what our current health care system produces is worthless for patients, the result of the profit incentive in fee-for-service.

The promise of a health care system based on value through primary care is exciting. But it remains a promise, and the biggest question in health policy as we move into the mid-2020s is, Can primary care deliver? Research says it can. Experts from many countries have long agreed that primary care is vital to the integrity of any health care system. The National Academies of Science, Engineering, and Medicine (NASEM), formerly the Institute of Medicine, in its comprehensive 1996 report on the future of primary care, stated that "primary care is the logical foundation of an effective health care system, because primary care can address the large majority of the health problems present in the population. Second, primary care is essential to achieving the objectives that together constitute value in health care—quality of care (including achievement of desired health outcomes), patient satisfaction, and efficient use of resource."[3]

This assessment has endured. In 2021, another group of experts assembled by NASEM delivered virtually the same conclusion: "High-quality primary care is the foundation of a high-functioning health care system and is critical for achieving health care's quadruple aim (enhancing patient experience, improving population health management, reducing costs, and improving the health care team experience). . . . People in countries and health systems with high-quality primary care enjoy better health outcomes and more health equity."[4]

Note that the key term is *foundation*, which suggests that everything else that is good in health care depends on primary care. Admittedly, these reports are written by people who are primary care experts, so perhaps they overstate their role. But no one is suggesting that any other medical specialty or discipline is as critical as this one. All other physical sites for health care, including hospitals, are usually seen as secondary to a primary care relationship. Thus primary care has a valid claim to be the foundation of our health care system.

Such blue-ribbon-panel assessments are buttressed by decades of empirical investigation. Much of the original research on the relationship between primary care and health care quality and equity was done by Barbara Starfield, a prolific and brilliant Johns Hopkins University researcher. I will go into detail about her work later in this book, but suffice it to say here that every major analysis of primary care in the past 30 thirty years has cited her work on the benefits of primary care within the US health care system. For example, a recent monograph by the California Healthcare Foundation for stakeholders involved in health reforms reached the following conclusion: "Studies have found that health is better in areas with more primary care physicians; that people who receive care from primary care physicians are healthier; and that the cardinal characteristics of primary care (first contact care, holistic person-focused care over time, comprehensive and coordinated care) are associated with better health."[5] For this broad endorsement, they rely on Starfield.

More recent research (Starfield died in 2011) done in both the United States and other countries has extended these findings and demonstrated improvements in quality and a reduction in overall health care costs (the holy grail in American health care) in areas where there is a strong primary care base.[6] In 2019, Sanjay Basu and colleagues at Harvard University reported on data from the United States showing that the supply of primary care doctors strongly correlates with lower rates of death.[7] Another group of researchers recently revealed that in areas of primary care shortage, there were higher rates of emergency surgery, serious complications, and readmission.[8] Based on this and similar evidence, today there is unanimous support among health services researchers for the proposition that primary care *can* and *should* be the base of a rational, cost-effective health care system.

Is primary care ready to step forward to be the foundation for an efficient health care system? The answer is resoundingly no. In a fee-for-service reimbursement system, the only service that a primary care clinician can bill for is an evaluation and management visit, a service that has chronically been undervalued by the systems of payment. Thus to make more money, and to make a practice profitable, the primary care clinician has traditionally had to jam as many patients as possible through an office every day. Many of these patients have some of the expectations of primary care as a foundation, so they may bring a host of complicated problems to each visit, where there is not enough time to address them all. Clinicians rush through visits and miss opportunities to ensure valued-based care. In short, primary care is a disaster in fee-for-service.

Fee-for-service reimbursement in itself is not bad; the problem is the incentives it creates when the fee-for-service determines clinician compensation. The financial signal is to see lots of people and see them fast, not tarrying to deal with their problems. In a foundational article from 2001, economist James Robinson correctly pointed out that fee-for-service, capitation, and salary all have potentially negative incentives if the goal is better health.[9] But prospective payment fits most neatly with an incentive for promoting health and preventing illness, emphasizing value-based care. That is the critical assumption of this book, and much of what one sees in cutting-edge primary care today.

Most primary care today remains mired in fee-for-service incentives. As a result, many primary care clinicians believe they are underpaid and underappreciated, and as a group they border on despondence. Burnout is rampant. The field is not sought after by medical students, who may see primary care as hard work with little financial return. Rhetoric about its foundational aspects is just that: Our current fee-for-service-based health care system demonstrates little belief in the value of primary care. The same is not true elsewhere. American primary care is underpaid and under-resourced in comparison with other developed and developing countries. The result is a widely predicted shortage of primary care clinicians.

Research on the sorry state of primary care in America is voluminous—and consistent. For example, in early 2023, the Milbank Fund published its first primary care scorecard, with nothing but bad news.[10] Primary care spending, as a percentage of total health expenditures, had dropped from 6.2% in 2013 to 4.9% in 2020. For Medicare, the amount was even less, 3.5%. For perspective, in many European countries, that number is 12% to 15%. There is some variation by state in primary care spending, but few if any approach European levels.[11]

As noted, lack of resources leads to less interest in this area of medicine. Milbank documented that from 2012 to 2020, only about 20% of physicians finishing their residency were engaged in primary care. Since about one-third of physicians have historically been in primary care, our reservoir of physician primary caregivers is shrinking. As a result, the percentage of Americans reporting that they have a long-standing relationship with a primary care clinician was 43%, compared to 76% in the Netherlands.[12]

Milbank's 2024 scorecard showed matters worsening. While 37% of physicians in training began in primary care in 2021, only 15% were practicing primary care three to five years after residency. The scorecard's title is apt: "No One Can See You Now."[13] Perhaps not unexpectedly, primary care is rarely studied in the same fashion as other specialties in medicine. The National Institutes of Health has consistently invested less than 0.3% of its total funds in evaluations of primary care. Instead, the NIH's focus is on specific diseases and expensive therapies.

The deficiencies in primary care are growing worse. NASEM's 2021 scholarly evaluation documented the problems with American primary care. The report's first page started with a devastating portrait: "This foundation remains weak and under-resourced, accounting for 35% of health care visits while receiving only about 5% of health care expenditures. Moreover, the foundation is crumbling: visits to primary care clinicians are declining, and the workforce pipeline is shrinking, with clinicians opting to specialize in more lucrative health care fields."[14] The authors brought this point home by noting that nearly equal numbers of people seek primary care and specialty care in a given year, but spending on the latter is more than three times the size of the former. The average primary care doctor earns less than half of what a radiologist or surgeon does.[15]

The rate of pay for primary care doctors is even worse in locales where patients' incomes are lower. There, Medicaid emerges as the primary source of payment. In areas within the lowest quartile of patient income, the number of primary care clinicians per 100,000 residents is about 40, compared with more than 60 in the highest quartile.[16] As a result—perhaps inevitably, but still regrettably—the deteriorating foundation of primary care will be worse in low-income neighborhoods, many of them home to people of color. This lack of equity will stalk the pages of this book and must play into any recommendations about the health care changes our country must make.

For primary care clinicians, it is not just that their pay is poor, but also that they feel as though their workload is becoming unmanageable. A substantial portion of their time is spent picking up the pieces for all their patients in what is essentially a chaotic and disorganized health care system. As one 30-year veteran of primary care told me, the electronic medical record system (used in most health care offices) and its inbox of messages is "like a Gatling gun, continuously firing at you." Given inadequate pay and a lack of prestige, as well as an unsustainable workload, it should come as no surprise that primary care clinicians' morale is low.

The statistics on the primary care mood are shocking. Even before the COVID pandemic, nearly 80% of primary care clinicians were reporting symptoms of burnout.[17] It is no surprise, then, that the number of medical students interested in primary care has continued to drop over the past decade.[18] Black primary care clinicians are in especially short supply, which is particularly unfortunate given that Black patients who have Black doctors have a longer life expectancy.[19] In sum, primary care does look broken.

In a health care system full of paradoxes, this is perhaps the most striking. Primary care delivering value-based care is seen by many as the solution for an inefficient, inequitable, and poorly performing health care system. Yet it is a shocking mess of burnout and depletion. With all the radical intention of Lenin, we must ask, "What is to be done?"[20]

Fortunately, there is no shortage of voices in health care that want to undo this harm and put primary care's Humpty Dumpty back together again. The federal government and various state governments have launched a host of medical payment reforms designed to promote primary care. So have small, state-based insurers and large corporate insurers, which are attempting to encourage value-based approaches. Some of these insurers have also begun to organize their own primary care groups, directly employing the primary care clinicians. Increasingly, large retail chains (such as CVS Health and Walgreens) have done the same in fits and starts. And private equity investors are organizing and buying primary care practices. All these interventions are based on both the rhetoric of primary care being foundational and the perception that, at present, much of primary care is failing. The proposals also share a common faith that we can move to a value-based health care system, which entails turning from fee-for-service to methods of prospective payment.

The goal of this book is to assess whether there has been real progress, and whether the primary care sector will do a better job of assisting patients with their health care journey, delivering value-based care, and producing a more efficient health care system. As noted, there is little research to this point on the evolution of primary care. The insightful blogger and commentator Kevin O'Leary recently revisited an article by Paul Keckley written in 2019, "Primary Care Is the Bridge to Health System Transformation: Who Will Build That Bridge?"[21] Keckley had outlined the transition from small practice Primary Care 1.0, to hospital aggregation of Primary Care 2.0, to primary care practices designed to manage care, Primary Care 3.0. Keckley argued that building Primary Care 3.0 was motivated by the perception that spending more on primary care would reduce specialist and hospital spending, and thereby total spending. He also recognized that traditional Primary Care 1.0 and 2.0 could not justify additional capital investment—the savings on total cost of care were critical. At the center of Primary Care 3.0 was the well-resourced team of clinician (nurses, doctors, advanced practice clinicians, pharmacists, care coordinators) who anticipated patient needs and avoided costly episodes of care.

Keckley proposed that the potential investors in Primary Care 3.0 would likely be hospitals, insurers, private investors, and retail health. O'Leary, writing five years later, found that hospitals really had not contributed. He pointed out that insurers, investors, and retail health had all made sporadic progress, punctuated by well-publicized retreats. In summary, he concluded, "it doesn't seem that any of the approaches have been consistently successful in investing in a new wave of Primary Care 3.0 that has disrupted the health care industry." Indeed, the health services literature contains few reports of disruptive innovations.

Ironically, some argue that existing investments and investors have had the opposite effect, essentially expediting the demise of primary care. Note that most of the investors enumerated by Keckley (and O'Leary) are for-profit corporations. Many commentators, perhaps best represented by Professor Timothy Hoff, have argued that the weight of insurer, regulator, and corporate influences on primary care "produces a healthcare marketplace that comes across as increasingly impersonal and transactional; coldly calculating and corporate in its strategizing; and relying on half-baked policies and delivery 'reforms' that lack a true appreciation for the deep complexity of health care work."[22] According to this line of reasoning, the would-be "saviors" are corroding what is left of primary care. They are not producing team-based Primary Care 3.0 but destroying Primary Care 1.0.

In its emphasis on the human touch, the moral commitment to the patient, this argument appealing. But it offers no way forward. No primary care policy expert believes the answer is a return to small group and solo private practice. More importantly, the financial basis for a return to the past is not apparent. Value-based primary care offers the promise of a health care system that is not only higher quality and more equitable, but also more efficient, something all payers seek. Given the runaway costs of American health care, it would be a welcome improvement. Traditional fee-for-service billing of individual evaluation and management codes is what has morally and financially bankrupted primary care.

There is one alternative that could allow a return to traditional primary care: a national health system, available to all, that is paid for by the federal government. Federalization of health care would allow the government to impose increased resources for primary care without the explicit expectation of savings. Over three years of interviews, most primary care clinicians I spoke to supported just this approach. Elsewhere I have argued that such a federalization/socialization may be the outcome of the long-term evolution of our health system. But in this analysis of primary care, I want to address the current reality, and the single-payer program is not part of that reality. What is part of the reality is a slowly growing penetration of value-based care on a primary care chassis. Moreover, primary care in a national health system would likely endorse team-based, value-based primary care, with an underlying incentive structure based on prospective payment.

Given that aperture, what can a qualitative review of a reasonable number of practices suggest about progress toward a value-based primary care? As noted above, there are good data on the degree of dissatisfaction with the status quo, Primary Care 1.0 and 2.0. And there is not much empirical evidence of a Primary Care 3.0–based disruption of health care. But value-based approaches to health care are taking seed in some areas, suggesting some promise for the future. Presuming that progress, the next natural question to ask is, What initiatives, which proponents of changes, which investors in the largest sense of that word, are having real—even if small—impact? Given that we have few alternatives for reforming our health care system beyond trying to build a primary care base, those questions seem vital. The stakes are high for us as a country, as well as for every individual citizen/patient, and the solutions are of extreme importance.

To uncover the progress, if any, of value-based primary care, I have spent much of the past three years talking to primary care clinicians and their administrative teams. Mine was an enriched sample, as I went first to primary care experts to identify examples of primary care teams that were focused on population health. I also used contacts in the insurance industry and in state governments to explore their initiatives. I tried to uncover not only each clinician's self-assessment of their practice, but also the financial incentives underlying their organization.

Over this period, roughly 2021–25, there has been substantial evolution in the activities of the various change agents. While I have argued elsewhere that long-term demographic and financial trends make some aspects of health care policy predictable, over the shorter three- to six-year period, there are fluctuations in the amplitude of waves of change.[23] That has certainly been the case for value-based primary care. While a few years ago, retailers, insurers, and investors seemed to be jumping in to provide capital, today there has been some pullback. The best example is Walmart, the largest company in the United

States, which five years ago intended to remake health care with its own primary clinics. In 2024, they announced an unconditional retreat, giving up on the health care business.

Some of this and related stories are the result of bad business planning. Some of it is because health care is hard. And a large part of it is the calculus of long-term profit. For Primary Care 3.0 to succeed, it must be supported by greater resources than have traditionally gone into primary care, and for that to occur, there must be the promise of profit from reduced health care costs. During much of the past five years, that strategy was bolstered by ever greater growth, in terms of both beneficiaries and payment per beneficiary, in the federal government's Medicare Advantage program, the managed care half of Medicare. Several well-known primary care companies had begun to demonstrate that team-based, value-based primary care could lower overall costs on a Medicare Advantage chassis. Taking payment in the form of capitation, they could support their primary care infrastructure and apparently reduce waste.

But concerns over the cost of Medicare Advantage, and even more so over the possibility that these primary care groups were inappropriately coding patient visits to make the patients appear sicker, thus gaining higher risk-adjusted payments, led the Centers for Medicare and Medicaid Services to change the reimbursement formulae. These leading clinics immediately claimed they could no longer profit sufficiently to maintain the value-oriented infrastructure of nurses, care coordinators, and pharmacists. The result has been some pullback by the investors, and general consternation.

Viewed from a decades-long perspective, these changes in reimbursement strategy are a consistent part of Medicare Advantage. The program was resuscitated by the Bush administration in 2003 with much higher per capita payments. Payments were reduced in the Obama administration but have risen over the past decade, at least partly due to risk adjustment strategies. A tack in the course of the program was inevitable.

But the reductions, which I will address in more detail, provide a stress test for the development of value-based primary care. Will trends that might have looked strong in 2022 prove to be sustainable? Will states and the federal government continue to endorse and support primary care risk schemes? How will insurers and retailers react—get out like Walmart, or double down? Does venture capital have a role, or will it be flighty, moving to other, surer sources of profit? The primary care landscape has some answers to these questions.

Overall, my guarded observation is that Primary Care 3.0 is continuing to grow. In particular, many state programs and most federal programs have continued to advocate for and more importantly find financial support for value-based primary care, including some based on capitated risk. This commitment has not flagged in the federal government's Centers for Medicare and Medicaid Innovation, nor in activist states like Oregon and Massachusetts.

Nor have the corporations all folded tents like Walmart. Insurers have health policy experts, and they have drawn the same conclusions as health policy experts everywhere: the only viable solution for the broken health care system is vibrant primary care. Primary care must be enabled to manage care with a team, which requires more resources. But insurers can only support those additional resources if it leads to reduced overall costs. As a result, they remain vigilant but in many cases continue to advance their primary care footprint. So have companies that are devoted to supporting primary care to take risk, companies that make their profit on reduction in total costs. Contrary to Hoff's thesis about abject corrosion, and to my surprise, private equity and venture capital firms are in some cases finding ways to assist primary care clinicians to do their work in more professionally and financially rewarding ways while decreasing costs and promoting quality health care.

It is not an entirely rosy picture, though. Most primary care professionals feel worn out and pessimistic. Many younger clinicians do not see a viable future. Most of these people are in practices owned by health care institutions, particularly hospitals, the Keckley/O'Leary Primary Care 2.0. They live in fee-for-service, paid on a per visit basis, without sufficient support to take good care of their patients. Those that can (because they have been at it a while) will retire early. Others have turned to unions to leverage their power and convince administrators that they need more support or caps on number of visits.

To provide a faithful picture, I report on some of the practices stuck in the no-win situation of fee-for-service with volume expectations. There are far more of these than there are practices taking risk, acting as a team of clinicians, and prospectively planning for their patients' health. But I will not give Primary Care 2.0 proportionate space because this book asks, Can Primary Care 3.0 come to dominate, and is there progress in that journey? Unfortunately, at this point and based on what I have observed, the answer is only potentially yes. It is a close call, and I cannot be definitive. Based on my interviews with primary care clinicians, I conclude by outlining a couple of alternative futures, some that I think are much less likely to solve the big problems of efficiency and quality in our health system.

One overwhelming impression does give me some optimism, however. Everywhere I went, clinicians and their teams demonstrated the special, altruistic, commitment to the patient that makes health care a truly moral endeavor. Even the most put-upon, dejected clinician could talk in warm terms about their commitment to their patients and their needs. Medical professionalism is not dead; it continues to thrive even in the face of burnout. I had not expected it, and with this other-regarded-ness comes some real hope.

To give a sense, I recount a couple of sunny days spent in Dallas, Texas, talking with physicians. While staying in University Park, near Southern Methodist University, I traveled north one day and south the next. The contrast in the clinics' locations was jaw-dropping. Heading up the Dallas North Tollway, I went through a vast landscape of upscale malls, office buildings, and affluent suburbs. The highways themselves are thrilling—even daunting—with high-flung bridges and complex interchanges. Everything seemed brand-new. And all the people were white. Going south the next day on Highway 352, past Fair Park, the housing quality deteriorated dramatically, there were few stores of any sort, and poverty was on display in most front yards. Almost everyone was Black or Hispanic. The two locales hardly seemed to be in the same country. This book is not about our nation's intolerable racial and socioeconomic disparities, although they do provide a context for our health care system.

But the primary care practices I visited over those few days had a critical element in common: a commitment to finding new ways to serve their patients. Up north, I met with Trevor Huber, a 35-year-old family practice doctor who had recently set up his office in a strip mall in Little Elm, Texas. Dr. Huber grew up in Beaumont, Texas, where his father also was a family practice doctor.[24] Trevor went to Nova Southeastern University's Patel College of Osteopathic Medicine, trained in Fort Worth, and opened up shop in Little Elm about five years ago. I met him because he is part of a practice of 1,200 physicians in the Dallas–Fort Worth area that has been organized by Dr. Christopher Crow. (I will spend more time on him and his group, Catalyst Health, in chapter 2.) For now, suffice it to say that Catalyst is preparing doctors to move away from fee-for-service medicine and into value-based care.

Huber loved to talk about this latter aspect of his practice, but much more so about his patients and his hopes for them. His oldest patient is 102, and his youngest that day was 2 days old. More patients were coming to him all the time. When he started, he had no patients and had to take a loan from the Small Business Administration to buy an electronic medical records license and pay rent. Then things moved quickly.

When I met with Huber, his team had expanded to three full-time physicians, one part-time physician, plus two full-time and two part-time nurse practitioners. They had just opened a new satellite practice. His wife had decorated the offices and done all the website design. The team was now doing more sports medicine and dermatology, but Huber still enjoyed family medicine because of the range of services he could offer. His ambition is for the practice to be the single stop for all a patient's medical needs.

Huber was committed to rethinking how primary care should be provided. He noted that when his father was in practice, he was isolated in the exam room with a patient. The only ways to reach him were by telephone or through the office door. For his father, fee-for-service billing made sense. Now, Trevor has data on patients flowing in constantly.

They call him or text him, and he gets messages from the practice's patient portal. Huber also receives patient information from the local health information exchange and from Catalyst Health's care management team. There is no solo episode of patient care; instead, he faces a constant flow of relevant information through an array of new technologies.

Moreover, patient care is continuous. Huber works with a multifaceted team—not only those who are part of his own practice, but also pharmacists, nurses, and care managers who work for Catalyst Health but see his patients. Health care has moved from being episodic to seamless, and Huber is proactive, not reactive. Still, he needs to get paid to make sure he can keep his patients healthy. Getting paid for discrete service made no sense.

Every point he made was illustrated by a story about a patient. For example, he had recently inherited a 68-year-old patient from another doctor. The new arrival was on Trelegy for chronic obstructive pulmonary disease, Eliquis for blood clots, and Ozempic for diabetes—all expensive drugs. Huber soon discovered that the patient was not actually taking the medications, though, because his out-of-pocket costs were approaching $1,400 per month. Huber got Catalyst Health's pharmacist involved, they identified a cost-effective regimen, and this patient is now doing much better. The previous doctor presumably had not considered the costs of what he was prescribing.

Huber asserted, however, that understanding the context for a patient's care is what it's all about. He tells his patients, "My goal is for you to have a long life and a good life." Little of this effort to improve his patient's health by getting to a cost-reasonable regimen would be reimbursed by fee-for-service. Yet it was the epitome of value-based care. Although I only spent an hour with Huber, I was convinced that his patients believe this motto. I did. His enthusiasm for his patients, and for new ways to practice medicine, was infectious.

Down in southern Dallas, even at seven o'clock on a clear morning, there was little shimmer in the surroundings. A couple of poorly dressed, apparently homeless men were walking next to the highway. As I turned onto neighborhood streets, a bridge crossed what looked like an open sewer. There was no new construction. Nearly everything looked dilapidated, although many homes were neat and well kept.

The Baylor Scott & White Health and Wellness Center and the City of Dallas Juanita J. Craft Recreation Center were exceptions to this gloom. They were warm and vibrant. The Health and Wellness Center is a public-private partnership between the City of Dallas and Baylor Scott & White Health. Baylor Scott & White Health is an integrated delivery system that operates 52 hospitals, 559 clinics and surgery centers, and 183 primary care clinics across Texas. The system has opened 6 community care clinics, 3 in the low-income area of South Dallas. In part, this was done to fulfill their community commitment as a not-for-profit health system. But in the case of Baylor Scott & White Health and Wellness Center, it is part of their effort to show that community-based primary care can lead to better outcomes.

Venita Owens is the engaging president of the Health and Wellness Center. She stated that originally the center was branded as the Diabetes Health and Wellness Institute, and membership growth was slow.[25] People often did not know they had diabetes or prediabetes, and the word "institute" was a deterrent for some. Once its name was changed to the Health and Wellness Center, membership began to grow and now exceeds 8,000.

Sitting in the heart of Texas, the center reflects the state's rather miserable commitment to public health care. The center and its clinic serve a patient population that is approximately 45% Black, 45% Hispanic, and an astounding 80% uninsured. The center is owned and operated by Baylor Scott & White Health, supplemented by some philanthropic support. Yet the programs are cutting edge and decidedly situated within the community, with outreach being a priority.

The Health and Wellness Center was built to demonstrate that there is continuity between medical care, chronic disease, education, nutrition, and physical activity. Situated in a food desert, the center's Farm Stand programs operated in various parts of the surrounding neighborhood. They are among their most popular community interventions. The center's mantra is for its staff to leave the four walls of the clinic and get into the community. Not surprisingly, then, 80% of their employees are community health workers.

The center's commitment to community health interventions is reflected in the programs its health care team develops and assesses. Dr. Andrea Harris has a doctoral degree in nutrition, and she has formulated several courses for the local community.[26] The best-attended one is her version of the renowned National Diabetes Prevention Program. Just behind that in popularity are Stay Active and Independent for Life (SAIL) classes for those over age 65, and Happy Kitchen cooking classes, oriented to those with hypertension and diabetes. Dr. Heather Kitzman assembled a research team that has evaluated the center's programs and shown that community interventions can reduce the severity of diabetes by lowering a person's blood sugar (measured through a hemoglobin A1c test). They also reduce the costs for care.[27] Their studies have garnered national attention. What the Health and Wellness Center is accomplishing, amid great poverty, is nothing short of remarkable.

I was especially struck by Dr. Lydia Best, the key primary care doctor in the center's clinic. She has a staff that includes two nurse practitioners, three medical assistants, and one licensed vocational nurse. The entire morning I was at the clinic, this team was busy with a nonstop flow of patients. After they huddle each morning to talk about that day's scheduled patients, they work through the day until 5:00 p.m., with only a short break for lunch. They interact constantly with a large staff of community health workers, as well as a diabetes team that is headed by a pharmacist. I had the sense that they share patient responsibilities with one another smoothly, a no-look pass. (Basketball metaphors come easily, as there is a nice and frequently used court in the Recreation Center. Former NBA All-Star Chris Bosh is a local legend.)

At the core of all this activity is the ever-calm Dr. Best.[28] When growing up in Detroit, an adult asked her what she wanted to be. She responded, "A nurse." When challenged as to why she did not want to be a doctor, Best replied that she did not know women could be doctors.

She changed her mind then and there, eventually going to college at Brown University and to the University of Michigan for medical school.

Best knew all along that she wanted to care for the underserved. One of her first jobs was working at a hospital in Detroit, but she was unhappy when she found out that they sent their poor patients to Detroit Metro Medical Center (the public hospital) for care. She wanted to be able to reflect her Christian faith in caring for her patients, and she could not accept this kind of situation. When she found out about the Health and Wellness Center, she knew it was the place for her.

Her current practice is challenging. Although the center is starting to see more insured patients—local people who work for the city or the transit authority—most patients are uninsured, and some are undoubtedly undocumented. In a Texas tradition, the county hospital (in this case, Parkland) is the last resort for specialty care for the uninsured. Patients who need such care must be referred to Parkland, but then communication with them can become difficult. The clinics at Parkland are frequently overwhelmed with the crush of patients, and wait times are quite long. (The specialists at Baylor University Hospital are generally in private practice and will not see uninsured patients.) As a result, caring for Health and Wellness Center patients involves doing everything possible at the center, and then working closely with their patients as they move to the uncertainty of necessary, but fraught, specialty care.

Best's practice is especially effective when its team identifies patients through the community program. If they get to patients with hypertension or diabetes early on, they can bend the curve and avoid the need for specialty interventions. Initiating medication prescriptions and wellness programs at the same time has a synergistic effect. If Best had a wish list, it would include (1) more behavioral health support for the "in-between" patient who needs more than the brief interventions they can provide locally but is not sick enough to require hospitalization; (2) better medication-assisted therapy for substance abuse (Baylor University Hospital may be providing this in the near future); and (3) an occasional miracle at Baylor Scott & White University

Hospital for her patients needing surgery or orthopedic care. Taking care of these patients, who have limited opportunities for care elsewhere, requires daily creativity and brings forth more than a little anxiety.

But Best is committed. When she first started her career, pre-Obamacare (and thus prior to the Affordable Care Act's prohibitions on insurance exclusions for those with preexisting conditions), she worked at a small, private practice clinic where every employee had a husband with diabetes. The entire group could not get health insurance. Best was pregnant, a doctor, and uninsured. She engineered a payment plan and paid out of pocket for her maternity care and delivery. But postpartum, she had complications, and the hospital put her into debt collection status. She understands firsthand the frustration and shame associated with a lack of health care insurance. Now she has a career helping those in a similar situation.

Both Best and Huber revealed a determination to change the nature of how primary care is delivered—a determination that is rooted in commitment to their patients. Each would probably not want to work in the other's medical practice, but that is not the point. They both can envision a better health care future for their patients, and they are fighting for that in the type of care they offer. Both practice value-based care, anticipating poor outcomes and working to prevent them. Both see the continuity of illness, and the doctor's relationship with the patient, as out of step with billing fees for service. These two physicians provide one with a sense of great hope for primary care, as well as for our health care system. Even more importantly, the attitude these doctors demonstrate is not an isolated case. Instead, in many places, it is prevalent. And there is a lot of institutional support, from a variety of sources, nurturing it.

This book, then, is about where primary care is headed, particularly whether a value-based future can obtain. In the first chapters, I offer a policy narrative, relating in more detail what primary care is and how it has gone wrong. I also describe some developments, generally not mentioned in the usual histories of primary care, that constitute important building blocks for future reforms, the foundation for the transition from Primary Care 1.0 and 2.0 to Primary Care 3.0. I then discuss how the federal government and state governments have attempted—sometimes ham-handedly, sometimes insightfully—to resuscitate primary care. I view these activities favorably, even those that have been characterized as unsuccessful, because I think they add to the base of attributes that can help propel primary care into a value-based future.

The last part of the book will be the more provocative, as I review the efforts of insurers, corporations, and entrepreneurs to prop up and cultivate primary care. It is anathema to much of the health policy community, and even more so to primary care cognoscenti, to suggest that for-profit entities could have a role in getting to a future where primary care is the overarching basis for health care. But that is what could happen—with emphasis on the "could."

All along, I turn to the voices of the doctors, nurses, care managers, and behavioral health experts who have advised me over the past three years and described the reality they face daily. In that vein, I intend this book to be a report from the front line. Its title is illustrative. One cold December Monday, I was in Lynn, Massachusetts, visiting with doctors at the Lynn Community Health Center, a large, federally qualified health center in the less-than-gracefully aging center of Lynn. All its patients were low income, either on Medicaid or uninsured. One of the doctors I met was Elizabeth Quinn. She grew up in Quincy, Massachusetts, went to Harvard University, and then attended medical school at the University of Massachusetts.[29] She trained in family medicine at the Lawrence Community Health Center and now specializes in obstetrics care for women with substance use disorders. In all of medicine, it is hard to imagine a more exquisitely difficult and subtle set of human interactions than those produced by this intersection of the strength of motherhood with the tragedy of addiction.

Yet Quinn seemed perfect for the job. Her language, particularly in the way she made certain points, was exceptionally keen and insightful. Just as impressively, she was so grateful for all the help she got from her colleagues, from the community health center, and from Salem Hospital. (I will come back to her medical practice later in the book.) Her response to my question about how she would describe her practice was slow in coming, yet measured and thoughtful. After a long pause, she said, "Wonderful, crazy, broken." Perfectly put. In this book I allow that yes, primary care is broken, and it is absurd that we have let this happen. Most primary clinicians are unhappy, and their practices are unable to fulfill all of their patients' needs. But I do see signs that primary care is moving to a value-based foundation, one that is driven by the marvel of the interactions of dedicated primary care clinicians with their patients.

One final note on verbiage. *Primary care office* and *primary care clinician* are terms that are familiar to most people. Primary care clinicians today consist of doctors, nurse practitioners, and physician assistants, or physician associates. I try to use the latter throughout this book, while recognizing that many individuals use "primary care physician" or "primary care provider," abbreviated as PCP.

WONDERFUL AND BROKEN

CHAPTER ONE

The Somewhat Recent History of Primary Care

TO UNDERSTAND THE POTENTIAL EVOLUTION of primary care, from solo practitioner to the team-based, value-seeking practice that we have called Primary Care 3.0, some historical context is helpful. The modern American health care system started in 1965 with the passage of the Medicare Act. At about this same time, the concept of primary care evolved from general medical practices. Rosemary Stevens has masterfully elucidated the various forces in play in the 1960s regarding the role of general practice in American health care.[1] First, medicine in our nation was already 50 years into a specialization-centric system, supported by fee-for-service. Over two decades, from 1949 to 1969, the number of doctors identifying themselves as specialists essentially doubled, to 77%. Specialization was the norm—and the expectation. Increasingly, general practice was considered second rate.

Second, American medicine had created no institutional home for general practitioners (GPs). In the United Kingdom, GPs were accorded the crucial role of being a patient's first medical contact, as well as the conduit to specialty care in that country's National Health Service. GPs in the United Kingdom were based entirely within the community, and all hospital care was undertaken by consultants. This contrasted with the situation in the United States, where general practitioners continued to seek hospital privileges to perform operations or deliver babies. Competitive conflict was inevitable in America and did not exist in the United Kingdom, where the swim lanes were well defined. The UK government had instituted this stratified system, whereas no governmental intervention occurred in the United States. Instead, patients expected to be able to decide when to seek specialty care on their own.

As Timothy Hoff has pointed out, American general practitioners were increasingly losing their ability to provide specialty care, and they were often no longer granted hospital privileges to do surgery or obstetrics by the late 1950s and early 1960s.[2] Something clearly was needed to replace the fading general practice subprofession, and the answer came in the creation of a new "specialty." The American Board of Family Practice was added to the club of medical specialties in 1969, with a training program that included pediatrics, obstetrics, office-based gynecology, and general internal medicine.

The leaders of what eventually became the American Academy of Family Physicians envisioned themselves as pioneers—radicals, even—within the health care academy and the medical profession in general. While what they did was considered a specialty, demonstrated by board certification, they staked out their domain as providing comprehensive care for patients, in some ways seeking a position like that of the British GPs. They wanted to have a lock on continuity with their patients. A single doctor could and would provide care for an entire family. (Of course, pediatricians continued to care for most children.)

Family medicine initially grew rapidly. In the late 1970s, there were 300 residency programs and 7,500 residents. By the early 1980s, it was the third-largest specialty training program in the United States.[3] Family physicians' only real competition for providing comprehensive care for adults came from general internal medicine. The same forces giving rise to the development of family medicine in the late 1960s also led first to introspection and then action in academic departments of internal medicine.[4] The upswing of interest in primary care led many to believe that three years of internal medicine training could produce a physician best placed—at least for adults—to be their comprehensive and continuous caregiver. By 1980, there were 68 divisions of primary care in academic medical centers; 30 years later, there were more than 150. But many of these faculty members were part-time practitioners, filling the rest of their schedule with research and teaching. Fiscal constraints, rooted in the relatively poor reimbursement rate for primary care services, meant that general medicine was often a beggar in academic medical departments. Yet many general internists did set up shop as solo or small group primary care providers.

While primary care came to play an important role in many academic medical centers as they morphed into what became known as integrated delivery systems, general internal medicine's place in the ranks of primary care initially rose but then fell rapidly. Today, less than 10% of internal medicine trainees are interested in primary care practices, and the field is increasingly dominated by family physicians, nurse practitioners, and physician assistants. Indeed, general internists were typically the most disgruntled of the doctors I met. But I am getting ahead of the historical narrative.

Over the 1970s and into the 1980s, the new family physician specialty grew in numbers and in strength. At first it was concentrated in rural areas and the Midwest, but then it spread, via new training programs, throughout the country. The specialty's mission has remained constant since that time: as Lindsay McCauley and coauthors put it, "to provide comprehensive, person-centered, relationship-based care that considers the needs and preferences of individuals, families, and communities. Primary care is unique in health care in that it is designed for everyone to use throughout their lives."[5] Continuity and comprehensiveness were and remain core values, resonating with the public's own view.

By the mid-1980s, general practice was finished as a field, rapidly being replaced by family medicine. No one book better captures the heady nature of the new specialty during this period than the suitably titled *Heirs of General Practice*, published in 1986 by John McPhee, the celebrated nonfiction author who is still writing at age 93. I was curious how McPhee, who has tackled subjects ranging from crofters, to shad, to oranges, to complex geology (and all stops in between) chose this subject, so I contacted him. He told me that he has long sought to observe people who are technically skilled, then to write about their vocation and insights.

In the early 1980s, Robert Bingham, a dear friend of McPhee's, was hospitalized with a form of brain cancer. McPhee often visited him in the hospital, as did Bingham's brother-in-law, Alex McPhedran. McPhedran ran the relatively new Dartmouth Medical School–affiliated family medicine program in central Maine. McPhee was fascinated by the program, and eventually McPhedran introduced McPhee to a number of its recent graduates in rural Maine. McPhee traveled to Maine to "observe and describe." (John McPhee never mentioned this to me, but his own father was a general practitioner who eventually became the head of student health services at Princeton University.)

McPhee's observations are priceless. Although he encountered a number of McPhedran's trainees, McPhee concentrated on a single practice in Skowhegan, Maine. It consisted of five doctors who were all recently minted family physicians from the Dartmouth program: David Axelman, Donna Conkling, Susan Cochran, Ann Dorney, and Cynthia Robertson. If a patient agreed, McPhee would sit in and report on the interaction with their doctor. *Heirs* is a short book, but its descriptions are unmatched in their characterizations of the way doctors navigate the confluence of a patient's illness and social situation. McPhee also beautifully captures the hectic atmosphere of the Skowhegan clinic.

At one point, McPhee was following Ann Dorney, who "does not have a choice about how many patients she sees in a day. She is there all the time, and patients keep coming through the door."[6] The interactions moved quickly, and Dorney was direct. But she knew her patients well. At one point, Dorney saw a patient with a fast-growing cancer in her stomach. Dorney commented matter-of-factly but also assertively, "You have to think about what you are going to do. For instance, you have to think about where you want to die." The answer was, "I will die at home." Readers get the impression of a superb professional doing her job, having laid the foundation to be able to ask that kind of question and to anticipate an answer.

Dorney's next patient was a 10-year-old boy with allergies. The father provided a family history, also mentioning that his own blood pressure had been high in the past. Dorney first dealt with the child's allergy problem. But then she put a blood pressure cuff on the father, and the reading was 170 over 110 (a normal reading is 120 over 80). Dorney treated him for hypertension and also diagnosed his adult-onset diabetes. The father's brother had recently died of a heart attack, which was probably where the boy's father was headed without Dorney's interventions.

After that, Dorney saw a 44-year-old woman who got the first complete physical examination she had ever had, and then a 12-year-old with a hydrocele (an accumulation of fluid around the testicle). The side comments she made with each patient and family were characteristic of many primary care interactions: earthy and human, eliciting key information and instilling confidence. All the admirable aspects of primary care were on display: long-term relationships with patients, varied medical problems, careful troubleshooting, and—especially—trust. Yet the patient load seemed to have been overwhelming, at least when seen through a 2020s lens.

I tracked down three of the doctors about whom McPhee wrote—Susan Cochran, Donna Conkling, and Ann Dorney—in spring 2023. All of them remembered their early practice, 40 years previously, vividly and fondly. Cochran, like most members of this group, had an unorthodox path to medical school. It included time spent on the southern side of the Alaska Range after dropping out of Harvard University, and then taking premed classes at Colby College while living part-time in a teepee. She recalled how fiercely and proudly independent their Skowhegan Family Medicine group was, but also how enervating it was to be on call every night for obstetrics, do rounds for all her hospitalized patients, and face a full slate of patients every day. Cochran's main joy came from intently listening to her patients' problems and trying to arrive at a durable diagnosis by drawing together their symptoms and her physical findings, but time was often at a premium. And she loved practicing with a group of respected colleagues who had the same approach to medicine that she did.

Donna Conkling had been an English teacher before she went to medical school. Her ambition was to carefully document her patients' histories and stories in her notes, gaining a deeper understanding of their lives. When the electronic medical record (EMR) system came in, she felt crimped, as she "could not fit the great American novel" into her EMR notes.[7] Along with this deep interest in her patients came a sense of privilege, which the other doctors in the Skowhegan clinic mentioned as well. Helping patients and families through difficult times created rich professional lives, and this was clearly sustenance for them. The first year, they were each only earning about $6,000 and had to moonlight to make ends meet. But they had no complaints, other than not having enough time.

Conkling made another point that seemed to resonate with her colleagues—and probably with a lot of other people practicing family medicine in those days. Skowhegan was just the right place for them. It was not a big city, nor was it too far "upriver" to be truly a wilderness. As a result, she was free to use all her family medicine skills. The family physicians were able to practice obstetrics, perform minor in-office surgery, and have multigenerational families as patients. (Many family medicine doctors speak in warm tones about this intergenerational aspect of their work.) The local hospital was run by surgeons, and at first they, along with the rest of the area's medical community, did not know what to make of these unconventional doctors. But there were enough patients for all, and soon the family medicine doctors fit right in with both the town and its medical community.

John McPhee and Susan Cochran both marveled about Ann Dorney's strong will and toughness. On a Zoom call I had with Dorney, this personality trait initially came across as Maine flintiness. She told me about trip she took for medical school interviews, where she rode in buses around the country, changing out of her jeans into a dress in the bus station's restroom before going to the next interview. She remembers getting off in Boston and going to Tufts Medical Center, where her interviewer harangued her for trying to take the slot of a male who would really practice medicine. After more than 40 years of working as a doctor, her anger was still visceral.

Dorney had a different recollection about the Skowhegan Family Medicine group's start, noting that she and her colleagues were not welcomed. They were told, "There is no real work here; go farther north." (A quick look at a map suggests that there is little north of Skowhegan but forest and moose.) The local general practitioners, who were all quite old at the time, felt especially threatened, but they all retired relatively quickly. Like the others, Dorney told me that the group's practice soon became busy.

The commitment to a full-service family medicine practice was important to Dorney. She proudly delivered more than 1,200 babies and never lost a mother or a baby, although she did encounter some friction with the "old-timers." For instance, one of her pregnant patients was having a difficult delivery, and the local obstetrician refused to leave his office to help. Dorney had to get one of the surgeons to assist her, and thankfully the mother and child did well. This behavior had enraged her, but she made no further comment on the obstetrician other than to note he retired a few years later.

All three of these family medicine doctors—both in their own recent words and those of John McPhee 40 years ago—highlight the kinetic and varied nature of their practice. The critical features of primary care (as defined by the National Academies of Science, Engineering, and Medicine) are on full display. Patients treated these doctors as their first and—usually—only source of care. Doctors accepted that they had longitudinal relationships with their patients, persisting over the long term. They understood the social and familial contexts for the diseases they were treating. They were also culturally aware, attuned to the structure of the community. Long before the term came into vogue, they naturally and automatically *integrated* considerations of the social determinants of disease into their work. They fostered close relationships—nearing friendship—with their patients.

The major gratification in their work was that patients returned that friendship and trust. That is why these three women, and so many other primary care doctors I have met, considered their occupation to be a vocation, a privilege, something wonderful. They implicitly recognized what Barbara Starfield stated so well in her unmatched book

Primary Care: Concept, Evaluation, and Policy: "Illness has meaning to patients far beyond its physical manifestations because every illness produces some disturbances in the person's life. Cure removes the physical abnormality of an illness, but healing requires restoration of the relationships disturbed by it."[8] Participating in that healing was an important part of the primary clinician's professional life.

The only problem with this picture of Skowhegan Family Practice, and the family medicine primary clinician stereotype, is that it was not sustainable. The three physicians recalled the 1980s as a golden period in their lives, and they cherished it. But the pace was impossible, as was the fee-for-service payment structure, which was based on discrete reimbursements. All the original Skowhegan group's doctors, except Dorney, stepped away to less demanding practices as they juggled raising children with professional demands. For them, it was simply too arduous to keep up with the stream of patient care and still have a life outside of work. Eventually, the practice could not make ends meet. It was bought by the local hospital, which has subsidized it over much of the last two decades.

The experience in Skowhegan was not isolated. The notion of a single doctor providing all your care—including aspects of adult medicine, obstetrics/gynecology, and pediatrics—was too much to expect in the context of fee-for-service. With low primary care compensation for individual visits, clinicians had less time to see more patients, which required more specialization. Family medicine, especially in urban areas, was whittled down, with obstetrics being the first part of the discipline that people abandoned. Today, talking to family medicine clinicians, some still do the entire range of specialties for which they are trained, but most do not do obstetrics, and many have left pediatrics. Those that stay in women's health tend to concentrate only on obstetrics, and they typically have access to high-risk obstetricians for difficult cases.

Perhaps more importantly, the fee-for-service reimbursement is antithetical to continuity and deep knowledge about patients. The typical productivity measure and determinant of income in fee-for-service is visit targets, or appointments per day. This puts the family practice clinician on the treadmill of four visits per hour, complicating the effort to anticipate patient needs. The better practices, those moving to value-based care, understand this and have put together resources to enable a team-based approach to care. This additional assistance can ensure a patient panel gets better care and that the clinicians do not burn out. But it requires greater financial support than fee-for-service can produce.

In summary, the typical primary care clinician cannot have the same temporal and emotional commitment that was the norm at the Skowhegan practice—a norm that defined the Primary Care 1.0 Marcus Welby image. So, even as that image took hold in the late 1960s, it was endangered, and by the 1990s, it appeared untenable as primary care moved out of small practices and toward employment in large centers, what Keckley referred to as Primary Care 2.0.

Health Care Reform, Managed Care, and Primary Care's Evolution

The evolution of primary care was sculpted by currents in health policy. Dr. Barbara Starfield, a singular figure in primary care, worked for many years as a pediatrician in the Health Policy Department at Johns Hopkins University. She was both the leading theorist of primary care and its most important empirical researcher. As her investigative career took off in the 1980s, she envisioned practices like Skowhegan Family Medicine. But this type of practice could not persist in the harsh financial reality of underpaid fee-for-service. As a result, the archetype of primary care outlined by Starfield rapidly became anachronistic, even as its goals and intentions persisted.

Concept, Evaluation, and Policy is Starfield's early tour de force. Writing in 1992, she set forth the parameters of primary care that she believed should define the field, and then created a research agenda. Her book begins by outlining the two goals of a health care system: optimization of health and equity in the distribution of resources. She argued that primary care is the means for accomplishing both goals. It provides preventive, curative, and rehabilitative services, and it integrates health care into social situations where there are multiple problems in play. Primary care also organizes and rationalizes resources. Its clinicians, who are close to the patient's milieu, appreciate the social and environmental influences on a patient's health. Starfield found a primary care doctor's roles to be "accessibility, comprehensiveness, coordination, continuity, and accountability."[9] These elements have continued to define the American Academy of Family Physician's expectations and goals for primary care, even though they have had to move beyond Starfield's image of primary care.

In retrospect, Starfield's foundational work failed to anticipate four fundamental changes in primary care. First, it is doctor oriented, and individual effort is placed at a premium. That was the situation in the early 1990s, well illustrated by Skowhegan Family Medicine. Each of the vignettes in McPhee's book features an individual doctor with an individual patient and the work done after that visit. There is no medical team involved. This sense of a heroic, isolated struggle against disease is a sturdy metaphor in health care, such as in Abraham Verghese's epic work *Cutting for Stone*.[10] Starfield acknowledged that in other countries, nurses and health aides were involved in primary care. What she did not foresee was the role of nurse practitioners and physician assistants practicing independently. She did, however, come to anticipate that the evolving role of a primary care clinician would be as a manager of resources and other personnel.

Today, that focus on teams is front and center. The 2021 report by the National Academies of Science, Engineering, and Medicine (NASEM) admitted that even its previous 1996 report did not adequately predict or encourage the use of an interdisciplinary team of clinicians.[11] As later chapters will demonstrate, the entire future of primary care is centered on teams, with a core of doctors, nurse practitioners, and physician assistants surrounded by care coordinators, medical assistants, and pharmacists.

Nor did Starfield anticipate the role that technology would play in a medical practice. The heirs of general practice medicine used old-fashioned methods of documentation. While John McPhee scribbled in his notebooks, physicians scratched away at their paper-based medical records. Through the early 1990s, everything was written down on paper with a pen. Yet even as Starfield published her book in 1992, Judith Faulkner was introducing her first version of EpicCare, a Windows-based electronic medical record. Starfield noted, with some wonder, how the Harvard Community Health Plan in Boston had introduced its COSTAR program, allowing any doctor at any of its 10 centers to access data on patients from another center. But she could not clearly envision what a critical part of primary care electronic medical records would become, even in some ways its bane.

The third consideration missing from Starfield's 1992 characterization of the structure and ambitions of primary care was an explicit measurement of the quality of health care. Oversight of physicians' practices by health insurers and regulators, through the surveillance of various process and outcome measures, was another aspect of health care birthed in the early 1990s. The National Committee for Quality Assurance was founded in 1990 and began to undertake provider accreditation for health insurers in 1991. Its main tool was (and still is today) their Healthcare Effectiveness Data and Information Set (HEDIS), which reports on more than 50 benchmarks derived from various domains of care.[12] Many of these measures arose directly from primary care relationships. Over the past 30 years, these criteria have grown in depth and breadth, and they play an increasingly important role in the primary care ecosystem. Unfortunately, in many circumstances, such quality yardsticks have come to resemble the panopticon (a prison where a centrally located guard can see all the prisoners) in Michel Foucault's *Discipline and Punish*.[13] But more on that later.

By the early 1990s, the image of a family physician as an isolated agent struggling against disease was fading. Technology was impinging, oversight was beginning to occur, and team care was nascent. But even more important were the many changes heralded by the Clinton administration's health care reform efforts, representing a fourth element missing from Starfield's original vision.

President Bill Clinton, elected in 1992, believed he had a mandate to remake the nation's health care system, manipulating the regulation of insurance and changing the balance of managed care versus fee-for-service. As others, as well as myself,[14] have discussed at length, the legislative proposal at the heart of Clinton's health policy reforms never went anywhere. It did not even come up for a vote in Congress. But this effort ushered in a focus on managed care that did have a substantial impact on the US health care system, especially on primary care.

The plan drawn up by Hillary Clinton and Ira Magaziner, the leaders of the Clinton Health Care Task Force, was based on Alain Enthoven's notion of managed competition. This entailed the use of cost-effective insurance plans, made available through health insurance purchasing cooperatives, which in turn relied on comprehensive care organizations that integrated health care financing and its delivery.[15] The model for these care organizations was Kaiser Permanente. It combined health insurance with an organization of physicians and hospitals—a health maintenance organization (HMO)—that managed care. In today's vernacular, we would say the HMO's goal was to produce value-based care.

Care management or value-based care entails considering treatment options *and* their cost when ministering to patients, emphasizing parsimonious and efficient interventions that meet the standard of care. This was not a new concept in the 1990s. Managed care had long stalked the dominant form of payment for health care services, fee-for-service. But the Clinton administration's health plan gave it a considerable boost. Even after proposed legislation for these reforms died quietly, many still thought a managed care revolution had begun. Health care systems began preparing for a change.

Enthoven's (and Clinton's) managed care began with a primary care clinician. This person is given a specified amount of money (a capitation) that must cover the cost of care for an individual, attributed, patient. This sum is usually paid in monthly installments (a *per member, per month payment*, or PMPM). The payment is *risk adjusted* depending on the extent of a patient's illness. Sicker patients get larger capitation fees. These fees, however, always entail a *group* of patients. Predicting the risk of illness each year for any one person is difficult—and hazardous as a business proposition. But a group (usually a large one) will have some people who unexpectedly get sick and others who remain well. Statistically, their overall health and the cost of their medical care become much more predictable.

Enthoven always referred to the marriage of financing and delivery in managed care, but it is really a marriage of *insurance* and delivery. A person or organization providing health care in a capitated setting is taking on an insurance risk regarding illness. In a traditional fee-for-service system, that financial risk stays with the insurer, whose actuaries make predictions about the risk of illness and set the premiums. The insurer also must address the health care supplier's moral hazard. In other words, providing and charging for more forms of treatment (using designated billing codes) is profitable regardless of whether a patient truly needs all those medical services. Moral hazard is inherent in a fee-for-service system. This financial motive for health care providers, when married to a patient's lack of knowledge about which treatments are essential, is a recipe for unnecessary, expensive care. In a fee-for-service system, insurers fight overutilization by requiring prior authorization of medical procedures or by using higher out-of-pocket payments to incentivize patients to avoid certain treatments.

In managed care, the incentives are turned 180 degrees. Taking capitation payments from an insurer means that clinicians and other health care providers make more when they do less. Here the moral hazard is that all of the necessary care would not be offered, potentially adversely affecting patient care. Managed care providers have the same moral and legal responsibilities to a patient as those in a fee-for-service system, so they should still be meeting the required standard of care. The profit margin in managed care should come from the fact that capitation is generally based on average fee-for-service payments. The latter include a waste factor—related to fee-for-service's inherent moral hazard—of between 10% and 30%, depending on which estimates are used.[16] So, if a managed care provider eliminates clinical waste, capitation becomes profitable.

Organized medicine (primarily the American Medical Association, or AMA) had long prized fee-for-service care, as it provided a maximum amount of discretionary treatment choices for physicians, handsomely rewarded specialty care in particular procedures, and kept concerns about the cost of medical care out of the doctor–patient relationship.[17] Early forms of managed care, primarily what were referred to as staff model health maintenance organizations, began to appear nearly a hundred years ago. Kaiser Permanente became the best-known example, being a combined insurer, medical group, and hospital system that was focused on managing care. As early as the Nixon administration, the federal government began to encourage the use of managed care. The Health Maintenance Organization Act of 1974 created incentives for employers to select health insurance plans that incorporated payment relationships based on capitation. By the late 1980s, many health policy experts thought managed care would come to replace the fee-for-service system. Having managed care at the center of the Clinton administration's health plan was therefore not surprising—it was cutting edge.

Nonetheless, capitated managed care had not penetrated deeply into the foundation of primary care by 1990. The Skowhegan Family Medicine group was typical of the 1980s, with their expectation of fee-for-service payments by billing for every patient encounter (although Dr. Dorney told me that even their group received capitated payment for their Medicaid patients over time). Starfield, writing in 1992, seemed to presume a fee-for-service foundation for health care in the United States, but she noted how managed care conformed nicely with primary care's commitment to longitudinal responsibility for a patient. Moreover, a primary care clinician's responsibility for coordinating medical services, including access to specialty care, did have a good conceptual fit with the management of health care.[18] Nonetheless, Starfield appeared to remain of two minds about how managed care—and the corporatization of the practice of medicine she feared it might bring—would affect the quality of this care.

Others were less reticent. Eric Cassell, in his influential 1997 book *Doctoring: The Nature of Primary Care Practice*, saw the future of primary care being linked to managed care: "If the corporate managed care of today leads to multispecialty group practices tomorrow under the leadership of physicians, and with capitated payment for patient care, we will have a much better environment for the care of patients and for the support of advanced ideas of primary care."[19] Primary care doctors, whose long-term relationships with patients involved advice and advocacy, including identifying necessary treatments from specialists, could be easily envisioned as "managers" in the health care industry. That is certainly how Kaiser Permanente saw its primary care clinicians.

The ascent of managed care that was expected by many, including eventually some primary care experts, never really occurred in the 1990s. There are numerous explanations for this failure, and for the persistence of a fee-for-service system. One prominent theme is that both physicians and patients became concerned about the potential for a lack of necessary health care in a program where a provider made more money when less care was rendered. Malpractice lawsuits regarding managed care incentives gone awry multiplied, and they often sought huge financial penalties against health insurers and organized physician groups.[20] In this scenario, managed care imploded as a result of its own cost-efficiency incentives.

I am not entirely persuaded by this rationale, however. My view, elaborated in detail elsewhere,[21] is that the prospect—or fear—of managed care caused a great deal of consolidation in the US health care system, particularly among hospitals, and between hospitals and doctors. The hospital industry realized that care management required an organic relationship with a large population of patients. They needed doctors—specifically primary care clinicians—who could be their hands-on representatives in managed care, ensuring continuity and coordination with patients. In essence, "owning" the primary care doctors meant that you "owned" their patients and could oversee their care. So hospitals merged, and they hired networks of doctors. In managed care, patients had to be *attributed*, meaning that they had a relationship with a primary care provider, so an organization needed primary care clinicians to get new patients. Otherwise, the patients would be attributed to others. Thus the *integrated delivery system* (combining doctors with hospitals) was born.

Many of these new systems, making use of a physician/hospital organization to create a single corporation, accepted managed care contracts, including full capitation. With the Clinton administration's health plan so clearly founded on managed care, the future seemed clear, even after that proposed plan faded quickly. But managing care is hard, especially if you are applying this approach to some contracts with health insurers, while other contracts are still based on fee-for-service reimbursements. Unlearning fee-for-service muscle memory proved to be challenging. As a result, these integrated delivery systems failed to manage care sufficiently and lost a great deal of money on capitation-style contracts.

At the same time, the lightbulb of market power went off for many integrated delivery systems. These merged hospital systems, employing both primary care and specialist physicians, had more market leverage than local health insurers. So instead of managing care, they sought much higher rates of payment from those with whom they could negotiate—that is, commercial health insurers representing employers—in fee-for-service contracts. This created a long-term trend where payments from commercial insurers far outstripped those from governmental payers. As a result, 1995 was the heyday for managed care and capitation payment, which has faded considerably since then.

The link to primary care has stuck, though, and today anyone interested in managing care realizes that they must have a trained primary care staff at the core of their health care team. Nonetheless, certain aspects of managed care were already giving Barbara Starfield pause 30 years ago: "Thus the issue of gatekeepers is controversial, and is becoming increasingly so as more types of health care organizations adopt it. There is widespread suspicion that in some plans the basis for gatekeepers is cost containment rather than rationality of organization."[22] Starfield's fear, like that of many in primary care, was that commitment to a patient's good could be diluted by the gatekeeping function. As a care manager, however, a primary care clinician was empowered and played a vital role in ensuring the cost-effectiveness of care, a role that meshed nicely with continuity and coordination for their patients. In some ways, the question was, Would primary care be simply at the front of the system, a gatekeeper, or at the center of the system?

Backing off from managing care did not mean that integrated delivery systems shied away from control of primary care. To some extent, having a large physician base gave them additional leverage. And "owned" primary care doctors could also be a vital source of referrals. Having a primary care division within an integrated delivery system provided a stream of new patients for specialists and hospitals' operating rooms. The value of such vertical integrations has remained relatively durable for these systems.[23] Some medical centers today get by with a small primary care base, but many continue to believe that primary care can be a feeder for profitable procedure and operating rooms.

The dynamic between the good and bad faces of gatekeeping/managing will continue to be a driving theme in this book. Timothy Hoff, who understands the value of primary care as being "relational"—that is, focused on the patient—has identified a critical distinction. Gatekeeping forces primary care to become "transactional." According to Hoff, "Instead of a one stop shop, the traffic cop role denoted primary care doctors as [the] first, quick stop on the way to other doctors and parts of the system."[24] He sees managed care, and its closely related conceptual cousin, value-based care, as ruining doctor–patient relationships, particularly primary care relationships. I argue that the opposite might also be the case, so long as its primary focus remains on a patient's health.

What was clear by the end of the twentieth century is that most primary care doctors were not becoming care managers. Instead, they were a source of fee-for-service referrals, and many were starting to work for integrated delivery systems. Their role was limited and functional.

Into the Twenty-First Century

By the turn of the present century, the employer-sponsored health insurance sector had gotten comfortable with plans that were relatively unmanaged fee-for-service. Only a shadow of managed care was still preserved, since doctors were organized by insurers into preferred provider organizations (PPOs), in contrast with managed care organizations (MCOs). To qualify as preferred providers, they had to comply with utilization rules and oversight of patient safety. But having to assume a financial risk regarding their patient populations was no longer on the table.

The reluctance of employers to insist on greater management of health care spending, including the elimination of financial waste, is not well understood. Employers have generally been unwilling to rock the health insurance boat, even though, in many ways, they are standing at the prow. Part of this has to do with the fact that promoting good health for employees does not really pay off for a company, as workers today change jobs more frequently. Another factor is that the Employee Retirement Income Security Act—the key statute defining employee benefits, including health insurance—does not call for a great deal of regulatory oversight, although it does insist that any health insurance policy be applicable to all employees. Managed care contracts that might reduce employees' choices must also curtail those choices for the executive suite. Instead of trying to get health care providers to manage care, companies generally lowered their overall health insurance costs by increasing the employees' share of the premium and out-of-pocket costs. Executives and employees with higher incomes could better afford the increased share of the cost.

In a preferred provider organization, a primary care doctor was not called upon to act as a gatekeeper, and the presumption that these physicians would provide coordinated, longitudinal care for their patients faded. Guided by fee-for-service incentives, integrated delivery systems promoted specialty care. This in turn kept hospitals' operating rooms and medical procedure suites full. Specialists and hospitals both profited from this arrangement. Competition for specialists and proceduralists grew, and integrated delivery systems had to concentrate their negotiating strength in this sector of physicians. Primary care networks could still be useful for feeding patients into the specialists' medical practices. But these networks were not highly prized, given the presumption by both patients and specialists that free choice, independent of a primary care relationship, was an inherent part of the American health care system.

Thus primary care—in many ways a safety net and a hedge against the return of narrow health care networks—became less important to integrated delivery systems. The result was less investment in primary care. With limited leverage in negotiating rates with an insurer, integrated systems tended to invest in procedures and operations, and generally on reimbursement for hospital stays. Thus primary care was slighted, with lower reimbursement rates and lower compensation as a result.

Stuck in a fee-for-service system, primary care clinicians billed on a per encounter basis, including both commercial payment and Medicare. Primary care clinician payment levels under Medicare were calculated according to a resource-based relative value scale (RBRVS). RBRVS payment levels are primarily set by the Relative Value Scale Update Committee (RUC), an advisory group organized by the American Medical Association.[25] From the point of view of primary care advocates, the RUC is specialist dominated and thus inordinately values specialty work, to the detriment of primary care practices. I examine these claims more closely in chapter 3, but suffice it to say here that because of these valuations, at the start of the twenty-first century, primary care doctors earned a good deal less per hour than physicians in other fields. That problem persists today. Primary care work is not as highly valued as specialty procedures by the RUC and hence by America's physician payment system. Medicare payment rates tended to act as the guide for commercial rates, another downward pressure on reimbursement for primary care.

The sizeable difference in incomes for general practitioners and for specialists began long ago. A detailed paper published by the Federal Reserve Bank of St. Louis in the 1950s revealed that in 1949, specialists made 70% more than general practitioners (with a mean net income of $15,014 versus $8,835).[26] But the authors emphasized that this differential was much less than it had been in 1929, and they predicted that it would decline further over time.

A generation later, the Health Care Financing Administration, a predecessor to the Centers for Medicare and Medicaid Services (CMS), evaluated physicians' income changes from 1975 to 1984.[27] After adjusting for the high rate of inflation over that period, the average income for physicians changed little, remaining at about $93,000 (in

1984 dollars). But the reverse was true for doctors in general practice, pediatrics, and internal medicine, with the pay for GPs dropping from $78,193 to $72,559. Meanwhile, inflation-adjusted incomes for those practicing general surgery and obstetrics/gynecology increased. More importantly, orthopedic surgeons and cardiovascular specialists were earning almost twice as much as general practitioners.

These disparities in income were already apparent to Starfield as she assembled her research agenda and policy recommendations. Presciently, she identified hospitals' financial dynamics as the source of a feedback loop that led to greater reimbursements for specialists. Hospitals gained revenue from the use of more intensive care, more operations, and more medical procedures. And they needed an ever-larger stream of specialists who could undertake this care. The training programs in specialty medical disciplines provided the infrastructure, at a relatively low cost, that allowed interventional medicine to grow. Starfield wrote, "Because primary care residencies generate less revenue than other specialties, teaching hospitals have found it increasingly difficult to support them."[28] Thus primary care was underemphasized—and in many ways was unneeded—by integrated delivery systems, including teaching hospitals, as long as patients had unrestricted access to specialty care.

Starfield thought this payment disparity situation would eventually correct itself, but (from a historical perspective) she labored under two false impressions. First, in 1980, the prominent Graduate Medical Education National Advisory Committee (GMENAC) predicted that the United States would soon have too many specialists and about the right number of primary care clinicians.[29] These views dominated policy circles for some time, leading many to conclude that earnings for specialists would begin to deflate, and the income level for primary care doctors would increase. But even by the 1990s, when Starfield was putting her thoughts together, it was becoming clear that medical innovations, profit incentives, and the structural relationship between specialists and hospital care were increasing the demand for specialty services. One new medical test or intervention often led to another, which required a new specialist.

Second, Starfield was caught up in the managed care wave at the time. As noted above, she was of two minds about whether primary care clinicians should act as gatekeepers. Nonetheless, she was convinced that they would have a leading role in managed care and hence garner better reimbursement. While lamenting the income disparity that was already evident in primary versus specialty care, Starfield did not concentrate on a solution, aside from suggesting that primary care doctors remain within a fee-for-service system and specialists move to a salaried structure—just the opposite of my ultimate recommendation.

Starfield's sanguine predictions did not come to pass. Into the 2000s, disparities in primary care versus specialty pay levels continued to grow. One report from 2003 showed both amounts dropping in real terms from 1995 to 1999 but less so for specialists, who were earning an average of $219,000 in 1999, compared with $138,000 for primary care physicians.[30] In 2006, Reed Abelson told a similar story in the *New York Times*, emphasizing that primary care doctors had experienced a steep 7% decline in income from 1995 to 2003.[31] The status of primary care physicians as low earners within the medical field was well established then and continues to be true today.

These comments about physicians' incomes, and for primary care doctors in particular, need some perspective. The median income in the United States was just over $71,000 in 2021. In early 2022, the Advisory Board website reported that the three worst paid specialties in American medicine were public health / preventative medicine, pediatrics, and family medicine, clustered at just about $250,000.[32] In contrast, plastic surgeons and orthopedists averaged more than $550,000. Cardiologists, otolaryngologists, urologists, and gastroenterologists all garnered more than $450,000. For medical students selecting a career path, all these disciplines are lucrative, but the income inequity between generalists and specialists points students toward performing medical procedures rather than developing the relationships with patients that characterized Skowhegan Family Medicine. Although primary care is underpaid as a medical specialty, it certainly is not when compared with what an average American earns.

The health care polity has continued to evolve. So far in the twenty-first century, the great health policy event was passage of the Affordable Care Act, whose provisions are often known collectively as Obamacare. But the ACA's impact on the structure of primary care was relatively muted. The act's main impetus was to improve coverage, and this it did, fantastically well, by expanding the Medicaid program and reformulating individual and small group insurance markets into the so-called exchanges. It also continued the expansion of support for federally qualified health centers (FQHCs) that the Bush administration had begun, which has been vitally important for primary care for lower-income people, as discussed in chapter 4. Finally, the act created the Centers for Medicare and Medicaid Innovation, which gave government regulators the ability to test new payment methods and organizations of care.

But there were no specific provisions for restructuring primary care. In recent years, it has become clear not only that primary care is not keeping up with other specialties in terms of physicians' incomes, but also that the flow of overall dollars into primary care is decreasing. Although the Affordable Care Act of 2010 created two new funding streams for primary care, one in Medicare and the other in Medicaid, neither has been sustained.[33] The Milbank Memorial Fund's scorecard on primary care makes the fundamental point that the percentage of health care dollars attributed to primary care continues to drop.[34] After peaking in 2013 at 6.2%, it decreased to 4.6% in 2020. Although the average in other Organization for Economic Co-Operation and Development (OECD) countries is 7.8%, it is much higher in some of these countries. In the United States, payment for and support of primary care should not be considered to be adequate for a well-functioning health care system.

Over the past decade, many primary care doctors complain that increasingly more is expected of them, even though they are (relatively) poorly paid and, in many ways, are an afterthought in a fee-for-service, PPO-dominated, nonmanaged health care system. Moreover, they believe, for good reason, that they are overworked. Only 17% of primary care physicians are extremely or very satisfied with their workload.[35]

Laurence McMahon and his colleagues from the University of Michigan have carefully explored the workload of primary care.[36] After lamenting the overall financial picture of primary care, they note that "managed care" was replaced by "pay for performance" in the early 2000s, coinciding with the shift from HMOs to PPOs. Realizing that a fee-for-service system had no incentives for promoting the quality of health care (and huge incentives for the overutilization of treatments and procedures), payers began using PPOs, which would receive bonuses if they performed well on measures of quality or utilization or face clawbacks if they did poorly. These measures often fell directly into the bailiwick of primary care: for example, average hemoglobin A1c measurements for patients with diabetes, or blood pressure control.

This effort to graft some responsibility for health care quality and utilization onto a fee-for-service backbone brought with it an emphasis on scorecards and new requirements for documentation. This in turn contributed to what McMahon and colleagues characterized as "three innovations that inexorably changed primary care clinical practice": (1) efforts to comply with the value-based care criteria, (2) consumerism, and (3) increased utilization of EMRs.

"Value-based care" became a synonym for "payment based on performance." Consumerism, which was seen as a positive in health care, characterized a patient not as a dependent person with an illness (a paternalistic view of the provider–patient relationship) but as an informed customer who should be served by the medical enterprise. Consumerism was consonant with empowerment. Responsibility for the customer's medical needs generally fell to primary care. In some ways, this makes sense, as it is the point of first contact for patients. But clinicians hate to see themselves as purveyors, preferring to have a partner rather than a customer.

EMRs rapidly became a larger part of health care in general and primary care in particular. It was clear to everyone that keeping paper records was not sustainable in the twenty-first century, and the federal government eventually provided a huge infusion of funds for the effort through the Health Information Technology for Economic and Clinical Health (HITECH) Act in 2009. More than $27 billion in incentives prompted almost all hospitals and most physician practices to adopt electronic medical records.[37] From 2012 to 2022, the degree of EMR penetration into physicians' offices went from 17% to more than 80%. EMR use in hospitals has become nearly universal, and it is generally seen as improving both the quality of health care and patient safety.[38]

These three innovations nonetheless created daunting new burdens for primary care clinicians. Their practices were not determining the path of a patient's care, as gatekeeper responsibilities had gone the way of managed care. But a primary care office was still the most likely health care site to be used by most patients, so the responsibility for complying with quality measures, promoting consumerism, and documenting these activities fell to primary care clinicians. Many primary care doctors complain that these jobs get dumped on them by specialists or by "the administration."

McMahon and his University of Michigan colleagues have done a great job in documenting the results of this vortex.[39] Tasks around referrals, insurance company requirements (including prior authorizations), and efforts to improve value-based care measures all end up in their EMR inbox. At the University of Michigan Medical Center, a full-time primary care clinician has nearly 400 inbox tasks per week, many of which require a reasonable amount of investigation. The authors estimated that this produces as much as 20 hours per week in additional work for a full-time doctor.

Consumerism adds to this workload, as patients can now access their health information through an EMR-linked patient portal, prompting more patient inquiries that are often based on background information gathered from Google searches. For example, all materials from laboratory and specialist visits now get to patients/consumers in a day or two, with new questions generated by these visits developing at an exponential rate. A patient's primary care doctor must digest this information and respond to it. As the University of Michigan team noted: "Facilitated by the EMR, primary care has essentially become the default decision maker for problems from scheduling to payment, with more members of the health care system forwarding issues directly to the primary care physician."[40]

Primary care clinicians—who are now the brokers of information for patients/consumers, the stewards of quality compliance, and the traffic cops between patients and specialists—find themselves chained to EMRs, doing more and more clerical work that they may not be able to delegate to others. Dissatisfaction with this role is ubiquitous. Primary care clinicians have less time to spend with their patients as they are burdened with more and more EMR keystrokes. It is no wonder, then, that in a recent study, a chatbot powered by artificial intelligence could provide more satisfactory (and more empathetic) answers to patients' questions than live physicians.[41]

This difficulty is perhaps most keenly felt in the large teaching hospitals I visited. During the 1990s or early 2000s, most hospitals saw themselves as integrated delivery systems, attempting to add a primary care component to what was otherwise a sizeable specialty/intervention-based medical center. These hospitals also tend to be the last bastion for internists in primary care medicine.

The result is that today, a good deal of primary care occurs in practices associated with hospitals and large medical groups. Another sizable proportion occurs at FQHCs. The American Academy of Family Physicians reports that 75% of its current membership is employed, and 75% of that is in hospitals or large groups.[42] The number is likely much higher for general internal medicine.

Few of these doctors are practicing what might be considered value-based care. The overwhelming majority are in the fee-for-service domain, and the currency in their practice is visits per hour, complicated by all the factors identified by the University of Michigan researchers. This is the norm in the United States. Likely one example suffices to illustrate it.

Primary Care at a Large Teaching Hospital

A visit to the University of Alabama at Birmingham Medical Center, known as UAB Medicine, in December 2022 crystallized a number of these points about the challenges faced by primary care. Arriving in Birmingham, it looked a bit tired and was smaller than expected. Getting out of the somewhat dilapidated cab I took from the airport, the driver warned me a second time to go easy on the vehicle's door, as "it has 600,000 miles on it." The town looks that way, too.

My hotel was surrounded by UAB Hospital, the largest single-institution medical center I have ever seen. And this in a city with less than 200,000 people. There are a lot of reasons why UAB has grown so large, but the most important one is that it provides much of the specialty medical care for the entire state. A series of hulking buildings, punctuated by the gargantuan I. M. Pei–designed ambulatory care center, stretches for blocks. The hospital has 1,157 beds. Perhaps no other hospital in the country plays as large a role in its state's and region's health care than does UAB.

A lot of medical care goes on at UAB, but not a lot of primary care. The entire complex has roughly 70 primary care clinicians, doctors, and nurse practitioners, including some in satellite settings. Nor does there seem to be a lot of unaffiliated primary care clinicians. The largest competitive primary care group, which is affiliated with an Ascension Health Care System hospital, is around a dozen people, I was told. Almost everyone you ask has the same response: people simply do not seek primary care. If they get sick, they go to specialists.

UAB Medicine owns Viva Health, an insurer with more than 100,000 members. It offers a Medicare Advantage plan as well as several group plans, including one for all UAB employees. (My taxi driver assured me that UAB was by far the biggest employer in the state.) Given this, one might expect that Viva Health's administrators would develop some programs with the university's medical faculty, especially its primary care team, to manage the financial insurance risk for these beneficiaries. (That is the strategy in most situations where health insurers and health care providers are combined in the same organization.) But such programs are not easy to find in the primary care practice at UAB.

Viva Health has apparently not depended on the medical center for care management. Instead, it employs its own team of nurses that do outreach to patients, and it has developed its own data on care interventions. Some of the data are transmitted to primary care practices, but the health insurance and primary care programs seem to be siloed. (Viva is nonetheless highly rated in the Medicare Stars program.)

The UAB administrative team in charge of primary care explained the situation. In the early 2000s, there was a general perception that the medical center's leadership did not support primary care and wanted to get rid of UAB's family medicine residency. (They did do away with the midwifery program.) The priorities have changed somewhat under new leadership, primarily through Dr. Selwyn Vickers, who departed recently to head Memorial Sloan Kettering Cancer Center in New York City. He supported family medicine and promoted a stronger relationship with Cahaba Medical, which is a large network of FQHCs. He also financed freestanding family practice programs in Huntsville, Montgomery, and Selma. But there was little effort to enhance primary care in UAB Medicine's core.

Nor does this seem to be a priority today. There has been almost no expansion of the number of their primary care doctors for years, even though any newly minted doctor would immediately fill his patient panel. (The UAB primary care team recently added a new physician whose patient schedule, within a week, was booked out eight months.) The only explanations for this situation are that the primary care department's bottom line is not profitable, and that there is already plenty of work for UAB's specialty-dominated hospital and its specialty departments. The medical center does not appear to need primary care practitioners. In this regard, UAB is not an outlier among academic medical centers. A recent McKinsey survey of academic medical centers listed reducing length of stay and revenue cycle management as the top priorities, reflecting a fee-for-service world. Value-based care arrangements were not among them.[43]

Another salient issue is the dominance of Blue Cross Blue Shield of Alabama, which has more than 90% of the commercial health insurance market. The explanation at UAB Medicine is that primary care payments under the Blue Cross Blue Shield plans are insufficient. Since the medical center would rather use what market leverage it has to boost fees in other departments, commercial health insurance payment rates for primary care have remained inadequate. Nonetheless, Viva Health and the UAB Medical Center have positive profit margins.

That profitability is all the more remarkable in that there is no city hospital, leaving UAB as the safety net for the city—and most of Alabama. A hospital in the Ascension chain is the only competition, and it usually has plenty of capacity. (Indeed, in mid-2024, UAB agreed to acquire Ascension St. Vincent's for $450 million.) UAB occasionally decants patients to them when the UAB Hospital emergency department is full, usually with 50–60 patients waiting for beds. UAB shares many of the challenges other large teaching hospitals face, acting as the place of last resort for impoverished peoples' health care while needing to remain financially sound. The strategy UAB is pursuing appears viable, but it does not entail a substantial role for primary care.

I got a tour of Prime Care, the main primary care practice on-site at UAB. Jaye Locks, its engaging and friendly practice manager, and Dr. Stuart Cohen, its medical director and leader, designed their new space. They had hoped to situate all of the team's clinicians in a shared open workspace, but the doctors ended up having their own individual offices. Prime Care is now facing a space crunch, as UAB administration, after moving primary care out of its main outpatient building (Kirkland Clinic), would now like to take over more of the current primary care space for dermatology. The medical center's reasoning was that primary care's use of space per visit was not measuring up financially to what orthopedists or other specialists could do, as these physicians spent a much shorter time with their patients.

All the doctors for Prime Care are trained in internal medicine. While UAB has a family medicine residency, its clinics are in a separate location. UAB's nursing school also silos its student nurse practitioners. A lack of cooperation between primary care training programs is pretty much the rule around the country (the exception being some programs championed by the Veterans Health Administration, or VA, a component of the US Department of Veterans Affairs). This situation is especially ironic, since most practices today expect all their professionals to work together in teams.

Stuart Cohen is a warm and thoughtful person who evinces the patience and wisdom that comes with providing primary care to patients for 30 years.[44] He still works multiple sessions, moving smoothly about the clinic with his veteran medical assistant. He is proud of Prime Care but laments about how hard everyone there works. Many of its patients are chronically ill, with "problem lists" (the standard term clinicians use in their notes summarizing a patient's visit) that often contain 10–15 items. The practice's full-time clinicians see 16–20 patients a day, in 9 sessions per week. It's much like the rapid-fire work of the Skowhegan Family Medicine group years ago.

Dr. Cohen reasonably takes some credit for helping Viva Health's Medicare Advantage Plan reach a five-star quality-of-care rating, the highest level awarded by the CMS. For years, his primary care practice carefully followed and excelled on what are now the CMS's health care quality measures: cancer screenings, treatments for chronic diseases, annual wellness checks, and periodic office visits. Viva would provide the clinicians with messages about gaps in care, such as interventions that patients were due to receive but had not yet occurred, for example, an annual mammogram. The practice would take this feedback and use it to encourage the clinicians to take steps to comply.

But none of this effort was ever automated. For example, data on the practice's care for patients with hypertension and diabetes were assembled by a staff member on an Excel spreadsheet, and hard copies went to the practice's nurses. But the Cerner EMR system they were using couldn't accommodate population health measurements or prompts delivered through text messaging. As Cohen laments, the UAB practices are about a decade behind industry norms in terms of data analysis. So, attention to these measures has waned somewhat. Nor is the practice taking steps to monitor and address its patients' utilization of costly services, like hospitalizations. Viva apparently takes responsibility for population health management for its members. Other insurers are not providing much feedback.

Getting new doctors into the practice is challenging. UAB has a huge, prestigious internal medicine training program, but most of the residents migrate into subspecialties. Other residents usually opt for hospital medicine, doing rounds for inpatients. Twenty years ago, there was a stream of general internists for UAB's primary care practice, but it has largely dried up. Nonetheless, Cohen and his team do manage to recruit a few new doctors each year, and they enter with the energy and optimism of youth, finding a professionally satisfying practice with colleagues they respect.

Dr. Cohen wanted me to meet with some of his more senior staff. I spoke with three of these physicians in depth, two of whom were recently retired. Although not representative of the entire UAB team, these doctors were fascinating and informative. (I should note that my visits to various medical centers and clinics were arranged by local leaders; therefore the individuals highlighted in this book are not a random sample. My stated intent was to study the field of primary care and understand its future, so the selection of people with whom I spoke could have been biased, representing the sunnier, more optimistic, and happier side of the spectrum. As this and later chapters will demonstrate, however, many of the doctors and nurses who spent time with me did not seem sunny and optimistic, but it is still important to keep that potential bias in mind. Things could be worse or better than I have reported.)

Dr. Jay Herndon was casually well dressed, relaxed, and self-assured.[45] Retirement seemed to be treating him well. Like the other physicians I met at UAB, he was polite, reserved, but also articulate, conversing in a matter-of-fact manner. He had grown up in Alabama, went to UAB's medical school, then trained at UAB. For more than 25 years, he was the senior doctor at a satellite practice UAB operated in Inverness, a nearby suburb. (There were also a couple of other satellites.) He retired at age 59, exhausted and convinced that he could no longer get sufficient resources to make his practice manageable.

When working, he was paired with a nurse practitioner (to help with the chronically ill patients) and a medical assistant. This arrangement was standard throughout UAB's primary care practices. When Herndon retired, he and his small team were seeing 3,200 patients. This huge number was dictated by constant pressure from UAB's administration. From Herndon's point of view, the administrators had long seen primary care as a money loser, so they pushed to have more patients in the practice, in order to reduce that financial loss. In addition, UAB wanted to increase access to specialists by having more patients enter through the portal of primary care. The result was a long working day: twelve hours in the clinic, with another two hours of EMR work afterward. Even so, patients were dissatisfied that they could not get appointments as soon as they wanted. Work became a real grind, so Herndon quit.

The compensation game at UAB was primarily based on points calculated from the number of patient visits. New patients and annual wellness visits received two points, and returning patients got one point. UAB's specialty maw wanted new patients, and Viva Health wanted to ensure that annual wellness visits occurred. The volume of patient visits constituted 70% of a doctor's income, and the volume from a paired nurse practitioner comprised another 10%. If a nurse practitioner saw more patients, then the affiliated doctor made more money. Panel size, or the number of patients cared for, accounted for the other 20%. Panel size is a nod to a more managed care approach. For example, some of the primary care practices I will discuss limit their number of patients (panel size) to 500 Medicare Advantage beneficiaries, contrasted with Herndon's 3,200 patients (a mix of individuals with either commercial health insurance or Medicare).

Herndon related that there was a good deal of transparency about the quality-of-care measures Stuart Cohen developed, so doctors paid attention to them. Three to five years ago, however, they faded in importance. Herndon also commented on the doctors' awareness that UAB employees and Viva's health insurance beneficiaries are essentially capitated, so their care should be managed with an eye to efficiency. But UAB never articulated any overarching strategy or specific incentives to do so. Not that Herndon was necessarily looking for such incentives. He noted that in a 20-minute visit, it was hard to set goals other than assessing the patient's health. Nonetheless, he always felt that the best care for patients involved a parsimonious approach, only referring them to specialists when necessary and taking care of as much as possible in his primary care office.

Herndon's average working day sounded intense. His main issue was completing notes for 15–20 patients a day. For years, the primary care practice used a transcription service but later adopted a voice recognition program. Recently they had tried a proprietary system in which doctors in India listened to what was said during a visit and then wrote a summary note. But this began to deteriorate when the employer in India had trouble hiring doctors there, and the notes backed up. Herndon did not mind tending to his electronic inbox, but he hated interacting with the EMR. He believed the program had a few microseconds' delay with each command; over hundreds of thousands of keystrokes, the delay was debilitating. He also thought the ergonomics of the screens were terrible. He had more detailed complaints about his computer than anyone should really have, but in the final analysis, he was still constantly clicking, clicking, clicking on the keyboard.

I asked Herndon what had happened over the past 20 years that led to his retirement. His bottom line was that the joy had gone out of his work. A couple of decades ago, his primary care practice was more varied. He could repair lacerations, perform pulmonary function tests, or spend time talking with older patients. More recently, everything was just a rush. Today, he said, UAB does not mind if their primary care teams send patients to urgent care facilities if their own clinics are too full. Years ago, that was not done. A patient was a friend with whom you had rapport, and you would extend your efforts in order to care for them. Today, the amount of data coming over the gunwales is just too much.

UAB is a tremendous medical center. Its primary care practice evinces the professional and compassionate commitment to care that is the hallmark of the institution. But primary care there, as seen through Dr. Herndon's practice, suffers from many of the same problems as hundreds, if not thousands, of similar practices in this country. Herndon's sense of having been overwhelmed and no longer enjoying his work is a symptom of the widespread burnout in primary care.

I spoke with two other physicians who corroborated Herndon's experience. Dr. Dave Gettinger is another native Alabaman, but he attended Stanford University for college and the University of

California, San Francisco for medical school.[46] He returned to UAB to train and be near family. Gettinger was a chief resident, an honor typically reserved for the best clinician among the house officers in a given training year. Former chief residents ought to be excellent doctors, and he certainly seemed to be one.

Gettinger identified two significant changes during the almost 40 years he practiced. The first was making rounds. The doctors in the Skowhegan Family Medicine practice visited all their patients who were in the hospital. They were the attending physicians who gave orders for a patient to be admitted and decided when that person would be discharged. Hospitalized patients saw either their own doctor or another doctor from the practice every day while they were hospitalized. This custom supported continuity, familiarity, and rapport. When Gettinger started at UAB, the same expectations were in place.

Generally speaking, though, it was not efficient to have doctors taking time out of their office schedule to do hospital rounds. Nor did these office-based doctors necessarily know and follow all of the hospital's protocols, which came to assume greater prominence over time. After Medicare changed its hospital reimbursement program in 1983, instituting a prospective payment system (PPS), the length of a patient's stay was a critical financial issue, and hospitals were incentivized to discharge patients as quickly as possible.

It was not long before hospitals hired their own doctors to make rounds. Dr. Robert Wachter and Dr. Lee Goldman dubbed these doctors *hospitalists*. Hospitals required hospitalists to be the attending physicians. Before long, a significant number of primary care doctors stopped making rounds for their hospital inpatients, as it seemed superfluous. But some, perhaps quite a few, regretted it.

Gettinger saw the rise of hospitalists as a sea change. He wanted to take care of his patients who were in the hospital, and he wanted them to expect such care. Using a hospitalist interrupted the continuity of care that he felt was vital to his practice.

EMRs were another blow for him. He refused to try to type a note while seeing a patient, as he wanted to maintain eye contact and concentration with that person. EMRs reduced his efficiency. Now he could only treat 80% of the patients he had previously been seeing, but his workload increased by 120%, since he had to fully document what went on during a patient visit, an essential medical care process known as *charting*. Moreover, he felt that EMRs left him with no excuse to not know everything about a patient. He found he was getting up at four o'clock in the morning to begin his pre-charting for that day's patients, thus ending up working a 14-hour day. He also wanted to write excellent, narrative-style notes, so that other doctors consulting those EMR notes would be completely informed. I found his thoughts about the workload to be a brilliant portrait of what happens when you combine electronic access to layers of data with a compulsive commitment to patient care. This underlies a great deal of the sense many doctors have of being chained to EMRs.

Gettinger regrets the way primary care medicine in general has evolved. He recalled the television show *Cheers*, whose theme song was called "Where Everybody Knows Your Name." As time went by in his practice, people no longer knew everyone's name. He had a sense that personal human contact had been lost. He was happy to be retired.

Dr. Alan Gruman was Gettinger's former partner, and they had covered for one another for years. When one of them was away, the other would deal with the scheduled patients, answer telephone calls, and, when needed, admit patients to the hospital. I saw them together as I was passed from one to the other, and their old camaraderie and mutual affection was touching.

Gruman was another Birmingham "lifer," going to medical school and training at UAB.[47] He is a large man, with a long, sympathetic face. He added two other important observations about UAB as we talked. The first was that many of the specialists at UAB were academically engaged and worked only part-time in their practices. Primary care doctors were the glue for UAB's medical system, as well as the conductor orchestrating treatment for patients with chronic diseases. (Starfield, a product of teaching hospitals, made the same point.) Now, that glue was slowly being lost.

Second, while Gruman had gradually accommodated himself to working with nurse practitioners and physician assistants, being chained to EMRs, and foregoing hospital rounds, the one thing he could not abide was prior authorization requirements. Insurance companies bear the financial risk for the cost of patient care, so they try to police overutilization. They require doctors to document why they are undertaking certain tests or procedures, or they will not allow payment. So, they want to approve the use of these often costly procedures or tests before they occur; this is known as *prior authorization*. These insurance demands typically land on the desk of primary care doctors—or, more accurately, in their EMR inbox. Dr. Gruman hated these interferences, as most doctors do. He especially detested peer-to-peer reviews, when he had to talk to an insurance company's doctor. The dislike of prior authorization is visceral throughout primary care.

Like his retired colleagues, Gruman felt the loss over time of what primary care should be. He went from "working *at* UAB to working *for* UAB." Once patient scheduling was moved to a centralized function, it seemed like he surrendered all control. His overall assessment: "I love what I do, but I hate to do the things I have to do to do it."

These sentiments are not unique but ubiquitous, especially in certain types of medical practices, and among middle-aged or older clinicians. But they are not restricted to those groups. I heard similar complaints from doctors in their thirties working at a Kaiser Permanente practice in California. (From the point of view of health policy, UAB and Kaiser Permanente could not be more different.) Dissatisfaction in primary care seems to be especially broad and deep. The difference among older doctors was the wistfulness in their comments, a regret for something that had been lost.

But depression and resignation were not the only stories I heard. The UAB colleagues I talked with revere their patients and have the same gratitude for their work as the doctors from Skowhegan Family Medicine did. I had every reason to believe that the patients in the Prime Care practice were getting great care. Dr. Cohen said that had I interviewed other, younger doctors, I might have gotten a different impression overall. But no one who studies contemporary primary care would suggest that the views of Drs. Gettinger, Gruman, and Herndon do not well represent a strong sentiment of dissatisfaction with practice today.

One final point about UAB's primary care practice is that it is an outlier, as all its doctors are internists. Today, newly minted internists are not choosing to go into primary care.[48] Family medicine has filled this void, and most of the young primary care doctors one meets today are trained in this field. As well, primary care residencies (family medicine and internal medicine) are no longer popular with doctor of medicine (MD) students from American allopathic medical schools. In 2023, there were more than 5,000 family medicine slots offered, with 1,484 filled by US medical school graduates (allopaths). Another 1,500 slots were filled by graduates from doctor of osteopathic medicine (DO) schools, which combine an interest in manipulation of the musculoskeletal system with an emphasis on whole person care and preventive medicine. The rest were filled by international medical graduates (IMGs) or were left unfilled.[49] Thus the majority of new primary care doctors have attended osteopathic medical schools or medical schools outside the United States. These are the doctors under 35 years of age found in primary care today. In addition, as we will see, their numbers are dwarfed by those of nurse practitioners.

Since UAB is the first site visit I related, I should emphasize at this point the four elements I use to characterize any primary care practice. The first is the composition of the practice team. Skowhegan demonstrated the traditional approach: a single doctor and that individual's patients, along with someone working the front desk. Today's primary care practice usually has a team of some sort, including nurses, nurse practitioners or physician assistants, care managers, medical assistants, and even pharmacists and behavioral health specialists. UAB's primary care doctors each have a medical assistant, plus a nurse practitioner to help with the overflow, but these latter individuals do not have their own panels.

My second element is the nature of financial compensation. The traditional approach was widely known as "eat what you kill" (one of many offensive aphorisms that populate clinical medicine)—that is, being paid a fee for every patient seen, minus some administrative overhead. Today, this is called relative value unit (RVU) payment, referring to the resource-based relative value system that assigns certain codes to physicians' work. (Dr. Herndon told me that UAB used to rely on RVUs, but the number of RVUs that doctors were doing got too ridiculously high.)

The third element is the percentage of patients who have some type of managed care arrangement. The extent of the need to manage care will dictate the parameters of a primary care practice. UAB's Prime Care was unusual in that it was overwhelmingly focused on fee-for-service payments even though there was a large proportion of Viva Health's insurance beneficiaries, where payment to the overall UAB organization was essentially capitation. But Viva did not move managed care downstream to Prime Care.

The fourth parameter is the dominant type of health insurance for patients in the practice: commercial, Medicare, Medicaid, or uninsured. Sadly, this insurance profile informs a great deal of what takes place in a primary care practice. Herndon's Inverness clinic was situated in a comparatively wealthy suburb, so most of its patients had commercial health insurance. Some primary care practices do not accept Medicaid and uninsured patients, while others have almost nothing but patients in these two categories. As I relate more site visits, various permutations of these four parameters will emerge.

As the differences in health insurance status show, American health care is not equitably distributed—not even close. Those with reduced incomes and people of color have less access to care, and that includes access to primary care. And where that access does exist in their neighborhoods, it is most often underresourced. Federal and state governments have taken steps to address and ameliorate access issues, but they have been only partially successful.

This is not a book about poverty, but about primary care. (Matthew Desmond's *Poverty, by America* is a great book on poverty.[50]) But any serious assessment of the American health care system reflects the devastating and unnecessary disparities in wealth that characterize the

United States. Nor is this really a book on health equity, or the emerging efforts to correct the differences in health care that people receive, based on their ability to pay, color, or ethnicity. All that said, those with low incomes and people of color are not as well served by our health care system as those who are wealthy and white. Recent research has shown that being in poverty creates a 42% greater chance of dying prematurely, compared with someone not in that economic state.[51] This blunt fact is buttressed by hundreds of studies that show that low-income populations, racial minorities, and recent immigrants get much worse care on a variety of measures.

Therefore it is no surprise when we find that primary care takes a different shape in low-income and minority neighborhoods. There is a whole sector of primary care that serves only those with low incomes, or Brown or Black patients, or recent immigrants. The contrast between the two medical practices in Dallas noted in the foreword is not an exception but the rule. Inequity in our society, in our health care system, and indeed to some extent in primary care, will be a consistent backdrop to this effort to understand how primary care evolves.

Where Is Primary Care Heading?

The future of primary care is difficult to predict. But the starting point is an understanding of the historical evolution of the discipline. From my point of view, the best way to see it is that primary care emerged from general practice as the health care system was moving into a fee-for-service-dominated payment structure, with operations and procedures being better compensated than evaluation and management of chronic disease. As a result, the currency in primary care practices became a measure of visits per hour, and the ideal of proactive management of a patient's health gave way to rushed efforts to deal with current problems.

In this setting, primary care clinicians do not have sufficient time to provide patients with care that leaves them feeling supported and healthy. Eventually chained to electronic medical records, and then saddled with all the paperwork and procedures that come from other specialists and insurers, primary care clinicians have broad responsibility but not enough resources or time to get their jobs done. So they have burned out and left. In a wide variety of practice settings, across the country, I heard this familiar story.

But it was not unanimous. For example, soon after returning from Alabama, I talked with Dr. Mirza Baig, who works for a physician group in eastern Massachusetts known as Atrius Health.[52] His practice is in Quincy, at a large site that Atrius Medical Group operates. (Atrius is now owned by Optum Health.) He grew up in India, trained in the United Kingdom, and came to the United States after finishing his Royal College of Physicians accreditation. He practiced as a hospitalist at Beth Israel Hospital in Boston for a few years and then joined Atrius 11 years ago.

Baig has a disarmingly warm style, and he was apologetic about being late for our interview, as he had been explaining an issue to a patient. Unprompted, he characterized his job as "excellent," relating that he "loves internal medicine, the diagnostic intrigue. It has been a great challenge throughout my career." The work does not sound easy. He has 3,000 patients in his panel and sees 18–20 of them a day, working four and a half days a week. He catches up with other tasks on Friday afternoons. He works with a team composed of a nurse practitioner, a licensed practical nurse (LPN), a registered nurse (RN), and a medical assistant (MA). They have all been together a long time, except for the MA. (Baig notes that "they cannot hold on to their MAs.") The Epic EMR system is "fine." It helps with reminders, and the inbox is an important way to keep up with patients.

The patient contact is what he loves. He wants to answer all the questions that patients have, and their satisfaction feeds his contentment. Baig, at age 60, is increasing his panel size. He believes that "if you wake up in the morning and see what you do as a burden, you will carry that all day. If you wake up excited about what you do, then you will remain excited." Lots of physicians feel this way, sustained by the rewards of taking care of patients. But in primary care, Dr. Baig notwithstanding, conventional practice is making this vocation harder to appreciate. He is an outlier, although nearly every doctor and nurse I talked to still has enthusiasm for their patients and wants their practice to be better. The range of primary clinician views falls much closer to UAB than to Dr. Baig.

In my view, fee-for-service is the root cause of the problems plaguing primary care. I have set out the alternative, like many others, as a value-based endeavor in which primary care has sufficient resources to quarterback the patient's journey toward health. Perhaps just better pay and lower volume expectations for primary care clinicians would accomplish this goal. But I believe real reform entails a turn toward prospective payment for primary care, where the financial incentives are such that the clinicians are charged with ensuring that care is value based, waste is avoided, and all efforts are aimed at anticipating and preventing future illness. More technically, this means capitated payment, either for the entire care of the patient, or at least for the primary care services.

I am not alone in this assessment. Nearly every other entity—mostly payers—who have the ability to drive health care reform see it the same way. The federal government, many proactive state governments, insurers both large and small, investors, and even some employers are pushing for more resources for primary care, but with the caveat that the financial incentives line up for proactive, value-based care. There are, simply put, no voices calling for maintenance of the status quo—the status quo is broken.

Some academic observers, and many physicians in practice, have come to a different historical diagnosis. Best articulated by Professor Timothy Hoff of Northeastern University, this thesis is that much of the current malaise, especially in family medicine, can be attributed to the influence of insurers and corporations on health care, and the abiding consumerism they bring.[53] What has been lost is the selfless commitment to the patient that was such an important part of the healing process, replaced by colder financial calculations. Professor Hoff has set forth the intellectual foundation for this view, but many others, especially practitioners, take it as a matter of faith. For example, many senior physicians with whom I talk today find the big problem in health care is private equity.

I do not see it this way, although it is impossible to deny that medicine is more like a business than it was 30 or 40 years ago. But that is the problem with the corporatization thesis: medicine is a business, and ignoring financial incentives is foolhardy. More to the point, if corporations are causing the problems in primary care, what are the reform alternatives? Some might say a single-payer system, where primary care is well paid and trust is restored. That could eliminate private insurers, and perhaps private equity, but it does nothing about the large hospitals and employers of physicians, which would still act according to the rules of commerce.

Therefore I am interested in how primary care is moving to value-based care, and the manner in which large change agents are encouraging this move. It may be that the push toward value-based care, founded on primary care, will be strong and lead to significant change in the outcomes our health care system produces. Or it may be that the fee-for-service backbone of today's health care economy is too strong, lacking the will to change how primary care is done, and the status quo is what we can expect for the future.

I do not, however, believe the status quo can persist. Too many people are too unhappy. If they do not move to value-based, proactive primary care, primary care clinicians will find ways to counter the assembly line demands put upon them. Two pathways loom for that. One is unionization, organizing to reset the parameters of practice, including better pay and fewer patients. This is beginning, and I will discuss it in more detail in the last chapters. The other escape hatch is to bow out of pure fee-for-service and enter a concierge practice, where wealthier patients pay out of pocket for membership and treatment. The concierge fees enable the clinicians to keep panels small and live a bearable professional life. I will also address the movement to concierge practice, both the good and bad, toward the end of this book.

But most of this project is on the developing practices that are trying to turn the table on fee-for-service and use notions of prepayment, managed care, and value-based care to treat patients the way they should be treated: by focusing on health and prevention and anticipating problems. Continuity and guidance are the key themes in such practices. The federal government, many states, insurers small and large, and even private equity are pushing models based on this vision. The question is, Are there signs of success?

On that note, I return briefly to Maine. Ann Dorney remained with Skowhegan Family Medicine for more than 40 years. Thirty years ago, the practice had trouble staying fiscally sound and independent, so it sold its assets to the local hospital, enabling Skowhegan Family Medicine to continue in business and recruit new doctors. In Dorney's view, they were blessed by the fact that Maine had several rural medical training programs. Over time, though, aspects of the practice became less enjoyable to her, as she was spending more time on her computer and less time with patients.

Dorney never lost energy, though. She ran for and became a state representative. In that role, she helped introduce the first naloxone (commonly known as Narcan, a nasal spray that can reverse an opioid overdose) availability bill in Maine and tried to help curb health care costs. She also became the first doctor in the area to prescribe suboxone (a medication that treats opioid use disorders by managing withdrawal symptoms and reducing cravings), focusing on the growing scourge of opioid abuse. Her team at Skowhegan grew and so did her responsibilities, so much so that she longed for the early days of her practice, when all her attention was focused on spending time with patients. "All the distractions," she lamented.

When COVID arrived, Dorney reached the end of her rope. She tired of having to explain why vaccines were important and disliked getting involved in family disputes, such as when one parent was enraged that the other got vaccinated during a visit with their child. So she retired in 2021. She thought she might continue to work in substance abuse but then decided that she could not, as she needed quiet. She got involved in rewilding a local land trust property, planting a variety of perennials—5,000 seedlings in a year. She spends as much time outside as possible, being quiet and contemplative after a lifetime of hard work.

Dorney emphasized with me that she considered herself "COMPLETELY burned out," and it took her more than two years to get into a good sleeping pattern. The lesson is that the current way much of primary care is being practiced is leaving its mark on capable people, and it is not a positive one. Something must be done to change this situation, for the good of the patients and the sake of the clinicians. Many *are* trying. It is important now to sort out what the best path forward is to redevelop a vibrant primary care medical field.

In a note she sent me after reading a draft of this book, Dr. Dorney endorsed the endeavor dryly: "Thanks for working on this issue—you have an uphill battle!"

CHAPTER TWO

Signs of a New Deal for Primary Care?

THE GLOOM OF PRIMARY CARE characterized in the previous chapter is the norm today. Many clinicians are dejected, feeling undervalued and overworked. Much of the work done by primary care policy leadership today centers on bringing a sense of crisis to the attention of policymakers. A fee-for-service industry that has for years valued specialty procedures and hospital stays centered on lucrative surgery has taken its toll.

Fortunately, efforts for reform are afoot, driven by the affinity between a vital primary care sector and value-based care. Health policy advocates realize that continued hospital- and specialty-dominated health care, and fee-for-service financing, are the root of our country's poor health outcomes and ever rising costs. Fee-for-service is just too prone to promoting unnecessary and ultimately financially wasteful care. The alternative is now widely known as value-based care. In their excellent new book *The Patient Priority*, Stefan Larsson, Jennifer Clawson and Josh Kellar rely heavily on the work done by Porter and Teisberg in the early part of the century. They define value as "simultaneously the value delivered to the patient in the form of better health outcomes and the value delivered by the health system in terms of the most efficient use of society's limited financial and other resources."[1]

Value-based or accountable care requires that a clinician take responsibility for those better outcomes and efficiency, and primary care is best suited for that role. The fee-for-service system does not require such sponsorship for the patient; instead, clinicians just do what they perceive to be necessary for their patients and then bill for it. Value-based care requires a structure where a patient is assigned to an organization and a provider. That provider must orchestrate the most cost-effective and equitable game plan for the patient. Where else would the foundation for this be found but in a primary care clinician–patient relationship?

It is easy to see how primary care gets sidelined in a fee-for-service environment, where a patient ping-pongs between different specialists. It is equally easy to see how valuable it is when a patient's care—and its costs—must be considered by a single responsible entity. Thus the consensus in health care policy is that comprehensive value-based care depends on a primary care foundation. The underappreciated primary care in fee-for-service is the center of value-based care.

Today, there are islands of primary care practices that are striving toward a value-based future. They are found where payers are willing to endorse and pay for future outcomes, using financing mechanisms that pay for health, up to and including capitation. There are generally two streams of value-based primary care. One comprises entrepreneurial-minded primary care practices that have become convinced that waste in our current system is huge, and that by taking prospective payment and eliminating unnecessary care while attending to preventive health measures, they can make primary care both professionally satisfying and relatively lucrative. The second stream of value-based care is found where meager resources make it a necessity to eliminate waste, especially in practices that serve the uninsured and people in government programs like Medicaid.

In both cases, the primary care clinicians want to be at the center of the continuum, taking full responsibility for the health care of their patients as these individuals make their way through the system. There are plenty of examples in a variety of settings. Survey data suggest that over three-quarters of American physicians believe risk-based reimbursement is important or very important to sustain primary care.[2] In my view, the health policy literature and the gloomy reports from expert committees understate the vibrancy of what is starting to occur as primary care endorses value-based care. Some examples help make that case.

Moving to Value-Based Care: Catalyst Health

I mentioned Catalyst Health in the preface. Dr. Christopher Crow (widely known as "Crow" by friends, colleagues, and business associates) is its charismatic leader. His story, and that of the Catalyst network of physicians across Texas,[3] provides a startling contrast to the hopelessness of the previous chapter. Crow grew up in Hillsboro, Texas. As a teenager, he realized that the town's doctors were prominent citizens and active members of the community. They contributed to the public welfare and—in his eyes—made a good living. This view was reinforced in 1987, when he was 16. An economic downturn occurred, throwing his family into bankruptcy, but the physicians in the community seemed to be immune to this disaster.

So, Crow went to college at the University of Texas at Austin and then to medical school at the University of Texas at San Antonio. He certified in family medicine and went into practice in the late 1990s. Even as a student, he thought the business aspects of a medical practice were rather dated. The Internet was producing a new type of service economy, while doctors and hospitals did not seem to understand this form of consumerism. No one at medical school questioned the status quo in health care. But he did, beginning in residency, when he used his elective time to work for insurance companies and in hospital administration. He also studied what was happening on the business side of the medical practices he rotated through.

Crow started his practice in Plano, Texas. At the same time, he got an executive MBA degree. He soon came to realize that there was a better path than traditional fee-for-service primary care. In his view, this form of payment undervalued primary care doctors and did not allow the field of primary care to improve overall health care in the ways he thought were possible. As Crow put it, he needed to "unlock physicians and patients from the time and space in the exam room."

That was not easy. Doctors were suffering from a version of Stockholm syndrome, realizing that they were trapped in unfulfilling practices, but not ready to change. Crow kept wondering, Why should a recurring relationship model receive payments on a per item or per event basis? He compared this cafeteria-style compensation method with Netflix's pricing format and argued that it was much better to get paid monthly than it was to try to charge for each transaction, especially if the goal was progression toward better health.

In 2006, Crow and seven other doctors started a new professional corporation called Village Health Partners. He proposed that they all try to get out of the transactional payment model and plotted out several steps. First, they began to undertake care coordination, making sure patients transitioned safely out of the hospital. The next step was to qualify as a Level 3 primary care medical home (more on primary care medical homes shortly). This status got the doctors in his group noticed by both health care payers and other doctors, and their practice began to grow. As a result, in 2008 and 2009, he was able to negotiate new contracts with better reimbursement rates, plus some *gainsharing* (additional payments) if the practice hit certain utilization and quality measures.

Over this same period, massive hospital consolidation took place in the Dallas–Fort Worth metroplex. Hospitals also began to buy physicians' practices. Crow and the doctors in his group wanted to remain independent, however. They had developed some expertise in population health management, and in 2010 they began to focus on the total cost of care for their patients. They resisted all entreaties from hospitals interested in purchasing their practice.

Health insurers were drawn to Crow's model. The insurers were "getting whipsawed" by the big consolidated health care systems (such as Baylor Scott & White and Texas Health Resources), having to pay higher fees to the hospitals for their commercial health insurance beneficiaries, given the leverage the big systems had. (Insurers and hospital-based integrated delivery systems always debate who has more leverage, but over the past two decades, most of the health services literature has shown that payments rise as hospitals merge.) In 2014, Crow created the Catalyst Health network, an accredited clinically integrated network. It was immediately an attractive alternative for many physicians. While the Catalyst group was still interested in better fees for services, it also strove to reduce the overall costs of care.

Catalyst did not employ doctors but instead contracted with them, forming a network. Crow noted that the general mindset among doctors in North Texas was that they wanted to remain independent, but they also saw the need to begin moving toward value-based care. Having better contracts, resulting in higher payments for the medical services they offered, was the calling card that Catalyst used to introduce itself to many physician practices. Crow and Catalyst, however, only wanted to work with practices if they were eventually committed to moving toward managing the total cost of primary health care.

It proved to be a popular proposal. His new partners found that they could increase their compensation by 30% to 50% with Catalyst contracts, which were based on better fees and successful gainsharing. But the organization was not as cohesive as Crow wanted. For example, he was saddled with 13 different electronic medical record systems among his practices. Nonetheless, Catalyst Health became a big player in the Dallas–Fort Worth area. By 2015, Texas Health Resources (a large integrated system) employed or contracted with 600–700 doctors, and Baylor Scott & White (the other large system) had a similar number. Catalyst had grown to 750 doctors. In 2022, Catalyst contracted with just over 1,000 primary care clinicians—real critical mass—while the big systems were starting to reduce their primary care base. Catalyst is now spreading to East Texas and the Panhandle.

By 2022, Dr. Crow and his team were ready to take the next step. At least a subset of the existing Catalyst Health practices planned to move to a financial/clinical data system with only a single EMR system for tracking their patients and an integrated *revenue cycle system*, which does patient billing and produces financial records. They selected athenahealth as their vendor. In addition, Catalyst is beginning to manage hospital stays and use only selected specialists. The primary care doctors in this leading-edge group are not employees but instead work under long-term exclusive contracts. As of mid-2024, there are more than 100 physicians in this tightly integrated group.

Under some of the insurance contracts, the Catalyst primary care doctors are paid on a fee-for-service basis. But their focus is increasingly on what Crow, hearkening back to the Netflix example, calls subscription contracts with health insurers, where the payments are population based. In other words, insurers hold the Catalyst group accountable for an annual, risk-adjusted sum for each patient. If Catalyst Health provides value-based care and pays attention to population health management for their beneficiary group—that is, if they manage care—they can reduce unnecessary and wasteful medical interventions and, by disbursing less of the yearly lump sum estimated by the health insurers, earn more money. Catalyst's doctors are essentially moving from cafeteria-style fees to Netflix-like pricing, consonant with their view that they are in a long-term relationship with their primary care patients. In this regard, subscription is equivalent to capitation.

Catalyst will also contract with agilon health (a company that shares a lowercase affinity with the EMR firm athenahealth, as well as with poet e e cummings), which assists primary care groups interested in population health management by providing them with tools for dealing with capitated risk contracts. For instance, agilon can help with efficiently managing specialists, analyzing hospital costs, and developing quality-of-care measures out of encounter data. They bring a playbook for success in managed care contracts, and their fee is based on the overall profit in a risk-based contract.

agilon can also proffer advice on contracting with insurers. The commercial health insurer lineup in the Dallas–Fort Worth metroplex is similar to that in other metropolitan areas, consisting of a Texas-based Blue Cross Blue Shield plan and national health insurers like UnitedHealthcare and Aetna. In their commercial health care offerings—either fully insured small group plans or self-insured large-employer contracts (most large firms and multistate employers prefer to self-insure, using the health insurer as a third-party administrator)—insurers tend to keep the various health care providers in fee-for-service contracts. The insurers are accustomed to a fee-for-service system, and their corporate customers often favor unmanaged contracts with preferred provider organizations (PPOs). Yet they are willing to consider alternative payment mechanisms, and Catalyst has so engaged them. With expertise in negotiations with insurers, agilon gives management advice, especially about diagnostic coding for various types of patient encounters.

Catalyst Health is also starting a relationship-based pharmacy business to augment the physician–patient relationship, called Stellus Rx. It focuses on *central fill*, or putting the medications in bottles and then making them available in doctors' offices (as opposed to sending patients to retail pharmacies to fill their prescriptions). Central fill and coordination with the ordering physicians improve patients' adherence to a medication regimen, which in turn generally improves patients' health and lowers their health care costs. Catalyst encourages the use of its pharmacy for patients who take more than six prescriptions, as adherence to their medications will bring about better outcomes. Adherence is also a vitally important measure for Medicare Advantage Star ratings. Doing well on Star measures means that patients are getting better care, and insurers and thus the clinicians receive a bonus from the federal government.

If this sounds like a different world than the part of University of Alabama at Birmingham Medicine I visited, it is. There are probably people at Viva Health (UAB's Medicare Advantage plan) that understand all these issues and are developing similar strategies. But this information is not percolating down to the individual physicians and nurses in UAB's primary care practice, whereas Catalyst Health expects its core clinicians to at least understand both the theory and the details. If all goes according to the plan, the clinician should focus on value-based care and eschew the churn of multiple treatments and specialist visits that creates profits under a fee-for-service system.

This description of Catalyst Health also includes a number of concepts that are not part of the vocabulary of everyday life: primary care medical homes, capitation, central fill, revenue cycle, and the like. I will fill in details on these recondite subjects as we move along. The point here is to demonstrate the contrast between Catalyst Health and traditional fee-for-service-based primary care. The former is entrepreneurial and moving toward aggressively managing health care, ensuring that it is value based. The Catalyst group sees better and more efficient care to be linked to better payment for primary care, while at the same time improving the patient's health.

Talking with Beth Martinez and Jenna Hemingway, key administrators at Catalyst Health, gave me a deeper sense of the complexity of their operation.[4] The first issue is growth. They had 50 to 60 doctors in 2013, and now they're at 1,200 clinicians. In health care vernacular (which relies heavily on acronyms), Catalyst Health is a clinically integrated network (CIN), not an accountable care organization (ACO). Up to this point, most of their contracts had been with commercial health insurers as opposed to traditional Medicare or Medicaid. For example, Catalyst does not participate in the Medicare Shared Savings Program (MSSP), a traditional Medicare vehicle that allows doctors to earn more money by managing care through an ACO. (MSSP is designed to introduce doctors and hospitals to value-based care, with shared savings accruing to the ACO. Many integrated hospital and physician systems, as well as physicians' groups without a hospital partner, have cut their teeth on value-based care through the MSSP program. More on this in chapter 4.)

Catalyst Health did not want to become integrated with hospitals, nor did it see any merit in participating in MSSP. Instead, Catalyst has moved more or less directly to contract with Medicare Advantage plans, guided by their relationship with another large medical group in Texas, WellMed. Medicare Advantage is the part of Medicare operated by private health insurance companies. Hence Medicare Advantage is distinguished from the fee-for-service-based traditional Medicare. When you qualify for Medicare, you can choose to be covered by traditional Medicare or a Medicare Advantage plan. In the latter, the federal government essentially transfers the average costs it would have incurred (with risk adjustments factored in, depending on your medical history) to a plan's private health insurer, and that insurer assumes the financial risk for the beneficiaries. Insurers presume they can manage care sufficiently well by eliminating enough financial waste to allow them to turn a profit on the government's per head payment (capitation).

A health insurer participating in Medicare Advantage may choose to use its own techniques (prior authorization; management of drug formularies, which are lists of drugs that will be covered by a pharmacy benefits plan; and negotiation of low-cost contracts on a fee-for-service basis with hospitals and doctors) to manage the financial risk of illness. Or, increasingly, they may simply handle the enrollment process and then hand off care management to physician groups or integrated delivery systems. In essence, health insurers simply take a cut of the amount paid and turn the rest over to the risk-bearing medical group—that is, capitation, based on a percentage of the premiums.

WellMed is another clinically integrated network, originally based in San Antonio. It was organized two decades ago by Dr. George Rapier. WellMed was bought by Pacificare, which was one of the original insurers in the 1990s to funnel capitated payments and managed care through physicians' groups, known widely at the time as independent practice associations, or IPAs. (Now they are more often referred to as CINs.) WellMed was successful in a region (South Texas) where there was previously little managed health care. Pacificare was eventually bought by Optum.

Optum is a health care conglomerate owned by UnitedHealth Group, the parent of health insurer UnitedHealthcare. For much of the past 15 years, Optum has been assiduously buying physician groups interested in managing care, seeing this as a key strategy in their health care business. Bringing health insurance functions and care functions closer together represents a crucial step toward value-based care.

Optum owns USMD, a competing CIN in the Dallas–Fort Worth area. But it allows WellMed to advise Catalyst Health on Medicare Advantage contracts, some of which originate with UnitedHealthcare, the health care insurer. Complicated enough for you? These kinds of tangled relationships and overlapping acronyms are the norm in health care. Twenty years ago, almost everyone who was eligible had traditional Medicare, where health care costs were paid on a fee-for-service basis. Now, more than half of Medicare beneficiaries are in Medicare Advantage plans, and relationships between the various players in the system are evolving to accommodate and promote the move to value-based care.

Cutting through the preceding jungle of organizations and acronyms, the critical point is that Catalyst Health is decidedly moving toward the management of health insurance's financial risk, which is passed along to them from insurers, particularly those who market Medicare Advantage plans. The federal government and health insurance companies are using Medicare Advantage to spread capitated contracting back through the American health care system, picking up where many in the early 1990s thought the health care system was headed. To do this, Catalyst needs tools, some of which they will develop and others will be acquired or rented from an organization like agilon health or WellMed.

Two central team employees gave me even more insight on the day-to-day operations of Catalyst's CIN. Matt Weyenberg is its chief medical officer (CMO).[5] He trained in family medicine in Tyler, Texas, and then went to work with Christopher Crow in 2004. By 2016, Weyenberg was burning out. He told me that he came to believe life has three mandates—spend time with patients, make enough money, and spend time with family—and he could only manage two. He was ready to quit the practice of medicine.

Crow told Weyenberg to go to work for WellMed. Crow figured that his colleague could learn the managed care ropes there and then perhaps come back to Catalyst Health. Weyenberg agreed, and WellMed welcomed him. But Weyenberg found WellMed to be hard-nosed, treating all affiliated and contracted doctors as if they were employees. (Most doctors participating in a CIN do not want a boss; they want an affiliation. A CIN does not employ its clinicians but simply gives them common management tools.) Weyenberg learned how to thread this needle, getting buy-in from physicians but allowing them to be independent. In 2021, Crow recruited him back to be CMO of Catalyst's Medicare Advantage business.

Weyenberg now coaches physicians who were formerly in a fee-for-service system, showing them how to operate in a managed care environment. He listens to the doctors and takes their views back to management. He also carries management's messages to the physician network. By late 2023, Weyenberg had 175 doctors participating in Catalyst's Medicare Advantage operation. Some of them have not been able to adapt to a managed care environment. Their biggest problem is that they continue to run on the fee-for-service hamster wheel and do not deal with issues such as gaps in care and patients' adherence to their medication regimes. He was anguished when he had to take two doctors out of the program, but through counseling and repetitive efforts, he has gotten them back. These doctors have had to back off on their patient volumes, however; one was seeing 28 patients a day.

These two physicians notwithstanding, Weyenberg believes that "doctors are really ready to jump ship on cafeteria-style reimbursement, now more than ever." This is true even in the Dallas–Fort Worth metroplex, where the average doctor is independent. As Weyenberg put it, most of the physicians in Catalyst's CIN can see the beauty of a capitated contract: you make more money if you keep a patient healthy. That also requires more time and more thought, but it feels less hectic. For many of them, these are the reasons why they wanted to practice medicine in the first place.

Weyenberg was also bullish about their new relationship with agilon health. This firm will help with specialty areas like kidney failure and stays in long-term-care facilities, assist in development of virtual behavioral health specialists, and provide some capital to help with Catalyst's EMR and revenue cycle makeovers. His doctors are "now excited about the prospect for primary care, more so than ever." They know they must modify the rapid visits aspects of their practice, but the larger prospective payments will enable them to be creative and come up with new ways to take care of their patients.

In 2021, Catalyst Health hired Christopher Abbott, a veteran health insurance person.[6] He had been president of the Texas and Oklahoma operations for UnitedHealthcare, so he brought a lot of insurer expertise to Catalyst's management team. Abbott noted that in the commercial health insurance business, insurers continue to maintain an adversarial position vis-à-vis health care groups. Medicare Advantage does not present that same problem; somehow medical practices and insurers can get on the same page. So Medicare Advantage is conducive to capitation in a way that much of commercial health insurance is not.

He reminded me that once Catalyst Health began to take on financial risk through Medicare Advantage, they did not need to obtain an insurance license. But payers did expect Catalyst to obtain a letter of credit or some other vehicle to act as a *stop loss* (a limit on their financial losses) in case they cannot manage their financial risk. CMS does have rules that state if there is no stop loss or reinsurance, then a primary care clinician's fiscal risk must be limited. So, the path for taking on the financial risk for illness from an insurer is not simple. It requires a good understanding of the dynamics of the health insurance market and its regulation. Meeting all of these people, I had an appreciation for the way that Christopher Crow had assembled a talented Catalyst Health team to change the nature of primary care practice.

Catalyst Health's tool kit is fairly well developed. One such tool applies when sending patients to specialists. Capitated primary care groups must find good specialist doctors who will be attuned to care management and not have inappropriately high fees. Instead of just telling patients to make an appointment with *a* cardiologist, they are referred to a *specific* cardiologist. Moreover, there should be a good deal of contact between the patient's primary care clinician and that specialist.

A referral management system, using an automated platform, helps with this process. Catalyst's program is called Leading Reach. It requires a reasonable amount of information to be entered by both the referring doctor and the doctor accepting the referral (or their staffs). This tool can then provide analytical insights into referrals and eventually allow the cost of that medical care to be tracked. It enables the primary care CIN to identify specialists who provide high-quality, parsimonious care, picking up on Barbara Starfield's notion of coordination and the promise of gatekeeping. Over time, a CIN like Catalyst Health will find the right set of specialists, and those specialists will learn the care patterns necessary to provide value-based care. (All Catalyst clinicians will be using the chosen specialists going forward, not just those on risk contracts—more information fine-tunes the program.)

A second key tool is a care management program for transitions in care. It identifies Catalyst patients headed to a hospital or emergency department and provides help as they move between these care settings. A care manager keeps track of patients when they go to an emergency department or during their hospital stays. The manager ensures that discharged patients have follow-up care with a primary care clinician, are on an appropriate regimen of medications, and know the warning signs of potential complications, thus avoiding unnecessary readmissions. Care managers are often physically present, although many are now experimenting with virtual approaches, a trend that will only accelerate as artificial intelligence moves into this space.

A third important tool for a medical group taking on financial risk is having a health promotion team—dietitians, social workers, and pharmacists—and a diabetes care program. This team works alongside physicians and nurse practitioners, helping with chronically ill patients and making sure they have the services they need to stay healthy and avoid hospitalizations. Pharmacy expertise and behavioral health support have emerged as being particularly useful.

Many clinically integrated networks are made up of a collection of physicians in primary care practices, each deciding which electronic medical record program to use once federal funding for them was made available a decade ago. The various systems do not communicate with one another, so they impair the clinical cohesion of an integrated network, creating a medical Tower of Babel. Thus a fourth tool for Catalyst Health involves moving to a single EMR program for tracking their patients, as well as an integrated revenue cycle system that bills patients and produces financial records, both of which promote that cohesion. This tool also provides a single platform for referral management and care coordination.

Insisting on a single EMR system is a big and expensive step for Catalyst Health, or for any loosely organized CIN, but it is absolutely necessary in terms of medical management, as it provides unified clinical and insurance claims data that can be used for the analytics that will guide all the teams enumerated above. Catalyst's choice of athenahealth is not unexpected, as this EMR firm has begun to gain ascendency for physicians' organizations. From my unscientific survey, it is the only competitor to Epic's EMR system, which dominates in hospitals and integrated hospital/physician groups. The crucial insight here is that team-oriented care is the wave of the future, and teams can best stay on the same page with a single EMR.

The new versions of an athenahealth or Epic EMR system come with modules that help spot gaps in care, identifying critical interventions that can promote the best health care for patients with chronic diseases. For patients with diabetes who need a hemoglobin A1c test, or patients with hypertension who are still having high blood pressure readings, these problems are often addressed by their primary care clinician. But many practices also have a central clinical quality team that tracks such measures and then alerts the patient's physician to any gaps, leading to better health and lower costs. Moreover, Medicare Advantage's quality measures focus on successful outcomes, and efforts to fill gaps in care can lead to bonus payments.

Catalyst Health must keep this central team small in order to remain profitable as an organization, so automation is critical. Nonetheless, adding these services entails a certain amount of overhead. Together, the cost of the programs represents a "soul biopsy" for clinicians as they ask themselves if they are willing to move beyond a fee-for-service system, which requires none of this. Clinicians also must be convinced that taking these steps, while adding to the practice's overhead, will lower its overall costs, thus paying for themselves vis-à-vis capitated reimbursements.

These concepts are not new. Most of them were outlined for me in the mid-1990s, when the physician-hospital organization I helped organize brought consultants in to help us with the new capitated contracts that our integrated delivery system had just signed. Large amounts of data move much faster today, however, and the data are more accurate and delivered on time. And the accuracy of interventions should only improve with better data analysis.

How does this change from fee-for-service to managed care look on the ground, where the primary care clinician meets the patient? I met with Dr. Jamie Albrecht, who gave me a tour of the new Village Health Partners clinic in Frisco, Texas—part of the Dallas–Fort Worth metroplex.[7] Village Health Partners was the original group founded by Christopher Crow, and it is now one of the anchor practices in Catalyst Health. The clinic was remarkably different from any other office suite I had seen. Village Health Partners has eschewed waiting rooms. Patients first complete all of their preliminary check-in information electronically, prior to their scheduled visit, and then, on the day of their appointment, they receive an electronic alert to enter an exam room. As Albrecht said, "People find their hotel rooms; they can find the exam rooms." Each exam room has two doors, and the team's work area is segregated from the exam rooms—an "onstage" versus "offstage" arrangement. A lot of attention was paid to the look and feel of the office, to make people comfortable during their visit.

Albrecht grew up in a small town outside of Amarillo, Texas. He has seven brothers; five are doctors and two are pastors. A couple of his brothers are orthopedic surgeons in Amarillo, and they wonder why Jamie is an apostle of value-based care and population health management, since they think these trends are going to lead to socialized medicine. His answer is, "I do have responsibility for the health of my patient, and that includes what she is paying for care." This kind of commitment was clear throughout our discussion and a tour of the facility.

Albrecht is the president of Village Health Partners, which has 60 clinicians in four settings. They originally cut their teeth on value-based care by getting National Committee for Quality Assurance medical home certification. Village Health has perennially acted as a flagship for the other practices in Catalyst Health, being the first to undertake certain care management approaches. For instance, they were the first to prioritize quality-of-care measures and be completely transparent about it. Their scorecards on these metrics are up-to-date, detailed, and fully identified by individual clinicians—and available for all in the practice to review. They also realized some time ago that free medication samples were just a marketing ploy for brand-name drugs, so they removed all such items from the office.

Village Health Partners provides a mix of onsite and virtual patient support. There are specialists in nutrition (dieticians) and behavioral health at the Frisco clinic, while Catalyst's health promotion team does a lot of the virtual follow-up. Albrecht described their pharmacy support group (known as Stellus Rx) to me in some detail. The pharmacists oversee a program that includes blister packs of pills, to encourage adherence to a medication regime; follow-up telephone calls; medication synchronization, so all of a patient's refills can be obtained in a single visit to a pharmacy; and quick referrals of problematic issues back to the primary care doctors. All of this is affordable, Albrecht reassured me, given Medicare Advantage's triple weighting in its Star Measures for how well patients stick to their medication programs. There are also virtual care coordinators, chronic disease managers, and social work counselors, who get messages from the central office about gaps in care that must be addressed.

Albrecht and Crow both thought that by 2020, the United States would have 50% of all health care payments be *prospective* (capitated in some fashion). Things did not move that fast, but this change is picking up steam now. As Albrecht described it, under Medicare Advantage, a doctor becomes the president of a health care panel and moves to proactively address patient issues. Albrecht was excited about Village Health Partners' new Leading Reach referral management program, which will eventually give them data identifying the most efficient (i.e., cost-effective) specialists. This program, described above, provides both the referring and the referral doctors with an app containing questions that must be completed. Thus it will eventually provide comprehensive data about the diagnoses and treatments by the various specialists.

Discussing Village Health Partners' recruiting methods, Albrecht found it best to try to attract physicians who have just completed their residency, since they are not already set in their ways and readily adapt to an ecosystem that uses a variety of technologies for communications. They also see the future of primary care as being a team practice involving many professionals, especially nurse practitioners. An integrated practice of this sort neatly coordinates with a multiple technologies approach. Almost all of Village Health's doctors are now paired 1:1 with advanced practice providers. Albrecht was confident and optimistic, yet understated and down-to-earth. It was difficult not to share his confidence in the vision and the future of both Village Health Partners and Catalyst Health. And, to some extent, of primary care in general.

Catalyst Health is miles distant in its journey from most primary care practices, especially those in big medical centers that are paid on fee-for-service and have little team-based care. But Catalyst Health is not alone. Other practices are moving in the same valued-based care direction. Several forces and movements, beyond the recognition of the importance of value-based care to righting our health care system, are driving this evolution.

Developments Facilitating the Growth of Value-Based Primary Care

The Catalyst Health story seems largely a matter of charismatic leadership, with one visionary doctor pulling a team along with him. But the ground was prepared for him and the organization. The techniques of managing care are not new. Rather, they are as old as the first HMOs, begun nearly a hundred years ago. More importantly, a series of developments over the past 30 years created at least some modicum of the culture and context necessary for the growth of financial risk–bearing primary care.

Through much of the twentieth century, managed care was primarily the domain of large-staff-model HMOs, such as Kaiser Permanente. Kaiser, especially in California, was then joined by large, risk-bearing primary care and multispecialty groups. During the push for health reform in the early 1990s, health care policy was dominated by the presumption that hospitals, doctors, and health insurers would move away from a fee-for-service system to managed care, impelled by the Clinton administration's push for health care reform, which relied on the notion of managed competition. But after hospitals pulled many private practice doctors into integrated delivery systems and merged with neighboring hospitals to form big systems—all to prepare for managing care—they turned instead to an easier solution: using market leverage to negotiate higher commercial health insurance payment rates. So, the percentage of health care payments through capitation hit its zenith in the mid-1990s and then collapsed. Primary care was treated as a feeder for the operating and procedure room maw.

But pockets of managed care still exist in many states—the remnants of what was once anticipated to be a big overall shift. Dr. George Rapier and WellMed offer a good example of that phenomenon. Rapier's clinically integrated medical group preferred contracts where WellMed assumed the full financial risk, and some health insurers had grown comfortable with that. But these were mostly niche players, and through the beginning of the twenty-first century, fee-for-service contracts dominated.

No one steeped in health policy believed that fee-for-service was the ultimate answer. Its incentives for overutilization—do more in order to get paid more—would eventually lead to a health care system that was too expensive. But Americans tolerated being charged more than double what other countries paid for health care, even as US health care outcomes worsened. Many health policy advocates continued to search for ways to reintroduce value-based care.

In this search, primary care and subscription or capitated payment remained front of mind, and linked. One crucial way to boost resources for primary care is capitated funding. Spending more money on primary care clearly produces better outcomes for patients—and the nation's overall health system.[8] It is also obvious that current spending on primary care in the United States is insufficient to adequately support interest in primary care careers, let alone comprehensive, prospective care. To make matters worse, primary care expenditures are declining.[9] Moving toward primary care–based capitation funding, and spending it wisely to eliminate financial waste, has persistently been seen by most value-based advocates as the best way to provide the resources necessary for primary care teams.[10]

Moving to a primary care–centered, top-down health system has not been contemplated since the brief Clinton reform effort. Moreover, incremental change is the hallmark of America's health care system. The field had to be prepared—fertilized, as it were—with value-based care concepts before large numbers of primary care groups could join something like the clinically integrated networks of health care managers, a WellMed or Catalyst. During the first two decades of the twenty-first century, there have been five significant cultivation efforts that have created at least attributes of an ecosystem that can foster the development of "new" primary care practices like Catalyst Health.

The first was the movement known as primary care medical homes. The idea is an old one. Pediatricians had long advocated for the coordination and oversight of interventions for children with special needs, in order to harmonize and coordinate their care. In 1967 the American Association of Pediatrics began to use the term *medical home* when referring to the way to provide health care for these children.[11] The chief aim was to avoid fragmentation, and over time, pediatricians began to apply the concept to *all* children. This movement was led by Hawaii's Dr. Calvin Sia, who advocated for the establishment of specific practice standards and recognition for those who fulfilled them.

Spurred by the Institute of Medicine's 1996 report on primary care,[12] family medicine began to incorporate the medical home idea into its advocacy efforts. In the meantime, the MacColl Center for Health Care Innovation, led by Dr. Edward Wagner, had developed the *chronic care model*, which was a framework for organizing care for patients with chronic diseases. It involved support for primary care practices throughout the health care system, including ensuring that these practices had adequate clinical information systems, appropriate support for clinicians' decisions, an orientation toward patients' self-management, and use of community resources.[13] Crucially, the MacColl Center, located in the Group Health Research Institute in Seattle, offered primary care practices a self-assessment tool to identify gaps in their current structure.

The concepts of chronic care treatment and medical homes merged, and in 2007 the American College of Physicians, the American Academy of Pediatrics, the American Osteopathic Association, and the American Academy of Family Physicians jointly promulgated the principles of a patient-centered medical home, or PCMH. Almost immediately, the National Committee for Quality Assurance (NCQA) launched the first PCMH recognition program.[14] For a fee, NCQA would evaluate a primary care practice and certify it as a medical home. Critical factors for this certification included promotion of immunizations; the use of preventive care via particular cancer screenings (such as mammograms and colonoscopies); chronic care measures (focusing on diabetes, hypertension, and the use of statins); behavioral health screenings; and follow-up and care coordination. The NCQA acknowledged that their recognition program mainly focused on measurements of these processes rather than the outcomes (better health) they were meant to produce, but such has been the state of technology.

Employers, led by IBM and Dr. Paul Grundy, encouraged their health care payers (insurers) to recognize and compensate primary care practices that gained medical home status. This created an incentive for primary care practices to change their methods. Leaders in internal[15] and family medicine argued that developing PCMHs could lead to greater work satisfaction among primary care practitioners.[16] Better health care, along with having a more enjoyable practice, offered quite a reward, but there were costs associated with making this transformation and then getting PCMH certification. So additional reimbursements from health insurers was crucial. Many insurers did so.

Almost every one of the practices I identified as doing cutting-edge work in population management, or accepting capitation, got their start in a PCMH model. In this regard, the development of and advocacy for this medical home concept by primary care's leaders—and to some extent by employers and insurers—gave those interested in a different primary care future a new step to follow.

While initial studies of the PCMH model suggested that it led to substantial improvements in both the processes it measured and their outcomes, an impartial analysis today indicates that this is not the case.

Two recent reviews have shown little difference between PCMH and non-PCMH patients. Investigators from the University of Florida evaluated a cohort of nearly 6,000 patients, over 40% of whom were in patient-centered medical homes.[17] They could find almost no difference in more than 30 of the health measurements, except for a slight improvement in cholesterol control in the PCMH cohort. That same cohort had less satisfaction with referrals to specialists. In an earlier publication, Anna Sinaiko and colleagues had evaluated 11 studies of PCMHs and reached a similar conclusion.[18] These authors did acknowledge that PCMHs were associated with a 4.2% decrease in total health care costs in a cohort of patients who were more chronically ill. They also emphasized, however, that the medical homes themselves were quite different from one another, and there may have been some organizational features associated with the better outcomes. Given the heterogeneity of the PCMHs, the authors just could not tell.

This is somewhat disappointing, especially considering earlier studies that were showing reductions in expenditures and improved health care quality. But from a different perspective, the evaluations did not matter a great deal. What really counted was that primary care had been given a template for improvement, and those interested in change had a path to follow. Not every PCMH was as assiduous as others, and the laggards would no doubt bring a regression to the mean in a study of any cohort of practices. But those that were successful could develop new relationships with health care payers, one in which stewardship for quality and costs could engender better reimbursements. In that regard, the PCMH movement has paid real dividends in awakening at least some subset of primary care clinicians and their practices, encouraging and allowing them to develop programs based on patients' *health* as opposed to concentrating on patients' *visits*. The PCMH contingent in primary care is not small. The NCQA currently certifies more than 70,000 physicians, or about one-fifth of all eligible primary care clinicians.[19]

The second major development of the twenty-first century has to do with the primary care clinician workforce. As discussed previously, primary care has become less popular with medical students as a career choice. Simply put, primary care means lots of work and not as much compensation as other medical fields. Not surprisingly, there are predictions of a future deficit of general internists and family physicians. The Health Resources and Services Administration (HRSA), a division of the US Department of Health and Human Services, is charged with oversight of the health care workforce in the United States. HRSA has developed a helpful calculator that predicts the supply of and demand for clinicians in the United States.[20]

The news from that calculator is sobering. By 2035, there will be 124,000 family medicine physicians, but demand would require 139,000. The situation with primary care internal medicine is even worse, with a supply of 89,000 physicians and a demand for 108,000. Thus about 34,000 primary care provider (PCP) positions will be unfilled. The crunch is already occurring. The Primary Care Collaborative revealed that the number of primary care physicians decreased by 14.2 PCPs per 100,000 population from 2018 to 2022.[21]

The diminished supply of primary care doctors is offset remarkably by the growth of nurse clinicians. Advanced practice registered nurses (APRNs) matriculate in masters-level programs to become practitioners. Traditionally there were four tracks: nurse anesthetists, nurse midwives, clinical nurse specialists, and nurse practitioners. The latter are filling the primary care gap left by doctors.

The profession is not an old one, dating from the birth of Medicare and Medicaid in 1965. Primary care leaders recognized that there would be a need for more caregivers as more people accessed insurance: Barbara Resnick and Charles Lewis at the University of Kansas, Joan Lynbaugh and Harriet Kitzman at the University of Rochester, and especially Loretta Ford and Henry Silver at the University of Colorado. These early programs set the template: advanced training, usually in a degree-awarding university program, for registered nurses interested in independent practice. The initial years of the nurse practitioner programs were somewhat fraught, as neither old line nurses nor doctors were certain they wanted this development.

By 1974 the American Nurses Association had endorsed the effort, setting up the Council of Primary Care Nurse Practitioners. In 1985 the

American Academy of Nurse Practitioners was founded, with 100 members. Perhaps most importantly, in 1993 the AANP began a certification program, and in 1997 the Balanced Budget Act created direct reimbursement for nurse practitioners. Certified and able to bill, the profession had the components necessary to thrive.

Since then, the growth of the profession has been nothing short of spectacular. A recent report by the leading researchers in the nursing workforce field underlines the tremendous increase in the number of nurse practitioners.[22] Between 2010 and 2017 the number of educational programs for them expanded from 356 to 467. Today there are more NPs graduating from educational programs than physicians graduating from medical school. This growth comes at the expense of the supply of registered nurses, as more and more nurses and nursing students go into advanced practice provider (APP) educational programs. Thus there is a net emigration from in-patient to ambulatory settings by the nursing profession. Moreover, the new nurse practitioners tend to be younger, while physicians in primary care are aging. In 2023, nearly 30,000 people graduated from a nurse practitioner school, while just over 5,000 physicians came out of primary care training programs.[23]

Every expectation is that the growth in supply of nurse practitioners will continue over at least the next decade. The HRSA calculator shows the nurse practitioners workforce rising from 79,000 in 2020 to 189,000 in 2035 (along with an increase in the number of physician associates from 36,000 in 2020 to 63,000 in 2035). By the next decade, these advance practice providers will outnumber physicians engaged in primary care. A 2021 report by the National Academies of Sciences, Engineering, and Medicine (NASEM) made the cautionary point that not all these APPs will end up in primary care.[24]

The same report also carefully documented state-by-state differences regarding nurse practitioners. For example, only 23 states allow NPs to practice independently and prescribe medications. Many of the rest require physician oversight for NPs. Such was the case in Alabama, for instance. But in many of the clinics I traveled to, all over the country, nurse practitioners were thriving in primary care. In most clinics, the APPs have little physician oversight once they have been in practice for some time. They seek help and advice on complicated patients, like any other member of the team would do, but they are not specifically monitored or audited.

Given the difficulty of recruiting doctors and the relative ease of finding nurse practitioners, the default position in many practices has become to add more NPs. Most APPs do not have a residency period lasting three to four years, like doctors do, so some graduates are not fully prepared for all the intricacies of patient care. But clinics are willing to train them, often in formal fellowship programs, where they get relatively careful oversight from senior APPs and doctors. One forthright physician I met told me he planned to partially retire and would only be mentoring APPs from then on, drily relating that they represented the future of primary care. In many ways, that future is already here. Anna Goldman and Michael Barnett reported that over the course of this century's first 20 years, the average number of hours a physician worked declined by 7.6%.[25] Meanwhile, weekly hours worked by APPs increased by 71% from 2010 to 2020.

The 2021 report by NASEM also commented on the rest of the members of health care teams now taking the field in medical centers and clinics.[26] Care managers, health coaches, nurses' aides, and medical assistants are often more representative of the patient care population than doctors and nurse practitioners. Community health workers in particular have a commitment to understanding the community in which the health care they offer occurs, with insights that can help promote health equity. This array of workers, and the notion of a primary care team, is much more prevalent in those practices that are self-consciously oriented toward value-based care. The exact number of these professionals—plus behavioral health specialists, pharmacists, and nurse midwives—is not well documented, but whether they are in small rural practices or in bustling urban health centers, these new, diverse teams are quite apparent.

The demographic die is cast. Primary care today, and especially tomorrow, will tend to have more APPs than physicians, giving rise to an emphasis on teamwork. If the value-based care movement makes progress against fee-for-service, the heterogenous team of MDs and APPs will be supported by an array of others. Some members of that team, such as medical assistants and health coaches, will reduce the workload of APPs or doctors, a trend increasingly enhanced by technology. Others, like behavioral health specialists and pharmacists, will offer cost-effective preventive treatments and counseling. All of this is much more readily supported by prospective payment.

This vision heavily depends on moving away from the fee-for-service system of financing.[27] Generally, the only source of revenue in traditional primary care practices came from individual health insurance payments for patient visits, where the necessary evaluation and management codes were completed by physicians and some APPs. It could be that APPs just come to replace physicians in the dreary fee-for-service march through as many individual visits as possible each day. If the nurse practitioner revolution simply turns out to be less costly clinicians grinding through fee-for-service, it will fizzle out. But it could facilitate the team development that is vital to advanced primary care.

One more point deserves attention in this discussion of workforce. For much of the twentieth century, primary care was dominated by allopathic physicians from American medical schools. Their longtime competitors had been osteopathic physicians. Over time, the training for both types of doctors coevolved, and these programs are now accredited by the same organization. But osteopathic physicians are more likely to go into primary care fields, and their numbers have grown. Currently there are 38 osteopathic medical schools in 60 locations. More than 80% of them are private, with some of the new ones being part of for-profit corporations. The number of graduating students in this field has increased by 77% in the past decade.[28]

Another large portion of the primary care workforce is composed of international medical graduates (IMGs). They comprise 25% of all physicians in the United States, and about the same proportion of primary care doctors.[29] Nearly 40% of these IMGs are US citizens, and the rest depend on immigration laws to work in this country. As is the case for osteopathic schools, the number of international medical schools geared toward producing doctors able to practice in America has increased, and many are for-profit institutions.

The rate-limiting factor for the development of more international and osteopathic medical schools is the number of training programs, particularly in primary care. If the number of training slots were increased, there would likely be an expansion in the number of graduates. This is an important point to keep in mind as I move to a comprehensive set of recommendations toward the end of this book. Importantly, graduates of international and osteopathic medical schools do as well on licensure tests and board examinations as allopathic medical school graduates.

The third major development in primary care over the past two decades is the increased use of technology in medical practices, which mostly hinges on EMRs. I have already detailed their growth—and dominant presence—in most practices. An EMR system is capable of aggregating data from a variety of sources and presenting these data to the clinical team as care suggestions. Perhaps more importantly, various sites that all use the same system from one of the big EMR companies can share these records among themselves. For example, people in a federally qualified health center (FQHC) can get comprehensive information on their patients hospitalized at a local hospital when both are on Epic.

As the team at the University of Michigan made clear, the EMR can become a burden, as more data are dropped into the primary care practice, much of it requiring and creating additional work. In my travels around the country, I heard this complaint repetitively as people spent increasing hours at home trying to keep up with the EMR. Recent data suggest some improvement in overall satisfaction with EMRs, but the results are uneven.[30]

Some primary care clinicians are boosters. Brooke Nicholls is a family nurse practitioner at OneCommunity Health Center, a two-site FQHC in Hood River and The Dalles, Oregon.[31] She is a great example of an evolving nursing workforce. Brooke received a bachelor of nursing degree from Portland State University and then came to OneCommunity as its diabetes support team coordinator. She then did virtual family NP training through Duke University and qualified/graduated in 2017. OneCommunity then employed her as a family medicine clinician, but they also let her do a yearlong residency, which she felt she really needed. She has practiced on her own since then, has a full panel of patients, and derives a great deal of joy from taking care of families.

When I asked Nicholls about Epic's EMR system, she responded, "It is great." Probing further, I inquired if its inbox could be overwhelming, to which she exclaimed, "Of course!" But she was clear that connectivity with Providence Hood River Memorial Hospital in Hood River and Mid-Columbia Medical Center in The Dalles was the most important attribute of EMRs in terms of improving her family medicine practice. In many ways, EMRs have replaced the need for Nicholls to make rounds when her patients are in the hospital. Continuity of care for them can be maintained by reviewing what is happening electronically and being in touch, if necessary, with hospitalists at the local hospitals, since all three care sites use Epic's EMR system.

This kind of connectivity is not the rule, and many clinicians and patients I talked to were distressed to find that often they had to obtain paper records to transmit information between practices or hospitals. The Office of the National Coordinator (ONC), which oversees regulation of EMRs, has placed a high priority on interconnectivity, but many see the ONC as falling short.

Nicholls also indicated that Epic's clinical messaging was oriented toward population health management, including prompts on the need to schedule screenings and callouts regarding values on lab reports that were helpful. She allowed there are a lot of messages and blinking lights, not to mention additional keystrokes, but nearly daily, things come up that otherwise might fall through the cracks. On the day we met, before seeing me, Nicholls had gotten a message about an overdue colonoscopy for a patient, so she promptly ordered it. In many ways, she was much more warmly appreciative of the support from EMRs than was the norm in other primary care practices. But grudging respect was prevalent elsewhere, especially on these points. In other words, there is some promise for the future.

The developers at companies like Epic are putting much more effort into health maintenance, quality-of-care oversight, and population health management than they were a decade ago, largely because their customers now demand it. Their installation base—across hospitals and practices with more than four doctors—is largely full now, and the current competition between EMR companies is to support the expanding needs and expectations of their clients. Their software developers realize that they must be careful, as they are well aware of the fatigue faced by clinicians, especially primary care clinicians, in their experiences with EMRs.

I spoke with the primary care team at Epic about their effort to improve the population health management segment of their EMRs.[32] Their next big step is to integrate generative artificial intelligence (AI)—which provides content in response to user prompts—into electronic medical records. The team's focus is to use AI to reduce administrative tasks and hence user burnout. Given a large language model base, clinician's interaction with a keyboard could become a thing of the past.

Three programs illustrated this commitment. The first entails ambient listening and clinicians' notes. Epic's team envisions a future where a machine listens in on conversations between clinicians and their patients and then automatically develops patients' progress notes. Such technology is not yet widely used, but soon it will be. Second, AI could draft messages on a patient's personal medical record (like Epic's MyChart) that would answer their questions. A patient's physician would no longer have to compose these replies. AI could also send messages directly to patients about gaps in their health care. Third, a physician needing information from a patient's chart would simply talk to a machine, eliminating keystrokes. It is easy to see how well this fits with a team that has both a physical and a virtual presence for its patients, prompting coordination and eliminating the use of medical scribes to enter information in patients' charts or EMRs. Many in primary care are excited about these possibilities, although I did meet a number of skeptics.

(I should note that I spoke to Epic and athenahealth team members throughout the writing of this book, mainly because I knew them from my work in the corporate sector. Many other good EMRs exist, but in the recent KLAS ranking of EMRs, the Epic suite of services was ranked first by a good margin. For physician practices, Epic ranked first, athenahealth third.[33])

The fourth major twenty-first century development that frames our understanding of the primary care industry is the emergence of federally qualified health centers. The federal government has long supported the establishment of local health centers in impoverished communities, starting with the first neighborhood health centers in Boston and Baltimore during the Lyndon Johnson administration.[34] But for much of the next 20 years, federal health policy did not countenance direct support for medical practices. Democrats in the US Congress kept up some funding, but the Nixon, Ford, and Reagan administrations saw the government's role as being limited to federal health insurance plans, not to direct patient care.[35]

Changes started in 1988 with the George H. W. Bush administration, and direct support began to flow through the US Department of Health and Human Service's Health Resources and Services Administration. New health centers opened. Even more importantly, the federal government changed the nature of health insurance reimbursements. After 1990, federally qualified health centers—which are controlled by local boards and approved by the HRSA—would receive predetermined fixed amounts from a *prospective payment system* (PPS), not only for their Medicare patients but also as a reimbursement floor for their Medicaid patients. Essentially, the FQHCs were reimbursed for the costs of their services, rather than being paid at whatever their state set as its Medicaid fees.[36] In addition, they could qualify for grants from HRSA, which would allow them to develop new programs. These funds, known as *Section 330 grants*, have grown over the course of the twenty-first century.

HRSA also has responsibility for funding workforce diversity and primary care workforce programs under Titles VII and VIII of the Public Health Service Act. While many of these training funds flow to hospitals, some go to FQHCs, and that could be expanded in the future. The funding for these titles has recently been in the $1.5 billion range, a relatively small amount given the size of our health care system.[37] The connection between FQHCs and training is critical, as these health centers have proven to be instrumental in training the providers who can help address the shortage of primary care workers and facilities in many counties.[38]

New FQHCs were constructed during Clinton's presidency, but his Democratic administration was not particularly supportive, with Secretary of Health and Human Services Donna Shalala favoring the development of hospital clinics. The largest expansion of community health centers occurred during George W. Bush's 2001–8 Republican administration, with 1,200 new centers serving 6 million additional patients. Thus FQHCs became a prominent part of primary care and Medicaid.

The Obama administration focused its efforts on improving health care insurance, particularly expanding Medicaid, which increased the insured patient population for FQHCs. In addition, the 2010 Affordable Care Act created the Community Health Center Fund, which provided $11 billion in support from 2011 to 2015.[39] Finally, part of the Recovery Act after the Great Recession (a financial crisis lasting from late 2007 to mid-2009) allocated more than $600 million for the construction of new health centers. As I traveled around the country visiting FQHCs, this infusion of capital was on display, with plenty of new buildings and renovated old ones. Over the course of the 2010s, Section 330 grant dollars also increased substantially, although this was slowed somewhat by the Trump administration. From 2010 to 2015, the annual appropriation for FQHCs rose from $2.2 billion to $5.1 billion, and by 2022 it had grown to $5.8 billion.[40]

Today, although there is substantial variation from state to state, about 40% of an average FQHC's income is from Medicaid, and 10% is from Medicare. The centers' receipts from Medicaid are much more generous than what is paid to private doctors and clinics in most states because of fixed amounts FQHCs receive through the PPS. Commercial health insurance pays for about 15% of the health care, and another 15% of funding comes from Section 330 grants. Most FQHCs scramble for a similar amount in grants from state and local sources.[41] Today, the HRSA's 340B drug-pricing program is also a reasonable source of revenue for FQHCs, although there is no good estimate of the average amount per center. Many FQHCs are busy building pharmacies to capture more of the 340B funds.

The result of this far-sighted effort over the past 20 years is a remarkably vibrant program found in many poor urban and rural communities.[42] Incomes for the patient population for an FQHC are generally quite a bit below the federal poverty level. On average, 23% of patients are uninsured. In 2018, there were 28 million patient visits at over 1,300 FQHCs. And 99% of FQHCs were accepting new Medicaid patients, compared with 73% of private physicians' practices.

FQHCs have enthusiastically endorsed population health management, outperforming other primary care sites on a range of measures, including immunizations, cancer screenings, Pap smears, hypertension treatments, and smoking cessation programs. A remarkable 77% of FQHCs have achieved primary care medical home status. Their per patient health expenditures come to $1,200, or 24% less than that of the other sites. In many ways, FQHCs are leading the way in primary care regarding population health management, providing better and less fiscally wasteful care. They are also beginning to use alternative payment models, often accepting a financial risk through capitation payments.[43]

In many ways, FQHCs are a separate sector of primary care. They have every incentive to provide value-based care, as their resources are always limited, and they have a largely fixed population of people for whom to care. They are also a federal creation, and as a result, changes can be made in reimbursement rather easily. Since Medicaid plays such a big role, and since states have a large say in Medicaid, the federal government must work with the states to address changes at FQHCs. Nonetheless, one could reasonably presume that value- and team-based primary care might be able to develop independently in the FQHCs, even if relatively dormant in other sectors of health care.

The fifth major health policy development molding primary care is the aforementioned emergence of Medicare Advantage. Almost since the start of the Medicare program, a government paid fee-for-service program that started in 1965, policymakers have sought ways to *privatize*, that is, to allow commercial insurance companies to fill in the role as payer for the federal government. Advocates of for-profit incentives thought this would lead to a more efficient program. Those who wanted the federal government to be a sole payer, seeing Medicare as the segue to a single payer, have been opposed. This tension has played out over the past 40 years.[44]

While it has taken various forms over the years, modified by administrations through rulemaking and by Congress through legislation, Medicare Advantage has the government pay the insurer a risk-adjusted amount for each beneficiary that signs up for a Medicare Advantage policy. Upon turning 65, one can decide whether to stay in traditional Medicare, paying the Part B premium, or to enroll in a Medicare Advantage plan. The plan has the risk for the patient's illness, thus moving the program from fee-for-service to prospective payment.

Over the years, the constant controversy has been the cost of the program, that is, how much (always more) does Medicare pay in Medicare Advantage than in traditional Medicare. The Medicare Modernization Act in 2003 famously boosted payment in the Medicare Advantage program to keep insurers in the game, the last bit of substantial Republican health policy. It worked, as enrollment has grown ever since. The Obama administration cut back payments, changing the risk-adjustment strategies, but that did little to reduce the momentum. Over the past decade, costs per beneficiary have increased significantly as overall enrollment in Medicare Advantage has moved past 50% of beneficiaries.

The Biden administration decided in the early 2020s to address the overpayment. Heeding advocate advice, and that of the Medicare Payment Advisory Committee, CMS has focused on the coding efforts by insurers. As noted previously, in a prospective payment program, the cost per beneficiary should be adjusted to fit the burden of the beneficiary's illness. This is done by the use of diagnostic codes for each illness. Insurers can game the system by *overcoding*, or attributing illnesses to patients that they do not have.

As was noted with Catalyst in North Texas, some insurers are willing, and some medical groups are eager, to take a capitated payment for a Medicare Advantage patient. Then the patient is attributed to them, and they must provide value-based care and prevent illnesses to earn a profit. With the capitation payment, they can hire the care team they need to address illness prospectively. But they also face incentives to overcode. CMS is addressing this in 2024 with new coding guidelines, and that process likely will continue, bringing Medicare Advantage spending back toward that of traditional Medicare.

The promise of value-based care in Medicare Advantage has spawned a number of different models of primary care prospective payment. These practices were blooming in the early 2020s, interesting for-profit investors. It remains to be seen whether that momentum will continue if CMS reduces the capitation spigot. It also remains to be seen whether successful practices really provided value-based care or were just more successful at coding and perhaps selection bias. In any case, Medicare Advantage–based risk compensation has become a major issue in the move to Primary Care 3.0.

Together, these five developments help create the historical context for value-based primary care. Importantly, Primary Care 3.0 is heterogeneous, showing up in lots of different practices, including those serving the poor and uninsured.

Value-Based Care at a Federally Qualified Health Center: Holyoke Health

There is no typical federally qualified health center. Some are in brand-new buildings, with lots of patients and a staff that is committed to providing care for low-income patients. Some are rural, oriented toward farmworkers, while others are situated in urban neighborhoods far from green spaces. Other facilities are decidedly tired looking, with staff that are even more fatigued. Some FQHCs are uncertain about the future, while others are bursting with optimism. Each has its own organizational character, which is almost uniformly expressed in the staff's attitude.

Holyoke Health Center is a good example of where thriving community health centers stand today, reflecting the five trends in the growth of value-based primary care discussed above. The town of Holyoke,

Massachusetts, made a real impression as I crossed the bridge from Chicopee. I arrived in a downtown industrial area that, 120 years ago, made most of the fine writing paper in the United States. Huge mills had stood along the Connecticut River, near Hadley Falls. Two great canals were dug through the industrial area to provide water for the plants' manufacturing processes. A fine town was built higher up the hill, reflecting the wealth produced below.

Now the town resembled Dresden, Germany, immediately after World War II. Its industrial area is completely dilapidated. Most of the buildings are falling down or burned out. Higher up on the hill, there are buildings with windows but few tenants. Holyoke's population is overwhelmingly disadvantaged. Many people are descendants of Puerto Rican immigrants, with many of their forebearers being drawn to central Massachusetts 50 years ago in a program designed to relocate Puerto Rican agricultural workers to the mainland United States.

The one vibrant enterprise in town seems to be the Holyoke Health Center, a sprawling FQHC that occupies a former furniture store. The center's executives claimed that it acts as an engine driving downtown revitalization, but the only sign of this I encountered was a lonely coffee shop across the street, where I got some soup with a taste of the Caribbean. (All the clinicians at the center brought their lunches to work.) Aside from that one boast, the staff members I met were uniformly grounded and practical minded. They were also loyal to and proud of the city, the region, and especially their health center. And they were optimistic about a better future.

Dr. Alejandro Esparza Perez is the chief executive officer, setting the health center's tone of quiet confidence that comes with making a difference.[45] He came to the Holyoke Health Center 21 years ago, as his first job after completing his medical training. He was born in Coatzacoalcos, Vera Cruz, Mexico—which he assured me was far more decrepit than Holyoke. He went to medical school in Guadalajara, Mexico, and trained at MetroWest Medical Center in Framingham, Massachusetts. Esparza had wanted to be a cardiologist but got involved with health care for the homeless in Framingham and decided he wanted to focus on the underserved. His former chief resident convinced him to go to Holyoke, and he lives with his partner and his dog not far from the medical center.

When Esparza arrived, the health center had about 150 employees. Today there are close to 400. That includes 31 primary care clinicians, about two-thirds of whom are allopathic and osteopathic physicians, with the rest being APPs (primarily nurse practitioners). The health center has a host of ancillary clinicians, residency programs in dentistry and pharmacy, and a family nurse practitioner training program. It also has a multispecialty suite for cardiology and other services, which is affiliated with Holyoke Medical Center, the only independent hospital left in Massachusetts. Holyoke Medical Center also collaborates with the health center on radiology and lab services.

One thing that stood out at the entrance to the FQHC was the pharmacy. It is expansive, with high ceilings and plenty of room for counseling. The health center has had an affiliated pharmacy for years, running it in-house for the past 10 years. All the center's clinicians talked glowingly about how they use the pharmacy's consultation services for diabetes care, medication reconciliation, patient adherence, and general counseling. This is now buttressed by the 340B revenues from the federal program that ensures lower costs for prescription drugs. The pharmacy is thus a profit center, although *how* profitable was not clear to me. It is always difficult to nail down the exact contributions from such programs, and pharmaceutical financial issues are uniquely opaque in health care.

The Holyoke Health Center's payer mix is dominated by Medicaid, providing over 60% of its revenues. Unlike other FQHCs in Massachusetts, Holyoke has few uninsured patients. Most people coming to the mainland from Puerto Rico previously knew about or were enrolled in the Medicaid program. The state of Massachusetts has also been assiduously expanding Medicaid coverage for more than 20 years. About 15% of revenues comes through Medicare, and the rest from commercial health insurance.

Holyoke Health Center and several other FQHCs in Massachusetts have come together to form the Community Care Cooperative (C3), an accountable care organization. Most of them were not newcomers to the population health management journey, having become certified primary care medical homes over the past decade. Two years ago, Holyoke Health Center was considering an ACO relationship with Holyoke Medical Center, but a program with other FQHCs made better sense. This new structure has brought about big changes, particularly converting all the centers to Epic's EMR system and preparing for Medicaid's impending switch to primary care capitation, mandated by the state.

The conversion to Epic was in full swing when I visited, and it was causing a good deal of angst. COVID relief funds had made the move to Epic's EMR system possible for Holyoke Health Care and the other C3 centers, and C3 was overseeing its implementation. This meant that for any questions or problems, the EMR "tickets" were going to a centralized team from C3, which was frustrating for the local staff. But already many clinicians liked the new EMR system, as aggregating preventive health measures and searching patients' charts now seemed much easier.

The other big issue facing the Holyoke Health Center when I visited it in late 2022 was the primary care capitation program from MassHealth (the Massachusetts Medicaid authority), headed their way on April 1, 2023. Esparza and the team were eager to take on capitated risk, although financial details did not abound in my discussions with him or others. They had been told by their actuaries, contracted through C3, that the center's revenue would be similar to what they got through billing codes in a fee-for-service program, which is good. But the actuaries could not tell them what percentage of overall costs this primary care capitation represents. Nor did anyone have much of a sense about how to document diagnoses to improve their at-risk patient scores (an issue I will discuss in detail later).

C3's administrative team was bullish, especially about capitation's philosophy of caring for the whole patient. Esparza also made the point that MassHealth has acknowledged that its fee-for-service payments had not increased much in 20 years. So the C3 health centers believe they are in line for a reasonable revenue increase through capitation. They are ready to "focus on quality, not quantity" and move away from a "fee-for-service mentality." Other good news included the reduced burden of being responsible for only 12 Medicaid quality-of-care measures instead of the previous 20-plus. Moreover, the new reports for Medicaid are being integrated with the quality-of-care reporting for HRSA. In the past, two separate reports had to be compiled.

My initial visit was in late 2022. By mid-2024, Dr. Esparza could report that the primary care capitation had been a financial success. Of course, other policy changes, like modifications of 340B eligibility, brought other challenges, but capitation was working for them.

Another critical strategic move is that the Holyoke Health Center will now provide their own behavioral health services. For years they had partnered with Behavioral Health, Inc., whose clinicians were integrated with the C3 practices. Holyoke Health Center now believes they must take this on themselves, given the press of behavioral health problems their patients are experiencing. Hiring is difficult, but they are making progress. They are also expanding their addiction program. They currently have nearly 300 patients enrolled in medication-assisted therapy.

The health center has not had a lot of primary clinician turnover, only one or two people a year for the past decade. For much of that time, departures were usually a matter of a spouse moving out of town. The same is not true with the center's medical assistants (MAs) and to some extent its nurses. The Holyoke Health Center cannot afford to match salaries and other benefits offered by hospitals in the area. Working with a local junior college, the center is developing its own MA training program in a downtown building it recently purchased. These kinds of resilient reactions to new problems were ubiquitous around the center.

The pharmacy is a real jewel. It filled 340,000 prescriptions in 2021 and heavily incorporated 340B pricing into the mix. They have 17 full-time-equivalent pharmacists and all do consultations with patients. The consultation rooms were a veritable hive of activity. Even though the interactions were short, the primary clinicians found them to be invaluable. The pharmacists also work with patients discharged from the hospital to reconcile their medications.

Esparza had a full plate. In addition to everything else, he was considering how to address the homeless problem in Holyoke—specifically, how the health center could develop affordable or transitional housing. He is a quiet man, always searching for ways to help his patients and the community. As a new CEO, he was afraid he might have to give up seeing patients, but that turned out to not be the case. Sharing this news with me brought the only big smile to his face that I saw all day!

Esparza introduced me to some of his clinical team. Dr. Monica Liao, like Esparza, had an interesting path to western Massachusetts. Her parents, who are from Taiwan, moved their family to Santa Cruz, Bolivia, when she was a small child.[46] Liao grew up there, speaking Mandarin and Spanish. She attended high school in Bolivia, a Christian university in California, and then went to medical school at St. George's University in the Caribbean, but she spent her first academic year in Newcastle, England. After doing most of her student clinical rotations in New York City, she attended Albany Medical Center in Upstate New York for a pediatrics residency. Holyoke Health Center was the first place she interviewed for a job. She wanted to care for the underserved and use her Spanish language skills—a perfect fit.

Liao had been at Holyoke Health Center for seven years. When Esparza was promoted from his old job of CMO to become CEO, she was named the new CMO. She was busy when I talked to her, dealing with Epic EMR nightmares. (The conversion to any new EMR system is indeed fraught for the person fielding the problems, and she was no exception.) Two days before we met, 10 different health centers went live, and all were having typical problems with an EMR conversion, including having to revert to paper for some medical issues.

Liao's other preoccupation was the shift to capitation. She forcefully uttered "you know" when emphasizing a point, punctuating her discussion of how the center's primary care practice must change with this new form of payment. Her key themes were that Holyoke Health Center's clinicians and their teams must anticipate patient needs before an office visit. Liao illustrated her point by enumerating the range of social determinants of health that routinely affect the treatment plans for their patients. For example, her patients live in food deserts and therefore have poor nutrition. She was trying to think of ways to promote better meal choices, such as purchasing food from farmers' markets.

Some practices readily discuss how their compensation system works. FQHC clinicians can be a bit more hesitant, but Liao was not ruffled when I asked. In the past, the Holyoke Health Center had a quarterly bonus system that considered relative value units (RVUs), the billing program developed by the American Medical Association, as well as quality-of-care measures. Full-time doctors were expected to see at least 57 patients a week, with a stretch goal of 69. The center's administrators will reassess this patient load as they adapt to MassHealth's new primary care capitation program, because its Medicaid payments will dominate their practice. The clinicians will also receive an annual bonus, based on several factors. One is maintaining an appropriate panel size, which for the team treating adults is 1,000 patients. This shift from counting *visits* to counting *patients* is the hallmark of moving to population-based capitation.

The starting salaries for Holyoke Health Center's physicians are in line with others around the country, ranging from $120,000 to $300,000 depending on the region and the setting. (Liao was much more precise about the salary range for her colleagues, but generally I will not quote exact figures for salaries and bonuses.) The center will maintain compensation for its clinicians at their current levels as it moves into capitation, but panel size will become much more important than the number of patient visits (RVUs).

Another colleague, Dr. Stephanie Billings, could not have been more clear and forthright.[47] Much more a product of Massachusetts than her colleagues, she nonetheless spent some time away from her home base. She grew up in Lawrence, Massachusetts, attended Smith College in Northampton, Massachusetts, then Albany Medical Center in New York State for medical school. She trained at Harbor–University of California, Los Angeles Medical Center in Torrance, California, then came to Holyoke on a National Health Services Corps scholarship. And here she has stayed.

Billings was a bit more skeptical about payment reform: "Every few years we see something new, first fee-for-service, then ACOs, now capitation." When I asked what would be better, she immediately answered, "A single-payer national health care system." Her reasoning was straightforward: since businesses cannot make money from low-income people, for-profit companies in health care will eventually bail out and be interested only in the wealthy and the well insured. A single-payer format would mean a level playing field for Billings's patients. But she did not dwell on this topic, moving right along to describe her practice.

Billings is a busy family medicine doctor, covering adult medicine, pediatrics, and gynecology. Friday is a procedure day: "Everything is sterilized and ready to go." Like the other Holyoke Health Center clinicians, Billings is expected to see patients every 15 minutes, and that can top out at 20–22 individuals a day. This is a large volume of patients, and many doctors would have trouble doing all their charting during the workday, but she gets everything done before leaving, at around 5:30 p.m.

Billings works part-time, which makes all the difference for her. As a result, she has only 500 to 600 patients in her panel. She would prefer a smaller panel size, since she feels as though she could do much more for her patients if she had more time. Still, her patient population is manageable, and she has a close relationship with the overwhelming majority of them, allowing her to anticipate their needs and intervene effectively.

Billings was enthusiastic about Epic's EMR, as it provides preventive medicine information much more easily than their former system. She could also work on patients' charts ahead of time, which she loved. She was excited to see some of her patients using Epic's MyChart to communicate with the Holyoke Health Center's clinicians. Long dissatisfied with their phone systems, Billings hoped MyChart might be a breakthrough for them. (These views are not the norm. Grudging respect for MyChart is much more common than enthusiasm.)

No one is quite sure what the new Medicaid capitation program will entail, but Billings believed she would have better access to case managers and improved care coordination. She hoped to be able to spend more time with patients, but that key issue was not yet clear, at least to her. The size of the center's panels and the rapidity with which its clinicians must see patients were her major pressure points. Her team of medical assistants and nurses, however, know the community well, and their patients very well. In Billings's primary care practice, the nurses play an important role. They schedule patients' appointments, *triage* (determine the priority of) any problems that arise, check a patient's blood pressure and glucose level, and consult with the pharmacists over medication issues.

But her practice had not yet developed a team approach, aside from the nurses, medical assistants, and clinicians working closely together. Billings did not interact with the care management or behavioral health support teams in the clinic itself. Given what is happening elsewhere in FQHCs on the cutting edge of primary care and population health management, the extended team concept will probably be adopted at Holyoke Health Center, especially with the new reimbursement program.

Billings wanted me to understand that she loves her primary care practice, and it shows as she described her clinical interactions. She did, however, worry about the center's personnel who work full-time, believing that they risk real burnout. Almost all of the center's doctors are National Health Service Corps clinicians or are on J-1 visas. Both avenues provide a pipeline of FQHC clinicians, and they both require recipients to work full time. (The National Health Services Corps is a program operated by HRSA. It offers tuition support for medical students, who then must work for a specified period in medically underserved communities.)

Lisa Connors, the chief operating officer (COO) for the Holyoke Health Center, is responsible for the care management efforts, which make up a large part of the center's population management strategy.[48] I met with her in the leadership team's offices. Holyoke Health Center's administrative offices are housed in an older industrial part of the building, with ceilings that must be 20 to 25 feet high, so the center has built modular offices with high walls that nonetheless stopped well short of the ceiling. The hallways seemed like narrow canyons, and enormous pipes and ductwork loomed over the top of the offices. The pipes and ducts above Connors's office produced a deep vibration that resonated through all the furniture and the floor. Given her rapid-fire speech and command of details, I had a sense that she did not have time to notice it.

Connors revealed that since Holyoke Health Center joined the C3 ACO, their care management team has expanded to help patients who suffered from severe diseases and required complicated care. More data, coming through to them from the ACO, has allowed the center to anticipate which patients will be at risk and get care management support to them sooner. Care managers work with individual patients, while care coordinators have lists of patients who need specific outreach, such as those recently discharged from the hospital. Care coordination is more administrative, with less patient contact. At other practices that are a bit further along the learning curve on population health management, these functions are tightly integrated with the patient care team.

Connors and the other administrative team members were considering a shift to that approach, making care management and behavioral health part of the team in the clinic itself. They were carefully weighing the benefits, noticing that most of the other C3 ACO's federally qualified health centers were building that kind of expanded team. To be able to receive capitation payments from MassHealth, an FQHC must have certain structural aspects of care in place, such as extended care management.

The Holyoke Health Center story illustrates how the concepts of population health management, value-based care, and capitated payments are being spread throughout the US health care system. Although Holyoke Health Center is in a geographic and socioeconomic setting quite different from that of Catalyst Health, the same tools are being applied, and the clinicians are excited about it. In Holyoke's case, one part of that impetus is the activism of C3, a second part is its leadership team's inclination to break away from traditional primary care, and a third part is related to the state's capitation initiative. But the overall result is similar to Catalyst Health, although North Dallas could not be more different than downtown Holyoke.

Are We Accelerating Toward Value-Based Primary Care?

Do care settings like Catalyst Health and Holyoke Health Center represent a new future for primary care? At both, EMRs and other digital interventions are providing much more information for clinicians, some of it overwhelming. Encouraged by primary care medical home models, the clinicians in both settings are now practicing in increasingly extended teams, with coordination possible through technology. New payment models are slowly infiltrating into the primary care practices.

Most primary care practices today are similar to the University of Alabama at Birmingham program, where doctors (primarily) stay on a fee-for-service treadmill, reimbursed by the number of visits they see, known throughout primary care as the RVUs. Catalyst Health and Holyoke Health Center provide a glimpse of a different future for primary care—and for the entire American health care system. Moreover, they resonate with what experts have long seen as the promise of primary care. Starfield's four pillars of primary care were: (1) a focus on patients' overall health; (2) an emphasis on health promotion; (3) clinicians who are generalists, not specialists; and (4) patients' active (rather than passive) participation in their own health care. That article has well stood the test of time.[49] She did not necessarily endorse a payment mechanism, but prospective payment, rather than visit-based reimbursement, would support this anticipatory posture of primary care.

Thomas Bodenheimer and colleagues have updated and extended the Starfield concept of good primary care.[50] It is worth enumerating their ten critical points, as they guide the possible future of primary care:

1. Engaged leadership, with concrete goals.
2. Data-driven improvement, using computer-based technology.
3. Empanelment—that is, every patient being assigned to a care team and a primary care clinician.
4. Team-based care.

5. Patient–team partnerships, with the patient engaged in shared decisions.
6. Population management, including health coaching and complex care management.
7. Continuity of care.
8. Prompt access to care.
9. Comprehensiveness and coordination in care.
10. Templates for a variety of different kinds of visits—including various lengths of in-person visits, e-visits, and home consultations.

This ideal primary care practice is not possible in a fee-for-service future. An RVU, widget-driven system, with expectations for clinicians to have a large number of patient visits per day, cannot obtain these goals. In a fee-for-service system, primary care does not have incentives to "own" the patient's health, or to anticipate problems and prevent them.

There is near unanimity in health policy today, insisting that population health management and value-based care must be the health care imperatives of the future. Nearly all of the experts see that the best means for achieving this is founded on having a strong primary care practice. And most believe that doing so entails empaneling patients and basing health care payments on prospective payment. Primary care clinicians are then charged with ensuring that health care is value based, that health is promoted, that disease is prevented, and that their relationships with patients are tight and enduring. That is what the inheritors of Starfield's premises want. In many ways, it is the rightful evolution of the kind of primary care practice that was started in places like Skowhegan more than 40 years ago.

But the yearnings of health policy experts and the realities of practice are miles apart. Most primary care practices remain volume oriented and struggle to provide a professionally satisfying practice for their clinicians. Change will come only as major payers, insurers and the federal government, change the nature of reimbursement.

Fortunately, many state officials, federal regulators, insurers, and patient advocates agree, and they are all pushing toward that future today. It is the only real hope we have for an equitable and affordable health care system in the United States—one that features a strong primary care base that manages care and eliminates financial waste, anticipates patients' needs, and is grounded in their community. As we will see, many governmental and corporate entities are advocating—indeed, pushing—for value-based care and trying to create a context for strengthening primary care. Catalyst Health did not need that push, but its focus today is on the Medicare Advantage program, which does facilitate prospective payment. Holyoke Health Center is certainly being urged forward by the changes in Massachusetts's Medicaid program. Tracking these various sources of pressure and impetus allows us to understand the full picture of how primary care might evolve.

I will start with federal government, the largest payer in health care by far. The federal government is moving, in many areas, to remake the American health care system into something more centered on primary care and population health. The Centers for Medicare and Medicaid Services relies on changes in reimbursements and special demonstration projects, promoted through the Center for Medicare and Medicaid Innovation. Nearly all of these advances reiterate the need to develop a stronger role for primary care. Politics plays a huge part in this process, and some dominant sectors in the health care system—particularly hospitals and their specialist doctors—are not too interested in change, especially something that puts primary care in the driver's seat.

State governments, as the founding fathers expected, can be engines of innovation. Currently some states are doing little, while others are actively remaking their health care systems. They have the same problem with lethargy in their large health care systems, but they also have an advantage in that states have historically regulated much of the nation's health care. With regard to financing, Medicaid is a state/federal program, and states can work closely with the CMS on Medicaid waivers that allow relatively radical changes in reimbursements. In chapter 4, I examine efforts in four states (Massachusetts, Oregon, Rhode

Island, and Vermont) that are promoting vibrant primary care, with varying degrees of success.

The next set of agitators for health care reforms are usually not discussed in the same breath as state and federal governments, as they are mostly for-profit companies. Primary care clinicians, as well as health policy experts, generally take a dim view of health insurers and health care corporations. Most of the primary care doctors I met with have the same attitude as Stephanie Billings; they've had enough with payment reforms and are ready for a single payer. That may indeed be the way our country eventually moves, but right now, private payers are a large part of our health care reality. Private health insurance companies—whether they are state-based Blue Cross Blue Shield plans or national companies like Aetna, Humana, or the UnitedHealth Group—are not stupid. They perceive the same weaknesses in a fee-for-service system as the government policy intelligentsia do, and these insurers are taking substantial steps to promote population-based health care. In chapters 5 and 6, I discuss a number of these initiatives, which could have as strong an impact as the federal government and state governments do.

The big question about these private corporations is their staying power. They may be convinced that primary care payment reform is necessary, and in some cases they might even own the primary care practices themselves. But will they persist if they accrue losses? Recent evidence suggests that large retailers, who were bullish about owning primary care as recently as early 2020s, are backing away. Might insurers as well, especially as the federal government reduces capitated payments in Medicare Advantage? The same question attends nascent efforts by employers to use value-based primary care practices.

The last set of influences comes from private investors. Surprisingly, at least to many in primary care, private equity firms are promoting start-up companies aimed at enhancing and improving value-based care (see chapter 7). In other sectors of health care (specialist aggregation, hospital ownership, nursing home ownership), private equity has been seen as sacrificing quality for high profit. Can primary care be different? Again, unless there are significant profit opportunities, will private equity be an enduring influence?

Who is absent from this mix of players in health care who might promote value-based primary care? Hospitals and integrated delivery systems. In my view, few of them have sufficiently abandoned the "turn and burn" fee-for-service format. Some large hospital systems have built a substantial primary care base, but the economics of fee-for-service health care are against them. Large hospitals generally follow the rules I learned nearly 50 years ago in my hospital management master's degree program: keep the specialist doctors happy, and keep the operating and procedure rooms filled. A fee-for-service system encourages that. It is no surprise, then, that most of the primary care in so-called integrated delivery systems looks a lot more like what I saw at the University of Alabama at Birmingham Medical Center than at Holyoke Health Center. This may be too harsh a conclusion, but I leave it to others to make a case for integrated delivery systems in value-based care.

In summary, a lot of what currently happens in primary care looks broken, at least in our crazy health care system, even though the human interactions at the center of clinician–patient relationships can still be wonderful. But exciting changes are occurring, and the entire range of these initiatives needs to be examined in order to understand whether primary care can be put back together again.

CHAPTER THREE

What Can the Federal Government Do to Promote Primary Care?

THE FEDERAL GOVERNMENT IS FAR and away the biggest payer for health care in the United States. More importantly, it is the main voice in health policy. While other key players in health care—states, employers, health insurers, hospitals, clinicians, and patient advocates—all make efforts to improve and modify the provision of patient care, most of the impetus for change in American medicine has been the result of federal initiatives. The states' financial lever is largely restricted to Medicaid (in which they share health care costs with the federal government), as well as to the power to regulate hospitals and insurers. The degree of state activism has been varied, but proponents of health care change in states have spurred impressive reforms. Employers have been relatively passive in helping determine the overall shape and path of health care—surprisingly so, given the large number of people who rely on their employers for health benefits.[1]

I turn first to the feds for health policy answers to the question, How can primary care be improved and reach its potential? The major problems with primary care are that (1) there are not enough clinicians; (2) their work in a fee-for-service setting is a daily grind, aimed at seeing as many patients as possible and thereby generating a significant number of bills for that care; and, (3) notwithstanding this frenetic activity, clinicians are underpaid compared with other physicians. The federal government should be a source of answers for all three of these issues. First, it provides nearly all of the financial support for physicians' training in this country, and it controls the number and types of slots for residencies that are available at hospitals and health care centers. Second, given the federal government's scope and vision, it is in the best position to change the nature of primary care practices by promoting new organizational structures for the delivery of care. Third, it is health care's biggest payer, and its payment policies tend to be echoed by commercial health insurers, so spending more for primary care but allocating it wisely would seem to fall under federal oversight. The federal government is active on all three fronts, with varying levels of success thus far, and some interesting initiatives are underway. Each deserves careful examination.

The Federal Government's Role in Training More Primary Care Clinicians

In health policy, controversy is the rule. So, it is telling that there is a consensus that our country has a shortage of primary care physicians. As I discussed in chapter 2, the federal government itself—specifically the Health Resources and Services Administration—predicts a substantial shortfall of primary care doctors for the foreseeable future. HRSA's projections for much of the 2020s through 2035 indicate that we only have about 90% of the family medicine doctors we need, with a deficit of more than 15,000 physicians in 2035.[2] General internal medicine is even worse, with a deficit of 17%, or 20,000 doctors. The Association of American Medical Colleges has even higher estimates: a deficit of 18,000–48,000 primary care physicians by 2034.[3]

This shortage is perhaps better portrayed by looking at patients' wait times. For example, in western Massachusetts (where Holyoke Health Center is located), the average delay in seeing a family physician was 45 days over a decade ago.[4] It probably is even longer now. The one phenomenon I found in my travels around the country (with the exception of a clinic in Selma, Alabama) was that the patient panel for any new doctor or nurse practitioner added to a clinic was completely filled within two weeks. It is clear that many more new doctors and advanced practice providers (APPs) are needed. Additions to their numbers depend largely on the federal government and the market forces surrounding medical education.

Support for physicians' residency training overwhelmingly comes from the federal government, in a program known as Graduate Medical Education, or GME. This system could not be more arcane—or more poorly designed from the point of view of developing a large, cohesive, well-trained primary care workforce. Medicare's funding for GME originally supplemented the costs of hospital training for doctors, and little has changed over the past 50 years, largely because this program well serves one of Medicare's key constituencies: large hospitals with teaching programs. This support is both direct and indirect.[5] Direct GME financing is based on a combination of the number of trainees and a hospital's number of Medicare patients. Indirect payment is meant to compensate for the higher costs a training program causes for a hospital, or inefficiencies related to the students' inexperience. These overlapping rationales are the result of legislative strategies from the distant past.

Since 1996, the number of residency slots that Medicare supports has been frozen (except for changes noted below). Nonetheless, this support is relatively impressive. In 2020, the program provided more than $16 billion in GME support ($4.5 billion directly and $11.7 billion indirectly).[6] The formulas for calculating these payments are complicated and imprecise. For example, the Medicare Payment Advisory Commission found that less than 40% of the indirect medical expenditures could be empirically justified by hospital needs.[7] Some economists have even suggested that GME training is profitable for hospitals.[8] Be this as it may, there is no serious consideration of changing the overall federal GME program. It supports teaching hospitals, which have a tremendously strong lobby in Washington, DC.

From a primary care viewpoint, two other significant problems result from this frozen-in-time system. First, the money goes to hospitals, which are really the last place where modern primary care doctors should be trained. The average family medicine or internal medicine resident spends an overwhelming portion of their training in hospitals, but once they begin to practice, they may never set foot in a hospital again. How can this system possibly make sense?

Second, the geographic dispersion of these Medicare-supported training programs reflects the US population in 1996 (or earlier). As Robert Orr persuasively argued, a physician's residency location is a substantial determinant of that person's eventual practice location.[9] There is a strong correlation between the density of medical residencies and the density of physicians per 100,000 people. Given the population shifts in the United States, the current geographic dispersion of programs is no longer defensible. Moreover, 30 years ago, few training programs were located in rural and urban communities that had a paucity of doctors. While Medicaid programs across the country do contribute to GME (about $3.2 billion in 2021), this funding has largely gone to hospitals already also receiving Medicare support.

Over the past 25 years, three separate committees of the National Academies of Science, Engineering, and Medicine (NASEM) have called for Medicare GME reforms.[10] There has been some progress. For example, the American Academy of Family Medicine has radically revised its program requirements for family medicine training programs, with a much greater emphasis on outpatient and interdisciplinary experiences.[11] Given these reforms, the GME training continues to fund a particular hospital, but the actual learning occurs elsewhere and is likely to be more applicable to a doctor's career.

Second, the Biden administration has shown an interest in reforming GME. The Consolidated Appropriations Act of 2021 provided new funding for 1,000 GME residency training slots, totaling $1.8 billion for the period from 2023 to 2031. The distribution of these slots is intended to repair some of the current deficiencies. Emphasis is placed on rural hospitals, states with new medical schools, and hospitals serving areas designated by HRSA as health professional shortage areas (HPSAs).[12] Such farsighted legislation gives me hope that the federal government can help solve the deficit in the primary care workforce. In this legislation's first tranche of 200 slots, 125 were allocated to primary care, and another 20 to psychiatry.[13] This is at least a start. Moreover, the proposed Resident Shortage Reduction Act of 2023 (H.R. 238), which is endorsed by most of the primary care and specialty physician organizations in the United States, would add 14,000 new residency positions.[14] If these slots are appropriately sited, and oriented toward primary care, it could make a real difference. The 2025 Trump administration's views on these subjects will be quite important.

To address the current shortage of primary care doctors, there must also be medical students interested in primary care to fill the residency slots. In 2023, there were 48,000 applicants for 40,000 residency training positions, but many primary care slots went unfilled.[15] Opening more slots in primary care would require more medical students to fill them, a problem that could be addressed by graduating more doctors.

Fortunately, there is a growing number of both allopathic and osteopathic medicine graduates. The number of allopathic graduates increased from 15,676 in 2002 to 21,051 in 2022, while osteopathic graduates increased over that time from 2,536 to 7,702.[16] The latter are a more important focus for primary care. Osteopathic students are far more likely to go into primary care than allopathic students. More importantly, the number of osteopathic medical schools is growing, resulting in the 70% increase in enrollment since 2011.[17] These students are exactly what primary care needs: high quality and commitment. On the quality issue, a recent paper in the *Annals of Internal Medicine* showed that health care quality and costs were similar between allopathic and osteopathic hospitalist physicians caring for elderly patients.[18] Leaders in osteopathy believe that more schools could be built if there were more training slots.

Expansion in the number of primary care doctors in America could also be accomplished by increasing the number of international medical graduates. Nearly one-quarter of the physicians practicing in the United States are IMGs, with their number growing by 18% since 2010.[19] IMGs are much more likely to choose primary care fields, such as family medicine, for their training.[20] These students are well trained to take good care of patients. Research suggests that the care IMG doctors deliver is equivalent to that by American medical school graduates.[21]

Regarding passing rates on US medical licensure exams, greater than 90% of American MDs, American DOs, and international medical graduates all pass the critical step 2 and 3 exams.[22]

The critical obstacle to further growth in the number of IMG graduates, similar to growth in the number of osteopaths, is the availability of training program positions and interest in those programs. Andrew Sussman is the CEO of Medforth, which operates St. George's University in Grenada, West Indies, and Rocky Vista University College of Osteopathic Medicine, which has campuses in Colorado, Montana, and Utah. He is certain that new medical schools, particularly osteopathic and international medical schools, would open if there were more training positions available.[23] Some of these, like Medforth, would be for-profit operations, which would need to depend only on market forces, and the lack of primary care doctors is certainly creating such incentives. Changes in state law like that enacted in Tennessee recently, which does away with the requirement that IMGs complete a residency in the United States, will help as well.[24]

Some experts think that new residency positions are unnecessary. Edward Salsberg and Candice Chen, longtime scholars of medical education, have recently made the point that the number of GME positions has continued to grow, some in the new teaching hospitals that were not affected by the 1996 cap on slots funded by the federal government.[25] Since 2013, nearly 7,000 additional slots were created. These authors also found that the quantity of positions and the number of applicants are evenly matched, even in light of the increases in osteopathic medicine and international medical graduates. But many of the additional medical school graduates are specialty physician training programs, which are preferred by hospitals. Hospitals need to support their surgical subspecialties. To increase the current number of primary care doctors, more primary care training programs are needed in ambulatory settings and in rural hospitals. Getting primary care slots filled might also entail the federal government paying bonuses to those medical students who opt for primary care. But again, this would be a short investment for a longer gain.

In addition to Medicare's Graduate Medical Education program, the other source of federal funding for training new doctors, especially in primary care, is the Health Resources and Services Administration. As noted, HRSA is the leading source of support for federally qualified health centers. But another big part of its mission is related to training, especially in primary care.

The hodgepodge nature of HRSA's responsibilities is reflected in its budget proposal for 2023.[26] The Biden administration requested a total of $13.3 billion, with $5.7 billion allocated to support FQHCs; another $2.7 billion designated for HIV/AIDS treatment efforts, including the Ryan White program; and $2.1 billion intended for health care workforce development. The largest part of this, nearly half a billion dollars, went to the National Health Service Corps (NHSC), which provides scholarships and loan repayment funds for residency graduates who are willing to work in underserved areas. (I discussed the role the NHSC plays in FQHCs like the Holyoke Health Center in chapter 2.) Today, there are more than 22,700 clinicians paid through the NHSC and the related Nurse Corps scholarship program. HRSA also provides nearly $400 million to programs that train behavioral health experts, and another $100 million for advanced nursing education.

This is an impressive list. But HRSA used to play an even larger role. In the 1970s, substantial funds for primary care training were available under Title VII, but these were cut to minimal amounts in the early 1980s and have never been reinstituted.[27] The Affordable Care Act came to the rescue in 2010 when it created a five-year initiative to expand primary care residency programs. Its Teaching Health Center Program, administered by HRSA, is targeted largely to community health centers, tribal health centers, and rural health clinics.[28] There were concerns that funding for this program might be lost after the first five years, as it requires periodic congressional renewal, but as of 2021, there were 769 medical school graduates in 60 primary care Teaching Health Center residency programs. They are much more likely to go into practice near their training sites and provide health care for the underserved.[29] The cost for this training is about $160,000 per trainee per year.[30] Yet its further funding remains in limbo, a sign of the dysfunction in training priorities.[31]

Still, some members of Congress recognize the need to train more primary care doctors. In late 2023, Senators Bernie Sanders and Roger Marshall began advocating for passage of the Bipartisan Primary Care and Health Workforce Act, which would add 700 new primary care residency slots to the Teaching Health Center Program. This legislation would also increase funding for community health centers, the NHSC, and medical schools where more than 30% of their graduates go into primary care.[32] As Leighton Ku and Sara Rosenbaum point out, the Congressional Budget Office's evaluation of the Workforce Act for the first time recognizes the value of primary care training investments.[33]

Compared with overall health care expenditures by the federal government (which approach $2 trillion), and the billions spent on direct and indirect graduate medical education, the Teaching Health Center Program for training primary care clinicians has a much lower price tag: $120 million. Training doctors in small hospitals and rural areas, and at federally qualified health centers, is inexpensive compared with other governmental interventions in our health care system. HRSA has recently published a Health Workforce Strategic Plan, with plenty of good ideas.[34] But this one seems simple—spend more federal money to train a larger number of primary care doctors in medical groups, health centers, and hospitals in underserved communities. For a relatively small amount of money, primary care's infrastructure could readily be repaired. The federal government also may have to consider paying primary care residents more than other residents, to attract a sufficient number of medical students to these positions.

The situation for APPs, including nurse practitioners (NPs) and physician assistants (PAs), is strikingly different. For example, HRSA counted approximately 80,000 NPs in primary care in 2020 and sees that number increasing to nearly 190,000 by 2035, which far outstrips their demand estimates of just under 90,000 NPs.[35] As noted in chapter 2, many registered nurses with bachelor's degree training are turning away from hospital work, getting advanced training and degrees as nurse practitioners, and moving into primary care facilities that need clinicians to care for their patients.

This rapid growth is producing unprecedented shifts in who patients see. Lower-income, rural-based, and disabled patients are more likely to see an APP. A recent study noted that in 2013, 14% of patient evaluation and management visits were done by NPs and PAs.[36] That proportion rose to 25.6% in 2019. For hypertension, 20.4% of visits were done by NPs, and for respiratory disorders, over 40%. Again, the quality appears to be very good. A 2020 study suggested that NPs render care equivalent to that provided by physicians.[37] The American Association of Nurse Practitioners reported that its 385,000 licensed NPs conducted more than 1 billion visits annually, and this profession is expected to grow by 46% by 2031.[38]

Another recent report evaluated nurse practitioner graduates going into primary care and compared them with physicians in primary care residencies.[39] From 2013 to 2023, the number of new primary care NPs increased from slightly more than 11,000 per year to over 27,000, while the figure for physicians went from 3,800 to 5,300. Of the latter, 40% were MDs from American schools, 31% were DOs, and 29% were international medical graduates. Most ambulatory patient practices are now pairing doctors and nurse practitioners, with the growth in NPs far outstripping physician recruits. I saw and heard about this in every care setting I visited. While the workforce future could be ameliorated by developing new residency programs for physician graduates from allopathic, osteopathic, and international schools, perhaps a better approach lies with APPs. The pipeline of nurse practitioners is gushing, creating a new approach in primary care.

A good example of the changing workforce was Reliant Medical Group's primary care practice in Leominster, Massachusetts. Visiting on a brittle day in January, I was impressed from the outset with this practice. Reliant is an offshoot of the older Fallon Clinic, founded by Dr. Michael Fallon and his son, Dr. John Fallon. They, like a number of other physician entrepreneurs around the country in the early and mid-twentieth century, wanted to follow the model of the Mayo brothers with a combination clinic and hospital. In 1977, the Fallons added a health plan, offering health maintenance organization (HMO) products, and their clinic emphasized managed care. In 2011, Fallon Clinic was restructured and the medical group became independent, renamed Reliant. In 2018, it was bought by Optum, a subsidiary of UnitedHealth Group, whose primary asset is the health insurer UnitedHealthcare. Reliant's primary care clinicians now wear white coats emblazoned with the name Optum.

The sleek clinic in Leominster was only five years old. The parking lot was full, and the waiting areas were humming with people. The design layout featured the modern workspace motif of a single open room with cubicles and tables, and Reliant's doctors, nurse practitioners, nurses, and medical assistants were constantly interacting. There was some rumor-sharing discussion among the practice's clinicians that these new buildings from the mid-2010s (Reliant has a number of sites in central Massachusetts) had ended up costing far more than predicted, ruining the medical group's finances and necessitating its sale to Optum. But the clinicians were not looking back.

The first person I spoke with was Dr. John Schneeweiss, a straight-talking man who is the medical director for the Leominster site.[40] He had a mask on, so I was never sure about his expression, but I suspected that some of the things he asserted so confidently were accompanied by a wry smile. He got started quickly in our discussion, recounting problems and solutions with impressive celerity.

Schneeweiss is a local. He went to University of Massachusetts for medical school, trained at the family medicine program in Fitchburg, Massachusetts, then started and stayed on at the Fallon Clinic. All along, he was committed to managed care. From his viewpoint, primary care suffers when it is on a fee-for-service platform, which is why he ended up at Fallon.

But the clinic's practice is changing. The dominant fact is that the Fallon Clinic cannot recruit doctors. Schneeweiss believed that in 10 years, their family practice group would consist of 90% nurse practitioners and physician assistants, with 10% doctors. In his eyes, this shortage is a policy failure, with the culprit being the American Medical Association's Relative Value Scale Update Committee, which determines payments for care rendered by doctors, and whose composition is 85% specialists. (I will spend more time on RUC in the next section.) To him, it was not fair that a gastroenterologist doing a procedure that takes 18 minutes gets 9 RVUs, while a longer primary care evaluation of a sick 82-year-old gets 1.8 RVUs. This kind of commentary from Schneeweiss continued to ramp up at quite a pace.

His strategy for recruiting at Reliant was succinctly put: "We suck less." In reality, though, he was proud of the medical group's commitment to value-based managed care. The practice today is still predominantly paid through capitation, a legacy of the Fallon Clinic days. There have always been some fee-for-service contracts, but the clinical team manages to ignore the differences in incentives—they stay in a single canoe. From Schneeweiss's viewpoint, capitated payment is so much better for their patients and the medical team that he could not understand why employers have not endorsed and insisted on it.

Reliant's Leominster family practice is very busy. They have three primary care pods, each with four to six clinicians. They care for more than 22,000 patients in their primary care panels and also have full specialty services in the building (another legacy of the multispecialty Fallon Clinic). Reliant's compensation structure is straightforward, with 40% of clinicians' salaries based on their panel sizes (2,000 patients for MDs, 1,000 for NPs), 40% on RVUs, 10% on patient satisfaction, and 10% on quality-of-care measures.

Their practice is assertively team based, usually with a formal pairing of a doctor and a nurse practitioner. The rest of the team includes two nurses, two medical secretaries (who greet patients), and two medical assistants. Their workspace is laid out in an admirably collegial fashion, with a large central office where everyone mingles. The clinicians do not appear to hide (as is the case in some centers that share this design). The visit rooms are equipped for electronic signal reception, with a tie-in to Epic's EMR system. The setup is impressive.

But even with all this farsighted design and a team-based approach, the clinic still has trouble with recruiting. Schneeweiss revealed that Reliant had been able to attract some doctors away from the nearby UMass Memorial Medical Center in Worcester. But according to his estimate, three of the clinic's doctors retire for each new hire. Initial salaries are greater than $200,000, and the clinic can offer a starting bonus of $50,000 to $75,000. The combination of Reliant's nursing support, the integration of population health management through Epic's EMR system, and appropriate financial incentives should be draws, but the physician pipeline is just not there.[41]

Today, Schneeweiss heads the Leominster family medicine practice, which occupies 30% of his time. He spends a reasonable amount of his administrative duties advising his nurse practitioner colleagues. He will retire as a clinician in 2024, at age 63, and plans to provide continuing education for the NPs, as they are the real future of primary care in his mind. He believed, as do many doctors and nurse practitioners, that when NPs graduate, they are not ready to take on a patient panel: "If you do not spend time training them, they flounder and leave." As he pointed out, a medical resident has 8,000 hours of postgraduate training, while a graduating nurse practitioner has 700 hours. So Reliant developed a formal teaching program for their NPs, which has led to much better retention.[42]

This is another area where the federal government could intervene. Support for development of nurse practitioners could involve financial support for the schools so they can attract more faculty. But more importantly, funding for residency programs for nurse practitioners after graduation would enhance the ability of clinics like Reliant to undertake formal training, fine-tuning what was learned in school.

Kelli Locke, Athena Crowley, and Lauren Katz are all NPs at the Reliant Medical Group's Leominster site.[43] Katz oversees the nurse practitioner program at Leominster. She and the others are proud that NPs are now assuming leadership posts at Reliant. Locke has been with Reliant for 7 years; Crowley, 15 months; and Katz, 10 years. They envision a future in which nearly all clinicians will be nurse practitioners. The Reliant clinic is now moving toward a ratio of two NPs for each MD. All three women agree that NPs are going to have to be trained on the job, starting with *precepting* (support by a mentor). Eventually, most NPs become self-sufficient, making careful use of an *e-consult approach* (electronic consultations between health care clinicians).

The biggest complaint from clinicians of all stripes is MyChart, the patient interface on Epic's EMR system. An average nurse practitioner faces 24 messages a day, which absorbs hours of their time. The work expectation for NPs is 12–18 patient visits per day from a panel size (when they are ready) of 1,000 patients. Their starting pay at Reliant is $115,000 to $140,000 (with no panel), increasing to $150,000 to $200,000 as the size their panel grows. The pipeline for NPs is not nearly as constrained as that for physicians, and Reliant is still able to recruit them, even though the UMass Memorial Health's system pays more.

According to these nurse practitioners, their jobs at Reliant are doable. Reliant is now using artificial intelligence–driven scribes, which helps. Notes are written when a clinician finishes with a patient visit, with a tablet having recorded and analyzed the discussion. Epic creates a lot of work for them, but they can see that the system is getting smarter, as well as better at gathering information from a variety of sources. All three Reliant NPs agreed that people in their field must have a passion for family medicine but should also be prepared for some long days. One bit of good advice they have for new clinicians is to keep a notebook of all the thank-you notes received, and to look at them at the end of a long day.

Even though the Leominster clinic is housed in a big, busy building, it is not accepting new patients. The three NPs I spoke with said its clinicians would be "flooded" if they opened up their patient panels. They also reiterated the need to manage care—capitated patients get a lot more non-visit-based care. MyChart helps with that. Overall, these NPs trusted their leaders, wanted to manage care for their patients, and were proud of their increased responsibility: "We are doing right by patients, and the practice is doing right by us."

The issue of not being able to recruit new doctors is simply accepted as a fact of life, like cold New England Januaries. This is especially remarkable given that the above conversations took place in eastern Massachusetts, which shares with New Haven, Connecticut, the distinction of having the greatest density of training physician slots in the world. Clearly, not enough of that training is in primary care.

In the future, perhaps primary care practices will not need physicians, or at least not many physicians. It may be that NPs or PAs, probably trained in postgraduate programs and aided increasingly by AI-based advice from EMR systems like Epic, will do an even better job than the current physician workforce. But no one—academics, policymakers, or the many clinicians I met during my interviews—sees that as optimal. Their primary care practices would be better if they had more physicians. So, how do we get more primary care doctors? The answer is to train them, and the federal government controls that.

Advocating for Change: The Federal Government's Mission to Promote Value-Based Care through Organizational Restructuring

Given the federal government's dominance of the American health care system—not just from a payment point of view, but also its regulatory breadth—it is the foremost voice in US health policy. Since at least the beginning of the Obama administration, and little interrupted by the Trump interregnum, that voice has been shouting about the need for value-based care and population health management. Much like the Medicare Modernization Act of 2003, enacted during George W. Bush's presidency, the Affordable Care Act, passed in 2010 under the Obama administration, was built on the concepts of managed care and prospective payments.

But the influence of the federal government was not restricted to specific legislative provisions and reimbursement policies. The federal government, since 2011, is empowered to promote change by creating demonstration projects in which hospitals, doctors, and health insurers could participate—projects designed to shift the nation from fee-for-service to value-based care. In essence, the federal government has pursued a path of education and influence to effectuate reform.

To be specific, the Affordable Care Act created a new function at the Centers for Medicare and Medicaid Services (CMS), called the Center for Medicare and Medicaid Innovation (CMMI), that could develop pilot programs without legislative action. Led since its inception by some of the most creative health care minds in the Obama, Trump, and Biden administrations, CMMI has inaugurated a wide range of programs to change the nature of health care in areas as diverse as oncology, orthopedics, and nephrology (kidney) care.

There have been criticisms of the CMMI programs. For example, the Congressional Budget Office estimated that the federal government spent $7.9 billion on CMMI programs to achieve $2.6 billion in savings—not a good return on investment.[44] But I would argue that the changes in the health care system wrought by CMMI are profound, although difficult to quantify. Essentially, they have led to a new set of presumptions: fee-for-service health care can be replaced by value-based health care.

A good deal of CMMI's programs have been designed to promote primary care delivery of value-based interventions. Using Medicare's compensation system and enlisting other health care payers as collaborators, CMMI built a series of innovative projects beginning with its Comprehensive Primary Care (CPC) program. The original CPC program provided bonuses for meeting population health management goals and specific supplements for care management functions. The program produced mixed results on quality-of-care measures and on the utilization of specialists, hospitals, and emergency departments. There were also concerns about the sustainability of the changes necessary to develop a primary care team within a practice.[45]

So CMMI backed up and tried again, with its Comprehensive Primary Care Plus (CPC+) program. CPC+ was a multiple-payer model. CMMI realized that leaving a practice with one foot in a fee-for-service system and the other in a capitated model was too difficult for clinicians. This duality meant that clinicians could not get the full commitment to managed care that was necessary to improve the quality of the health care they offered and lower its costs. CPC+ had care management fees, but it also attempted to push primary care practices toward much more meaningful capitation. CMMI also tried to provide quicker data feedback, as well as outreach services intended to help counsel these practices on care management techniques.

Nonetheless, primary care practices and participating health insurers were hesitant to move toward a higher percentage of payments that were based on capitation. Most opted to limit capitation to 10% of their total revenues. The CPC+ results on the quality of care and health care costs, like those of CPC, were somewhat mixed. In its near-final analysis, CMMI concluded that when taking into account all the expenditures associated with data development and outreach, CPC+ was largely a break-even proposition.[46] A 2022 peer-reviewed analysis of two large Michigan private payers' participation in CPC+ suggested little improvement in either costs or quality.[47] A comprehensive analysis published in December 2023 showed that CPC+ reduced inpatient expenditures and overall utilization, but total expenditures rose over five years.[48]

Economists want to see the data. And the data on CMMI's interventions in primary care are not overly compelling. But my talks with experts in primary care health services brought a slightly different perspective. Asaf Bitton, the director of the Ariadne Labs at Harvard Medical School, noted that the federal government's analysis loaded all the expenditures for training and data analytics onto the cost side of the ledger. Without these costs, the savings through the CPC+ program were substantial. Bruce Landon, a professor on the faculty at Harvard Medical School, has been involved in nearly every major evaluation of large programs intended to promote value-based care. He pointed out that there were real successes with CPC+ among certain primary care practices, and that there is a learning curve in developing the kind of team management that is necessary to make their health care efforts more efficient—doing so takes time. The conclusions from NASEM's 2021 report, *Implementing High-Quality Primary Care*, on efforts to change primary care practice are worth quoting at length.[49]

- Though participating practices valued the care delivery innovations, they often struggled to find the time or resources necessary to fully implement desired changes, even with multi-payer models.

- Busy primary care clinicians need education about what they are required to implement and why. They also require simplified and harmonized reporting requirements across payers to reduce administrative burden on practices.
- Practices need some flexibility from payers to adapt payment models to their circumstances.
- Involving an extended care team other than those in primary care can enhance model impact.
- The redesign of care can take time to yield impact.

In summer 2023, the CMS announced a new initiative, the Making Care Primary (MCP) model.[50] It was to feature a 10-year time frame and involve multiple payers. The MCP program would provide primary care clinicians with payments in advance, as well as tools and various supports to improve care. There would be an emphasis on care management for chronic diseases, integration with specialists, and ties to community services. The federal government was thus continuing to design models for primary care clinicians to manage population health outcomes. This persistence was admirable, and necessary, as Professor John Ayanian has pointed out. Reflecting on the CPC+ results, he noted simply: "CMS will have a steep challenge to achieve its ambitious goal of accountable care for all traditional Medicare beneficiaries by 2030."[51] The new Trump administration canceled the MCP in March 2025.

Persistence is the hallmark of the CMS's primary effort to inject value-based care into other segments of the US health care system, the Medicare Shared Savings Program (MSSP). MSSP was established by legislation and is not a formal CMMI project. CMS's promotion of accountable care organizations grew out of earlier efforts to try to inject managed care into the operation of integrated delivery systems and medical groups. In 2005, the CMS started its first program to bring some financial risk back onto a Medicare fee-for-service chassis: Medicare's Physician Group Practice (PGP) demonstration project.[52] This project, which involved only 10 medical centers, topped fee-for-service payments with bonuses for improved performances on quality-of-care and utilization measures.

The Affordable Care Act built on the PGP initiative by endorsing the ACO concept. The term *accountable care organization*, or ACO for short, was coined by Dr. Elliott Fischer at Dartmouth Medical School and doggedly promoted by the remarkably energetic Dr. Mark McClellan. The ACO concept was holistic: all physicians and health care institutions should share accountability for the costs and outcomes of the care they provided. It was a natural progression for integrated delivery systems to become ACOs, although physicians' groups were also welcome. CMS believed that the fee-for-service foundation of ACOs should be incrementally replaced over time by value-based payments, moving away from bonus payments for outcomes into up- and downside financial risk for participating organizations.

The Affordable Care Act required development of the Medicare Shared Savings Program, subsequently launched in 2012 by CMS. ACOs were able to retain shared savings so long as quality measures were met. Over time, there were more than 1,000 participating ACOs with over 11 million traditional Medicare beneficiaries assigned to clinicians in the accountable care organizations. That number has plateaued, but a new program, ACO REACH (Realizing Equity, Access, and Community Health) has rapidly grown, encompassing over 2 million beneficiaries.[53] CMMI has documented the improved quality of care and lower costs in the population participating in the MSSP, but much more of that has occurred in the affiliated physicians' groups, rather than in the integrated delivery systems.[54] And many skeptics will point out that the savings from the MSSP have been, at best, a tiny portion of Medicare's overall budget.

Nonetheless, the MSSP has established the ACO concept in American health care. Many state Medicaid agencies have begun to experiment with ACO contracts. Perhaps more importantly, value-based care, delivered through ACOs, has begun to percolate into the realm of commercial health insurers, and then into executive suites at medical centers. Speaking as someone who worked in commercial insurance for 15 years, almost none of the senior insurance executives can describe the current evaluations of the MSSP, but they—and, to some extent, employers, who are their clients—expect that accountable care contracting must be part of their health care portfolios. There is also a strong presumption that ACO-style contracting will continue to grow. In many ways, ACO leaders like Fisher and McClellan, and their disciples at the CMS, have done their job. They have begun to create a presumption that value-based care is the wave of the future.

One more point is worth making. As we will see, many primary care groups track a series of quality measures upon which they base some bonus reimbursement for clinicians. As well, the groups often face requirements from the federal and state governments, as well as private insurers, to do well on specific measures, leading to bonuses and penalties from the payers depending on performance. Needless to say, this tends to produce a welter of measures, and high costs with compliance. Parsimony and alignment are needed. CMS has recognized this and has recently outlined a small set of foundational measures. These have been greeted warmly by many,[55] but some primary care experts have raised questions.[56] The movement to a single, small, universal set of measures will hopefully gain momentum.

Meanwhile, the consensus is that more effort to spread accountable care is warranted. The Congressional Budget Office in 2024 argued that greater savings from ACOs was possible. The CBO cited three moves toward that goal: increase provider incentives to participate in ACOs, increase provider incentives to reduce spending, and increase beneficiary awareness and engagement.[57] Accountable care seems to transcend party affiliation, so that even a Republican administration seems likely to continue this momentum.

Interestingly, the Medicare Advantage program, and the opportunities it creates for at-risk primary care groups, rarely makes it into discussions about the federal government's support for value-based care. Democrats face a progressive wing of the party that assertively advocates for a single-payer program and abhors Medicare Advantage, which is seen as privatization of Medicare. So there is little to be gained for a Democrat administration to characterize the Medicare Advantage program as a facilitator of value-based care, especially since there is so much concern about gaming of the system today. Republicans stand by Medicare Advantage, preferring private to public systems. Their commitment to small government can, in Medicare Advantage, permit efforts to promote value-based care. But they are generally loathe to give the government credit for innovation. Thus Medicare Advantage can be a key driver of primary care–based population health, no matter who has control of CMS, but that fact is little discussed by politicians. Time will tell where Trump 2.0 comes out.

Value-Based Care in Action: SSM Health

Not every physician's practice or integrated delivery system is preparing to take capitation from insurers and reduce financial waste. But many have increasing doubts about a fee-for-service format and are considering how to participate in value-based care, even while much of their revenue is still based on fee-for-service payments. Leaders in big health care systems, now exposed for over a decade to the federal government's rhetoric about accountable care, seem convinced. They are moving their increasingly large base of employed physicians slowly, albeit unevenly, toward accountability for population health management.

I saw an apt example of this in Missouri. SSM Health is a major St. Louis hospital system that employs many physicians, including primary care doctors. I talked to various clinicians there, and with the primary care management team (headed by Dr. Kalyam Katakam), but to no one in the executive suite. It is worth presenting these clinicians' frontline views in some detail, drawing a picture of value-based health care in a system that wants to move toward accountable care.

SSM Health was originally part of the string of Sisters of Charity hospitals in the Midwest, including St. Louis, Oklahoma, southern Illinois, and Wisconsin. The Wisconsin group recently merged with the Dean Clinic, and some management views and skills are percolating through the system from exposure to Dean Clinic's health management portfolio. The St. Louis part of the system has five major hospitals, and it competes with the large BJC HealthCare and Mercy systems. In addition to its suburban hospitals, SSM has recently bought the inner-city St. Louis University Hospital, signaling its intent to compete directly with BJC, which has long been the dominant academic medical center in eastern Missouri and southern Illinois.

SSM Health has been pursuing an integrated doctor/hospital strategy for over a decade, buying primary care physicians' practices and starting others de novo. The SSM system in St. Louis in late 2023 has more than 550 physicians, over 200 of whom are primary care clinicians, including both physicians and APPs (NPs and PAs). SSM now also employs the over-800-member St. Louis University medical group, almost all of whom are specialists, hospitalists, or pediatricians.

I discussed SSM's strategies with Dr. Jason VanGundy. He is the chairman of the primary care group, working largely a physician-liaison role.[58] By his own account, he is in practice 95% of the time, with 5% devoted to administrative tasks. VanGundy is a likable, soft-spoken, and reasonable family medicine physician. He grew up outside of Des Moines, Iowa, went to Cornell College in eastern Iowa, attended medical school at the University of Iowa, and then trained in Iowa's Quad Cities. He loved his training, as he had the opportunity to participate in the full range of a family medicine physician's services.

In 2001, VanGundy joined a fellow trainee in a primary care practice located in Wentzville, Missouri, which at one time was quite rural but now is on the western edge of the St. Louis metropolitan area. In 2003, he joined the SSM Health practice in Lake St. Louis, the next town over from Wentzville. SSM had built a new hospital there, replacing an older facility. They were adding primary care practices around the new hospital to feed it—a well-honed strategy. To this point, the SSM story neatly conforms to the pattern of hospital network expansion that has now dominated for 30 years, which is decidedly built around fee-for-service.

The physician consolidation story is a well-recognized trend. VanGundy believes that the practices of most of the primary care physicians in eastern Missouri are being bought by hospitals. In many cases, the conversion to EMRs has instigated this move. Hospitals, which all compete to recruit the same clinicians, believe there is a shortage of primary care clinicians. The typical starting pay for a PCP is around $210,000, which includes benefits. The SSM Health practices use Epic, as do the hospitals. This, too, is part of the consolidation story—using the same EMR system for hospitals and ambulatory care facilities. The clinicians no longer engage in any direct hospital care, but a single EMR system allows them to follow their hospitalized patients and integrate their care with the hospitalists.

The primary care practice at SSM's Lake St. Louis facility has a fee-for-service feel. While VanGundy would not describe it as such, patient care appeared to be a grind. Their clinicians average 20 patients a day, but the range is from 16 to 30. Most doctors work 4.5 days per week. All of this could fit into the standard story of fee-for-service primary care in the United States.

But SSM Health is consciously introducing the precepts of population health management. Its system had long relied on robust RVU production, but about five years ago, SSM introduced a new compensation plan, with 10% of the salaries based on population health measures. At the same time, SSM became an accountable care organization and enrolled in the MSSP program. They received additional payments, through gainsharing, for the first three years of the experiment.

These value-based bonus payments are determined through specific clinical metrics, which are focused on chronic diseases like hypertension and diabetes. SSM Health also considers panel size. VanGundy's panel consists of more than 3,000 patients, while practitioners at Essa Health, the only purely managed-care primary care practice in St. Louis, have a panel size of 1,800. At this point, SSM's administrators are not narrowing their clinicians' panel sizes, and there is little cost-of-care information transmitted to their physicians. But that could change.

In early 2022, the SSM system carefully switched over to a 75:25 split in reimbursements, boosting the portion based on population health measures. VanGundy noted that "physicians get pretty squirrely when you start changing reimbursement." In the past, their 10% reimbursement portion for value-based care came to them as a reconciliation, after the fiscal year had closed. Now they will get their 25% value-based portion in real time, relying on cost estimates. According to VanGundy, physicians like that approach much better, as they have more trust in this form of reimbursement. I sensed that VanGundy is good at his administrative job. His explanations were so honest and crisp, and his manner so steeped in positive intent, that even skeptical clinicians must trust him.

SSM Health still relies on quality-of-care metrics in calculating the 25% of its clinicians' compensation that is value based. To some extent, these metrics are dictated by their local health insurers, and they vary according to individual contracts. Clinicians are also strongly encouraged to have their Medicare patients make annual wellness visits. In addition, they are trained in and evaluated somewhat on coding. Both wellness visits and coding initiatives were introduced as new Medicare Advantage contracts were signed. SSM's next step will be to stratify the physician panels according to their clinical risk in order to make an apples-to-apples comparison, although this has not yet been completed.

Some—perhaps most—of these changes were prompted by the incorporation of financial risk parameters into payer contracts. But SSM Health seems to be advancing this theme by taking on more financial risk from local health insurers, impelled by a sense that the future of health care is in value-based care. Most of their commercial health insurance contracts, and the Medicare Advantage ones, now contain some value-based financial risk. Physicians get trained on all the value-based contracts, and new doctors participate in an onboarding session to understand expectations. Group meetings to review data are held either quarterly or monthly. There are also continuing training programs on value-based care.

SSM's primary care practice arrangements do not exactly exemplify an organization that is at the forefront of managing care. Each doctor has a medical assistant as well as a receptionist. VanGundy's four-physician practice has three nurse practitioners. NPs in Missouri cannot see patients on their own, so they are not assigned a panel of patients. NPs can provide complex care, but they need direct supervision. Some doctors in the SSM Health system have a number of NPs working with them, so they can handle many more patient visits. Physicians working with nurse practitioners do well on their quality measures, according to VanGundy.

Other population health management resources reside outside the practice, at the central SSM Health facility. This care management organization, which consists of case managers, social workers, and pharmacists, is networked through their EMR system. SSM does use a team-based approach here, with weekly huddles. The care managers follow patients through their hospital stays, identify at-risk individuals, and communicate with the clinicians. SSM's central care management function has focused a good deal on their Medicare Advantage patients, generally on high-risk individuals. Care managers and doctors identify care gaps using Epic's care-gap guidance, which is part of their EMR population health management suite.

Nonetheless, the daily primary care practice in Lake St. Louis resembles the typical fee-for-service approach I saw at University of Alabama at Birmingham Medicine. VanGundy generally saw 20 patients a day. Working efficiently, he gets most of his tasks done during the work day, only leaving about three to four charts per evening to finish up. He did not use a medical scribe—less than 20% of SSM's clinicians do. He noted that Epic's MyChart personal health record and patient portal has increased their workload, especially since COVID. Staff does help with these patient-generated inquiries, but they still take time. In the evening, in addition to finishing his charting, he must deal with the MyChart queries. VanGundy himself sees all his patients—as do the majority of SSM Health doctors. He performs some primary care procedures, such as biopsies, joint injections, and cryotherapy, but no longer applies casts to broken bones. Like most family medicine physicians, he lamented the loss of a broader range of health care services delivered in the office.

VanGundy is realistic, yet unassuming, combining quiet confidence and self-deprecation. It took a bit of time for me to discover that for years his peers elected him as their primary care leader, but that choice immediately made sense. As chairman of the primary care group, he acts as the liaison between SSM's doctors and its administrative staff. The previous year, SSM Health ended such elections, and he is now appointed by the administration. The doctors understand that they are working for SSM, and Drs. Katakam's and VanGundy's are the faces they see. All of this is very much in line with an evolving organization and its bureaucracy.

I asked VanGundy about the changes in both SSM's primary care practice and the organization itself. He immediately ticked off a series of points.

1. Their doctors are good at doing RVU-based work, but "change will come when we convince them that the insurers are serious about value-based work."
2. Approximately half of SSM's physicians work with nurse practitioners. Based on their previous fee-for-service experiences, some physicians remain concerned they will not get credit for their RVUs if work is passed to other team members.
3. SSM's absorption of St. Louis University Hospital should bring gains in terms of doing value-based care with specialists, as the specialists are uninvolved at this point.
4. More pilot programs for concentrated care management are needed, such as a practice concentrating on older patients, led by a geriatrics specialist, that they have been talking about.
5. SSM needs to train more primary care clinicians, perhaps by shifting St. Louis University Hospital's teaching program in that direction. As VanGundy asserted, "It is dumbfounding that we can see the lack of primary care so clearly, and the government cannot do anything about that."
6. SSM must focus more on the social determinants of health. They recently undertook a program to increase their rate of noninvasive testing for colon cancer, after finding Medicaid patients were more likely to miss their screening. Follow-up after interventions has shown substantial improvement.

Asked how he was doing, VanGundy replied with a wry smile that while "COVID was weird," he "is not burned out yet!"

SSM Health also has a rural health mission. A branch of the religious order that started St. Mary's Hospital in St. Louis (the original SSM hospital) also founded hospitals in two other Illinois cities, each with a population of about 45,000. St Mary's Hospital in Centralia and Good Samaritan Hospital in Mount Vernon are now part of SSM. These two hospitals are aging, but they are still financially viable. SSM operates a series of rural clinics in the surrounding area. There are still some independent doctors left in southern Illinois (although fewer every year), and SSM is working to recruit the remaining ones. SSM Health appears to perceive a threat from Deaconess (a large health care system in Evansville, Indiana), which is moving into southern Illinois. I presume that SSM wants to head that off by sweeping up the last of the region's independent primary care doctors.

What I found during my travels from 2022 through 2024 is that rural health care is fundamentally thin. There are not enough clinicians, and those who are on-site are overworked. In addition, the notion of value-based care has a difficult time penetrating the rural scene. All of them are simply too busy keeping their heads above water within the fee-for-service status quo. Thus I was interested to see how SSM Health was faring in the value-based journey in its Illinois practices.

Driving out to the flat landscape of southern Illinois in early fall 2022, I saw miles of corn and soybeans ready to be harvested by huge combines, interspersed with clusters of forested areas and small towns. One of these is Nashville, with about 3,000 residents. Its downtown is little changed over the past 100 years, as any development has taken place on the periphery, out near the interstate. The SSM clinic where I spent a morning is housed in a neat, brown brick building located on the road to the interstate, out past the railroad tracks and grain elevators.

All the Illinois clinics in the area surrounding Mount Vernon (including the one in Nashville) are overseen by Candy Guern, a small woman who was largely hidden behind a light blue mask, which periodically slipped below her nose. While SSM seemed to be open to the removal of masks (following recent Centers for Disease Control advice), she "likes to follow the rules."[59]

Like her colleagues in Lake St. Louis, Guern is dealing with SSM Health's new expansion into value-based care, with 25% of the clinicians' compensation now based on population health measures. She said that this has made a big impact, as the clinics have been more aggressive about outreach, especially with regard to filling gaps in care. In her opinion, their patients are getting much better, more proactive therapy. The new focus on annual wellness visits adds to her sense of taking care of health problems before they become too serious. But her clinicians are somewhat agitated about the change, with "everyone harping on it." In terms of value-based care measurements, their key performance indicators (KPIs) look pretty good, Guern remarked, as she pulled up a series of spreadsheets on her computer.

The team in the Nashville, Illinois, clinic consists of one nurse practitioner and one physician assistant. Nicole Vetter is the practice's NP. She was trained in a three-year program at Maryville College in St. Louis and had years of floor experience as an RN before that. She supervised the occupational health unit for SSM Health in southern Illinois, but now they needed her as a primary care nurse practitioner.[60]

Vetter's work is fulfilling but exhausting. She sees 14–16 patients a day and never finishes her charting within normal work hours, often putting in 12-hour days. She likes Epic's EMRs but would prefer to have a medical scribe, which is not possible right now. Vetter had physicians she could consult, but she only called them about once a month. She was much more likely to use *UpToDate*, an online medical textbook, and work through questions by herself. Asked for an example, Vetter recalled a patient she diagnosed with Marfan's syndrome (a genetically inherited disorder that affects connective tissues) using this method— an impressive result. She was now trying to line up cardiology and rheumatology support for the patient.

SSM Health's new value-based approach has added complexity to and extra work for the Nashville clinic. Vetter has some support from a medical assistant and another nurse who worked in the practice. This team helped her with follow-up telephone calls and the like. Vetter also relied on Epic's EMRs to identify gaps in care. While the focus on population health management created more work for her and her team, she admired SSM's commitment to primary care and the values the company evinces. Perhaps unsurprisingly, she did not have much information on the economics of the Nashville practice, its health insurance arrangements, or SSM's strategy regarding financial risk.

Vetter was clearly immersed in her patients' care, making sure to follow up on every problem. She discussed this in a wan fashion, giving the impression that her job was a bit overwhelming. In particular, Vetter seemed to have difficulty identifying the boundaries between what she *can* and what she *must* do. This is best illustrated by her patients with complex health issues, as she found that specialists will see a patient and then drop the follow-up back on her, offering little real help. For example, while clearing a patient for surgery, Vetter diagnosed atrial fibrillation (an irregular and often rapid heartbeat). Vetter sent that person to a cardiologist, who initiated a regime of rate control and anticoagulation medications but provided no plan or parameters for further monitoring. My impression of Vetter was of a committed clinician, but one facing a lot of patient morbidity—sometimes an overwhelming amount. It seemed a bit doubtful that she and her team had time to undertake the forward-looking aspects of population health management.

Just the opposite impression came through talking with Dr. Michael Kirk, who oversaw an SSM Health practice in Columbia, Illinois.[61] He is hale, confident in his work, and exuberant. He grew up in central Kansas, went to Kansas University Medical School, and trained in family medicine at the Medical College of Georgia. From there, he went to a practice in far northwestern Kansas to pay off his medical school debt through Kansas's tuition credit program. He worked with four other family medicine doctors and a general surgeon, and they "did everything," he recalled, with joy in his voice. But his wife wanted to get out of rural Kansas, since they had both grown up there.

What happened next is a representative history of entrepreneurial primary care in the late twentieth and early twenty-first century. Kirk joined a friend from residency who had a practice in Waterloo, Illinois, which today is almost a suburb of St. Louis. That practice, which included three family physicians, a cardiologist, and a general surgeon, lasted from 1995 to 2007, but it came apart when malpractice insurance premiums in St. Clair County, Illinois, rocketed from $40,000 a year to

$200,000. In 2007, Kirk and his original partner moved to a practice with four other family medicine physicians and four midlevel clinicians. They cared for about 16,000 people in Waterloo's population of 36,000.

Kirk, a savvy medical businessman, noted that Waterloo was a great place in which to have a medical practice, with its residents having a median income of $90,000. The practice's patient population was well insured, with only 3.4% on Medicaid and 0.3% uninsured. The new practice did well, eventually adding ancillary testing such as magnetic resonance imaging (MRI), computed tomography (CT) scanning, and nuclear imaging. About a year after they initiated this testing, however, the American College of Radiology ruled that except for cardiologists, urologists, and radiologists, referring physicians could not own these assets. So that revenue stream was lost.

In 2010, they faced competition from a new group just to the north, in Columbia, Illinois. Kirk and his partners had to open a second practice in Columbia and outcompete these newcomers, and they were successful. By 2010, their practice also had two operating/procedure rooms, and they were performing about 400 endoscopies and colonoscopies per year.

But their overhead was rising, from 45% to 78% of the revenues over the course of the 2010s. Their volume of patient visits and procedures was increasing, but their take-home pay was not following suit. The clinicians were doing more but earning the same amount. At that point the practice had 34 employees and 8 physicians. But they had no leverage with the insurers, so they had to accept the set rates for the community—about the same as those for Medicare. As a result, they hired an acquisitions/merger consulting firm and put themselves up for sale, hoping to find a hospital partner that would boost their leverage with insurers.

BJC HealthCare, one of the giant systems in St. Louis, was not interested, and SSM Health was not yet buying practices in their area. They sold their practice to for-profit Community Health Systems (CHS), which also bought the hospital in Red Bud, just south of Waterloo. Kirk and his partners were paid for both the practice itself and its real estate—a very good deal. But CHS wanted the practice to use the Red Bud hospital, which was designated as a Medicare critical access hospital (a federally funded program for small hospitals in rural areas, serving residents that would otherwise be a long distance from emergency care) and was reimbursed for its health care expenditures on a cost-plus basis. That was good for CHS, but Kirk and his group did not want to use Red Bud exclusively.

Eventually, CHS's stock price crashed, and in 2016 they sold out to Quorum, which now owned both Kirk and his partners' practice and the Red Bud Hospital. The family medicine practice was compensated according to their patient volume, and they were becoming a fee-for-service mill. Nor was Quorum's revenue cycle system particularly effective. From Kirk's point of view, this situation was not sustainable.

In 2019, Kirk took the practice's seven other doctors out for a meal at the local Twisted Tree restaurant and suggested that they resign. Six of the eight agreed. Litigation ensued, as Quorum sought to enforce a noncompetition clause in their contract with the family medicine group. Eventually, five of the six were allowed to open a new practice, which contracted with SSM Health and set up in Columbia, but Kirk was exiled from practicing in the Red Bud/Waterloo/Columbia area for a year. Instead, he went to an SSM family medicine practice in St. Peter's (over 50 miles away!) for a year, taking about 1,500 of his patients with him.

The remaining Quorum primary care practice has faded, and the SSM practice is going great. Kirk himself, back now in Columbia, had 3,000 patients in his panel again. He sees up to 20 patients a day, and afterward he spends a few hours charting. He loves Epic's EMRs and has no interest in a scribe, since his workload is not overwhelming. Kirk also oversees all the business aspects of the practice. His practice, exemplifying primary care's traditional feeder role, uses SSM Health's St. Clare Hospital in Fenton, Missouri, about 15 miles away. In 2021, the practice had 2,700 admissions there. Kirk would also like to bring SSM specialists into his practice, but SSM's central administration is not ready to do that yet.

Kirk has a huge amount of energy and lots of ideas about organizational excellence. He made his team read Dale Carnegie's *How to Win Friends and Influence People*. When recruiting people for the primary care practice, he hunts for individuals who "show appreciation and do not complain or condemn." He also commanded an amazing number of facts, all delivered smoothly and efficiently in an offhand manner. On medical economics, he said that 40% of what a family medicine physician does is deal with medications. So, he uses the Canadian website DrugMarkDirect, where his patients can get lower-cost medications. (He showed me that website and compared its prices to the posted list prices on America's GoodRx.)

Over lunch with Kirk at the excellent Thai Garden restaurant in Columbia, Kirk raised some insightful issues about population health management. For example, he was not a big fan of annual wellness visits, since he felt like he already knew his patients' health issues, and more than 2,000 of them had his cell phone number. But annual wellness visits are important for Medicare Advantage contracting. Kirk thought a value-based approach was being pushed by the insurers, which boils down to having him (1) increase the number of annual wellness visits, (2) expand care management by SSM Health's central nurses, (3) add a series of population-based KPIs (which he endorsed), (4) place an emphasis on panel size, and (5) carefully code hierarchical condition categories (HCCs), which are diagnosis codes assigned by the treating clinician. Kirk closely follows their practice's progress on these measures. He also watches their net operating income, to keep costs under control.

Kirk believed that SSM Health will continue to try to grow its primary care base, and that they will move toward capitation. He admires Laura Kaiser, SSM's chief executive officer, and believed she had been importing expertise from Intermountain Healthcare, where she previously worked. He did note that SSM is putting together its own Medicare Advantage program, called WellFirst. If this strategy is going to be successful, however, Kirk said that primary care training must change. It must be a team approach, with nurse practitioners and physicians working together from the start of their training (a common theme everywhere I went).

After this colorful and bracing morning and lunch with Michael Kirk, I went to SSM Health's regional headquarters, housed in a rather aseptic and stunningly empty office building in the western St. Louis suburbs. There I met Jayceen Ensrude, vice president of operations, and Dr. Kalyan Katakam, who oversees the St. Louis clinicians: 370 physicians and 200 APPs, with 220 clinicians among them providing primary care. Their mantra is growth and value-based care. SSM's progress on value-based care was slower than these two might have expected, but they were continuing to move it along. Both were certain that fee-for-service reimbursements would continue to dwindle. Ensrude oversaw the central care management team of 111 full-time-equivalent employees (FTEs).[62] The team, which supports all of SSM Health's medical practices, includes behavioral health specialists and care coordinators. They help resolve gaps in care and encourage medication reconciliation.

SSM Health began its journey in value-based care with the development of accountable care organizations, but that focus is now being de-emphasized. SSM still participates in the Medicare Shared Savings program's ACO enhanced track, but their focus has turned toward value-based contracts with UnitedHealthcare, Blue Cross Blue Shield of Missouri, Aetna, and Cigna. All of these contracts vary in their parameters, and some (in Medicare Advantage) include partial financial risk. SSM also has its own insurance plan, WellFirst, which initially was an Affordable Care Act exchange plan and now enrolls about 500 people in Medicare Advantage.

Dr. Katakam outlined SSM's value-based strategic plan.[63]

- Get more contracts that have a population health management approach. Currently, these constitute less than 40% of SSM's contracts.
- Their insurers are bereft of care management resources, so these contracts must allow development of such resources by SSM.
- Their medical staff, particularly specialists, must get on board, as they need to be the ones to deliver this form of health care.
- SSM cannot stay with one foot in each canoe, so everything must move from fee-for-service reimbursements to capitated payments, including the acceptance of financial risk.

My general impression is of a big ship turning slowly and carefully. Something about the federal government's promotion of ACOs has turned big insurers and large integrated delivery systems toward a future of value-based care, and that is changing the nature of the primary care they are providing. Much of this progress is attributable to constant pressure from CMMI and the CMS's Medicare Shared Savings Program. CMS's policies seems much more impactful when talking to people in the field than they do when being analyzed by economists.

Importantly, CMMI and CMS show few signs of relenting in their push for value-based care, which probably helps keep SSM and other health care organizations moving along the evolutionary path toward managed care. For example, the Making Care Primary model was to be integrated with ACO concepts, shifting toward prospective population-based payment.[64] It was supposed to be a 10-year program, however, and there would have been time for even small practices to learn. The Biden-era US Department of Health and Human Services had recently outlined its commitment to primary care, emphasizing the Innovation Center work and promising new payment programs.[65] Trump 2.0 may or may not be like-minded. Places like SSM are watching, listening, and engaged in change.

Paying More and Paying Right

The CMS/CMMI strategy is to slowly change the basis for reimbursing health care providers, moving to a primary care–centric system that pays for the quality and efficiency of health care. Over time, this should lead to a greater opportunity for capitation reimbursements and a more gratifying primary care practice that is not based on the treadmill of relative value units. There is some evidence that this strategy is succeeding.

There is also a direct alternative for increasing primary care salaries, in turn attracting more students to this specialty. If primary care clinicians were paid better on the existing fee-for-service system, they could then develop the teams they need. This was one of the main recommendations from NASEM's experts in 2021, who reexamined the history of physician pay along the same lines that many other studies have over the past 20 years.[66] While often told, this health policy story is so bizarre—and so central to our country's current primary care demise—that it is worth reviewing briefly.[67]

In a fee-for-service system, doctors submit bills for the medical care they provide and then are paid by the patient's insurer, either the federal government or a commercial health insurer. Fee-for-service payments have dominated American medicine for years. They were highly favored by the American Medical Association (AMA) throughout the twentieth century and were more than acceptable to most hospitals. Since insurers do not want to customize payments for each physician and procedure, they need to use codes for these services and the various fees for them.

Fortunately, and perhaps not unexpectedly, the AMA concluded that code standardization would be crucial to ensure control over payments to physicians. Thus the AMA published its first current procedural terminology (CPT) code book, aiming to help automate payments, in 1970. This initial code manual focused on surgical services, but the second edition was much more comprehensive, relying on a five-digit classification program. By the mid-1970s, a system of annual code updates was in place. Everything a clinician might do, from a physical examination to removal of a brain tumor, had its own code. It may seem odd that a professional organization like the AMA published and owned the CPT manuals, but the AMA has long been intimately involved in payment policies for physicians, with the express purpose of improving physician pay.

By the 1980s, the federal government began to seek ways to rein in medical care costs, and it needed some payment standardizations. Since the existing CPT codes were available to provide infrastructure for this standardization, the Health Care Financing Administration (HCFA) did not have to construct a new payment program from scratch. It based its Healthcare Common Procedure Coding System (HCPCS) on the CPT program and required all physicians who were billing Medicare to use CPT codes. The same requirement was applied to Medicaid in 1986. Going forward, CPT/HCPCS codes would be the common currency for payments to physicians from federal sources. Commercial health insurers soon fell in line.

The CPT code book is a living document. It has been updated continuously by an editorial panel, its 17 members approved by the AMA Board of Trustees. The CPT provided the *language* for billing but did not determine the *amount* to be paid. Commercial health insurers set these amounts through negotiation, but Medicare generally accepted "usual and customary charges." As Medicare costs and its number of beneficiaries grew in the 1980s, its leaders realized that they must begin to set health care fees, and not simply pay what was charged. In order to set these fees, the government needed some basis for assigning values to physicians' time and efforts.

William Hsiao, an economist at the Harvard School of Public Health, had received several grants from the federal government and other sources to develop a methodology for rational reimbursements for physicians' services. He called his methodology the resource-based relative value scale (RBRVS), designed to identify the value associated with specific physician interventions. The basis for this scale was part economics, part psychology. It used three factors: the physician's work, expenses for their practice, and professional liability costs. Each CPT would then be assigned a relative value unit, which, using a geographic modifier and then a monetary conversion, produced a rate of payment.[68]

This research was incorporated into the Omnibus Budget Reconciliation Act of 1989, and Medicare switched over to the new payment schedule on January 1, 1992. The RBRVS determined the appropriate payment for a huge range of services. As a result, Medicare had control over the health care fee schedule. Perhaps more importantly, the RBRVS system allowed the federal government to set up a zero-sum game: raising fees in one area would lead to decreases in others.

Significantly, the assignment of RVUs to the CPT code, as well as the reevaluation of specific codes, was left in the hands of the AMA's Relative Value Scale Update Committee (RUC). To be precise, the Centers for Medicaid and Medicare Services (HCFA in the past) delegated this responsibility to the RUC. Many saw regulatory capture in this arrangement. The AMA fox appeared to be guarding the CMS henhouse—while the CMS determined the payment for RVUs, the determination of RVUs remained in organized medicine's hands. The RUC has been accused of favoring surgery and interventional subspecialties to the detriment of primary care,[69] with codes for the latter being systematically undervalued.[70] (Recall the complaints of Dr. Schneeweiss at Reliant, presented earlier in this chapter. Many primary care clinicians voice the same complaints.)

These accusations continue to this day, with NASEM's 2021 report having focused heavily on the need to change the valuation process.[71] From the perspective of leaders in primary care, RUC is hopelessly specialist oriented, and over time its valuation of fees has moved dollars from primary care to specialty care. There have been several efforts to improve primary care clinicians' pay, with the most significant being changes in Medicare and Medicaid as part of the Affordable Care Act. But the bottom line (discussed in chapter 1) is that the proportion of health care dollars devoted to primary care continues to drop.

NASEM's 2021 report, which was admirably assertive on policy issues, suggests that the CMS could simply develop its own advisory committee.[72] The RUC could stay in place and formulate its views, and these would be considered by the CMS. But the CMS would have its own group, perhaps modeled on Medicare's Payment Advisory Committee, whose members would make the final decisions. In this fashion, at least Medicare and Medicaid could begin to funnel more money into primary care, and commercial health insurers might follow suit. But all of this would still operate in a fee-for-service economy.

An assertion of authority over the RUC by CMS seems unlikely to occur in the current political environment. The zero-sum-game aspect of physicians' reimbursements means that specialists continue to guard their turf, and they have strong advocates in Congress. In addition, the economic engines for hospitals are the procedures and operations performed by specialists, so the financial interests of hospitals and specialists are aligned. While many large hospital systems support a primary care base to some degree, their stake in a battle over a restricted pie of physicians' pay would lie with specialists. Hospitals also have strong supporters in Congress. So, while the NASEM report's authors were forthright—as have been long-term scholars in the area of physicians' payment, like Dr. Robert Berenson[73]—wholesale change in who calls the shots in payments to physicians under a fee-for-service system seems unlikely.

The difficulty in changing the proportions of physician payments was well illustrated in late 2023. Back in 2020, the CMS had created a new code for billing patients' complex office visits: G2211. It was intended to apply to primary care situations. CMS predicted that it would be used frequently, thus draining away money from Medicare reimbursement payments for codes used by specialists. The specialists' lobbyists got Congress to delay its implementation until 2024.[74]

In 2023, the CMS proposed further cuts to Medicare's 2024 physician fee schedule. If this version of G2211 had come into effect, some of the savings gained from the cuts could have been allocated for primary care reimbursements under the new code. The surgical specialties voiced their opposition to the overall cuts in reimbursement and also to G2211, maintaining that use of the new code "would penalize surgeons and negatively affect surgical patients."[75] The American College of Physicians and the American Association of Family Physicians have fired back, pointing out that the CMS has already trimmed away a good deal from Medicare reimbursement payments for primary care physicians' services, and inaugurating a G2211 code "will allow physicians to be more fairly compensated for complex primary care visits,"[76] but they face long odds of effectuating substantial fee shifts to primary care. In late 2023, CMS finalized the roll out of G2211, adding an extra $16 per evaluation/management visit.

Much of the foregoing refers to federal health care payments, and that is appropriate, as the federal government leads the way in terms of reforming the US health care system. Private health insurers—whose business (outside of involvement in government-sponsored programs) is primarily serving the employer-sponsored health insurance sector—have generally followed along with Medicare, paying most small physician groups at Medicare rates for the CPT codes they submit. While employers did play a role in advocating for the primary care medical home concept (the IBM physicians who oversaw their company's health benefits were especially important), they, too, have passively allowed primary care to decline.

Higher payments for evaluation and management (E&M) CPT codes would lead to higher incomes for primary care clinicians, perhaps making the field more attractive to medical students. It is not clear, however, that this would provide what America's health care system needs to foster: the kind of team-based community care necessary to create a focus on the prevention of illness and the promotion of health. Nor it is clear, at this point, how effective a boost in E&M codes would be in terms of improving clinicians' working conditions. A recent study showed that the payment increases that have occurred in E&M codes over the past decade have had little impact on physicians' overall incomes.[77]

Paying primary care physicians and nurses more for the care they provide by substantially amending the RUC process would perhaps solve some of the problems associated with primary care's workforce shortages. But it also shores up fee-for-service, when what is really needed is a value-based program. Pouring a bit more money into E&M codes is treating a symptom, rather than the illness, that fee-for-service will never support team-based, outcomes-focused care. Recognizing this shortcoming, key advocates for primary care have begun to incorporate calls for more experimentation with prospective payment along with their suggestions for greater overall spending on primary care.[78]

Robert Berenson has for years been the leading voice on reform of physician payment. He does not advocate for a hard turn to alternative payment as a replacement for fee-for-service, noting the political improbability of that scenario. Echoing Professor Robinson's thesis on the drawbacks of both fee-for-service and capitation, he argues constructively for mixed-compensation models that can be accommodated in the current fee schedule.[79] Laurence McMahon and Zirui Song have recently made the same argument, but emphasizing the foundational work necessary to improve the operation of the physician payment system.[80] These are persuasive arguments, but for purposes of primary care, I believe the focus should continue to be on what can be done with alternative payments that emphasize value-based care.

Getting Population Health Done on Federal Revenues

It is reasonable to ask, Can a newly transformed, value-based primary care practice lead to better care and happier clinicians? And can it be done solely on what the federal government pays? The answer is yes. Many experts in primary care suggested that I visit the Southcentral Foundation (SCF) in Anchorage, Alaska, to see the best example. The Southcentral Foundation, which is mostly supported by the federal government, provides ambulatory health care for Alaska Natives in Anchorage, Matanuska-Susitna Borough, and 55 rural villages in the Anchorage Service Unit.

The organizational structure for the care of Alaska Native people is unique. The Indian Self-Determination and Education Assistance Act of 1975 finally gave Alaskan Native and American Indian people in the United States the option to take control over their health care.[81] Most of the tribes outside of Alaska chose to stay with the Indian Health Service (IHS), whereas 26 tribes and tribal organizations in Alaska signed the Alaska Tribal Health Compact, which authorizes the management of services beyond what was previously provided by the Indian Health Services. According to SCF, assuming full funding and control over their programs has allowed local decision-making, setting of priorities, and collaboration.

The Alaska Tribal Health System now comprises 17 autonomous regional tribal health providers (SCF is one of the largest) serving specific geographical areas across the state. They also operate a tertiary hospital complex in Anchorage, which is co-operated by the Alaska Native Tribal Health Consortium (ANTHC) and SCF through a Joint Operating Board. On the same campus, SCF has numerous buildings for ambulatory care, including primary care, behavioral health, and pediatrics.

The SCF cares for 70,000 patients, 74% of whom are residents in the Anchorage area. SCF has approximately 2,700 employees and an annual budget of more than $500 million. The physical setting is jaw dropping: a campus of beautiful buildings, many seemingly new, surrounded by what appeared to be primeval forest, with huge, serrated mountains in the distance. I stayed at a hotel nearby that was mostly used by visitors referred from rural Alaska, and I was warned to watch out for moose on my morning walk to the clinics. Most people working at SCF remembered the old tuberculosis sanitarium in downtown Anchorage, which until 1997 was the health care center for Alaska Native people. They recalled it as being worn out, smelly, overcrowded, and incredibly depressing. Their pride in what they have brought to life is palpable—and universal.

The structure they have built for their care team is equally impressive. SCF received the Malcolm Baldridge National Quality Award in 2011 and 2017, becoming the second health care organization in history to win the award twice. SCF hosts visits from doctors, nurses, and administrators from the Lower 48, and abroad, on such a frequent basis that they offer the services of a Learning Institute. The institute makes available consultants for training and technical assistance on primary care team development, as well as other practices. There is nothing like the Southcentral Foundation anywhere else in the United States.

Until recently, Doug Eby was the head of the Medical Services Division at SCF. He is currently their executive vice president for specialty services. He outlined their program for me before I arrived in Anchorage (he was on vacation when I actually visited). For the past 20 years, every family they care for has been empaneled with a primary care team and offered same-day access as needed. The core team includes a primary care provider, a nurse case manager, a case management support person, and a certified medical assistant. The team is also supported by shared behavioral health specialists, pharmacists, care managers, dieticians, and certified nurse midwives, providing consultation to the team and the families served. They are all colocated in a common space where the entire team works. Private physicians' offices do not exist. This unique health care arrangement generates superb patient satisfaction.

The clinic's structure and its staff lived up to their advance billing. Melissa Merrick, who is now the executive vice president for primary care, related to me that all members of the extended team are available to patients, and all consultations are frequent and thorough.[82] The clinics are designed with plenty of space. There is a decentralized check-in area, so waiting patients do not feel like they are clustered on top of one another, and a seamless flow of people can move to exam rooms and what they call demedicalized talking rooms. Expectations are set for the clinical team to see 12–14 patients per day, but the average is closer to 10–12.

Two of SCF's management techniques are especially striking. First, they frequently survey their patients and will make changes based on the trends they find. Their ubiquitous theme is "continuous improvement." Second, they employ more than 50 people in their workforce development section who identify people from their base of customer-owners (the name they use for their patients, reflecting the fact of Alaska Native people ownership of SCF) who might become employees. They invest heavily in recruitment, onboarding, and training, and they provide career paths and mentoring for employees to move up through the organization.

An employee training on Core Concepts is offered monthly and required of all new employees. Lessons from Core Concepts reinforce (1) the importance of relationships and personal connection with the health care system, (2) healthy communication, and (3) how to share and respond to a personal story in a ways that promote healing. It works, as their teams appear to be cohesive and are constantly involved in discussions about customer-owners as the latter flow through the main work area, which is surrounded by exam rooms. Several people told me that they sometimes must reach out to get the clinic's doctors involved with the team, revamping physicians' usual mentality of "just calling the shots." But to my eyes, the teams appeared to have little in the way of hierarchy.

Compensation is generous, with Southcentral's primary care physicians earning more than $200,000 per year. There is no bonus for relative value units, as the foundation has eschewed a fee-for-service mentality. Clinicians can earn more, however, with extra compensation based on a series of wide-ranging quality-of-care measures, including clinical aspects (blood pressure and blood glucose monitoring) and service metrics (empanelment and same-day availability for patients to see their own physician).

The team resources are somewhat fluid. For example, like elsewhere in the country, the clinicians have encountered an increasing burden of behavioral health problems, seeing more people experiencing homelessness and substance use disorders in their customer-owner population. Every team member carefully accounts for social determinants of health (SDOH) and helps develop care plans accordingly. SCF's leadership points to this as an area of increasing emphasis.

Quality-of-care measures are continuously calculated. Southcentral's information technology (IT) team downloads data from their Cerner EMR system into an electronic data warehouse on a daily basis. David Fenn, manager of data services, and Steve Tierney, senior medical director of quality improvement, proudly told me that they can produce more than 1,500 separate reports.[83] But the clinicians are not overwhelmed by data. Rather, SCF is deliberate about what is emphasized in the quality-of-care realm. The data and evaluation team annually develops a strategic plan involving new care measurements and intervention approaches, which is then modified after discussions with their data stewards and is finally approved by senior management. Another aim is to exploit differences between the teams by understanding the variations and developing new interventions.

What are these quality-of-care measures? Jerry Markus, an operations director who evinced easy competence, took me through the key ones.[84] One important metric is for clinicians to be available at 8:00 a.m., and 25% to 40% of the appointment slots in most pods open at that time, encouraging availability. The goal for a match rate between primary care clinicians and their empaneled patients is 60% to 65%, which they do attain. The aim is to meet 75% of Healthcare Effectiveness Data and Information Set (HEDIS) goals—50 benchmarks from various domains of care set by the National Committee for Quality Assurance—and that is generally exceeded. Overall, these are extraordinary numbers. The IT team also compiles data on other quality measures, such as well-child visits, emergency department utilization, and hospital utilization.

Pride in what they do seems to motivate most of the SCF employees. I spoke with two Alaska Native nurses, Chelsea Ryan and Rona Johnston, about their outreach work at local homeless shelters.[85] The range of problems they must address, particularly in a political environment that is not always hospitable to social activism, was daunting. But they clearly drew energy from their shared mission, talking proudly about how they themselves had come from small villages, attained their professional goals, and wanted to give back to their communities.

April Kyle, the foundation's relatively new CEO who has worked at SCF for more than 20 years, made many of the same points in a more polished but nonetheless sincere fashion.[86] She characterized the SCF mandate as uprooting the health care hierarchy and putting the customer-owner in charge: "The community drives and intentionally pushes against hierarchy.... Families know best what families need." She provided a recent example of utilizing test strips that can detect the presence of fentanyl to decrease overdoses. Doctors and experts agree that the technology behind the test strips is a good one, and recommended that they should be distributed to local people so they could test drugs before using them,[87] preventing fatal overdoses.

Kyle had asked how the test strips would be distributed in the community, and what villages would do with them. The answer was for SCF to seek input on this issue from the communities themselves. On large maps in her office, Kyle proudly pointed to the villages she had visited in the SCF service area over the past year, stressing the importance of constant community dialogue.

Southcentral's primary care clinicians have bought into this community-based approach. Dr. Verlyn Corbett is a senior medical director.[88] His mother is a member of the Walker River Paiute Tribe, and he grew up in Nevada. He went to the University of Southern California for medical school and trained at the University of New Mexico. From there, he started in practice at the Mescalero Apache

Reservation, staying for eight years. It was, from his point of view, a "typical" Indian Health Service outpost—dingy and worn. He was working 60–80 hours a week, seeing an overwhelming number of patients each day. Few of them were empaneled, and most needed urgent care. (He admitted, with a wry smile, "I was 30 years old and figured I *should* be working 80 hours a week.") There was always more work than he could handle, with no continuity of care and no way to appropriately manage chronic diseases. He ran into Doug Eby at a meeting and liked what he heard about SCF. Corbett soon moved to Anchorage, and the contrast with his practice in New Mexico could not have been greater.

Corbett's enthusiasm for Southcentral's mode of operation, and its contrast with the situation for Mescalero Apaches, prompted the question, How can SCF afford this care model when other IHS facilities could not? His answer was thoughtful but not detailed. He noted that in New Mexico, his clinic had so many patients with kidney failure from diabetes that the IHS built a dialysis center (which is now defunct). Meanwhile, among the 78 people with advanced diabetes at Southcentral, only one has needed dialysis. Managing care leads to lower costs.

Dr. David Lessens, one of SCF's medical directors and a primary care provider, made the same point.[89] His team had inherited a patient with cerebral palsy who had been in the hospital for 140 days in 2018. The team worked out all the social issues surrounding this patient's care, and now that person has been at home for two years, with no hospitalizations. Lessens concluded that the result of this care was great financial savings, a great health outcome for the patient.

April Kyle reiterated this insight. She believed that SCF has such great continuity with its base of customers-owners that patients can count on follow-ups. This means that the primary care clinicians do not need to "throw the kitchen sink at the patient." They can take their time and use a stepwise, probably less costly, diagnostic approach, all the while taking into account the social context for an illness. She commented that most of the clinicians Southcentral hires are initially not ready for such an approach—they must be mentored, but they learn.

Doug Eby said that Southcentral's clinicians refer 65% fewer patients to specialists than the average number for other physicians.[90]

The SCF shows what is possible. It makes a great case for the proposition that a primary care team, with deep roots in its community, can provide excellent, population-based health care. Moreover, most of the revenue comes from federal funds, including the Indian Health Service Compact, federal grants, and Medicare and Medicaid patient service revenues.

The Indian Health Service Compact is essentially an annual block grant from the federal government. This accounts for about half of the SCF budget for its population. Under a block grant, as SCF sees it, there is no incentive to increase the volume of services, as this would just increase costs without more revenues. This understanding drives the care model. SCF and ANTHC (the partner in joint management of the hospital) operate cohesively, sharing a similar approach to population health management. While Medicare and some private insurance revenues are paid on fee-for-service, as is the Medicaid contribution, SCF stays in the single canoe of value-based care. As a result, SCF can support a robust health care model without taking on exclusively prospective risk contracts (although the IHS Compact block grant is essentially prospective).

This raises the question about how much revenue must be prospective before a practice can convert solely to a population-based program. Sanjay Basu and colleagues have suggested the threshold is 63%.[91] With the culture developed at place like SCF, it appears that number can come down. This is a critical point, as many practices persist with fee-for-service mentality even as their proportion of value-based contracts grow. SCF demonstrates that need not be the case.

I was reminded of this a few weeks after my trip to Alaska, during a visit to an urban community health center. The medical director was excited about a new approach he was advocating: adding one more medical assistant, who would be present during each visit, to help with documentation and provide advice for the patient. This new person would act as a case manager and health coach. The health center had none of the fine woodwork and thoughtful architecture of Southcentral.

Instead, its cement block walls were covered with thick greenish paint. It had a standard waiting room, with tired furniture and few magazines, and a small number of exam rooms surrounded it. It did, however, have a lot of risk contracts.

Thus I was disappointed when, talking to other clinicians and some of its medical assistants, it was clear that "the administration" had decided against the medical director's proposed innovation. The center could not afford an extra body, so its health care "team" was to remain as it was—a single clinician, working at times with a medical assistant. The mandate from above was that everyone had to see more patients.

To get to anticipatory, value-based primary care requires shifting from a conventional fee-for-service system. The Southcentral Foundation shows how can be done while still relying on federal governmental payments that are not entirely prospective risk.

Summarizing the Federal Government's Support for Value-Based Primary Care

What emerges from this review of the federal government's role in the promotion of primary care is that a quick cure—paying more for primary care services through a fee-for-service system—is an unlikely solution. Our nation's medical/political deck is stacked against primary care, blocked by the formidable joint interests of hospitals and specialists, since hospitals need well-paid specialists to continue to profit from fee-for-service health care. In the zero-sum game of Medicare's physician reimbursements, paying primary care clinicians and facilities more means that others are paid less. That is not likely to happen, at least to the extent necessary to convert fee-for-service primary care from a hamster wheel to a community value.

Perhaps more fundamentally, neither a hospital administrator nor a specialty physician necessarily wants to see primary care in the driver's seat, making decisions about value-based health care that eliminate wasteful medical spending, since unnecessary treatments provide a good profit margin for them. As a result, they are unlikely to support a US health care system based on primary care. In today's fee-for-service world, hospitals and specialists have a profit horizon that is broad and deep, as long as a specialist can get a patient into a procedure room or operating room. Given their political power, a direct attack on the current RUC-based reimbursement program seems unlikely to succeed.

What might be more politically feasible is to train more primary care clinicians. There is every indication that the nursing profession is managing this feat with existing federal support, although concerns exist about the pool of professors and instructors needed at nurse practitioner training programs. Over the next two decades, nurse practitioners—and, to some extent, physician assistants—will be the backbone of the primary care workforce.

The supply of primary care physicians will be constrained for years to come, however. Much of this shortage results from the lower compensation primary care doctors receive in comparison with specialists. Some also comes from the perception that primary care's fee-for-service treadmill is especially dreadful. But there is every indication that many medical schools, especially offshore and osteopathic ones, would be able to produce more potential primary care clinicians if there were more training slots available. For around $750 million per year, 5,000 new primary care residents could be trained in appropriate settings, such as community health centers. When combined with loan forgiveness, and/or primary care career bonuses, new slots could make a real difference in the primary care physician shortage.

Even if allopathic medical schools stay on the sidelines, there is every indication that with additional training funding, international and osteopathic medical schools would expand, enrolling more students interested in primary care. The influx of new doctors would improve the primary care field immensely, for a price that, on the federal scale, is essentially a rounding error. One estimate indicates that the federal government's current graduate medical education program is overpaying hospitals to the tune of $1.25 billion per year,[92] so this could be the source of funds for additional primary care training programs. Specialists—and particularly hospitals—might oppose the addition of more primary care training programs, fearing that federal funds for these GME efforts might eventually come out of cuts in governmental support for traditional medical education, but political pressure will probably be less intense with this approach, rather than a direct shift from specialist slots to primary care ones.

One other point about medical training deserves mention. Today, primary care clinicians are almost universally trained in silos. Yet the best clinics are those where everyone functions as a team. Thus initiatives like the one the Veterans Health Administration has pursued—co-training physicians and nurse practitioners—must become the rule.[93] Many community health centers, like OneCommunity Health Center in Oregon (see chapter 2), are informally undertaking postgraduation "residency" programs for nurse practitioners, where the NPs are integrated into a team, but this effort should be accelerated and become standardized.

Perhaps the most important thing the federal government can do, in addition to supporting the expansion of primary care training, is to continue to advocate for value-based care, both in the Medicare Shared Savings Program and the primary care programs sponsored by the Center for Medicare and Medicaid Innovation, such as Making Care Primary. While admittedly not yet decreasing costs,[94] the value-based training these initiatives offer appears to be having a real effect in slowly turning health care's mindset toward value-based care. The realization that value-based care is the only true alternative to the current US health care system is percolating down to commercial health insurers, as well as to negotiators who work on behalf of physicians and integrated delivery systems—and they are responding. While fee-for-service is still king, there is a growing sentiment that it cannot last. Continued efforts by CMS administrators to emphasize the management of care, something that—fortunately—seems to transcend divisive politics, will bear long-term fruit. Once primary care controls capitation dollars, even if only in primary care, this money can be used to build teams and manage care, taking medical waste out of our health care system. Increasingly, CMMI seems to understand that this is a long game, as it is building a foundation for value-based, managed care.[95] The fruits from CMMI's efforts are slowly taking shape; hopefully, the Trump 2.0 administration will continue the effort.

I should note one other intersection of federal authority with primary care practice: labor law. There is increased interest in physician and health worker unionization today, especially in clinics and hospitals where the practitioners are overworked and underpaid.[96] I heard whispers about unionization at many large academic medical centers. The AMA has somewhat tentatively endorsed the right to unionize.[97] A collective bargaining unit in primary care could be a good thing, helping to build the kind of teams I have encountered. I will return to unionization in a later chapter.

CHAPTER FOUR

The States' Role in Primary Care Reform

STATES PLAY A SUBSTANTIAL ROLE in health care policy. Most commercial insurance oversight is state based, including health insurance, although in recent years many employers have moved to self-insurance (acting as their own health insurance company, including covering their losses), enabling them to largely ignore state requirements. This displacement of the states' role in health insurance and health system reform was largely not deliberate. It is the result of the federal government's intent, stated in the 1973 Employee Retirement Income Security Act (ERISA), that employee benefits have some federal protection that preempts state law. It became clear in the 1990s that this ERISA preemption had essentially shielded employers who self-insured from being subject to a state's insurance and health care financing requirements, relocating the fulcrum of health care insurance oversight and reform to the federal government.

That remains the case today, although the segment of employers who still buy commercial health insurance (i.e., are fully insured, as opposed to self-insured)—mostly small companies—is significant. Of greater importance, however, is the states' control over Medicaid, the health insurance plan for many people whose income is at or near what the federal government considers poverty level. Medicaid has received much of the focus in the states' promotion of primary care. Indeed, these state programs centered on Medicaid have become some of the most exciting areas for improving primary care.[1]

The States' Overall Role in Medicaid

Medicaid, the federal/state collaborative health insurance program for low-income people (among other beneficiaries like children and people with disabilities) is the same age as Medicare; both were founded nearly 60 years ago.[2] The operation of these two programs, however, is largely distinct, with Medicaid resembling the governmental welfare programs on which it was based. Under the original Medicaid legislation, states and the federal government were required to co-fund health care for the categorically needy, with a focus on low-income families, especially those with dependent children.[3] But the states could choose the income level at which coverage would begin for these people, which in some states was quite low. Thus there have always been states that covered a broad swath of their citizens under Medicaid, and others that have set narrower criteria, so a smaller proportion of their populations qualified for this program. Massachusetts and Texas are often viewed as the paradigms for generous and skimpy state health care support.

Over time, the federal government has unilaterally increased the number of Medicaid recipients by adding new categories of coverage and changing the requirements for funding levels. Moreover, certain types of services—such as for children, pregnant women, and the disabled—have become mandatory. States could also participate in optional programs. New mandatory requirements put increased pressure on state budgets, slowly but surely pushing Medicaid to the top of the states' funding lists.

Pressure on state budgets is created by the fact that, under Medicaid, federal dollars were matched by state dollars. States generally paid less than half the costs, and the federal government provided the rest. The more optional programs under Medicaid that states took on, the more federal funding they received. Some states (such as Massachusetts) viewed the arrangement as a bargain, while others (such as

Texas) saw it as a burdensome overreach by the federal government. Over time, Medicaid's architecture has boiled down to mandatory and optional categories of beneficiaries, mandatory and optional benefits, and varying levels of federal matching funds.[4]

States can also modify or customize aspects of Medicaid through a waiver process, spelled out in Section 1115 of the Social Security Act.[5] These waivers have allowed both Republican- and Democrat-dominated legislatures in the states to pursue changes in the program. More often it has been Democrats seeking new coverage approaches, while Republicans have tried to reduce coverage, most recently through work requirements for Medicaid beneficiaries.[6] States also originally used the waiver process to experiment with managed care. Traditional Medicaid required that beneficiaries be able to choose their clinicians and other health care providers, so not much managed care percolated into the program in the first 15 years of its existence. But over time, many states sought federal waivers to be able to bring managed care firms into their Medicaid programs, hoping to reap savings.[7] So, while the states were charged with administering their respective Medicaid programs, they were free to use contractors to do much of the health insurance work.

The Balanced Budget Act of 1997 allowed states to use Medicaid-only HMOs (health maintenance organizations that only accepted Medicaid beneficiaries) and reduced the need for a formal waiver from the federal government.[8] As a result, in Medicaid, managed care became more the rule than the exception. In 2020, the Kaiser Family Foundation found that 69% of Medicaid beneficiaries were in a managed care program.[9] Thirty-five states now predominantly use managed care contractors for their Medicaid populations.

Most of the contracts state officials sign with managed care organizations are capitated. The federal government's main role is to ensure that the capitation amounts are appropriate on an actuarial basis. The use of managed care in Medicaid does not necessarily conform to standard politics, as both some Democratic and Republican states are managed care bastions. By 2020, nearly half of all Medicaid dollars ($600 billion) flowed through managed care contracts. But this is not to say that the managed care companies necessarily embrace value-based approaches or primary care capitation. This is only starting to develop. For much of the twentieth and early part of the twenty-first centuries, fee-for-service reimbursements remained the standard means of Medicaid payment for health care providers, buttressed by a good deal of prior authorization. But much of Medicaid is based on capitated payments to administrators who have taken on a financial risk, so an impulse to manage care is embedded in the program.

Medicaid fee-for-service payments are generally paltry—to a fault. As recently as 2019, Medicaid's fee-for-service reimbursements were on average only 72% of what Medicare paid, which in turn was less than half of the amounts doctors received from commercial health insurers.[10] (Payments in managed-care Medicaid are similar.[11]) To give an example, Rhode Island's fee-for-service Medicaid reimbursements are only 37% of what Medicare pays to an average health care provider in that state. This means that many physicians prefer not to care for Medicaid patients. For instance, in 2020, 90% of all physicians were accepting new patients, but only 71% accepted new Medicaid beneficiaries.[12] These bare facts prompt a critical question for health care in the United States. While there are a great many efforts to improve equity in US health care, how can we pretend that we are committed to this concept when clinicians who care for those with low incomes are not paid the same? Improving Medicaid payment is in many ways the fundamental equity step in our health care system.

Health care reform in states usually starts with a federal Medicaid waiver program. This does not mean, however, that other forms of health insurance do not come into play. Often a state, working with the Centers for Medicare and Medicaid Services (CMS) on its waiver, will also try to engage Medicare, and that state's Medicare beneficiaries, in the reform proposal. Moreover, a state may attempt to jawbone commercial health insurers into developing policies like those intended for the federal program, creating all-payer programs where all third parties use the same reimbursement rates. Such programs are rare, and the self-insured contracts portion of the commercial health insurance sector is mostly immune from state oversight because of the federal government's Employee Retirement Income Security Act. Somewhat ironically, the states are far more likely to innovate using state/federal Medicaid plans than they are to use commercial insurance plans in the private sector. But the fully insured population does heed state rules and can be rolled into statewide reform efforts.

The Biden administration proposed new rules for Medicaid's managed care program, not only encouraging it, but also strengthening requirements concerning the actuarial viability of the states' payments.[13] This administration also intended to rein in large state-directed reimbursements, which had been used to supplement paltry capitation payments in some circumstances. Overall, moves by the Biden administration demonstrated the federal government's continued commitment to population health management through the promotion of managed care in Medicaid (twinned with its efforts in Medicare, discussed in chap. 3). This creates a substantial opportunity for innovations by the states interested in value-based care. Difficult to predict, but a Trump administration likely would move in the same direction, although a more radical move might be to use block grants, essentially removing federal oversight on the use of Medicaid funds.

There are two substantial, structural problems with Medicaid-based health care reform, especially if such measures incorporate value-based payments. The first, highlighted by Rajaie Batniji and William Shrank, is that Medicaid beneficiaries shift in and out of the program, with a turnover rate that can approach 25% in a given year.[14] Such a turbulent patient population makes it difficult to engage in chronic care management. This contrasts with Medicare, where there is relative stability in the patient pool. Second, many states contract with multiple managed care organizations. The states must be willing harmonize their health care contracts if they want to undertake overarching care management efforts.

Some states have focused their Medicaid-based health reform efforts on promoting a stronger primary care base for their health care systems. Vermont, Rhode Island, Massachusetts, and Oregon are considered the most active, although they emphasize different approaches to building primary care capacity. A few others, such as Minnesota and

Washington, are also progressive in this regard, but their policies are generally similar to at least one of the other four leaders.

Vermont's Comprehensive Health Care Reforms

Tiny Vermont is a good place to start. It is a blue state, voting Democratic in most presidential and congressional races, and is the home of Senator Bernie Sanders, a liberal firebrand and former socialist. But it has also developed a tendency to elect middle-of-the-road Republican governors. On health care reform, this state has had a history of supporting universal access, and its small size, plus its manageable number of hospitals, has long made it a likely candidate to create a single-payer program. Moreover, Vermonters are generally healthy, doing well on most state-to-state comparisons of public health. Blue Cross Blue Shield of Vermont is the primary health insurer (although Cigna and UnitedHealthcare have made inroads), which brings some simplicity to health care reform plans. But even with all these assets, a single-payer arrangement and universal access have been difficult to achieve.

When Peter Shumlin ran for governor in 2010, he made single payer the centerpiece—first of his campaign and then of his new administration.[15] The bill creating the Green Mountain Health Care program passed Vermont's House and Senate in 2011. But financing the new health care system, while avoiding the federal government's ERISA obstacles, proved to be difficult. Every financial estimate the state made over the period from 2011 to 2014 showed ever higher costs for Vermonters in terms of income taxes and payroll taxes, and Shumlin eventually had to back away. A single-payer system was put on the shelf—and remains there.

Shumlin's single-payer attempt was not Vermont's sole health care reform initiative. Value-based payments and the promotion of primary care have also been on the state's agenda. In 2005, state officials had sought federal Medicaid waivers that would let them expand Vermont's community health–based services, and some type of waiver authority has remained in place to the present time.[16] For years, these waivers have supported the state's Blueprint for Health (known simply as "the Blueprint"), which was aimed at improving overall health care and controlling costs for those with chronic conditions. The focus in 2005 to 2010 was on the development of primary care medical homes for Vermont's primary care practices, and the addition of community health teams to help these practices with care management.

When extra Medicare funding became available in 2010 as a result of Vermont's participation in the CMS's Multi-Payer Advanced Primary Care Practice initiative, the Blueprint expanded from 18 practices to 123 by 2014. The state's three commercial health insurance payers also helped fund this program.[17] Today, the Blueprint still functions throughout the state, helping to support primary care practices in several ways: maintaining their patient-centered medical home (PCMH) status, providing case management services, and treating substance use disorders through a hub-and-spoke mechanism to ensure that medication-assisted therapy is available.[18] The Blueprint has also recently added a women's health initiative to support pregnant women and promote long-acting reversible contraception.

The Green Mountain Care Board (GMCB), which was created to oversee the proposed single-payer program, has survived. It is an independent, five-member board, with each member appointed by the governor for a six-year term. According to GMCB's website, the board's present role is to advance innovation, serve as a transparent source of information on health care in Vermont, and regulate the state's health care system.[19] Many people I talked with in Vermont tended to see the GMCB more prosaically: as a regulator, dealing with health insurance premium rates and certificates of need. Importantly, the board also supports Vermont's All-Payer Accountable Care Organization Model.

The All-Payer Model—a collaboration between Medicare, Medicaid, and commercial health insurers—is a statewide accountable care effort, involving both primary care and the state's hospitals. The All-Payer Model has been envisioned as a replacement for (or a precursor to) another try at a single-payer program. Negotiations with the CMS for a federal waiver to set up the All-Payer Model, which went on for several years, were finalized in 2018. The end result was signed by the governor on behalf of Vermont Health and Human Services (Vermont's Medicaid program), the GMCB, and CMS. At that point, funding for the Blueprint fell under the All-Payer Model.

The main administrative structure for this model is OneCare, a private 501(c)(3) nonprofit organization that has the University of Vermont Medical Center (UVM) as its single member. OneCare had originally been started by UVM and the Dartmouth Hitchcock Medical Center (DHMC) in New Hampshire to promote the development of accountable care organizations (ACOs) in Vermont. (DHHC is no longer a board member but still participates.) OneCare was intended to develop a global budget for hospitals to promote value-based care. All but one hospital in Vermont now participate in OneCare.

Today, OneCare focuses primarily on Medicaid and Medicare beneficiaries.[20] Blue Cross Blue Shield of Vermont did participate, but it has now dropped out. Cigna and UnitedHealthcare were never part of OneCare. The Medicaid dollars from OneCare come straight from the state (through an appropriation from the US Department of Health and Human Services) and are paid to the participating ACOs on a capitation basis. Medicare still adjudicates claims on the basis of fee-for-service payments, but OneCare develops a shadow budget for each ACO, using the All-Inclusive Population-Based Payment mechanism. At the end of the year, OneCare oversees a financial reconciliation, and the hospitals generally share the amount of savings. The goal under the federal waiver for OneCare is to keep Vermont's health care growth rate under 3.5%. Only about 50% of the state's Medicare recipients are part of OneCare, but 85% of its Medicaid beneficiaries are.

Just to make things a bit more complicated, the 2018 federal waiver also called for a primary care program, known as Comprehensive Payment Reform. This involves a blended payment from Medicare, Medicaid, and Blue Cross Blue Shield of Vermont for primary care clinicians, which is based on the number of OneCare's members and its entailed practice financial risk. Fifteen independent primary care practices participate in OneCare, but thus far the state's federally qualified health centers (FQHCs) have stayed out of it. OneCare now also oversees Blueprint payments, which the Blueprint's long-tenured administrators aren't happy about.

Vermont is a small state, and all its key leaders in health care and government know one another. But even given that manageable size, this description of the state's health care reform is an excellent example of how complicated relationships among health care payers, the state and federal governments, and health care providers can be.

How does all this convoluted infrastructure look in practice? It depends on whom you talk to. There is clearly overlap—and some lack of cohesion—in what the Green Mountain Care Board, the OneCare team, and the Blueprint staff do. Moreover, there is some mutual skepticism about each other's overall value. The major thrust of the state's health care reform is not clear. Is it a single-payer program, state-supported primary care, an ACO approach, or a new format involving global budgets? Perhaps most disappointingly, the signals regarding value-based care do not appear to be coming through to clinicians on a consistent basis, at least in the practices I visited.

I went to St. Johnsbury, in the northeastern part of the state, and Bennington, in the far southwestern portion. The Blueprint staff have a cohesive story of support for primary care practices and the treatment of chronic diseases.[21] Physicians' offices have maintained their PCMH status, and the newer substance use disorder and women's health initiatives have been real successes, with their good outcomes demonstrated through careful empirical evaluations. The Blueprint teams have lost some of their community health team staff recently, and there is some angst about being funded through OneCare, which they feel is more oriented toward financial measures and hospitals. These teams work with all of Vermont's primary care practices, which are largely associated with either a hospital or an FQHC. In the two regions I visited, as well as throughout the rest of the state, there are few independent primary care practices left. Almost all of these doctors have retired.

I talked on the phone with Dr. Laura Newell, who oversees the primary care practices for Northeastern Vermont Regional Hospital

(NVRH) in St. Johnsbury.[22] Of the 15 hospitals in Vermont, 8 of them are critical access facilities (having fewer than 25 beds), including NVRH. Newell works closely with the Blueprint staff in her district. She supervises the primary care practices the hospital owns: Kingdom Internal Medicine (adult primary care), a family medicine practice, and a pediatric practice. She also works closely with Northern Counties Health Care, the local FQHC. Generally speaking, Newell's catchment area is the lower half of what is known as the Northeast Kingdom: the wild, sparsely populated northeastern section of Vermont. There are no longer any private primary care practices in her area, as the last one closed several years ago.

Newell readily described the role played by the Blueprint: primary care medical home support, community health workers, women's health, and a hub-and-spoke arrangement for substance use disorder treatments. At NVRH, Blueprint provides funding, but NVRH hires the health care workers, often having to fund part of a position on the hospital dime. Newell had a lot more trouble describing OneCare, although she knew that NVRH has been paid a lump sum for its Medicaid population (which is about 30% of its total patient population) and has done well on this capitation-based payment. This suggests at least a bit of a disconnect between the state's programmatic operations (the Blueprint) and its value-based financial architecture (OneCare).

At NVRH, I was able to meet with Shawn Tester, its chief executive officer, and Michael Rousse, its chief medical officer.[23] Both are experienced health care administrators, familiar with governmental programs and managed care. Tester came up through FQHC programs in New Hampshire. Rousse trained at University of Vermont, completed his residency at the University of Massachusetts Medical Center in Worcester, and eventually became chief of staff at NVRH.

It was an unseasonably warm and gray day in November when I was there, and perhaps that affected their mood (or mine), as optimism was in short supply. Tester was clear when stating, "We have a problem. Health care is too expensive." Moreover, "all the reformers are looking for 20% solutions, and we need some 1% solutions. Vermont's problem is that it wants to be a leader in health care reform, but nothing is really happening. The state is moving the deck chairs around a lot. There is a parade of new themes: single payer, then ACO, now considering global budgets. I really do not care how I get paid." But it is difficult for a small system to adapt. Global budgets now seem to be gaining steam, and Vermont's legislature gave the Green Mountain Care Board $4 million to evaluate this format, according to Tester.

The big problem, both administrators believed, is that in Vermont, there is not a lot of fat in the system. Significant cost savings are not available, as most of the excess utilization aspects have been wrung out, with COVID exacerbating the problem: "We are fighting yesterday's battles. . . . The system has been throttled. . . . Most hospitals have negative [profit] margins. . . . The population is very old and getting older. . . . We are not ready for the tsunami. . . . The ERs are overwhelmed with old people. . . . The big problem going forward is agitated dementia. . . . And now the work force is collapsing." Not a pretty picture. Nonetheless, Vermont's health care system has "done a great job of keeping people healthy." The title of John Knowles's famous book *Doing Better and Feeling Worse* comes to mind.[24]

Tester and Rousse had some doubts about the state's ACO effort, asserting that it is "not health care reform, it is payment reform. It really involves only about 10% of the payment. . . . But it does involve part of Medicare, and all of Medicaid and some commercial [health insurers]." All of this means that NVRH has a partial managed care approach but is still firmly in a fee-for-service system elsewhere. The executives suggested that the somewhat flawed presumption for an ACO is that if the clinicians were given some data, they would adapt their practice. Tester and Rousse noted, however, that emergency department visits had decreased, and NVRH's readmission rate was already low.

In terms of further system-wide reform, though, Tester and Rousse were not convinced that this would occur: "The lever was supposed to be primary care, but can they really ask people to do any more?" Primary care practices wanted more care managers, and NVRH's two administrators hoped that this would reduce the number of hospitalizations for the chronically ill. But new care managers required more funds for salaries, and it seemed doubtful that these additional full-time-equivalent employees would cover their costs in terms of decreased utilization. As the two men remarked, "The accounting is a little tricky." In short, Tester and Rousse seemed to be experienced, sharp, and committed to the care of their patient population and the overall health of hospital. But they seemed unconvinced that Vermont was on an entirely correct path.

Visiting Kingdom Internal Medicine, the main adult medicine clinic affiliated with the hospital, reiterated the gap between theory/policy and practice. The clinic's milieu was neat, with the clinicians' diplomas and certification documents proudly framed in the front hallway. But it was set up like my primary care practice 40 years ago: one big waiting room, with a bunch of exam rooms and clinicians' offices, none of which suggested a lot of team collaboration.

I met with Dr. Irene Krechetoff and Dr. Thomas Myrter, both osteopathic physicians trained in internal medicine.[25] They have each been at Kingdom for about five years. Between the two of them and three nurse practitioners, they empanel 2,545 primary care patients. Neither doctor really had a team, although there were some medical assistants and nurses in the practice. They use the hospital's MEDITECH EMR system, but they were not too pleased with it. It provided some information on gaps in care but was not comprehensive. Kingdom's affiliated specialists, mostly at DHMC in New Hampshire, are not on MEDITECH, so they get EMR information on about 60% of their referrals, and that only after expending a significant effort. A care coordinator, partially funded by the Blueprint, does help with some of this. The coordinator also searches MEDITECH for information, although the doctors were not too sure for what: "HEDIS something, not sure what it stands for."

They see 12–15 patients a day—whoever shows up on the schedule. They are open to adding patients but see someone new perhaps one to two times per week. Myrter works four days a week, and the others, only three days. They are paid a straight salary, with no bonuses for reaching preset productivity measures. Krechetoff and Myrter have heard the terms "value-based care" and "population health management" bandied about but do not actively associate much with these concepts. For instance, they were not certain if they are in an ACO or not. Both noted that there is a continued focus on making sure that codes are appropriately entered. They are also supposed to have their patients make annual wellness visits. But the underlying rationale for all of this was not something they paid much attention to.

Krechetoff and Myrter have access to a clinical pharmacist, who helps patients with their diabetes and psychiatric medications, but the pharmacist is available weekly at best. Both doctors wish they could have more contact with pharmaceutical representatives. The practice also has a behavioral health resource person—someone who is at the clinic for two to three days a week—who can help with some patients. Myrter provided medication-assisted therapy for opioid use disorders, but he did not currently have many of these patients. While there is some discussion in the practice about population health management, there was also a major focus on ensuring that the clinicians see an appropriate volume of patients. According to Krechetoff and Myrter, "the signals get crossed," "the incentives do not align," and there is "a patchwork."

The situation in St. Johnsbury was mirrored in conversations I had with clinicians in the far southeastern part of the state, near Bennington. Dr. Reija Rawle works at a family medicine practice in Pownal, Vermont, while Dr. Kim Fodor's practice is at the Southwestern Vermont Medical Center (SVMC) hospital in Bennington. SVMC operates both clinics. The consistent story at SVMC is that there is too much work, with an insufficient number of clinicians.

Rawle works with two other allopathic physicians, two osteopathic physicians, and one nurse practitioner.[26] The team in Pownal had recently turned over completely, but the clinic was able to replace the doctors who left. Meanwhile, other private doctors in the area are retiring. Recently, one of them abandoned 5,000 patients overnight, but the Pownal practice could not absorb all of them. The clinicians all work long hours and take work home with them. The clinicians deal with over 20 visits a day.

None of the accoutrements of a cutting-edge practice are present. At Pownal, the clinicians are supposed to have a dedicated medical assistant, but these employees don't stick around for long, so new ones must constantly be trained and acculturated. Rawle stated that the clinicians' reimbursement is all driven by relative value units (RVUs), with no tracking for quality-of-care measures. The case managers from the Blueprint do help with social determinants of health (SDOH) issues for some patients, and its hub-and-spoke substance use disorder program does work, but there are no real teams. A nurse assists with injections, vaccinations, and blood draws. Nonetheless, Rawle did not see any future possibility of not being overwhelmed. The fact that the state is supporting primary care does not seem to resonate with her.

In Bennington, Fodor believed the hospital was trying to be supportive.[27] SVMC is moving toward an affiliation with Dartmouth Hitchcock Medical Center in New Hampshire, giving them access to Epic's EMR system. She also noted that SVMC emphasizes managed care for her practice's patient population, with compensation based 60% on panel size and 40% on RVUs. The crush of patients was impressive—and time consuming—requiring two to three hours of work at home each night for her to keep up. She saw even less support from the Blueprint than Rawle did. The case manager for Fodor's practice was overwhelmed, the behavioral health position had constant turnover, and there was little training in the use of buprenorphine, a drug to treat substance use disorders. Fodor had heard of Vermont's OneCare ACO, but she had not seen any signs of its existence. Her views were not entirely encouraging:

- She "feels abused" as a primary care clinician.
- "Not much of what I do really makes a difference."
- "My personal greatest power is listening and compassion."
- "Patients do say 'thank you,' every day."

While Vermont has an impressive health care infrastructure and a commitment to reform, based on my interviews, it is hard to say, at least from these brief visits, that medical care is improving for patients, or that the state's primary care system has improved. The practices I visited were not a scientifically drawn sample. I could have gone to ones that were outliers, or been there on a bad day. Nonetheless, it is hard to conclude that the state's comprehensive reforms are changing the nature of primary care in Vermont, despite the best intentions of its state regulators. Nonetheless, CMS is convinced they are working. An analysis CMS commissioned by the well-regarded NORC at the University of Chicago showed that over the first four years of the program, Medicare spending decreased a remarkable $1,177 per beneficiary per year.[28] If not primary care, then perhaps hospitals are responding.

That impressive performance notwithstanding, OneCare Vermont announced in early November 2024 that it was going to cease operations at the end of 2025. The press release made no mention of what reform approach might ensue.

Rhode Island's Support for Better Primary Care Pay

Rhode Island has been focused in its approach to primary care. As I noted in chapter 2, spending on primary care in the United States does not measure up to that in other wealthy countries. Yet spending in the primary care domain is associated with better outcomes. The direct approach to improve care through greater support for primary care is to force insurers to shift a higher percentage of health care dollars into primary care. The most recent estimates are that private insurers in the United States disburse 8.7% of their total health care dollars on primary care, whereas Medicaid only uses 7.4%, and Medicare, 5.3%.[29] These estimates, taken from the Medical Expenditure Panel Survey, are higher than other estimates of American primary care spending, but they are still quite a bit lower than in most European countries.

In 2008, under the leadership of Christopher Koller, the state's commissioner of insurance, Rhode Island developed affordability standards for commercial health insurers. The key elements of these new standards were to cap the growth in health care spending going to hospitals, encourage new payment methods for clinicians, and increase the percentage of health care dollars directed toward primary care. The first step in this latter goal was to increase primary care's share of total health care dollars by 1% a year for several years. Under updated regulations, the total outlay for health care must be 10.7%, with 9.7% of that going to directly to primary care.[30] Since the insurance commissioner's office approves insurer rates, compliance with Rhode Island's rules on primary care spending and total expenditures is measured on a yearly basis. A widely cited study has suggested that overall health care spending slowed under these new regulations.[31] Most of this slowdown, however, was attributed to inflation caps on, and diagnosis-based payments to, hospitals.

The increase in primary care spending in Rhode Island has not been empirically assessed, and there is reason to believe its impact may be small. First, the required payments apply only to the state's population covered under fully insured commercial contracts. Self-insured companies do not have to adhere to the increased amounts, owing to the federal Employee Retirement Income Security Act's preemption clauses. While 59% of the state's population has commercial health insurance, the requirements only apply to the roughly 55% of that 59% with fully insured health care plans,[32] or one patient in three. The insurance commissioner's office was not empowered to address spending in Medicare and Medicaid, and the Medicaid situation is especially fraught. On average, Medicaid reimbursements for primary care in the United States are about 54% of what Medicare pays, and Rhode Island has a notoriously penurious Medicaid program.

Primary care spending in Rhode Island's fully insured commercial market has increased slowly since 2015, to about 12.5% of total health care dollars, or just over $80 million.[33] In 2008, when the state's new standards were initiated, over $40 million was disbursed in direct payments to clinicians, with little spent on value-based care incentives or on support for primary care medical homes. But the new law's affordability standards had specified that this money had to support team development and could not go into base rates. By 2018, about $35 million went directly toward clinician payment, with an equal amount allocated for incentives and for PCMH development. Moreover, from 2018 to 2021, the fully insured population in the state declined by about 14%.[34]

The data from Rhode Island's rate filings suggest that approved primary care claims came to about $22 per member per month, compared to total health care expenditures of nearly $400 per member per month—in other words, a little more than 5%. This implies that Rhode Island's primary care practices have seen little improvement in their fee-based income under the state's reforms. While Rhode Island's support for primary care is much discussed in health policy circles, on close scrutiny, its impact seems to be small. The state appears recently to have reached much the same conclusion; a 2023 report from the Office of the Health Insurance Commissioner suggests there has been little progress in access.[35]

Rhode Island's reform measures regarding primary care payments were not overly visible at the one practice I visited in the Ocean State. While it might be an outlier, there is reason to believe that it is not. Coastal Medical is the largest primary care group in Rhode island—the product of numerous mergers between primary care practices over the past 20 years. In 2020, Lifespan, the largest hospital group in Rhode Island, bought Coastal Medical, and the primary care practices historically affiliated with Lifespan's hospitals are being merged into Coastal's groups.

I went to Coastal Medical in East Greenwich, one of the wealthier suburbs of Providence. Luis Echeverria Jr. is the manager for this practice, proud of both his clinicians and the Coastal team.[36] In the past, some of Coastal's physicians were partners, but the majority of clinicians were affiliates, contract-based physicians and nurse practitioners. After Coastal Medical was bought out by Lifespan, all of its doctors became employees. Each practice had formerly had its own profit/loss financial status and made all decisions locally, but that is no longer the case. At East Greenwich, one of the larger Coastal practices, the team consisted of three (former) shareholder doctors, one contract physician, three physician assistants, and one nurse practitioner. A central Coastal office handled the revenue cycle for Echeverria's group, but neither he nor anyone else I talked with there was aware of any primary care premium payments being made by commercial health insurers.

Some changes have taken place in the practice over time—scheduling more annual wellness visits and entering additional codes on patients' charts—which are not unexpected occurrences, given the growth of value-based care. But not much teamwork was evident, other than the clinicians being paired with a single medical assistant. Notably, however, Coastal had some central teams focused on population health management. One of the most effective was a diabetes team that managed patients by making substantial use of its pharmacists. A central pharmacy team also took care of all medication refills and reconciliations. It appeared that Coastal was using at least some of its extra primary care money for these purposes.

I also spoke with Dr. Kristen Hubbard, a (former) partner in Coastal's East Greenwich practice, who had been there for seven years.[37] She was calm, sincere, and direct, with thoughtful observations about that group's dynamics. She stated that in 2017–18, finances were failing, at least for Coastal's physician partners. Their primary care practices had been "boats on their own bottom," paying a tax to Coastal's central team and strictly following an RVU-driven production pattern. The partners were doing more but getting paid less, even in their affluent suburb. Coastal had been a Medicare Shared Savings Program ACO and had received some funds from that, but it dropped out of the program in early 2018. The partners' compensation was decreasing even though they were hitting a target of 4,500 RVUs a year, seeing 16–22 patients a day for four days a week. A sale became inevitable, and Lifespan's bid looked better than those from Optum and others.

Hubbard listed a set of recent developments. The Coastal team had begun to consider a set of quality measures to supplement their RVU targets. Some of these measures—those related to effective care for patients with chronic diseases—were tracked by the clinicians, but no reimbursement was tied in with them yet. Coastal had also become more panel oriented—the average size was now somewhere around 1,850 patients—but panel size was not part of their physicians' compensation at this point. The team would also have liked to bring on some behavioral health support, but these professionals were difficult to hire.

The population health management path was starting to become clear at Coastal Medical, although RVUs still appeared to be king in terms of compensation. The state's payments into primary care might be helping, although the clinicians were unaware of them. Coastal has had trouble hiring new doctors and staff, and the East Greenwich practice was now closed to new patients. All at the practice agreed that if they could hire someone, this new doctor's patient panel would be filled in no time, but it was not clear that the additional reimbursements would be sufficient to justify a new position. An article in the *Providence Journal*, which reported a statewide primary care shortage, confirmed the perception.[38] The article noted that a researcher at Brown University had called 15 different practices, and none of them were accepting new patients. (Notably, a few months after I visited, Coastal initiated a long-term plan to support patients and clinicians, including a nurse triage system, a medical assistant and scribe for every clinician, a practice clinical navigator, and a triage service for night and weekend calls.[39])

The problem with access probably should not be a surprise. The Rhode Island state government's control is limited to fully insured commercial health insurers. Furthermore, the state can only force these insurers to pay a limited additional amount for primary care. If Medicaid, Medicare, and self-insured employers continue to pay less, over time the premiums on fully insured health care contracts will begin to bloat, and small businesses will no longer be able to afford coverage for their employees. Furthermore, insofar as those insurance dollars simply go toward fee-for-service reimbursements based on RVUs, there is no movement down the path toward population health management. Thus, while it may be good for a state to require more health care payments to go directly into primary care, nearly all payers must be involved for it to work. And long-term benefits will only accrue if such payments are paired with more effective transformations in primary care practices. Rhode Island is currently navigating this conundrum.

Massachusetts's Innovations in Medicaid

Just to the north, Massachusetts has long focused on access to primary care, as well as on transformations in Medicaid. Massachusetts's efforts are admired by the health policy cognoscenti. One of the state's health care reforms—creating health insurance for those who fell into the gap between Medicaid and individual or employer-sponsored health insurance policies—was emulated by the Obama administration in the Affordable Care Act (ACA), sparking a tremendous national movement toward universal coverage.[40] Massachusetts continued its expansion of Medicaid in concert with the ACA, and today only 3% of this state's population, many of whom are undocumented immigrants, remains uninsured—the lowest rate in the country.

Medicaid officials in both Republican and Democratic administrations in Massachusetts have not been satisfied merely with expansion. They have also assiduously pushed toward value-based care.[41] Going back nearly 30 years, MassHealth (the Medicaid authority in Massachusetts) has had Section 1115 waivers in place, first to add new eligibility criteria, and then to support safety net hospitals in Massachusetts. The Commonwealth has also long employed a set of health insurers to act as managed care organizations (MCOs), taking capitated payments from the state to finance health care for their Medicaid beneficiaries. Some of these—such as Tufts Health Plan and Fallon Health—are divisions of private insurers. Others are subsidiaries of hospitals, like the Boston Medical Center's HealthNet Plan, now known as WellSense. These MCOs have had close ties with health care providers, particularly with the network of federally qualified health centers.

The 2017 waiver was intended to push the state's primary care groups toward value-based care by having them form accountable care organizations. An ACO would be responsible for the costs of its health care services and could gain upside (or suffer downside) financial risk, depending on how well it did against its preset, calculated budget. Massachusetts's ACOs began to prepare for this approach by adding new care team members and developing care management protocols, using state funds that were part of the Section 1115 waiver, known as delivery system reform incentive payments (DSRIPs). MassHealth also funded Community Partners, which are organizations that could help ACOs with beneficiaries needing either long-term care or support, or substantial behavioral health services. Its Flexible Services Program could assist ACOs in finding food or housing benefits for MassHealth members. An independent 2021 analysis suggested that Massachusetts ACOs were generally staying within budget, as well as that their primary care visits had increased, as had beneficiaries' satisfaction with the care they received.[42]

A new waiver for 2022–27 was approved in late 2022. In addition to maintaining the levels of coverage, it has three other main goals: (1) to reaffirm and improve the value-based care provided by ACOs, (2) to improve health equity, and (3) to increase people's use of primary care by linking it up with behavioral health care. The Community Partners program is no longer funded by DSRIP dollars. Instead, ACOs are receiving monies to purchase services from Community Partners, which increases both the ACOs' control over and responsibility for these services, especially for ones related to behavioral health. The new waiver extends the Flexible Services Program in a number of directions, including a longer period of support for postpartum mothers, and nutritional support for an entire household (not just the beneficiary). Behavioral health support is also being expanded, and it will become more community based. Through this waiver, MassHealth programs will be available to those who are incarcerated, enabling smooth transitions upon their release.

The new waiver's biggest changes are in its focus on primary care and health care equity. Having prepped the ACOs during the period from 2017 to 2022, MassHealth will now direct primary care practices to receive capitation payments and no longer rely on fee-for-service reimbursements. To be eligible for MassHealth funds, primary care practices must have firmly established care coordination and behavioral health capabilities, as well as the ability to offer urgent care services and telemedicine support. Some primary care practices can qualify for higher capitation payments if they meet certain tier requirements, including the provision of evening and weekend care, as well as care navigation/management. This push is to be combined with workforce initiatives, where MassHealth will pay for student loan forgiveness for new physicians, nurse practitioners, and behavioral health specialists over a four-year period.

Regarding equity, MassHealth will support ACOs in first gathering health care data and then addressing identified inequities. Data collection will focus on social risk factors, including race, gender, socioeconomic status, and gender identification. Any deficiencies found in the data must be addressed, with efforts to do so leading to incentive payments. Over time, these payments will move to equity targets set by MassHealth.

MassHealth's emphasis on placing more responsibility on primary care practices to address costs—first by playing a central role in ACOs, and now reiterated by basing payments on capitation—underscores the concept that producing value-based care requires managing care.[43] This, in turn, means a primary care practice must pay heightened attention to the attribution of its members and their risk of illness. Capitation means that payment follows an individual patient, so now a primary care group's payments will be based directly on the number of patients they are caring for, not on the quantity of patient visits and related services. *Attribution* simply means that a particular patient (or *member*) is attached to a specific primary care practice. This is essential for comprehensive health care management, since care teams must feel like they "own" their patients, being responsible for both the patients' general health and appropriate treatments when they are sick. MassHealth's administrators, working with the intermediary MCOs and health insurers, has become adept at attribution. Primary care practices must follow this lead, particularly in knowing who their assigned members are.

Regarding risk adjustment, some people are healthy, while others are sick. So there must be a process to identify the risk for disease borne by an individual member and then modulate the payment for that individual. In the federal Medicare system, there is a single approach. But each state has had to develop their own method vis-à-vis Medicaid, so they can pay any health insurance subcontractors they hire the correct amount for their financial load from the patients' health care burden.[44] Many states use the Chronic Illness and Disability Payment System, which was developed specifically for Medicaid's risk adjustments. Massachusetts has its own approach, which considers SDOH. Its model involves standard adjustments based on age and sex, uses a proprietary diagnosis-related modifier called DxCG, incorporates markers for mental health and housing status, and adds a neighborhood stress score.[45]

Attribution and financial risk adjustments determine the amount that ACOs will eventually be paid. And primary care budgets are explicitly based on capitation. So, it behooves a primary care practice to understand who is assigned to them, anticipate their medical needs, keep them healthy, and ensure that their care is both effective and parsimonious. To some extent, it also requires a primary care practice to develop appropriate documentation for the clinical and social factors that go into the risk adjustments for their patient pool, to ensure appropriate payment.

There have been several well-studied efforts to promote primary care capitation. Perhaps the best was in Hawaii. The Hawaii Medical Services Association—that state's Blue Cross Blue Shield plan—had long been interested in system reform. Working with a team from the University of Pennsylvania, they launched a primary care capitation program in 2016.[46] When it was evaluated two years later, the program showed few changes in overall utilization measures. Specifically, there was no change in 11 of its 15 prespecified endpoints, including in the mean total cost of health care. The number of primary care visits declined. Some quality measures, however, did show improvement. The researchers suggested that more time might be needed to identify changes in the number of patient visits to specialists and emergency departments, as well as hospitalizations, but a follow-up study has not been done.

From this and other studies regarding capitation, some lessons appear to be clear.[47] In particular, it is important for most practices to phase in capitation, and they need operational and financial support for this transition. It is best if the new payment structure can be aligned across all payers, or at least to have the dominant payer promote capitation. This latter bit of advice has received some empirical support by Sanjay Basu and colleagues, touched on briefly in the previous chapter.[48] After analyzing 969 primary care practices in the United States, 95% of them would attain financial gains through managed care if more than 63% of their health care payments were capitated. If less than 23% of their patient population was capitated, then 95% of these practices lost money. This being the case, Massachusetts can probably expect some success with primary care capitation in those practices that have a high percentage of Medicaid beneficiaries. And certainly, with the stepwise progress of its sequenced Section 1115 waivers, MassHealth has prepared the state's primary care practices as well as possible.

The Holyoke Health Center (see chap. 2) and the Lynn Community Health Center (discussed below) are now paid the new form of primary care capitation. They, along with over 20 other federally qualified health centers, are members of the Community Care Cooperative, or C3, which is an accountable care organization. This allows the FQHCs to take financial risk payments directly from MassHealth. Unlike most other participants in the MassHealth capitation program, the Community Care Cooperative does not have an intermediary managed care organization. Instead, C3 has knitted the health centers together, putting many of them on a single iteration of Epic's EMR system and counseling them about care management and coding.

The latter issue does not come up often when talking to health care groups taking on financial risk through Medicaid, which contrasts sharply with what occurs in Medicare Advantage (which I treat in later chapters). Risk coding is an essential part of ensuring adequate revenue, no matter the nature of the financial risk program. But as many clinicians at FQHCs reiterate, they are not practicing medicine to generate revenue (even though they do). So, discussions of risk coding are always guarded, and most of the efforts to ensure appropriate coding are done administratively by an organization like C3.

The issue of financial risk at FQHCs is a bit murky. The Health Resources and Services Administration, which provides a lot of federal health care funding, does not want to jeopardize the special treatment of Medicaid funding for FQHCs, so there are some who believe that FQHCs themselves cannot take on financial risk. CMS, in contrast, is promoting risk and sees no problem for FQHCs taking risk. As a result, many FQHCs participate in financial risk reimbursement in their Medicaid contracts, even though HRSA is not always on board. So goes American health policy: if we can make reimbursement rules more complex, we will. The good news is that recent research suggests that performance in FQHCs improves substantially on quality measures when they utilize alternative payment models.[49]

In chapter 2, I related my impression of the Holyoke Health Center, one of Massachusetts's federally qualified health centers, as it prepared for MassHealth's launch of primary care capitation in fall 2022. But perhaps an even clearer picture emerged at the Lynn Community Health Center, a FQHC in Lynn, Massachusetts. I was introduced to its operation by Dr. Kiame Mahaniah, a veteran of FQHC care after spending ten years at the Lawrence, Massachusetts, FQHC before coming to Lynn ten years ago.[50] In April 2023, Mahaniah went from Lynn to become the undersecretary for health in Massachusetts's Executive Office of Health and Human Services. He left behind quite a team, as I came to realize.

The Lynn Community Health Center is impressive. Their patients speak over 30 languages, and the center has on-site translators for Arabic, Creole, Khmer, Portuguese, and Spanish. Many of their newest refugees are from Afghanistan and the Democratic Republic of the Congo. The Lynn FQHC grew out of a mental health center, so behavioral health is heavily integrated, with over 70 clinicians. A total of 43,000 patients use the center, served by 660 employees in a couple of buildings in downtown Lynn. When I visited, a new pharmacy was being put together to take advantage of funds from the HRSA's 340B drug-pricing program and integrate pharmacy care into primary care, as the Holyoke FQHC has done.

Mahaniah was a big advocate for disease management within primary care, and he supported primary care capitation as a way to do that. He has argued that this capitation should include behavioral health, since, in a place like Lynn, patient care by the family medicine doctors and the behavioral health teams are meant to be totally integrated. But the current Section 1115 waiver does not quite accomplish this goal.

I got to Lynn early on a cold morning at the beginning of December, and people were already streaming into the building. Many looked as though they could be experiencing their first bout of cold weather, some with ill-fitting winter clothes that had a secondhand look. Among the center's patient population, 70% are covered under Medicaid and 15% are uninsured. The latter percentage makes the center an outlier in Massachusetts, which has an overall uninsured rate of around 3%. One explanation for this higher figure is that many of the Lynn Community Health Center's patients are recent immigrants needing assistance services and seeking legal status. There were also lots of kids—25% of the center's patient population is under age 18. The inside of the building was bustling—and polyglot.

Mahaniah set me up to talk with his team, led by Dr. Geoffrey Pechinsky, the center's chief medical officer.[51] Pechinsky (who is an imposingly large man) graduated from Notre Dame University, received his medical degree from Boston University School of Medicine, and trained in family medicine in the Greater Lawrence Community Health Center. (The training site there is one of the preeminent programs for family medicine in the state.) Pechinsky is strikingly friendly, greeting everyone throughout the center with a mixture of joy and respect. We went out for a Vietnamese lunch (in Lynn, a city with a lot of refugees, there is a wide variety of cuisine), and ran into one of Pechinsky's patients, who was smoking and drifting around a bit on the street. Responding to a cry of "Hey, doc," Pechinsky's greeting was warm and familiar, although he immediately admonished his patient for missing their last appointment. This person guaranteed that he would come in soon, and both wore big smiles as they parted company.

Pechinsky remarked that the Lynn center's doctors and nurses are like a lot of people in primary care: fatigued by the COVID pandemic and wondering if their jobs are really doable. Yet in his view, their level of commitment to their patients is extraordinary, and this was borne out by the several interviews I conducted. One clinician after another reiterated—unprompted—that Lynn's low-income population and its even poorer new immigrants are exactly who they wanted to serve. This sense of social justice magnifies the altruism that is a part of primary care, and it was deeply gratifying to this visitor.

Dr. Clark Van Den Berghe, a family medicine physician, was raised in Upstate New York. He looks like he is right out of central casting for a midwestern father or doctor.[52] Van Den Berghe knew when he went to medical school that he wanted to practice anything but primary care, choosing Northwestern University for medical school with that in mind. But during his first year, he heard a lecture by Dr. Mark Loafman (now the head of community medicine at Cook County Hospital in Chicago) that catalyzed a change of heart. After that lecture, he wanted to take care of poor and underserved people as a family medicine doctor. He trained in family medicine at Greater Lawrence Community Health Center, with Pechinsky as his boss—there is a huge Lawrence mafia at Lynn. Van Den Berghe and seven other family physicians at Lynn include obstetrics as part of their practice and deliver at nearby Mass General Brigham (MGB) Salem Hospital.

Van Den Berghe, who was a missionary in France for the Church of Jesus Christ of Latter-Day Saints, speaks French and its variant, Creole, a helpful skill when treating the Lynn Community Health Center's recent influx of Haitian refugees. In addition, he speaks Spanish and gets along in Portuguese, so he is expert in the multilingual aspects of his job. He also gets to do plenty of different procedures, which he greatly enjoys.

Our conversation started with the changes in health care financing. His boss (Geoffrey Pechinsky) believes that with the new primary care capitation program MassHealth rolled out in spring 2023, he and his colleagues will be able to move away from fee-for-service's shackles and really practice cost-effective medicine. As Van Den Berghe saw it, this change in financing at FQHCs was a boon for social justice—clinicians will get paid properly for keeping people healthy and happy: "Once you get unburdened from the visit as the only way to get paid, you can do tons of good things."

Van Den Berghe thought that the Lynn Community Health Center had sufficient infrastructure to thrive. Some of its success comes from

Epic's EMR system, and C3 will provide other tools. The Lynn FQHC teams are integrating capitation payments into their ideal care model, which will involve more formal teamwork. Going into family medicine, Van Den Berghe was sold on the team model, but his current primary care practice consisted only of him and his medical assistant. He is a strong advocate for family group visits, especially for hypertension and substance use disorders. The center is also building a pharmacy, and its pharmacists will be part of the care team. The CVS pharmacy across the street will be closing, and the Lynn center hopes to hire several of the pharmacists from there.

I turned the conversation back to the current finances of the center's medical practices. Its clinicians do not have volume incentives, but their daily schedules do control the patient density. The physicians are expected to see 10 patients in a four-hour session, with the advanced practice providers (APPs) seeing only 8. The recommended panel size is 1,300 patients. Most of Van Den Berghe's patients are Medicaid beneficiaries, but he does have some uninsured patients. The health center gets partial reimbursement for them through the state's Health Safety Net Program, but there is no local specialty support available. Instead, uninsured patients must travel to Boston Medical Center (BMC), a designated safety net hospital, and they can get lost there. It is rare for a primary care doctor to hear from the clinicians at BMC, so there are coordination and continuity concerns, but the Lynn teams can pick up most of what happened using Epic's Care Everywhere feature.

I asked Van Den Berghe about the health of the Lynn center's clinical teams. He responded that he had 10 coresidents at the Lawrence Community Health Center, and they have all stayed in primary care, focusing on the underserved. He is the most pathologically optimistic among them, but even he felt a bit run down by the COVID pandemic. He was bolstered by the prospect of MassHealth's new payment approach, but he knew he needed to temper his expectations. It is already clear that the state will not roll behavioral health into its primary care capitation, a big blow at the Lynn center, which has historically championed the integrated care model. Overall, Van Den Berghe could not say that everyone at Lynn is happy, but he thought they all agreed that it is better than most FQHCs. And he was clear that he never wants to work in a private practice with affluent patients. His Lynn patients are so appreciative of the care he renders that "it picks me up every day."

But Van Den Berghe also admitted that practicing in a center that is chronically underfunded can create anxieties and tensions. Its lack of resources plays out in several ways. The clinic's call center and customer service have not been great historically, but they are improving. Good outside consultations are often difficult to obtain. In contrast, the care payments through Medicaid are quite reasonable, and Lynn manages care so well that Medicaid provides a steady revenue stream. And the center can hire new staff. It will have nine new primary care clinicians joining the practice in the coming year, mostly physicians. Their $185,000 starting salary for doctors is competitive. While it may be as much as 30% less than at other primary care practices, people are attracted to the Lynn Community Health Center's mission. The center also qualifies as a site for National Health Services Corp physicians, as the city of Lynn is a health workforce shortage area.

Van Den Berghe's enthusiasm as a relative newcomer to the center was shared by Dr. Brian Faherty, who has been with the Lynn FQHC for nearly 40 years.[53] He is a slender man with a casual style, sporting a bright blue shirt and a tie featuring the Grateful Dead's Jerry Garcia. His sharp features suggest his Boston Irish Catholic background. He also has these Hibernian credentials in his schooling: Cardinal Spellman High School and then Boston College, where he studied psychology. Professionally, he started at Cambridge City Hospital and was providing therapy there as an unlicensed counselor before going back to school to earn his doctorate in psychology.

When he arrived at the Lynn Community Health Center in the late 1970s, his first workplace was in a trailer, then in the second floor of a house, and finally in a converted office building. The clean and new-appearing building in which most of the center's care occurs today was built in the 2010s with Affordable Care Act money, and it has an atrium that links up with the old building. Faherty was proud—and impressed—by the expansion of the center and the role it plays in the community.

Behavioral health integration is a crucial aspect of any progressive primary care practice. This is especially true today, when there is a relative dearth of mental health professionals and primary care settings deliver 60% of patients' mental health care.[54] The history of the Lynn Health Center is grounded in this commitment to collaboration. One of its buildings is named after Steve Hayes, who was Faherty's mentor. Hayes pushed relentlessly for behavioral health's integration with primary care. Originally, the Lynn center was dedicated solely to mental health care, and it has retained both respect and broad ambitions for behavioral health care. Faherty clearly relished his work with his primary care clinician collaborators.

He recalled specific patients with substantial mental health problems, and he noted how caring for them alongside his medical colleagues saved these patients from real harm. But Faherty acknowledged that truly integrated care is always hard to accomplish. The key elements for him were colocation, shared electronic medical records and shared problem lists, and the camaraderie that the first two criteria create. The members of the care team must know and respect one another, and work together to bring in additional care when needed.

While Faherty found nothing but joy and gratification in his work, he admitted that recruiting is difficult today. He would not provide specific numbers, and I did not press him, but the behavioral health team may be operating with as many as 30% to 40% of its budgeted positions filled. By way of a roundabout explanation, Faherty noted that new people prefer not to come to a fixed work site. They want to be "only remote," with jobs that provide better reimbursement and part-time work. The COVID pandemic pushed a lot of people toward private practice.

When asked about the problems he faced, Faherty admitted that he is saddened because behavioral health is not in the new Medicaid capitation program. He and his team were going to have to remain responsible for coding patient visits and trying to pigeonhole these encounters into specific 18- or 37-minute slots. He also worried about the EMR communications system the center's teams use. Behavioral health notes go over to the primary care outbox, where they might be lost or ignored. The primary care people, however, complain that the behavioral health clinicians use too many words, and Faherty has been working with his team on streamlining their notes. They need to be succinct and outline exactly what the next steps are.

Faherty's reasonable bottom line was that behavioral health must be aware of a patient's medical problems, and medical personnel must understand that individual's behavioral problems. That takes commitment and exemplifies his daily work. I was impressed by this discussion, particularly because of the progress it suggests in terms of a health care team addressing the manifold problems presented by their patients. It offers some evidence that primary care is evolving toward a more effective foundation for health care, albeit in starts and stops.

Dr. Roopa Chari is another family medicine physician at the center.[55] She devotes one day a week to obstetrics at MGB Salem Hospital, the center's local care partner. She also runs the satellite clinic at Market Square, several blocks from the main Lynn Community Health Center buildings. She pushes the clinic's caregivers into a team approach: the right person does the right job. She commented that some people resent this arrangement, seeing work now coming their way that they did not have to do in the past. Nor did she think that a team approach could be taught during residency training—it is too chaotic there. But coordinated teamwork is the only means she saw to address the burnout that comes with the crush of patients she and her clinicians faced. Chari, too, was looking forward to MassHealth's new payment model, which meant "getting rid of a lot of clicks" on the EMRs.

As the day progressed, it became clear to me that the management team at Lynn had empowered individual clinicians to do their jobs effectively. Doctors and nurses would take on problems that otherwise might seem "administrative," largely because these clinicians could perceive the benefits for their patients. They no longer saw their role as beginning and ending at the exam room's door.

Dr. Elizabeth Quinn is another of the Lynn Community Health Center's family medicine doctors, practicing obstetrics and family medicine.[56] She grew up in Quincy, Massachusetts, going to Harvard University as an undergraduate, to the University of Massachusetts for medical school, and then to the Lawrence Community Health Center for training. She was the person who described her practice as being "wonderful, crazy, and broken." Quinn was grounded, matter of fact, and extraordinarily articulate. She specializes in care for pregnant women with substance use disorders.

Quinn believed the Lynn Community Health Center is doing a better job of addressing the medical/social duality than anywhere else in the Commonwealth, particularly for the patients she sees. A lot of them have behavioral health problems, and she has been getting a good deal of support from the center's integrated team and from the staff at MGB Salem Hospital. Some of her patients have been successful in dealing with their substance use disorders over the long term, but many relapse. As one might expect, childbearing while being addicted is incredibly difficult for both these patients and their clinician team.

Quinn took the initiative and made herself the champion of social determinants of health at the Lynn Community Health Center. I told her that this sounded like taking coals to Newcastle, and she laughed. But she made a trenchant point. As part of the reward structure under the state's new Medicaid contracts, the health center could get financial rewards for ensuring that an SDOH questionnaire was filled out. I had to fill out this questionnaire before seeing my own primary care doctor, and I wondered, as Quinn does, whether there was any underlying mechanism to address problematic answers provided by patients.

Dr. Quinn took the initiative to create workflows to provide support for people needing help with such social issues. She made sure the center could help patients who were not able to access healthy foods complete food stamp applications. She reached out to the Massachusetts Coalition for the Homeless to help people find housing. She was instrumental in developing a food bank program that now serves 500 households. And she is working to do more—seeing these efforts as all being part of her job.

Quinn was anxious about some aspects of the new primary care capitation program and the ACO concept, and she brought up several good points. Like many progressive doctors, she was suspicious of financial incentives, believing that that those who have the most money to set up and then cull information from a data structure will do well. The FQHCs are understaffed, so they are at a disadvantage in having to rely on the Community Care Cooperative's ACO to provide the necessary infrastructure. The question is, Will C3 be able to do so? Quinn also raised sophisticated questions about attribution, with the inherent unreliability of some of their patient populations. Most of the clinicians at an FQHC like Lynn would prefer to skip an accountable care transition period and roll right into a single-payer format.

Quinn also struggles to meet the demands of her practice. Her child goes to daycare right next to a Cambridge Health Alliance Center—working there would greatly uncomplicate her life. She wonders how much longer she can do the commute to Lynn. But she is committed to her patients, and that sustains her for now.

The last person I visited with at the Lynn Community Health Center was Ryan Griffin, the director of psychopharmacology.[57] He trained as a nurse and then as a nurse practitioner at Massachusetts General Hospital's Institute of Health Professionals. Griffin made some great points about capitation. First, it would let him promote more telemedicine for behavioral health patients. Its usage is now at about 50%, but it could be higher. And with capitation, he would not have to worry about billing for this type of patient visit. Second, capitation would eventually reduce the paperwork associated with fee-for-service billing, which he thought would be incredibly important. Anything that could allow more time with patients is crucial.

Finally, Griffin had an insight that put into perspective many of my visits to health care sites caring for the medically underserved. He asserted that for many of Lynn's patients, the fundamental root of their problems is trauma. The clinics see a lot of very low-income patients, many of whom are refugees. During their lives, these people are traumatized. They may develop depression, substance use disorders, schizophrenia, or attention deficit hyperactivity disorder (ADHD), but trauma often underlies these conditions. Without articulating it per se, Griffin was communicating to me that coming into contact with all of these traumas was also tough on the clinicians. The treatment of psychological trauma, he reasoned, required a sustained and continuous care effort. For that, paying for a single, coordinated program to achieve good health—rather than being billed on a piecemeal, per visit basis— made real sense. In Massachusetts, primary care capitation in Medicaid is forging ahead with great promise yet some foreboding.

Oregon's Comprehensive Value-Based Program, Built on Primary Care

The promising future for primary care in Rhode Island (perhaps not yet obtained) and Massachusetts (still to be assessed) prompted me to visit Oregon, which has perhaps the most comprehensive effort to support primary care of any state in the country. Oregon has long been a leader in health care reform at the state level.[58] As early as 1989, Oregon began moving toward universal access to health care. The major tool was an expansion of Medicaid. In order to achieve this, the Oregon Health Authority famously came up with a list of benefits that were cost-effective and planned to include all of them as part of the state's Medicaid coverage, while leaving some other treatments unfunded. This caused an incredible health policy fuss and raised concerns about rationing. But the benefits package proved to be generous, and Medicaid did expand, under a series of Section 1115 waivers.

After 2000, though, this expansion began to falter. A set of policy miscalculations, including failing to anticipate the impact of cost-sharing measures, caused diminished enrollment. In addition, the 2001–3 nationwide economic downturn reduced state revenues and led to further problems in funding Oregon's Medicaid program. Bipartisan support waned, and the state's number of uninsured patients rose. The important lesson here is that health care reform ebbs and flows, and its sinusoidal curve can be exacerbated at the state level.

But Oregon health care advocates fought back, and today the array of initiatives makes Oregon perhaps the leader in promoting value-based access to care at the state level. Four main policy efforts form its backbone: (1) a statewide cost-control program; (2) primary care payment reform, including targets for primary care spending; (3) coordinated care organizations (essentially Medicaid ACOs that are paid on a financial risk basis); and (4) a statewide, payer-wide compact to encourage value-based care.

Oregon's statewide cost-control effort is new, but it is not unique. Massachusetts has been the leader in this approach to reducing health care costs, setting budget targets and enforcing them in the delivery system.[59] The Massachusetts Health Policy Commission sets benchmark expenditure rates and then requires hospitals and integrated systems that exceed these amounts to submit performance improvement plans to get back into line. It also oversees any new provider-consolidation proposals and has halted some that could lead to increased costs. Connecticut, Delaware, and Rhode Island have followed suit, but unlike Massachusetts, they have not granted enforcement authority to their respective health policy commissions. Oregon has, setting a benchmark in 2022 for annual statewide health cost increases not to exceed 3.4%. In many ways, Oregon has emulated the Massachusetts model.

The other three major Oregon reforms focus more on primary care. For over a decade, Oregon has provided support for primary care practices to become patient-centered primary care medical homes. Today, 650 of the state's 800 primary care practices have attained this certification, at one of five tiers. The certification process includes requirements for addressing health equity and SDOH.[60] In 2015, the PCMH effort was supplemented by the Primary Care Payment Reform Collaborative, a multi-stakeholder program aimed at further improvements in primary care, specifically by increasing spending on this aspect of health care.[61] In some ways, Oregon has followed the lead of Rhode Island.

Unlike what happened in Rhode Island, however, Oregon's effort has been sustained. Even more importantly, since 2017, it includes requirements that apply to commercial health care insurance, Medicaid, and Medicare Advantage.[62] Medicaid payers (known as coordinated care organizations, or CCOs) and commercial health insurance payers in Oregon were required to allocate at least 12% of their medical spending to primary care by 2023. Moreover, these payments are reported annually. In 2022, the CCOs spent 16.2% on primary care, and the commercial health insurance plans, 13.9%. Each of the state's regional CCOs reports these amounts separately, with some of them spending over 22% on primary care.[63]

These improvements in the amounts paid for primary care are carefully integrated with Oregon's Medicaid reforms, which are focused on the CCOs and the compact that promotes value-based payment statewide. The CCOs evolved from Medicaid's managed care organizations in Oregon. They are now regionally based, all funded as part of the state's ongoing Section 1115 waiver.[64] CMS granted Oregon $1.9 billion to develop these coordinated care organizations, and in return, the CCOs' annual spending increases were to diminish from 5.4% to 3.4%. Under this arrangement, the CCOs receive capitated payments, and their affiliated health care groups must manage care to gain upside profits, or risk downside losses. The program provides care for more than 90% of Oregon's Medicaid beneficiaries in what is best understood as an ACO structure.

The CCOs use the typical methods for managing care: (1) data analysis to find the patients who need interventions, (2) behavioral health integration, (3) the use of primary care medical home techniques, (4) care management for those who went to an emergency department or were admitted to a hospital; and (5) careful attention to social determinants of health. A thorough analysis completed in 2017 indicated that this new organizational structure was working.[65] The researchers found a 7% relative reduction in expenditures, with the biggest factor being a decrease in the use of emergency departments and hospitals. There are now 15 CCOs spread throughout the state. One of these is Pacific Source Community Solutions–Columbia Gorge, which serves Hood River and Wasco Counties.

Each new Section 1115 waiver brings further evolutions in Oregon's contracts with the CCOs. From January 1, 2020, to January 1, 2024, the CCOs were to focus on integrating behavioral health with managed primary care, increasing the value of performance measures, paying attention to SDOH and health care equity, and maintaining sustainable cost growth.[66] A new waiver was granted in late 2022 for the period 2022–27. Crucial new features include two-year continuous coverage (a huge issue in Medicaid today); more funds for social needs, including housing and food assistance; and protection from climate changes.[67] In short, the CCO structure constitutes a durable and comprehensive accountable care foundation for those who provide health care for Medicaid beneficiaries.

Moreover, Oregon is attempting to move all its payers in a similar direction. Senate Bill 889 (passed in 2019) had set forth a vision for statewide value-based care. It established the Sustainable Health Care Cost Growth Target Implementation Committee, which in January 2021 recommended an all-payer growth target of 3.4% for 2021–25 and 3% for 2026–30.[68] The committee's key strategy was to develop a compact between all payers and all health care providers to promote value-based care. Many organizations quickly signed on to the compact, which although not legally binding, still puts reasonable pressure on payers in particular to coordinate efforts to promote parsimonious care.[69] The signees have now committed to a goal of having 70% of their contracts with primary care and general acute care clinicians entail shared savings at a Health Care Payment Learning and Action Network (HCPLAN) category 3B financial risk level or higher by 2024.[70] Plans for regional multipayer global budgets are taking shape.[71]

Oregon's steady move toward value-based care—with state leadership on the Medicaid front, followed by outreach to other payers and primary care practices—is nothing short of breathtaking when compared with health care efforts in many other states. The report I got from on-the-ground health care providers in Oregon is equally impressive.

I drove to The Dalles, Oregon, one dark May night, with a lot of traffic on the interstate. Little did I know that I was on one of the most scenic interstates in the country: I-84 along the Columbia River. I had no respect for it that evening, as the highway was crowded with trucks, and I was prejudiced just by the name, knowing well the ignominious end of a different I-84 at its Stockbridge, MA, intersection with the Mass Pike. Only the next morning, viewing the river from my motel, did I realize my mistake.

I was visiting One Community Health, an FQHC with locations in The Dalles and Hood River.[72] The staff at the health center eagerly shared information about their twin cities (about 10 miles apart) and their differences. Both towns have long been dominated by agriculture, particularly fruit orchards. (The health center was originally founded as a farmworkers' free clinic, called La Clinica.) In June, especially toward The Dalles, thousands of migrant workers would move into the area to pick cherries. Harvesting pears and apples would occur later. Everyone was highly attuned to the agricultural pulse of the area.

But agriculture is no longer the whole story. Over the past two decades, Hood River has gentrified somewhat, with a lot of people moving in to buy second homes in its picturesque downtown, overlooking the majestic river. The city is a windsurfing mecca, but there is also plenty of bike riding and hiking. The Dalles, however, remains more hardscrabble. It is also more politically red, compared with blue-leaning Hood River. One Community Health saw this division in its COVID vaccination rates—they were much lower in The Dalles.

The main One Community Health campus is a brand-new building in Hood River, up the hill from the river. Their old building was torn down, and its former site has now become a parking lot and community gardens. The new health center, constructed with a loan grant from the US Department of Agriculture, is open and spacious, reminding me of the buildings at the Southcentral Foundation in Anchorage, Alaska.

In Hood River, I met first with Dr. Connie Serra, the lead clinician, and Max Janasik, One Community Health's chief executive officer. Janasik had an odd background for an FQHC administrator, having come from Regence Blue Cross Blue Shield, where he was the director of e-business, and Cambia Health Solutions, where as vice president of innovation he focused on digital interventions.[73] He emphasized that the trajectory of One Community was ascending. They had been pushed by COVID to be more proactive, and they now are. A great example was their renewed commitment to get out into the orchards in June as the migrant workers came into the area for the harvest. Janasik's patois was decidedly corporate, but convincing.

Serra spoke more from the heart.[74] By her own account, she grew up in a low-income neighborhood. She went to Ohio State University's College of Medicine for medical school. She knew she wanted to focus on rural health—specifically, combining family practice with obstetrics—and was convinced that she had to get west of Mississippi River. She then trained at Oregon Health and Sciences University (OHSU) in Klamath Falls and practiced there for three years. Serra moved to Hood River 20 years ago as a single mom with a toddler, with a starting salary of $80,000. She has been in Hood River ever since.

Serra was enthusiastic—even ebullient—about her family medicine practice and One Community, clearly energized by her work. The center's health care payer mix is dominated by Medicaid, at greater than 70%. The Medicaid payments come from Pacific Source, which is their MCO partner as the CCO. One Community also has a huge outreach to the area's uninsured population of farmworkers, with some supplemental funds coming from various state and federal programs. While The Dalles and Hood River seem like large towns, the health center's family medicine practice is decidedly rural, ranging over a 75-mile area that extends from the Hood River up through southern Washington State.

One Community Health is delivering great care now, but the situation was not so sanguine when Serra joined the Hood River center. During 2008–10, 50% to 60% of their patients were uninsured, and the board had to begin to limit the types of patients the clinicians could see. Accessibility was dictated by the patients' insurance status. Managing the payer mix—shorthand for limiting who could be seen by insurance status—was heart-wrenching for the staff. During one all-staff meeting in this period, there were tears in many of the eyes, including Serra's.

The Affordable Care Act saved them. They renegotiated their prospective payment system rate with Medicaid, and then the state's health care reforms began to kick in. One Community Health enthusiastically endorsed gaining primary medical home status and began to focus on value-based care. Serra did not articulate this history in terms of Oregon's health reforms, but the collinearity of the two stories is striking.

The first step to achieving PCMH status was empanelment, and from that came a focus on anticipating and preventing diseases. The One Community teams huddle every morning to discuss the incoming patients and their problems. This type of huddle is probably the number one feature I saw in my travels that distinguishes *proactive* from *reactive* primary care. Patients are assigned to specific teams and stay there, creating stability for the clinicians and their patients. The clinicians continue to push forward on team-based care criteria, led to some extent by Pacific Source paying them more as they hit new tiers. Serra was clear that the Medicaid per member, per month payment gives the team the flexibility it needs to address various patient issues.

Pacific Source employs One Community Health's care managers, who work closely with the clinical teams and focus on hospital utilization, both for admissions and visits to the emergency department. Electronic medical records help with this integration. The center had been on a Next Gen EMR system but switched to Epic, which better tracks patients who use other providers. Both the OHSU's medical center and Providence Portland Medical Center's hospital systems are on Epic, so One Community's clinicians can follow their hospitalized patients. The usual praise and complaints about Epic's EMRs come through. As advice from Epic's population health management feature grows better, the MyChart boxes fill up, but the main phone center gets relief.

Serra foresaw a bright future, but it depends on the whim of politicians. The state's Medicaid expansions have helped the center's patients. But the anticipated contractions are making her and her colleagues profoundly uneasy. She was afraid that politicians just do not realize that coverage makes a difference, such as having an inhaler when you need one as opposed to doing without. She is also a bit skeptical about some of the aspects of value-based care. One Community Health is now working with Aledade on Medicare Advantage plans, and the need for better coding has come into play. Serra saw this as an administrative burden, as do most people at FQHCs. They realize that better coding means more revenue. But the problem is time and resources: clinicians have not been trained on coding, and that takes time alongside other continuing medical education and training responsibilities. Dr. Serra is just trying to figure out how to keep all the balls in the air.

Brooke Nicholls filled me in on more of the clinical details at One Community Health's Hood River campus.[75] She went to nursing school at the University of Portland, became a diabetes educator, and then decided to go back to school to become a nurse practitioner. She felt well trained, but she was able to do a yearlong residency at the Hood River clinic, bringing her up to speed. These types of informal residencies for nurse practitioners have become an increasingly familiar story. Nicholls has her own panel and does not seek out supervision but instead works with her team in caring for her patients' difficult problems. This looks like the future of primary care.

Nicholls receives a salary, and she has a panel expectation of 690 patients. Her weekly workload consists of 30 patient-facing clinical hours, plus 4 additional hours outside of that. She does urgent care work on Saturdays, a different schedule than most NPs. There is no scrutiny of her team's RVU numbers, although there was in the past, and no bonuses. Her team consists of three physicians and one nurse practitioner, as well as a registered nurse. Each clinician has a medical assistant. There are also staff at a welcome desk and a referral coordinator. The Hood River site has three master's degree–trained behavioral health consultants that cover all three of its teams. One Community Health has not developed its own pharmacy but nonetheless derives revenue from HRSA's 340B drug-pricing program. The center continues to work with the local Walgreens for prescription dispensing.

Not everything is going well at the Hood River clinic. In the past six months, they lost most of their nurses—with two of them leaving nursing altogether, and one switching to traveling nurse status—but they have been able to hire replacements. And One Community Health has had a boost in physician hiring because it is now part of a rural health primary care residency with OHSU. Nicholls's team specializes in women's health, follows patients who deliver their babies at the local Providence hospital, and does lots of pediatrics. As for many family clinicians, this care for the community and for extended families brings great professional satisfaction for her.

Nicholls and the other 30 clinicians in her family medicine practice have a real voice in the evolution of One Community Health. Their CEO, Max Janasik, meets with them frequently, and they discuss longer-term strategy. Grants are critical, as they provide for new health care interventions, such as acquiring a mobile van that they are now using in several locations. Perhaps more importantly, they are taking steps to combat burnout. Clinicians have more flexibility in their schedules now, and certain tasks are being spread throughout the team members. Nicholls also mentioned that she uses a medical scribe, which reduced her workload by six to eight hours per week and allows her to address population health management issues while using Epic's EMR inbox.

For most FQHCs, and many other health care sites in rural areas, specialty care can be sketchy—it is distantly located and not always well coordinated. One Community Health has a great diabetes team, but for other issues, they must rely on OHSU in Portland. The local Providence hospital has some specialists, and OHSU operates a phone line that helps the Hood River family medicine team manage their patients without formal consultation. This is especially important for their uninsured patients, including migrant farmworkers.

As we were finishing our discussion, Nicholls wanted to be sure that I understood how important their community health worker team is. Some of them are assigned to the diabetes team and the prenatal clinic. But several other community health workers do nothing but outreach, and they are vital in terms of identifying emerging problems and building trust. This, plus One Community Health's emphasis on behavioral health consultations, greatly increases the value of their team to their patients.

I got a completely different but complementary view of One Community Health talking to Harley Davidson.[76] A gentle giant (I told him he must be the biggest person in Oregon, and he laughed), Davidson is the paradigm of a self-made individual. He has been working full-time since he was in high school, including while putting himself through college and graduate school. Moreover, most of his previous work was at for-profit companies, including Hospital Corporation of America (HCA). He considers the FQHC environment to be an exciting challenge.

As One Community Health's chief operating officer, Davidson is in charge of its revenues, so he spends a good deal of time with the Pacific Source CCO team diving into the intricacies of Medicaid's prospective payment system rates. One Community Health is also working to strengthen its Medicare revenues, especially from Medicare Advantage plans. HRSA grants are another key portion of One Community's financing. These federal funds do not change much over time, but the health center must reapply for them every couple of years. One Community Health is also always looking for other grant sources. From Davidson's point of view, enhancing and improving the center's payer contracts are crucial, and he is afraid they can get too dependent on grants. When we spoke, their total budget was over $30 million, with $4.5 million in HRSA grants and $4 million in other grants.

Davidson was certain that there are health care access problems in the state. In Idaho, where he is from, patients were waiting two to three *weeks* for appointments, while in Oregon, it takes two to three *months*. The bigger contrast is that the state of Oregon is involved in health care, and Idaho had not been. In Idaho, he had doctors seeing 30 patients a day, which would not be possible in Oregon, given the state's requirements for managing care and ensuring quality of care. Davidson thought support for primary care is generally insufficient throughout the United States, but less so in Oregon than in Idaho.

In terms of addressing key problems, Davidson's clear passion was how to get everyone to "the top of their license" in order to lower costs and ensure they could improve access to health care. (An article in *Forbes* gives a cogent explanation for this phrase: "Highly experienced healthcare professionals trained to diagnose and manage complex illness should not be burdened with routine tasks and documentation requirements whose fulfillment don't require their skills and intellects."[77]) He had been studying a clinic in Providence, Rhode Island, that was composed entirely of registered nurses who were supported by telemedicine. He thought One Community Health could do that in Oregon and had started a "test-to-treat" program for Paxlovid (an antiviral pill used to help reduce the progression of COVID to its severe stage) during the COVID pandemic.

In another example, Davidson calculated that on One Community Health's primary care capitation budget, three visits per year with a senior clinician was a break-even point, yet they had plenty of patients making 15–20 visits per year. So, he helped create a diabetes education program, including culturally relevant nutrition counseling, that could substitute for a number of clinician visits. The center's mobile van was also his idea, and getting to distant patients in a timely fashion had prevented poor outcomes.

Davidson was also charged with the center's relationship with the federal Health Resources and Services Administration. One Community Health wants to "get out of the box" in terms of treatment protocols, but HRSA reins that in. The center must pay attention to HRSA's definitions of acceptable therapy, as the malpractice insurance protection One Community Health receives under the Federal Tort Claims Act depends on HRSA's approval. HRSA is a constant presence, as its staff members make site visits and regulate community oversight. One Community has not had to give up any of the programs it wants to put in place to serve patients, but some of them must be modified in light of HRSA pressure. Davidson's short answer to a lot of my questions was, "There are always new fires." One occupying him as we talked was having to pay market prices for vaccines for One Community's patients that had lost their Medicaid benefits. Trusting to previous experience, he was confident that a solution would be found.

Davidson's key staff at One Community Health's clinic in The Dalles are Amy Marquez and Kendahl Caminiti.[78] Marquez previously worked at Mid-Columbia Medical Center, the hospital in The Dalles. She was a local, grew up on a farm (mostly with pear orchards, but now moving into cherries). She had an excellent feel for both local and health care politics. Caminiti was the clinic's nursing supervisor, with responsibility for clinical care.

When I visited in mid-May, they were dealing with a crisis. Migrant cherry pickers were due to arrive in June, and the Mid-Columbia Medical Center (MCMC) had just had a meltdown, losing all ten of its primary care physicians. They were employed by OHSU, on contract with MCMC, and new terms could not be resolved, so these ten doctors went back to Portland. MCMC, under new ownership, was moving to replace the decamped doctors, but that would take time. One Community Health in The Dalles was doing the best it could to absorb some of MCMC's patients, taking on 168 new patients in the previous month. But they had room for only two health care teams, with eight clinicians, and the increased demand would call for at least three more. The current solution was a series of temporary modular structures in the parking lot. The only solace in this situation was that The Dalles was quite a bit warmer and drier than Hood River.

Dr. Jennifer Jehnsen was one of three physicians on the eight-member clinician team at The Dalles office.[79] She had a remarkable and peripatetic background. She grew up in New Jersey and went to college at the University of California, Berkeley. She then spent three years in rural McGee, Arkansas, teaching high school. She applied to medical school without great test scores but got into the University of Michigan, as they were looking for students with varied backgrounds. She then trained in the Waco Family Medicine Residency Program in Waco, Texas, where she and her fellow residents were the only residents at a large Baylor Scott & White hospital. That gave her a great experience in family medicine and obstetrics, since, as Jehnsen commented, she "got to do everything." The National Health Service Corps tuition support she received required her to initially practice in a medically underserved locale, and The Dalles appealed to her. Jehnsen liked the weather, could use her Spanish-language skills, and took care of people who needed her help. Her varied practice includes prenatal care (without obstetrics) and a reasonably sized group of patients with substance use disorders. (She noted that the introduction of fentanyl into the Hood River area meant that she had to prescribe huge doses of suboxone for those patients.)

Jehnsen's one big problem was the insurance companies' prior authorization requirement. She recently had trouble getting an MRI approved, and she had another issue with a prescription drug that was not covered under a patient's health insurance plan. She wondered why "insurers cannot simply trust doctors." But mostly she was pleased with her practice. Epic's EMR system was "great." It created some work overload for her, but it also provided a great deal of good data. Jehnsen did have a medical scribe, which saved her a lot of time in charting after a patient's visit. She enjoyed the number of Spanish-speaking patients she had.

There were challenges, however, often related to a lack of specialists, such as the nearest endocrinologist being 60 miles away, in Portland. Jehnsen had taken to talking through problematic cases with OHSU's consultants. For example, one of her new patients, a young woman, had upper abdominal pain and was losing weight. Jehnsen ordered thyroid tests, and her patient was diagnosed with Grave's disease (an autoimmune disease affecting the thyroid), which Jehnsen had never treated. Her patient developed liver toxicity with the first treatment, methimazole, so now she was taking a second-line drug, all this guided by telephonic consultation. Despite these difficulties, because Jehnsen had consultant support, she felt was up to the task of managing this patient's health care.

A recent participant in the job market, Jehnsen provided insight into the choices faced by new doctors, especially those in primary care. She could have gone to a fee-for-service medical group, gotten a huge signing bonus, and then been confronted with an RVU treadmill, having to deal with more than 24 patient visits each day. Instead, she opted for an FQHC, One Community Health, seeing 14 patients a day. Its capitation payment structure ensures good outcomes for her patients. She commented that in some ways, "RVU-based clinical care seems unethical." Jehnsen's work here is manageable. She is in the clinic from 9:00 a.m. to 6:00 p.m., with a half hour of precharting at home, followed by one to two hours of additional work after her kids go to sleep. She has four full days of patient visits a week, with the fifth day spent in administrative follow-up.

There is stress, but it is mostly related to how tattered society is. One area of concern is pediatric mental health. Jehnsen recently had a pediatric patient who attempted suicide and was then treated in the emergency department. With a psychiatric bed unavailable, this patient was discharged. Now Jehnsen and the youth's mother were using medications to care for the patient and waiting for psychiatric follow-up. A reasonable health care system would have offered the child hospitalization from the time of the event.

Even in a well-planned and well-honed program of value-based care, like the one Oregon has developed, there are holes in the care being offered and other deficiencies. But overall, I was impressed by what thoughtful health care planning—oriented toward a primary care base and taking on financial risk for patients' health—can accomplish. I was fascinated that no one at One Community Health mentioned or discussed the decade of Oregon health care reforms. But the outcomes of that reform are well reflected in their practice structure, and their patients seem to be getting excellent care. Some of that is a tribute to the people providing the health care, and some of it to the community. But part of it, at least, must reside in the health policy structure Oregon has carefully built.

In Summation

States can and do have an important role to play in bolstering primary care and improving health care outcomes. The ones I have reviewed here—Vermont, Rhode Island, Massachusetts, and Oregon—are widely seen in health policy circles as leaders in health system reforms. The paradox in our American health care regulation scheme is that the states have much more influence on their Medicaid programs than they do on health care plans from commercial insurers. As a result, more change is occurring in Medicaid as a whole, as well as in the sites where health care for its beneficiaries is delivered, particularly the federally qualified health centers. In some circumstances, that change is abiding, and there is a real move toward value-based care. Furthermore, the fulcrum for this shift is primary care, leading (at least in some circumstances) to a more gratifying situation for its practitioners.

While not comprehensive, state-driven changes in health care are bracing and important. There are various sources of change that are promoting an alliance of primary care and value-based care. By building new capacities in Medicaid, the states are influencing the overall system. States—as well as the federal government's initiatives under the Center for Medicare and Medicaid Innovation and the Medicare Shared Saving Program—are shifting our country's health care framework in a positive direction, heading from predominantly broken to something manageable. Of course, this may be occurring mainly in practices that care for the poor because they have no alternative: fee-for-service is simply not affordable.

By no means have any states solved the puzzle of making primary care viable through value-based payment, but the FQHCs I visited generally were the closest. That said, I met many overworked and pessimistic FQHC clinicians. Research has also suggested that in areas like cancer screening, FQHCs demonstrate some substantial gaps.[80] As well, low-income people generally have less access to high-value care.[81] So, more progress is needed. All that said, there does appear to be progress toward a sustainable primary care in those states that are thoughtfully reforming Medicaid and the health safety net.

CHAPTER FIVE

State-Based Health Insurers' Role in Primary Care

INSURERS PAY ATTENTION TO HEALTH policy and economic literature and have an oddly intimate and adversarial relationship with their network of providers, including primary care doctors. Therefore it should be no surprise that they are interested in promoting primary care as a way to lower health care costs and improve the overall quality of care. That impetus has gathered momentum as more health policy experts extoll the virtues of care management based on primary care and raise concerns about the current fee-for-service system. Even if the health insurers remained relatively uncommitted about the shifting tectonic plates in health policy, their clients (employers) are not, and the latter have come to expect some acceptance of value-based care.

How are insurers cultivating and supporting primary care? The insurance industry can be divided into two major segments: large, for-profit, national commercial insurers, and state-based insurers, which are likely to be not-for-profit concerns. During my 40 years in the health care business, I have found that nonprofits and for-profits generally behave in the same way, reacting similarly in any given market situation. They maximize their financial gains, whether they are for-profit or nonprofit hospitals, private doctors, or doctors hired by a nonprofit entity, and insurers of all stripes. But state-based nonprofit health insurers must conform to specific regulations and have tighter relationships with state bureaus and regulators. They are expected to have some regard for a state's interests and, perhaps, protections for its citizens.

The large national commercial health insurers are wholly corporate. Their main concern is their quarterly earnings report, which must show a profit. For them, profit is the only real issue. This lesson came home to me when I joined one of these firms after spending more than half of my career at nonprofit hospitals and universities. The company's chief financial officer and I were talking about a variety of initiatives, and I was expressing some thoughts about initiating new programs aimed at improving patient welfare. His reply was rather short. He was okay with my ideas if they led to new business. "I want to make a lot of money," he told me, meaning both personally and for the company. His attitude was jarring to me, but it should not have been. In a university-based nonprofit hospital or a nonprofit insurer, a lot of people probably were often thinking the same thing, but it was not okay to state that out loud. In a corporation, it was.

This is not to say that corporate employees are inherently greedier or less committed to their beneficiaries. It is just that, at the margin of any decision, the need to profit likely plays a larger role. As well, conversations about the ethical or moral implications of any decision are more circumscribed and tend toward what is "legal," as opposed to what is "right."

Smaller, state-based nonprofit health insurers are also profit driven, but they more frequently must assert the thesis that their actions are in line with improvements in patient welfare. So, their embrace of primary care will be informed by some commitment to their beneficiaries, independent of the financial implications. State-based health insurers can and will pursue some things because they are the right thing to do. These companies have more freedom to do so than the national for-profit insurers, whose stock analysts are incessantly looking for profitability. The moves of large commercial health insurance corporations will always be aligned with their interest in profits (with the smarter ones realizing that improvement in patient welfare should generally align with profit motives). No distinctions are ever this clear, so there will be some shades of gray, but the nonprofit/for-profit gulf must be acknowledged, providing a context for my segmentation of insurer types.

Blue Cross Blue Shield Plans

The main players in the state-based, nonprofit health insurer camp are the Blue Cross Blue Shield companies. They are chartered in an individual state but are members of a national organization, the Blue Cross Blue Shield Association (BCBSA). Historically, Blue Cross plans provided hospitalization insurance. Blue Shield plans came later and focused on insurance for doctors' visits. Over time, in most states, these separate plans merged into a single, comprehensive insurer. (For simplicity's sake, I will refer to Blue Cross Blue Shield as *Blue Cross*.)

Blue Cross companies generally had special state charters under which they were classified as nonprofits, although they did pay some taxes and could not receive tax-deductible donations. They were often heavily regulated, with state insurance commissioners carefully evaluating their annual filings and requiring that community ratings of patient illness risk be used in their actuarial data analyses. As a result, Blue Cross's health insurance plans are more likely to work closely with state regulators. In Vermont, for example, Blue Cross participated in that state's health policy reforms much more assiduously than did UnitedHealthcare and Cigna—commercial insurers with a significant Vermont-based market share.

Blue Cross companies are often well positioned to bring about significant policy changes. In many states, more than 50% of commercial health plan beneficiaries are participants in the local Blue Cross plan, reaching as high as 94% in Alabama.[1] If an insurer with this kind of market share makes a shift toward value-based care, health care providers—particularly doctors—are going to have to pay attention and change the patterns in their practices.

Unfortunately, there have been few such initiatives, as many Blue Cross firms are content to play the fee-for-service game they have participated in for 80 years. Given their market share, Blue Cross can expect hospitals and doctors to offer them discounts unavailable to other insurers. They do not have to change in order to retain a reasonable reserve balance, their key measure of financial success. With a substantial share of the provider market, and the leverage it enables, comes lassitude.

Their warm lagoon, however, is slowly draining. The great advantage that most Blue Cross companies have enjoyed is that they each had a monopoly in their own geographic region, usually a state, policed by the Blue Cross Blue Shield Association. In addition, any large employer in that state who wanted to choose Blue Cross as the health insurer for its employees had to use the local Blue Cross plan. That employer could then access other Blue Cross plans in different states—along with their excellent low rates of reimbursement for hospitals and doctors—using what was known as the Blue Card. So, a small provider like Blue Cross Blue Shield of Arkansas was in the driver's seat when supplying a health insurance plan for a huge employer like Walmart, headquartered in Bentonville.

This chummy set of relationships was challenged somewhat in the 1990s as entrepreneurial heads of some Blue Cross organizations, especially in California and Indiana, began to move their companies away from nonprofit status, becoming for-profit entities. They then worked to convince other Blue Cross groups to do the same, forming the conglomerate that became known as Elevance Health, which now encompasses 14 Blue Cross companies. The wave of for-profit conversions came to a halt in the early 2000s, as some state regulators began to balk at Blue Cross plans' efforts to switch to for-profit status, particularly because the regulators did not perceive that for-profit status offered any better health care or new efficiencies.

More change is in the air today, however, as a private antitrust suit has successfully fractured the BCBSA's rules of competition.[2] (Neither the Federal Trade Commission nor the US Department of Justice's antitrust division ever saw a problem with the division of markets that sat at the heart of the BCBSA-policed state monopolies.) The settlement with the antitrust suit's class of employer clients required that the monopoly on bids from Blue Cross insurers be curtailed, and Blue Cross firms were now free to engage in other lines of business. This put substantial pressure on the smaller Blue Cross companies, some of which will now seek mergers with their larger compatriots. Soon after the announcement of the settlement, Blue Cross Blue Shield of Louisiana announced its intent to join Elevance Health, and Blue Cross Blue Shield of Vermont has begun to pursue a merger of its operations with Blue Cross Blue Shield of Michigan.

For now, the market-dominant but relatively pedestrian Blue Cross Blue Shield health insurance plans remain a fixture of many states' health policy structures. Because Blue Cross has such a large market share, giving them an advantage in terms of payments to hospitals and doctors, its health insurance plans have not had to undertake innovative efforts in value-based care. A good example is Blue Cross Blue Shield of Alabama, which provides paltry reimbursements to primary care clinicians (see chapter 2). Most primary care groups have no market leverage in payment negotiations and must accept whatever rates the Alabama Blue Cross team offers. A fee-for-service system can work well for a health insurer if it has enough market power to keep its reimbursements small enough to outstrip provider-induced health care demands.

Some Blue Cross companies have bucked this trend over the past decade, focusing on value-based care to improve overall health care and lower the costs of that care. Perhaps the best example is the accountable care organization strategy pursued by Blue Cross Blue Shield of Massachusetts (BCBSMA). Beginning in 2009, it paid ACOs serving beneficiaries under its HMO plan on the basis of global budgets, with patients assigned to ACOs through their primary care relationships. These budgets entailed up- and downside financial risks based on the patients' utilization of health care. This program, called the Alternative Quality Contract (AQC), also included 64 quality-of-care measures, and BCBSMA would advise ACOs about potential areas for improvement.[3]

The Alternative Quality Contract ought to have had trouble getting traction, given that BCBSMA's market share is not as great as that of some other Blue Cross firms. The AQC program was also largely restricted, at least at the outset, to the subset of beneficiaries that were in a health management organization (HMO) plan, as opposed to the more popular preferred provider organization (PPO) or high-deductible plans. But serial evaluations over the subsequent eight years have shown that these contracts reduced overall health care costs and improved the quality of care.[4] During the initial years of the program, savings were derived from referring patients to lower-cost primary care centers or clinicians. Later, health care utilization reductions led the way—particularly for lab tests, imaging, and the use of emergency departments. As the program matured, its savings began to outstrip its incentive payments.

Today, the AQC program is part of the infrastructure of Blue Cross Blue Shield of Massachusetts and has been bolstered by a new set of initiatives on health equity. It demonstrates that dominant Blue Cross companies could be pursuing broader initiatives in value-based care. Notably, AQC is not a primary care–based program, although many ACO participants undertook strategies that were based in primary care.

Other state Blue Cross firms have been more assiduously focused on primary care. Those in Maryland and Hawaii are the most prominent examples. The Blue Cross Blue Shield insurer in Maryland is CareFirst, which also spills into Washington, DC, and Northern Virginia. Starting in 2008, under the leadership of Chet Burrell, CareFirst began to emphasize the concept of patient-centered medical homes, offering additional payments to PCMH practices. CareFirst did not require external certification, but it did have guidelines based on the typical PCMH parameters—care coordination, complex disease management, behavioral health access, and the like. Primary care practices that joined got an immediate 12% increase in their fee-for-service payments. CareFirst did not use capitation but had a reward structure based on the quality of care and spending outcomes. About 70% of CareFirst's members were eventually distributed among PCMH practices.

An evaluation of Maryland's CareFirst program through 2013 showed that overall health care costs and utilization were reduced for those patients assigned to a PCMH practice.[5] After three years, spending was

2.8% lower in the participating group, much of this coming from reduced inpatient, emergency department, and medication spending. Care coordination and hospital follow-ups seemed to be the key interventions. A subsequent evaluation suggested that CareFirst's PCMH program—which extended well beyond just PCMH status into value-based performance payment—had shifted their traditional trend of an 7.5% annual increase in health care costs to approximately a 3.5% increase over a five-year period.[6] Again, reductions in hospital admissions and emergency department visits appeared to lead the way. CareFirst's overall quality of care and patient satisfaction scores also massively improved.

In 2018, Burrell—who had been the champion for health system change that was led by primary care—retired and was replaced by Brian Pieninck. Pieninck retained CareFirst's primary care medical home model but moved toward an ACO-based strategy, reasoning that 5% to 6% of CareFirst's claims were for primary care, with the rest applied to hospitals and specialty physicians.[7] Under Pieninck, CareFirst believed it needed to get more financial risk into larger health care systems. Eventually, the many primary care groups owned by such systems were absorbed into an ACO scheme that included up- and downside financial risks. About one-quarter, or 1,000, primary care doctors and nurses remained in the PCMH program. Similar to what happened in Massachusetts, CareFirst has come to concentrate on the integrated delivery systems rather than on primary care.

Hawaii's Blue Cross program, known as the Hawaii Medical Services Association, or HMSA, has continued to focus on primary care-based financial risk. After careful consideration through the early 2000s, the HMSA began to work with health services researchers and behavioral economists from the University of Pennsylvania to design a new financial risk program.[8] The result was the Population-based Payments for Primary Care (3PC) program, which had two major features and three subsidiary ones. Its two primary features were a new primary care capitation payment (ranging from $7 to $80 per member per month, depending on risk adjustments) and an incentive payment of up to 40% of the shared financial risk savings. The secondary features, in many ways just as important as the other two, were (1) a quality-of-care bonus system, based on few key performance measures; (2) a penalty on per member, per month payments for failure to show appropriate engagement; and (3) a comprehensive health care dashboard monitoring quality of care and health care utilization. Previously existing PCMH reimbursements were rolled into the capitation payment. The primary care doctors in Hawaii had little choice but to participate in the 3PC program, given the HMSA's market share. Nonetheless, the company had extensive collaborative conversations with these physicians before initiating it.

The same group from the University of Pennsylvania that designed the 3PC program did a follow-up evaluation based on claims data from 2012 to 2016.[9] They focused largely on whether the quality-of-care measures had improved—which they did, slightly but significantly. They also found that the number of visits to primary care clinicians decreased, meaning that doctors no longer believed it necessary to funnel large volumes of patients through their offices to maximize income. Finally, they saw no significant differences in the mean total cost of care. While the HMSA was pleased with improvements in the quality of care, the 3PC program's lack of impact on spending was disappointing.

Capitation proved to be a savior for Hawaii's primary care doctors during the COVID pandemic, when patient visits decreased enormously.[10] Since the pandemic's waning, primary care doctors have begun to complain about the administrative burden posed by the 3PC project. The HMSA, however, is not going back to fee-for-service reimbursements for primary care. The larger practices have adopted new systems, using integrated teams, to manage costs. Their engagement with patients is much better, and their clinicians now have a better work/life balance. In 2023, the HMSA was discussing its next steps with the state's primary care doctors and the University of Pennsylvania team.

For many Blue Cross firms, and smaller insurance companies generally, the theme today is that an incremental approach to value-based care is necessary. A good example outside the Blue Cross universe is the primary care capitation program designed by the Capital District Physicians' Health Plan (CDPHP), a 350,000-member nonprofit health plan in the Albany, New York, area. In the mid-2000s, CDPHP pushed its primary care practices to attain PCMH accreditation. Beginning in 2009, it started a pilot program to pay primary care capitation, based on Arlene Ash and Randall Ellis's model of primary care activity level.[11]

As its pilot program expanded, CDPHP developed a two-part approach: a learning stage, followed by a maturity stage. In the learning stage, primary care practices were paid a per member, per month bonus, which was based on utilization, patient satisfaction, and Healthcare Effectiveness Data and Information Set (HEDIS) quality measures. Once a practice had shown signs of transformation, it moved to primary care capitation for a specified list of codes. A primary care practice could earn up to 40% more for its services under the new approach. The entire two-stage program is known as enhanced primary care (EPC). In 2009–11, a study of the EPC initiative suggested substantial decreases in hospital admissions and emergency department visits, as well as improvements in the quality of care.[12]

The CDPHP has maintained and deepened its EPC program over the last decade. Today, this health insurer asserts that its capitated payments are 50% higher than fee-for-service reimbursements, with the possibility of adding 20% more in quality-of-care incentive payments. At the same time, the EPC program remains profitable for CDPHP, with a positive financial return based on lower health care utilization by patients. Its returns on quality-of-care measures are also excellent.[13] CDPHP has recently instituted programs that emphasize the addition of behavioral health support and substance use disorder treatments to primary care practices, as well as care transitions. The next step is to begin to align specialists who had stayed in a fee-for-service payment system but could now earn quality-of-care bonuses on patients referred to them. After meeting quality-of-care thresholds, specialty practices (starting with cardiology and nephrology) can participate in upside savings on utilization.[14]

The CDPHP has avidly shared information about its experience with primary care capitation, and other insurers have taken notice. Blue

Cross Blue Shield of Rhode Island (BCBSRI) had undertaken an extensive ACO-based financial risk program with the state's large health care systems, which had gone well.[15] After hearing a presentation by Eileen Wood (the senior vice president at CDPHP who has quarterbacked a number of their innovations over the years), however, BCBSRI decided to try a primary care capitation scheme using the CDPHP model.

Like the HMSA in Hawaii, BCBSRI was interested in reducing the number of unnecessary primary care visits that were used to increase the quantity of reimbursements paid under an RVU-based system. Christopher Bush, BCBSRI's senior vice president of network management, pointed out that Rhode Island is among the top three states in the country in terms of the number of its primary care clinicians per capita, but access in the state is not good (see chapter 4). He attributes this lack of access to the unnecessary churn of patients caused by a fee-for-service system. Given the development work that the BCBSRI has funded as part of the primary care payment requirements in Rhode Island, Bush's team believed that primary care practices would be ready for some form of capitation. BCBSRI is proceeding with this program.

Other State-Based Private Insurers: Rocky Mountain Health Plan in the Roaring Fork River Valley

After conversations with health insurers across the country, in both Blue Cross companies and other nonprofit insurers, I have a growing sense that slow changes are occurring in American health care, spurred by experiments with ACO programs for integrated delivery systems as well as primary care payment reforms, starting with quality-of-care measures and moving toward capitation. These developments should be empowering for primary care practices, and they are certainly in concert with the efforts that states are undertaking. Slowly, the foundation for health care payments, and the expectations for overall care, are changing.

In my research, two other state-based plans best illustrated this for me, but neither are Blue Cross Blue Shield companies. Nor are they similar. One is Rocky Mountain Health Plan in Colorado, which was a nonprofit firm but is now owned by UnitedHealthcare. The other is Kaiser Permanente, which is certainly not small and not entirely state based. Both show what changes can be wrought by private insurers. And both have undertaken their care management strategies with a high degree of commitment to patient welfare.

Rocky Mountain Health Plan is located on the Western Slope of Colorado, the part of the state that is west of the Continental Divide. The Western Slope is heterogeneous ecologically and politically. There are high mountains, meadows, and great forests, as well as a lot of territory consisting of desolate buttes. Residents in its ski areas tend to be politically blue and wealthy, but its overall population is low income and politically red. Lauren Boebert, one of the more conservative members of the US House of Representatives, hails from the small town of Silt. Many of the poorest inhabitants in this part of the state did not vote for either her or her opponent, as they are undocumented immigrants working in agriculture or servicing the ski areas.

Grand Junction, the main town in the Western Slope, had its day in health policy circles. Atul Gawande, following up on his extraordinarily influential article in the *New Yorker* on McAllen, Texas, and its high per capita cost of health care, found that per capita costs were low in Grand Junction. He attributed this to the operation of an independent practice association (IPA) that took its patients' utilization of health care seriously and worked closely with the two Grand Junction hospitals. After Gawande portrayed Grand Junction as the opposite of McAllen, President Barack Obama visited this Colorado city and commended the leaders. Although remembered fondly by some of the old-timers, Mesa City IPA has now evaporated and per capita costs in Grand Junction have risen, albeit more slowly than national averages.

Today, the entity at the center of health care reform in Colorado is the Rocky Mountain Health Plan, emphasizing value-based care and the role of primary care. In at least two ways, it is a strange health care leader. Rocky Mountain Health Plan (or Rocky, as it is called by everyone locally) has always been Western Slope based and Medicaid focused. The latter is its initial oddity in that Medicaid in Colorado has historically been a fee-for-service operation, rather than a managed care one, based largely on the 1990s crisis in managed care litigation. But Rocky Mountain's use of managed care programs predated this crisis, and it was allowed to continue in a managed format. Rocky Mountain also had a role in Colorado's individual and group health insurance markets and still offers a Medicare Advantage plan. In addition, Rocky Mountain's work with the Grand Junction–based Mesa County IPA was part of Gawande's explanation for the low health care costs in western Colorado.

The second odd aspect of Rocky Mountain's health care leadership role derives from a financial crisis, when the company got in over its head on the exchange markets created by the 2010 Affordable Care Act (ACA). The company suffered massive losses, and its reserves were threatened to such an extent that the state of Colorado was ready to intervene. This prompted its "fire sale" to UnitedHealthcare for $50 million in 2016. Rocky Mountain Health Plan's leaders have said that UnitedHealthcare has tended to leave strategy and focus up to Rocky Mountain's team, but it is nonetheless the case that what was once and still is the chief instigator of improved health care in the Western Slope is now part of what is arguably the largest conglomerate in health care—the UnitedHealth Group.

Nonetheless, Rocky Mountain Health Plan's reputation is sustained. My travels took me through two regions of the Western Slope. First, I went along the Colorado River, taking I-70 through Rifle and up to Glenwood Springs, and then followed the Roaring Fork River Valley to Aspen. Most of the traffic in the morning was headed toward Aspen, which sucks up a great deal of low-cost labor from the towns downriver. As the altitude rose, so did the property values. The second region was the greater Grand Junction area, which serves as the hub for most of the Western Slope's regional efforts and has its own health care ecosystem.

My chief guide in Roaring Fork Valley was Dr. Gary Knaus, from Carbondale, Colorado. I had a chance to speak with him on the telephone before arriving in Colorado and then met him at a brew pub just off what is known as the "speedway" from Aspen to Glenwood Springs.[16] He has seen things change quite a bit. He was born in 1949 and grew up in Glenwood Springs, noting that there was not really any skiing at Aspen until the early 1960s. The Roaring Fork Valley was originally dominated by coal mining and ranching. The coal mines have all closed, but some ranching still takes place. The predominant industry today, however, is tourism—to be more accurate, "feeding Aspen."

Knaus has practiced in Carbondale for the past 43 years. By his own accounting, he knows just about everyone in town. Knaus was in the vanguard of family medicine physicians trained to take on everything they could handle in their primary care practices. In addition, he and his longtime partner were fundamentally community based. Their patient panel *was* their community. They knew where people lived and could visit them at home. They also had a good handle years ago on social determinants of health (SDOH). The combination of an exciting medical practice and intimacy with the community was obviously gratifying for him. Knaus reminded me of the way that George Eliot has Dr. Tertius Lydgate describe himself in *Middlemarch*: "I should never have been so happy in any profession that did not call forth the highest intellectual strain, and yet keep me in good warm contact with my neighbors."[17]

By his reckoning, Knaus was the ideas guy and his partner the detail person when they started their family medicine practice in 1975. They (especially Knaus) wanted to try every innovation available. They installed an EMR system in 1996, years ahead of many other practices. They began population health management in the late 1990s. They became a patient-centered medical home certified by the National Committee for Quality Assurance. As the Center for Medicare and Medicaid Innovation rolled out the Comprehensive Primary Care Plus program (CPC+), they enrolled. To them, population health management seemed like the correct direction for primary care, as well as the most humane approach. The practice used CPC+ funds to pay for care coordinators and a pharmacist, and the latter found a couple of great interventions every day. They also integrated a social worker into their practice. They now have a team meeting every morning to discuss the day's patient schedule, and to check notes with one another. Knaus believes that creating a feeling of community in their medical practice promotes a sense of care for the larger community.

Through all of this, their family medicine practice got great support from Rocky Mountain Health Plan, which pushed CPC+ and made funding available to help prepare the practice to begin working on population health management. This was crucial, especially for their Medicaid population. Knaus and his partners eventually sold the practice in 2012 to the local hospital in Glenwood Springs (Valley View Hospital). Since that time, the 12 clinicians in Knaus's practice—eight doctors, two nurse practitioners, and two physician associates—have worked closely with the local integrated system, which includes Valley View Hospital and some of the primary care practices in the area. He has now retired from patient care but is still busy as the medical director of a skilled nursing facility in Carbondale.

Knaus maintained that the Valley View Hospital has continued to invest in population health management, spurred somewhat by the lead from Rocky Mountain. He noted, however, that the hospital does pay its primary care clinicians a salary, with an RVU-based incentive, which Knaus does not like. He would prefer getting rid of any focus on RVUs.

Valley View Hospital has not been the leader in population health management in this locale. That role is played by Rocky Mountain. Knaus's view was that the "Rocky Mountain Health Plan taught us all we know about advanced primary care." He is a great admirer of Patrick Gordon, the CEO of Rocky Mountain, whom Knaus views as a true visionary. The Carbondale family medicine practice now participates in Rocky Mountain Health Plan's Medicaid contract, where they take on up- and downside financial risks, although this contract does not yet involve primary care capitation. The clinicians in Carbondale screen patients with regard to SDOH, and under the Rocky Mountain plan, they can get funds for food vouchers and housing. They also participate in a local community health plan, the Valley Health Alliance, which is organized by the large employers in the county, including the ski areas and the local municipalities' employees, as well as Valley View

Hospital's employees. This is another primary care innovation in the Roaring Fork Valley.

Up in Aspen, Dave Ressler gave me background information about the hospital scene in the Western Slope, as well as specifics on the Valley Health Alliance, the innovative effort to deliver value-based care to local employers.[18] To set the table, Ressler explained that there are 30 hospitals in the Western Healthcare Alliance, most of them small, with less than 25 beds. An entity called the Western ACO helps all these hospitals participate in ACO opportunities. The 300-bed hospital in Grand Junction, St. Mary's, plays a big role. Until 2022, this hospital was owned by the Sisters of Charity. St. Mary's Hospital is now owned by Intermountain Health, and everyone expects changes to occur. But the Valley Health Alliance is distinguished from Western Healthcare—the former is much smaller and based in the Roaring Fork and Upper Colorado River Valleys.

Ressler is the CEO of Aspen Valley Hospital, where he has worked for much of the past 20 years. Aspen Valley is a district hospital, which means that part of their revenue (about 4% of the budget) is from local taxes. Aspen Valley is also a critical access hospital, which means that Medicare payments are received on a cost basis. Both of these are important for the finances of the hospital, but the big funding source in Aspen is philanthropy.

None of these sources of additional funds kept the cost of care under control. Nearly 85% of the care they provide is outpatient. Historically, the hospital and its outpatient medical practices were fee-for-service driven. Over time, the costs of care mounted to a crisis point.

About 15 years ago, Aspen County's head administrator came to Ressler and said, "We cannot afford health insurance," including care at Aspen Valley Hospital. The health care costs were too high, too many procedures were being performed, and health insurance premiums were out of control. Ressler heard the administrator's challenge: "If I need to, I will start to hire my own doctors and get it done." A coalition of the county's employees, as well as those from the school districts, the city, and the major ski area companies, were all on the same page.

Ressler took on this challenge. He encouraged population health management and integration, eventually hiring his own primary care and specialists who would work closely with the primary care clinicians on clinical guidelines. He also established wellness programs with the county's various employers. But he felt as though he could not do this by just depending on support from Aspen. (Everyone else in health care in the Roaring Fork Valley is envious of Aspen, given its tax base and fundraising prospects.)

So, Aspen Valley Hospital reached out to the other hospitals in the Roaring Fork Valley, since the towns in which these hospitals were located were the places where most of Aspen's workforce lived. Eventually, the Aspen team, Valley View Hospital in Glenwood Springs and Grand River Health in Rifle, along with the Mountain Family Health Centers (a large FQHC), formed the Valley Health Alliance and agreed to work with the region's large employers on population health management. Ressler was disappointed that the Valley Health Alliance's other hospitals have not brought the big employers in their towns on board yet, but all of these hospitals support the goal of investing in more support for primary care to improve population health management for their patients.

At this point, along came Patrick Gordon and Rocky Mountain Health Plan. Gordon was trying to reestablish an exchange plan under the ACA, so he collaborated with the Valley Health Alliance to get better rates and is now able to offer a lower premium health care plan on the exchange. Employers in this part of Colorado, even though they are self-insured, see this as a big win for their independent contractors, who need a reasonably priced exchange plan. Rocky Mountain Health Plan's expertise in Medicaid care management is spilling over into the Valley Health Alliance primary care practices participating in the exchange plan, such as Knaus's former practice in Carbondale. As a result of these primary care offices' focus on population health management, employers are seeing some moderation in their health care cost increases, so they are happy. The collaboration within the Valley Health Alliance and the presence of Rocky Mountain at each intersection are bearing fruit.

Ressler is not declaring victory. He is not sure he has the data to show that these innovations are making a difference. But he has a path to get this information—endorsing radical transparency. He has opened all his own financial data to a citizens' group put together by the area's big employers. They are going over the fiscal dynamics of the hospital, including such things as the pay levels for its administrators and the medical staff. Ressler thinks that there must be trust on all sides, and transparency is one way to accomplish that. Premiums and claims information from the employers and their insurers will add another piece to the puzzle.

Mountain Family Health Centers is the critical health care entity for towns "down valley," where the cost of living is lower and where more low-income people can afford to live. Mountain Family does participate in the Valley Health Alliance, but its focus is on Medicaid and the uninsured. Ross Brooks was the CEO of Mountain Family, a federally qualified health center in western Colorado.[19] (Brooks retired after I visited, in mid-2023.) Brooks related that they are the health care home to 24,000 patients in a three-county service area. There are ten different locations for Mountain Family's primary care clinicians: the five clinics that integrate behavioral health and primary care, and five others that are school-based sites. They have a total of 22 primary care clinicians and 8 dentists, as well as 12 behavioral health specialists.

All of this represents tremendous growth for Mountain Family Health Centers. In 2010, they only had approximately 9,000 patients. The Affordable Care Act's expansion of Medicaid was a big part of their overall growth, but the ACA also provided them with more tools to help the uninsured and do more outreach, a story repeated across the country in every FQHC I visited.

The headquarters for Mountain Family is in Glenwood Springs, but it has a catchment area from the Utah border to the Continental Divide—a sector that encompasses both tremendous wealth and an inordinate amount of poverty. Most of their programs are based on Medicaid, but only 33% of their patient population has Medicaid insurance, while 40% are uninsured. Commercial health insurance covers about 15% of their patients, with the rest of them on Medicare or the Medicaid-related Children's Health Insurance Program.

The uninsured are a vast mix of people, ranging from those who have sufficient income but simply choose not to participate in an exchange plan to impoverished, undocumented Central Americans. Like most FQHCs, Mountain Family's health care support for these individuals is cobbled together with monies from federal outlays, progressive partnerships, and a reasonable amount of grant writing. As I toured the facility one hot September day, the team proudly showed me their new pharmacy. The pharmacist was labeling several vials of Ozempic, a prescription drug for diabetes. Ozempic, which comes in injectors, normally costs about $1,000 a month, but the health center, through the federal 340B drug-pricing program, could provide it to individuals without health insurance for between $2 and $7. This was a remarkable example of the complexity of the American health care system, combining the role of HRSA's 340B program for the poor, and some entrepreneurial spirit at this FQHC.

Art Fernandez, Mountain Family's chief operating officer, joined us on the tour. He has been with Mountain Family for 15 years, and Ross Brooks, for 10. For them, Mountain Family's story feels like a Dow Jones stock market average: it is up overall, but there's a lot of variation. COVID retarded their progress for quite a while. They had to use parking lots and a drive-thru system in caring for patients. More importantly, COVID made it difficult for them to recruit clinicians, and they are only slowly recovering from the shortfall.

The worsening economic conditions of the post-COVID era have also hit Mountain Family hard. They have recently increased their entry-level pay for medical assistants to $20 an hour. (In comparison, the local fast-food chains are now offering $18 an hour.) They are also having a great deal of difficulty filling spots for nurses and case managers. All this slows the progress toward clinical support for care management and value-based care.

The starting salary for Mountain Family's primary care physicians is around $215,000, which is about $30,000 below the median in the Western Slope area. They do, however, have access to clinicians from the Colorado Health Services Corps and the National Health Services Corps. These programs enable the FQHC to offer debt repayment for individuals who join them right out of residency training, which has proven to be an important recruiting perk. But recruiting is still slow for dentists and dental hygienists. So, like other FQHCs I visited, Mountain Family is now reaching out to their local junior college to begin a dental hygienist training program.

The biggest problem for Mountain Family Health Centers is the cost of living for this region of Colorado. As one goes northeast from Grand Junction to Rifle, and then to Glenwood Springs, the cost of living increases dramatically. This makes it difficult to recruit clinicians in their up-valley health care sites, so they rely on employees who must drive relatively long distances to get to work.

Brooks got out of college and started working for the Advisory Board (a health care consulting and research company) in Washington, DC. He decided he didn't like trying to make money for hospitals and pharmaceutical firms and eventually got hooked up with the Colorado Community Health Network, the primary care association for Colorado. Brooks soon discovered that he wanted to work at an FQHC, and he eventually joined Mountain Family Health Centers.

As we had lunch in Rifle (just across the street from where Representative Lauren Boebert's gun-themed Shooters Grill restaurant once was), Brooks reflected on the challenges his health centers face. The most prominent is health insurance for those who do not qualify for Medicaid. While Colorado itself is progressive politically, the state has found it difficult to develop a low-cost ACA exchange market. The hospitals are so expensive that there is no way to get around charging high rates in the state's exchange plans. Right now, Rocky Mountain Health Plan and Anthem Blue Cross Blue Shield are the major players in the exchange market. Rocky Mountain's return to this market has helped, but the average health insurance premium for an exchange plan has until recently been as high as $750 per month, with a $7,500 deductible. Brooks hopes that, locally, Rocky Mountain's emphasis on care management will help create a lower-cost product. The state's health insurance problems cut close to home for Brooks. His wife and Art

Fernandez's wife were uninsured for a period of five years. The clinic could not offer a family health care plan because the exchange's product was too expensive. Both women were healthy, so they gambled on going without health insurance.

The second big challenge is that Mountain Family's relationships with local hospitals are somewhat fraught. Aspen Valley Hospital subsidizes the uninsured for Mountain Family's clinic in Basalt, Colorado. This clinic serves the people in Pitkin and Eagle Counties, the Aspen area. So, the hospital pays a per member, per month payment for uninsured patients. Valley View Hospital in Glenwood Springs and Grand River Hospital in Rifle, however, are not willing to provide support for the uninsured seen by Mountain Family, although there is some support for rent for Mountain Family's Rifle and Glenwood Spring's clinics. Brooks works carefully and diligently with the area hospitals' presidents to increase this kind of support.

Each of these hospitals is also building its own primary care base, which reduces Mountain Family's patient population. The FQHC's primary care doctors and the local primary care physicians do work together in a collegial fashion, however. There are few independent private practice primary care clinicians left.

The third major issue is value-based care through Medicaid. Brooks, being a former policy person, provided some further background on Colorado's Medicaid program, Rocky Mountain Health Plan's role, and support for primary care. Colorado had a real backlash against managed care in the 1990s, and its Medicaid program became almost completely a fee-for-service system. The state was divided into regions, one of them being the Western Slope. Rocky Mountain Health Plan, as the major payer in this part of the state, pushed forward with value-based, managed care, with the state's approval.

It began by making a small primary care coordination payment to Medicaid's health care providers. The next step was a true managed care pilot program known as Medicaid PRIME (Payment Reform in Medicaid Expansion). It entailed true primary care capitation, paid at between $58 and $63 per member per month. There are no fee-for-service reimbursements in this program, and all of Colorado's FQHCs would like to completely transfer their Medicaid patients to the PRIME program, according to Brooks. It allows gainsharing, with an FQHC getting a share of any leftover funds. Rocky Mountain has been a great partner for Mountain Family Health Centers with this program. For the present, however, it applies only to adults and the disabled, and it is only administered in two of the three counties served by Mountain Family. Expansion plans are on the table for the mid-2020s.

In regions where PRIME does not exist, Mountain Family can undertake care coordination and case management with funds that are made available by Rocky Mountain Health Plan. The current tragedy is that they have not been able to recruit clinicians into these programs. They also have funding from Rocky Mountain for a program referred to as Social Health Advocates, which bridges the gap for patients with social determinants of health issues. But again, the health center has been having a difficult time finding trained personnel to work in this program.

Rocky Mountain Health Plan is clearly highly valued by the team at Mountain Family. The Rocky Mountain team made the dollars available for behavioral health support and encouraged its integration into primary care. They have also strongly championed care coordination, as well as community hospital integration with FQHCs. Mountain Family's only concern is Rocky Mountain's purchase by the UnitedHealth Group, over five years ago. Thus far, the ethos at Rocky Mountain has persisted. Nonetheless, Brooks was worried because there seemed to be some turnover of personnel at Rocky Mountain, so he tries to follow the situation closely.

The leaders at Mountain Family support the evolution from a fee-for-service system to managed care. This makes sense, given their patient population. As a result, Mountain Family is building a delivery model where the workflow moves to managed patient panels, nurses are integrated into a team of clinicians, and telephone outreach increases. The doctors and NPs themselves, however, are only slowly making that shift. The management team is trying to get the physical plants reconfigured to support team-based primary care. They've managed to do so in Rifle, but in Glenwood Springs the clinicians are still siloed, and behavioral health is located in another part of the building.

Brooks understands that digital infrastructure is also important. Mountain Family's clinicians use a NextGen medical record system, which he characterizes as "satisfactory." For example, the EMR uses a scoring system that enables the primary care clinicians to identify patients that might need help addressing social determinants of health. Rocky Mountain has provided financial support for this effort, but it has been difficult to operationalize because Mountain Family does not have a coordinator for SDOH services. Still, some of the aspects of the strategy are coming together. Their local health information exchange, the Quality Health Network (QHN), has developed an inventory of social support agencies, called the Community Resource Network. The Mountain Family team anticipates that this information can eventually be integrated into their electronic medical records.

The clinics usually have one doctor paired with either two nurse practitioners or two physician assistants. For now, Mountain Family's management team believes that this ratio is appropriate, although, like everywhere else, there are questions about exactly *how many* physicians they need to have as part of the team. They also try to have one nurse for every two physicians or nurse practitioners. The critical initiative today is to get all their patients empaneled with a team, and to increase the number of their visits to that team.

Integrating primary care with behavioral health has been a consistent goal for Rocky Mountain, and the Mountain Family Health Center has responded. Its managers would like to reach a goal of 700 patients per behavioral health expert. They use all sorts of clinicians for behavioral health, including family counselors and licensed social workers. They can offer a salary of about $70,000 a year to people in those positions, while a hospital can pay around $90,000 per year. Nonetheless, Mountain Family is making strides toward value-based care, aided and abetted by Rocky Mountain Health Plan.

How does the view of their operation by Mountain Family's management compare with that of the clinicians seeing the patients? Maddie Nieslanik, a physician associate at the clinic in Rifle, seems to represent what Mountain Family and Rocky Mountain are trying to attain.[20] She grew up locally (in Carbondale), wanted to take care of patients, and eventually enrolled in the Physician Assistant Program at Colorado Mesa University in Grand Junction. During her training, she rotated through Mountain Family, loved it, and got a full-time job there. "This is exactly what I wanted to do," she said, adding that the other clinicians in the practice have been helpful. Every day that she spends with patients, Nieslanik realizes the heavy burden of their health care costs. She must make decisions to help people avoid the emergency department or visits to specialists. As in many FQHCs, health care for the uninsured highlights the need to provide parsimonious care—sometimes, unfortunately, to a substantial degree. For example, Nieslanik recently saw a patient with a wrist fracture. *UpToDate*, the online medical textbook, was not much help, so she consulted her peers and placed a splint design that she found online. It worked out well for the patient.

Nieslanik is expected to see a set volume of patients, although this is not explicitly tied to her compensation. She was seeing two patients per hour, but she would have to move up to three eventually. She charted patients during her lunch hour and from 5:00 to 6:00 p.m., and got her EMR notes done before going home, which usually made for a 10-hour workday. She could rely on nursing support and case management services, but most of her focus was on treating patients with behavioral health problems, with the help of a behavioral health clinician colleague. This relationship is no doubt part of the payoff from Rocky Mountain Health Plan's support for the integration of behavioral health and primary care.[21]

Since joining the practice, Nieslanik has encountered many challenging medical conditions. Her clinical acumen impressed me, as did her interest in talking about her cases. For example, she identified a case of endocarditis, an infection of the heart valves that can be difficult to diagnose. When this individual was in the hospital earlier in the week, the hospital staff had failed to pick up on a positive result in the patient's blood culture, indicating an infection. When seen by Nieslanik during a posthospitalization clinic visit, the patient looked "sick," and the QHN allowed her to find the blood culture report. Subsequent hospitalization confirmed the infection. Another of her patients had a prolonged headache, so Nieslanik scheduled follow-up soon after the initial visit. When this person developed double vision, she ordered further testing, which revealed that the blood flow through an artery in the central part of the patient's retina was blocked.

Nieslanik's clinical work was clearly gratifying to her. So was the environment in the practice. She was diligent with regard to quality-of-care items, such as hemoglobin A1c tests to measure blood sugar, hypertension follow-ups, and Pap smears. But she never felt as though she was alone. The nurses who do follow-up visits and outreach telephone calls on issues like nutritional education and anticoagulation therapy are integrated into the primary care practice. There is a great sense of community—of a genuine team working together. Her experience put Brooks's reservations about Mountain Family's progress toward value-based care into perspective. Brooks, as its CEO, was appropriately focused on where Mountain Family could do better, but a lot of things were going well.

The Mountain Family primary care practice in Glenwood Springs is up the valley from Rifle. Anneliese Heckert and Matt Percy, Mountain Family Health Centers' co-chief medical officers, were more circumspect about their care model, perhaps a little jaded after having spent eight years at this clinic.[22] Heckert hailed from Delaware, went to osteopathic school in Philadelphia, and then trained in Pueblo, Colorado. Percy grew up in Cortez, Colorado. His parents both practiced medicine for years on the Navajo reservation, and he loved rural health care. He went to Stanford University, then to the University of Colorado for medical school, and trained in family medicine at the University of Utah.

In addition to these two physicians, there are three other doctors in the Glenwood Springs practice, plus an adult nurse practitioner, a pediatric nurse practitioner, and a physician assistant. Nursing support, with a focus on diabetes and hypertension, is integrated into the team. Like the rest of Mountain Family, this clinic suffers from hiring difficulties. Their case manager works remotely, and they have not been able to hire a coordinator to oversee SDOH, even though they have funds for this position.

The grind of seeing 20 patients a day, four days a week, is difficult. Heckert and Henry have both downsized to two sessions of patient visits a week, as their administrative duties take up another two days per week. They do manage to get their charting done on the days when they see patients, but it is not easy. These logistical problems pale in comparison with the stress related to their patients' poverty, however. While their clinic sits in the shadow of Valley View Hospital in Glenwood Springs's sharp-walled canyon, that hospital has its own primary care practice. These two practices are collegial, but Mountain Family's Glenwood Springs clinic, with 40% of its patients being uninsured, is unique. The Mountain Family doctors must work hard to keep people away from medical imaging tests, as well as out of specialists' offices, the emergency department, and the hospital. They do a lot of *curbsiding*—informal consultations—and their specialist colleagues are accommodating.

This parsimonious health care approach is not something Heckert and Percy were trained for; no one really is. Sometimes their shared decision-making in trying to keep the entirety of their patients' care within the clinic is just too risky, so Heckert and Henry must tell them that there is no other choice but to opt for expensive medical care. These two doctors hope—and lobby—for charity care from the hospital, but it is not always available. (In Glenwood Springs, Ross Brooks is unable to get Valley View Hospital to support any capitated payment for the uninsured, which he has been able to do in Aspen.)

The dissatisfaction I picked up on is based on resources. There is too much patient volume, and health care for the uninsured is spotty. At times, it sounds as though the situation is frankly demoralizing. COVID did not help, as it fostered staff absences and closed clinics.

Percy had joined the Glenwood Springs practice with great altruism, and that attitude persists. But it was wearying to have to keep such a close eye on costs, foregoing radiology, specialty care, and certain types of pharmacy products, although their 340B drug-pricing contract has helped with the latter. More pointedly, Henry thought COVID decreased people's trust in the medical profession, and this was spilling over to other forms of care, such as pediatric vaccinations. He found the vaccine situation to be especially disheartening.

The Glenwood Springs clinic has been able to recruit clinicians, with financial help from the National and Colorado Health Services Corps programs. But there is still a cost-of-living problem, which is much worse as one gets closer to Aspen. Any new clinician the clinic hires must speak Spanish and be mission driven—and, just as importantly, be able to deal with a significant lack of resources. For example, Heckert and Henry might ask a prospective employee, "What do you do with a new patient whose blood sugar level and hemoglobin A1c test are elevated?" If the answer is "consult an endocrinologist," then that person is looking for a job in the wrong place.

As co-chief medical officers, Heckert and Percy were not convinced that the population health management aspects of their practice were having much of an impact. They had integrated behavioral health into the clinic's primary care agenda, and that worked well. But the clinic does not have care coordinators and SDOH assistants. Heckert and Henry would like to embrace the care management paradigm with patient panels, but Mountain Family's volume expectations still hang over them. EMRs do allow the clinicians to stratify some of the patients' health risks, but these electronic records are not yet integrated with the clinic's SDOH inventory. The Glenwood Springs clinic was making progress, especially with patients in Rocky Mountain's Medicaid PRIME program, but COVID killed their hiring ability, so they have backed off from these goals for now.

Percy saw the clinic's future as being guardedly better—they will get better data and develop managed care panels. Heckert thought the clinic needed to be on a single-payer system, or there will continue to be fragmentation. She saw their team as rebels, railing against private primary care practices.

Rocky Mountain Health Plan: Grand Junction

Moving back down the valley to Grand Junction, the gravitational tug of Aspen plays a much smaller role, but Rocky Mountain Health Plan still casts an outsized shadow. The ecosystem of doctors and hospitals in Grand Junction is evolving. Historically, the Mesa County Independent Practice Association—celebrated by Gawande and Obama, among others—played an important role. But this IPA's influence has largely faded, which is not surprising. Health care's ecology goes through phases, with new developments succeeding institutions that have run their course. The main players are still present but have grown new adjacent structures. St. Mary's is the big hospital in Grand Junction. With 346 beds, it is the largest hospital between Salt Lake City and Denver. Family Health West is a critical access hospital in Fruita, just 10 miles west of Grand Junction.

Primary care has become perhaps more concentrated in Grand Junction than was the case when Mesa City had its heyday. St. Mary's Hospital employs the doctors at one of the primary care practices, and there is one large independent practice, Primary Care Partners, that provides the lion's share of the primary care and is now working closely with Aledade (see chapter 7). The town's specialists are largely employed by St. Mary's. Today, Monument Health provides Grand Junction's value-based organizing architecture.

Monument Health is what is known as a clinically integrated network, not dissimilar to Catalyst Health in Dallas. The CIN concept was originally developed to consolidate health care insurance contracting, but it now provides a structure for legally separate entities to manage care effectively. Monument Health is a for-profit limited liability corporation, originally capitalized by St. Mary's Hospital (45%), Primary Care Partners (10%), and Rocky Mountain Health Plan (45%). Now Rocky Mountain has backed out. Monument Health contracts on behalf of its members with many of the local health insurers. It also contracts directly with local employers, supplemented by a third-party administrator.

Ashley Thurow is the thoughtful leader of Monument Health, a relatively recent arrival from the health policy community in Denver.[23] She patiently explained the intricacies of the Grand Junction health care scene. The purpose of Monument Health is to improve the quality of care and reduce costs by promoting value-based arrangements between hospitals and doctors. Her team contracts with insurers (and employers) to produce shared savings for its member organizations, utilizing financial incentives at the practice level and providing system-wide care coordination and case management. Monument Health also participates in the Medicare Shared Savings Program. Thurow anticipated moving to full capitation, starting with Rocky Mountain Health Plan's Medicaid program. She has the capability to do so, as Monument Health encompasses 260 primary care doctors and hundreds of specialists.

Thurow's crucial success factors included oversight for specialist referrals (Monument Health has a hotline for this), case management, a careful weighing of the need for hospital admissions, guaranteed primary care clinician access, a wellness program (especially important for employers), and patient empanelment in a primary care medical home. The original—and primary—mover for Monument Health was Rocky Mountain Health Plan. And today, Monument Health's most important contract is with Rocky Mountain's Medicaid plan, which has 41,000 medical beneficiaries and 35,000 behavioral health ones. Rocky's exchange market product is also beginning to thrive.

It is an impressive array of services, and a creative concept in a relatively small town, undergirded by the influence of a farsighted health insurer. And Monument Health is efficient in terms of its staff. There were only 10 employees when Thurow and I met in September 2022.

Monument Health, and the health care providers in Grand Junction generally, are well served by the Quality Health Network. The QHN is a health information exchange (HIE). HIEs are typically local entities intended to consolidate information from health insurers' claims and hospital medical records, so anyone taking care of a patient can get up-to-date health information on them. (The Mountain Family clinicians were following their hospitalized patients using the QHN.) Data can also be analyzed to track various care interventions and assess which ones are working.

More than a decade ago, HIEs were seen as a key development in American health care, but that is no longer the case. In many metropolitan areas, HIEs grew but did not thrive. Over the course of the past

15 years, many clinicians became integrated into their integrated delivery system's own data systems, and they did not see the need for an external information source. For example, Epic's EMRs offered information from all its locations in a program called Care Everywhere, obviating the need for an HIE. In some broad but relatively isolated geographical areas, however, HIEs have persisted. The Western Slope fits that description.

For an HIE to be successful, stakeholders must commit to this system. In the case of Grand Junction (and the Western Slope), its initial members were St. Mary's Hospital, the Mesa City IPA, and Rocky Mountain Health Plan. Now the HIE encompasses 100% of the area's hospitals and 1,800 medical practices. Marc Lassaux was the long-term chief technical officer, and he is now Quality Health Network's CEO.[24] He effusively acknowledged the support of Patrick Gordon and Rocky Mountain, who recognized the need for an HIE backbone through the QHN.

Today, the QHN covers the entire western half of Colorado. Lassaux gets 28% of Monument Health's funding from its affiliated hospitals, 16% from ambulatory primary care practices, and 56% from health care insurers and the state. Medicaid and eHealth innovation dollars lead the way in terms of the state's share. Monument Health has 29 staff members and a budget of $5.9 million, receiving data downloads from nearly 30 different sets of electronic medical records and 10 health insurers. Bringing data into the QHN is relatively easy, but Lassaux needs help from the different EMR systems (and their clients) to get this information back into the original EMRs—and the EMR systems vary a good deal in their capacity to do so.

There are two major groups of users for this data. One is the clinicians, who can track the health care their patients receive across specialty practices and in hospital. The QHN is successful at such tracking, mostly because its key customers are the doctors, care coordinators, and hospital discharge coordinators in the network. The other major group is the insurers interested in utilization data, especially Rocky Mountain, which tracks their Medicaid members' use and the coordination of their care. Rocky Mountain and Humana also use QHN data to calculate HEDIS results. Right now, QHN's new initiative is gathering SDOH data and building an inventory of potential interventions. Together, Monument Health and the QHN provide a strong framework for managing care in the Western Slope. Thurow shared in the summer of 2024 that they are making more progress on value-based care, weathering some headwinds that have come with the Medicaid redeterminations.

To get some sense of how all this has helped or changed primary care practices on the ground in Grand Junction, I talked to Dr. Gregory Reicks, who has been in practice for over 30 years.[25] I met him at the spanking-new facility SCL Health (a Sisters of Charity organization) built down the street from St. Mary's Hospital. Reicks is a relative newcomer to SCL Health, but he is a seasoned player in Grand Junction's health care arena.

Reicks trained in family medicine at the University of Colorado and came back to Grand Junction in 1989. He bought into a primary care practice when another doctor retired and had a single long-term partner. Back then, Grand Junction's physicians were all in private practice, and as was the fashion in the 1990s, they formed an independent practice association—in this instance, the Mesa County IPA. It included almost all the town's primary care physicians and its specialists, providing a negotiating platform with health insurers. The IPA followed the typical 1990s fiscal model: payment withholding (based on reimbursements), reconciliation (based on assigned budgets), and then bonuses. This IPA took its role seriously. It examined data, used the best specialists, and undertook care management.

Reicks was the president of the Mesa City IPA. He and his team worked closely with Rocky Mountain Health Plan on all aspects of the business, and Rocky Mountain provided resources for care management. The IPA did not negotiate with the hospital, as the health insurers did that. Mesa City performed well with regard to their commercial health insurance contracts (there was no Medicare financial risk-taking back then). The IPA had no idea that it was performing well on a national basis, so the notoriety stemming from Gawande's *New Yorker* article and President Obama's visit took them by complete surprise.

As Reicks put it, the game was always about fee-for-service reimbursements, and the IPA's doctors eventually found that they could increase the monies they received if they joined St. Mary's Hospital, as it was able to negotiate better health insurance contracts (higher fees) for its doctors. The Mesa City IPA slowly dissipated and finally was terminated in 2021. As a result, health care utilization and its costs most likely increased in Grand Junction.

SCL Health, which had long owned St. Mary's Hospital, has also long dabbled in primary care. They entered the primary care field during the 1990s, then backed out, and now have returned during the past five years. Reicks's partner retired a year ago, and he could find no one else interested in joining his private practice, so he finally sold it to SCL and became part of its cadre of physicians. Now SCL has four doctors and four advanced practice nurses in its Grand Junction location.

The way Reicks saw it, St. Mary's Hospital and SCL Health were now working with Rocky Mountain on care management. Together, they supported the QHN. They also built Monument Health to replace the Mesa City IPA. Five to eight years ago, none of Grand Junction's eligible residents were in a Medicare Advantage plan. Now about 50% of them are.

Reicks was not overly impressed with Monument Health. The Mesa City IPA was lean and agile. Its members could quickly make decisions and take action. The execution of such ideas is much more cumbersome with Monument Health, as "a lot of people have to check off on changes." Reicks chairs the board of the QHN and serves on the Clinical Effectiveness Committee at Monument Health.

From a health care provider's point of view, Monument Health tracks a series of outcome measures (such as hospital readmissions and emergency department visits), as well as common primary care quality measures. The CIN operates a withholding mechanism—where a health insurance plan withholds a portion of the payments that are otherwise owed to its clinician participants, and these withheld amounts are then placed in one or more financial risk pools created by the health plan—with a bonus earn-back after reconciliation between the budget and actual spending. Monument Health continues to work closely on

Medicaid issues with Rocky Mountain Health Plan, and they have value-based care arrangements with UnitedHealthcare on its Medicare Advantage plans. But the total financial risk for a primary care clinician through Monument Health is approximately 10%, not like it was in the past, Reicks noted, when the Mesa County IPA took on a lot more risk.

How does this translate in a clinical setting? Reicks believed that the clinicians in his practice were largely focused on the volume of patient visits. They were expected to see 16–20 patients a day, with a total panel size of 1,800 patients. Most are slowly building up to that number, but recruiting was not easy. The practice increasingly relies on nurse practitioners. Reicks agreed with the medical literature that suggests that advanced practice nurses may provide more expensive care, as they tend more frequently to refer patients to specialists. In his view, their training is like going to medical school but without a residency period, so APNs are not comfortable with some clinical issues, he gave as an example *osteoporosis* (a condition that weakens bones and makes them more likely to break).

Nonetheless, the clinicians act as a team. The SCL Health clinic has case managers and social workers who are integrated into the practice. There are also nurses who do outreach, and there is a team huddle every morning. The standard features of an advanced primary care practice are in place.

For SCL Health doctors, the starting salary is pegged at $240,000, with some bonus opportunities. Reicks made "a lot more money" in private practice, but he worked longer hours. He would still prefer to be there, but he really had no choice. Moving from his private practice's eClinicalWorks EMRs to Epic's system "nearly killed me." In his view, it is not user-friendly in an ambulatory primary care setting.

Given Reicks's long history of leadership in and careful reflection about primary health care, I asked how he sees the health care system evolving. His long-range view was that health insurers are slowly but surely taking the topic of utilization seriously. Rocky Mountain has consistently been way ahead in this regard. In the past, the financial game for insurers was a matter of trying to minimize each fee-per-widget/

service. That ended in a standoff, however, caused by the hospitals consolidating the provider market and boosting per widget reimbursement. Today, if health care costs equal the rate of payment for a treatment times its frequency of use, health insurers must address utilization. They are doing so through care management and a new focus on SDOH. Reicks was impressed with the latter and its potential for improving primary health care. He seemed bemused toward the end of his career—there has been a great deal of change, but the same challenges persist.

During my last evening in Colorado's Western Slope, I had dinner with Patrick Gordon. In light of the role that Rocky Mountain Health Plan has played in developing primary care in this part of the state, and how closely intertwined Gordon the person is with the company, I was not sure what to expect. Surprisingly youthful in appearance, Gordon is intellectual in demeanor, with a decidedly self-effacing style.[26]

When I got to the table, he was in an animated iPhone discussion with a colleague. As that conversation ended, he explained that his team was placing their claims adjudication engine onto a UnitedHealthcare chassis. He went deep into details on the attribution of patients, partial capitation, and the like, lamenting that the big health insurers are not ready to properly pay capitation. His grasp of technical minutiae was impressive, especially for someone who had been described so often as a visionary. He seems to understand both the details and the big picture.

Gordon explained that Rocky Mountain Health Plan had been influential for years in western Colorado, well before he was its chief executive. The older program—the one that produced superlative data for that part of the state on the Dartmouth Atlas of Health Care, which led to Gawande's *New Yorker* article, was the result of closely knit IPAs that have largely disappeared. His diagnosis on that demise was the same as Reicks's (one I have long endorsed): managed care in the 1990s disappeared as hospitals and doctors realized that consolidation could lead to higher fee-for-service payments. As a result, the Medicare numbers in western Colorado no longer look so good.

Rocky Mountain Health Plan and Patrick Gordon have focused on being a managed Medicaid plan in a state that has largely eschewed managed care in Medicaid. Its use in the Western Slope has been an experiment for the state, one that now it is going to expand into other regions of Colorado. Rocky Mountain has about 140,000 Medicaid members and participates on the ACA exchanges. The company's commercial health insurance and Medicare Advantage plans are now operated by UnitedHealthcare. Gordon proffered no excuses for Rocky Mountain Health Plan's initial enthusiasm on the exchange market, which got it so deeply in debt—they simply miscalculated. And he maintained that UnitedHealthcare has been a great partner. They bring scale to Rocky Mountain's operations, although not sufficient flexibility, I surmised.

Gordon was articulate in his support for primary care and for physician-based management of health care budgets. He has pushed for a fully capitated model, believing that his Medicaid health care providers can work with it. Even more adamant was his support for the integration of behavioral health into primary care—not based on a calculated return on investment, but on a commonsense need for counseling and similar efforts in a primary care setting. He felt the same way about case management, at least when it is "boots on the ground" who are reaching out to patients. On both counts, Rocky Mountain Health Plan is renowned throughout the country. Note that there is no distinction between value-based care and managed care in the discussions in Colorado, nor are there any doubts about the value of prospective payment.

Getting great care for Medicaid recipients is the current priority for Patrick Gordon and Rocky Mountain Health Plan. But he knows that the number of uninsured individuals is too high. These people need a viable set of exchange plans. Applying the same set of methods Rocky Mountain uses with Medicaid to the ACA exchange market can do that. And the tools, including the Quality Health Network and Monument Health, are in place. Gordon's commitment to and understanding of the tools Rocky Mountain needs to succeed in primary care and increase heath care access in Colorado are admirable—and impressive—showing what a state-based health insurer can do.

Kaiser Permanente

On a much larger platform, and over a longer period, Kaiser Permanente has remade health care in California. Yet it is much more than just a California health plan. It is really three entities: (1) a health insurance plan, (2) a hospital and ambulatory care chain, and (3) a semi-independent Permanente Medical Group. Founded in 1945, Kaiser Permanente now has 12.7 million members, 39 hospitals, 623 medical offices, 23,982 physicians, 68,218 nurses, and 226,539 employees.[27] It also operates in Colorado, the District of Columbia, Georgia, Hawaii, Maryland, Oregon, Virginia, and Washington State.

But nowhere (except perhaps in Hawaii) does it offer the depth and breadth of primary health care that it does in California, where Kaiser covers nearly 25% of the population. That number, however, understates its role in commercial health insurance. California has nearly 40 million citizens, but 15 million of them are enrolled in Medicaid, where Kaiser Permanente has a smaller share of less than a million.[28] Kaiser's share in commercial health insurance and Medicare Advantage plans, however, approaches 40%, similar to a good-sized Blue Cross plan. More importantly, a Kaiser beneficiary is completely enveloped in the Kaiser system. Once you sign up for their health insurance, you use Kaiser for all your health care: seeing Permanente doctors in a Kaiser-owned office building, getting your outpatient tests in their centers, and going into a Kaiser hospital when needed. You have no other choices—you have signed on for the whole affair.

What Kaiser Permanente provides is value-based managed care to the greatest degree possible. The Kaiser Permanente system is built on high-quality, efficient, and cost-effective care for individual patients. Clinical algorithms that emphasize parsimonious and guideline-driven care dominate their clinicians' decision-making. Everyone is on the same EMR system, so continuity is seamless. No one is paid through an RVU-based fee-for-service system; everyone is on salary, and at the primary care center I visited, there are few bonus incentives. People work there because they believe what they are doing is the best way to care for people, and they are highly supportive of the quality of care they deliver.

The managed care backlash of the 1990s never affected Kaiser Permanente. Its health care model continued to cast a long shadow in California, where a number of other large physicians' groups were formed to take on capitated risk from health insurers—a development virtually nonexistent outside of California in the late 1990s and early 2000s. Some of these competitors took business away from Kaiser, but in the past decade, its health plan has roared back, with a nearly 50% increase in enrollment. Kaiser has created an ecosystem in California where primary care–based financial risk is almost the norm.

Kaiser Permanente has grown its care structure around this capitated risk. Early on, Kaiser's leaders adopted Epic's EMR system, allowing broad sets of teams to access patient information. They built care management into their format, with chronic disease teams that primary care doctors could access. They used group visits and endorsed virtual care long before others did. In my wanderings within the US health care system for 40 years, I encountered two especially visionary leaders: James Mongan (with Partners HealthCare System) and Per Lofberg (with CVS Health). They could not have been more different in their orientations—socialist versus capitalist—but they had one core response when faced with a strategic issue: let's understand what Kaiser is doing in this situation. Kaiser Permanente is deeply and widely admired by many in health policy.

While Kaiser Permanente is much more than a health plan, one can see the instincts of the health plan structuring the care model: capitation with an emphasis on high-quality, appropriately parsimonious care. All the care the patient needs, but not excess care pushed by fee-for-service incentives. Kaiser Permanente's strongest model is in California, and much of the rest of the state's health policy takes place in its shadow.

So it was with great interest that I approached Kaiser Permanente, asking to visit one of their primary care clinics. I was surprised at first how difficult this was. For most of my visits to such clinics, I knew one person or another who was affiliated with them—old acquaintances—and a couple of initial telephone calls would suffice to make the appropriate arrangements. No one would really ask any more about my project beyond accepting my initial statement: I was studying primary care. At Kaiser Permanente, however, I could not break through. I finally had to approach friends who had been in senior leadership positions and work down the chain.

I was eventually put in touch with Dr. Grace Firtch, who was the physician-in-chief at the Redwood City Medical Center in Redwood, California. Kaiser has a hospital there, and a medical office building housing a large primary care practice. It is part of the Northern California (NorCal) division of Kaiser Permanente, which has more than 8,000 doctors and 2,000 primary care clinicians. The scale is huge. Redwood City is imposing and busy.

I had anticipated seeing a model of the future of primary care in the United States. The reality was more complex, as I should have expected. Every doctor I met was a true believer in the Kaiser Permanente system, wanting their own relatives to be taken care of at their center. They thought the quality of care was incomparably better than elsewhere, and many found the fee-for-service system to be morally repugnant. The doctors I spoke with also thought highly of their administrators in Redwood City, especially Dr. Firtch, who was seen as "brilliant" and a "breath of fresh air."

With that as background, the overall mood was not entirely upbeat at Redwood City. Some of the physicians felt overworked, embedded in a care administration program that had many professionals in many layers, yet the entire team looked to a primary care doctor when action was needed. As a result, what awaited the primary care doctors in their Epic EMR inboxes often seemed overwhelming, at least for some of the clinicians. The crush of information was such that some team members had doubts about the sustainability of certain aspects of the model.

Dr. Marc Todd Philippe had a fascinating perspective.[29] He grew up in northern Kentucky, opposite Cincinnati, and was educated at the University of Kentucky. He trained in northern Kentucky and went into family medicine there in a fee-for-service, traditional primary care practice, where RVUs were king. In his seven years there, he saw over 30 patients a day, and many of these visits would have been considered unnecessary at Kaiser. He then moved to Redwood City and has been at this Kaiser Permanente facility for seven years.

Philippe believes the Kaiser program is much better for patients because it is not tied to counting RVUs. He was clear that the "infrastructure of care matters so much," and that "patients and physicians have a cohesive relationship," with "no tension on how dollars are exchanged in an episode of care." He is as enthusiastic a supporter of Kaiser's managed care system now as he was when he joined. But the big problem for him was the onslaught of patient data and subsequent communications, much of it overwhelming.

In my interviews with Philippe and other Kaiser physicians, two trends intersected, with huge work implications for primary care doctors. The first is the evolution of the care management process for patients. For example, a patient who is suffering from diabetes or hypertension has appointments with a team of nurses and pharmacists who help ensure that person's adherence to a medical regimen, finetune dosages, and the like. In Kentucky, that patient would only see a primary care doctor, and medical visits would occur often. At Kaiser Permanente, the *team* provides that care. The patient's primary care doctor is kept in the loop but has few visits with that patient. Yet when there is a problem, it comes back to the primary care physician. So, while the *number* of patients Philippe now sees (16–18 a day) is less than during his fee-for-service days, they are sicker. The easy problems stay with the care management teams. Still, there is lots of signaling from those teams back to the primary care doctor.

Since the COVID pandemic, the number of telemedicine visits increased. So did the use of Epic's patient portal, known as MyChart. Patients got more used to communicating virtually with their doctors. To emphasize the advantages of a primary care clinician–based model, Kaiser Permanente encouraged direct contact with primary care. Increasingly, at least some of the primary care doctors felt bombarded by the increased patient communication.

Philippe saw himself as being resilient. (I would agree, based on my hour with him.) He comes in at 8:00 a.m. and leaves at 6:00 p.m. Outside of that, he catches up on patient charts for an hour or two on weekends. About 25% of his visits are virtual (he does not have to worry about billing). His time is 80% clinical, with 20% spent as the quality leader for the Kaiser outpost in San Mateo, California. Like others whom I met at Kaiser, he wanted to work at the top of his license, and he was supported by helpful care algorithms that are accessed from the EMRs. He is able to keep many patients in his practice, not needing to refer. And he has plenty of support from the care teams.

For example, if one of his patients has atrial fibrillation, Philippe can use an algorithm called CHADS that provides a score indicating the severity of the problem. Based on this score, he can decide whether his patient needs to be referred to a cardiologist. In another example, a patient with diabetes and hypertension might be taking six different medications. Philippe does not need to see this patient, as the hypertension care team keeps tabs on him. Any problems, though, come his way.

Philippe believed the attitudes of his colleagues could be represented by a bell curve, and he was on the happier side. But everyone agreed that the workload was stiff. Two solutions have surfaced. One is to use more artificial intelligence "bots" in dealing with patients' emails. The second is to hire more clinicians, most likely more advanced practice nurse practitioners, something Kaiser has not completely embraced in the past. Nonetheless, Philippe was hopeful they could hire more help.

Another doctor, who did not want to be identified in this book, provided some insight into the care management team process.[30] A Kaiser doctor for seven years, she leads the local cardiovascular team, working with pharmacists and project managers. The team is constantly reviewing the data for their patients, trying to figure out new ways to improve blood pressure control, cholesterol management, and diabetes care. They consult with a regional team, gathering the best practices from all the Kaiser Permanente health centers. Together, they search the medical literature to identify new solutions. They have a similar team working on disparities in social determinants of health. This is the kind of continuous improvement effort for which Kaiser is widely admired.

The results are gratifying. Redwood City is number one in NorCal on a variety of cardiovascular, diabetes, and cancer screening measures. Their team does substantial outreach to patients, and they work with doctors in outlier Kaiser clinics. They currently have a special focus on Latino patients. This doctor also works hard at getting clinicians to code properly. Kaiser Permanente doctors need accurate codes in order to plan for their patients' care and any required interventions.

Ultimately, though, any problems land on the primary care physicians. Her patient panel is well over optimal size. She believed that many clinicians were in a similar position, and that is why some were burning out. She realized that Kaiser is trying to come up with virtual solutions in dealing with emails, but patients still want to talk with doctors face-to-face. This doctor related that she works two hours every night, from ten o'clock to midnight, to keep up with EMR issues and answer emails. The conflict between having this great health care system, yet too much work, spilled out.

- "There is no joy in practicing medicine this way" (referring to portal-based messaging).
- "I believe in the KP [Kaiser Permanente] model; it is the best care."
- "It comes at a personal cost."
- "There is so much momentum and so much inertia."

To this doctor, Kaiser was trying to do the best for their patients by building the right system. They just needed more ancillary help and reduced panel sizes.

Not all of the doctors I spoke with felt this burdened. Dr. Baonhan Le received his MD from Ross University School of Medicine in the Caribbean, and then did his medical rotations in the New York metropolitan area.[31] His residency in family medicine was at the University of California, Riverside, and he came to Redwood City in 2019. His outlook was almost entirely optimistic. He went into primary care out of a sense of altruism and interest in people. He trained in the Inland Empire metropolitan area, where there were many patients on Medicaid, and he had to jump through a lot of hoops, especially those associated with prior authorization, to get adequate care for his patients. There is none of that in Redwood City, as the Kaiser Permanente program is designed to serve patients. He knows his entire specialist team and works with them on shared patients.

Le had the second-largest panel in the Redwood City practice, but he got in at 7:00 a.m. and left by 5:00 p.m. Although he did not dictate his patient notes, he asserted proudly he could type quickly. He dealt with his Epic inbox during work hours. His succinct summary of his inbox contents bears repeating.

1. Laboratory results
2. Medication changes
3. Messages from other clinicians, include triage nurses, nurses seeing walk-in patients, specialists, home health clinicians, and those providing ancillary services
4. Transition teams' notes
5. Complex care coordinators' messages
6. E-consults
7. Messages from patients

Traffic from patients skyrocketed during COVID, and it has not slowed down since people have started coming back into the clinics. But to his mind, the job is doable, and the Kaiser Permanente team is keeping patients healthy.

Dr. Helen Lin is another person who has experienced both private primary care practice and the Kaiser model.[32] After she trained at the University of Arizona, she went into private practice for eight years and has now spent eight years at Kaiser Permanente. She was worried about burnout, and her team had decided to try to hire more advanced practice nurses to fill in the gaps. Lin is the team leader for a pod of 20 primary care physicians, and she personally found hiring to be difficult. Her schedule was grinding, as she saw three patients an hour from 8:30 a.m. to 12:30 p.m., and then from 1:30 to 4:00 p.m. Firtch and her leadership team had recently approved an hour of administrative time at midday—a much applauded move.

Most of the Kaiser Permanente doctors I interviewed were under 40 years old. One physician, who wished not to be identified, was a comparative old hand, having been with Kaiser since 1998.[33] His take on the Kaiser Permanente system was that technology is a double-edged sword. It has greatly improved the clinicians' ability to care for and follow up on patients, and it has brought a large virtual care team into play. But it has also stultified the clinicians' professional development and is to some extent grinding down the doctors. Offering access to physicians through email meant that the doctors "went from back office to front desk," and it was wearing them out.

This doctor also made an incisive point about the foundation of Kaiser Permanente's health care being its primary care clinicians (usually physicians): it is both a cure and a curse. A primary care doctor guides the care for a patient. That is good. But that person must also fill in all the gaps. The problem is that when a primary care physician sends a patient to a specialist, all the phone calls regarding that patient come back to the primary care doctor. An orthopedist does an operation, and the patient experiences pain afterward—call the primary care clinician. If a patient needs to remain on disability benefits longer—call the primary care clinician. This works only when a clinician's panel size is reasonably sized.

Everyone I met reiterated that primary care at Kaiser Permanente was superior: better quality-of-care outcomes that are carefully monitored (and backed up by the five-star status of most Kaiser health plans); cost-effective care, because the clinicians have no incentive to provide more care than is necessary; and no fee-for-service payments. So, in many ways, the Kaiser Permanente model can be seen as the future of health care—at least in a managed care world. But the system must be monitored closely, with sufficient resources and appreciation of the panel size, at least from what I saw during my visit to Redwood City. Kaiser Permanente's reshaping of a lot of care management, which is no doubt efficient and effective, still must be funneled to patients through their primary care doctors. Every primary care practice suffers from "inbox exhaustion," but at Kaiser Permanente, it may be exacerbated by the care architecture.

Another point is worth mentioning. Many of the other primary care clinics that I visited, especially the federally qualified health centers, have the additional burden of caring for Medicaid patients, who have few medical resources, and uninsured patients, who have none. The latter in particular require time-consuming workarounds for clinical problems. The Kaiser Permanente doctors had none of this. Patients needed a Kaiser health plan to get a foot in the door, and there are relatively few Medicaid recipients with a Kaiser plan (at least until recently). So, Kaiser's clinicians did not experience the additional stress of having no resources for some of their patients that other clinicians have.

Just one more issue deserves mention: the gender gap. Recently, an article by Lisa Rosenstein, Richard Gitomer, and Bruce Landon in the *New England Journal of Medicine* addressed this problem, noting that not only are female physicians paid less, but they also generally spend more time with patients and with electronic-messaging activities.[34] These authors believed that the gender differences in physicians' approach to primary care must be addressed in compensation formulas, and they thought that capitation might be the answer. That may be, but even in a capitated program, the panel size must be moderated or electronic messaging will become burdensome for all, perhaps especially for female doctors.

The Impact and Influence of State-Based Health Insurance Plans

State-based health care plans appear to make a difference in promoting value-based primary care. Two insights stand out. First, the integrated model—care delivery plus an insurance function—can be a strong foundation on which to build such a program. Thus there are a number of larger, vertically integrated corporations that emulate the Kaiser Permanente model (see chapter 6). But even the vaunted Kaiser Permanente system cannot solve the basic problem with primary care: there is often too much work and not enough support. Getting that right will be critical for America's health care future. Yet if anyone can get the work/life balance for primary care doctors right, it should be Kaiser.

Second, state-based health care plans can make a difference, even when they do not employ the clinicians in primary care practices, by just contracting wisely and putting appropriate support in place. My visits with a number of the Blue Cross plans, as well as the history of the Rocky Mountain Health Plan in western Colorado, show that a health insurer can have a real impact on the breadth of care. The health care program an insurer promotes, the nature of its payment structure, and the clear expectations and guarantees that an insurer can make for health care providers can all change the way primary care is delivered—and improve it. Every one of these efforts by state-based health insurers is slowly pushing the US health care system toward more value-based care. It is incremental and can act alongside what we see from the federal government and state governments.

CHAPTER SIX

The National Health Insurers (and Other Corporations)

LIKE THE STATE-BASED HEALTH INSURERS, national commercial health insurers are interested in how they can lower costs and improve the quality of primary care. This may come as a surprise to some, including many in the health policy and primary care communities. Historically, national health insurers have taken the most direct routes to reducing costs in a fee-for-service world. They negotiated for low rates of reimbursement for clinicians, and they used prior authorization requirements to reduce unnecessary utilization. Primary care doctors, historically disaggregated into small practices with little negotiating leverage, had to take what the insurers offered to participate in their health care plans. Moreover, utilization review obstacles often landed on a primary care clinician's desk. Thus the UnitedHealthcares, Aetnas, Cignas, and Humanas of the world were not seen as being friendly to primary care.

The enmity between primary care and national health insurers perhaps goes deeper than just these historical business relationships. Primary care is generally and genuinely imbued with a strong nonprofit ethos. People who go into primary care know they will not make as much money as other clinicians will. But they like the relationship with their patients that primary care offers, and they value guiding people through the health care system. Many have patients who cannot afford certain kinds of medical interventions, so the financial structure of health care obstructs their patients' health. Primary care clinicians are not trying to take profits out of the health care system, and they resent those who are. To some extent, this leads to antagonism with their own administrators—who they sometimes see as unnecessary overhead. But this combativeness really comes to the fore with regard to health insurers, especially the for-profit insurers, who are seen as providing no real value-based care and inducing greater costs for patients.

As a result, many of the primary care doctors I met support the idea of a national health care system that would provide access for all patients at no direct cost to them and would fairly reimburse primary care clinicians for the work they do. They see little or no need for large corporations in the health care business, as such companies are perceived as simply bringing administrative costs and no extra value in their contracts with providers. Who can blame them? When you are a doctor at a federally qualified health center, spending long hours on a workaround treatment for a patient who cannot afford to see a specialist or get an expensive test, how else would the world look? Moreover, taking responsibility for that person's health and not being able to employ all that medicine offers today can only be extraordinarily stressful. The primary care clinicians' voice for change is compelling and must be heard.

But if you believe that profit-taking is not going to be eliminated from health care in the United States, and that most health care institutions—physicians' groups, individual doctors, hospitals, health insurers, pharmaceutical companies, medical device manufacturers, and even ambulance companies—are profit driven, then you might reasonably wonder how these rapacious influences can be oriented toward improving the health care system. Some of that involves appropriate regulation to ensure that this greed is limited.[1] In addition, you must have some belief that firms will rationally seek profits, supporting primary care to ensure that it is efficient and of high quality, and so aligned with their own corporate interests. As Gregory Reicks in Grand Junction put it, the old game of low reimbursement rates has been outstripped by high patient utilization, so health insurers of all stripes now need to understand how to limit this excessive utilization at its source—at least in part by working with primary care clinicians.

Some clinicians and policy analysts will not buy this. They will see any involvement of health insurers and other for-profit entities as polluting—and even destroying—primary care. Timothy Hoff, a professor at Northeastern University, has written a series of books based on extensive interviews with family medicine physicians. He makes the case that retail medicine is not a good thing, and that it is replacing the type of primary care practices we really need in our American health care system. This tone is well encapsulated in the subtitle of his most recent book, *Searching for the Family Doctor: Primary Care on the Brink*.[2]

Taking a slightly different approach, primary care physician Gregg Coodley has reached much the same conclusion as Hoff, seeing that for-profit influences in health care, along with other negative developments such as electronic medical records, will soon eliminate access to primary care for all but the wealthy, who can afford concierge practices (personalized medical care where members pay a monthly or annual fee for direct access to their doctors).[3] Although Hoff's and Coodley's positions differ in substance and nuances, they (like many others) have come to the conclusion that part of the failure of primary care in the United States is the result of interventions by for-profit corporations.

Kevin Grumbach, long one of the leading theorists and activists for primary care is much more explicit, and he well captures the tone I heard in conversations with primary care doctors. He recently posited that "a market-based health system captured by extractive capitalism is inimical to primary care as a common good," and that "primary care doctors . . . must join with patients, primary care workers, and other allies in a social movement demanding fundamental restructuring of the health system."[4] His prescription is a publicly financed system of universal coverage for direct primary care, with 10% of all health care spending allocated to primary care. Presumably, in his world, for-profit companies would be eliminated from the health care arena.

This may seem like a radical suggestion—any title in a health care journal article that includes the verbs "dismantle" and "liberate" is provocative. But elsewhere I have suggested that a single-payer approach with little involvement by private health insurance companies is one of two likely outcomes in the evolution of the American health care system.[5] Primary care would probably be the centerpiece of a single-payer system, modeled on that of Great Britain (although its health care system is experiencing many travails at present).[6] My sense was that the majority of primary care clinicians I met would find a single-payer format wholly preferable to our current system.

This book is about the future of primary care, and that future might involve a single-payer program written into federal law, with a set of specific provisos about funding for primary care. But an equally likely future is that health care stays in the market economy, with for-profit companies deeply involved. Indeed, such companies are having substantial influence on the development of primary care today. For-profit entities—health insurers and private equity firms—are pouring billions of dollars into the primary care practices. The practices they support look and feel much like the ones described thus far, with grateful patients and committed clinicians. So, they and the forces impelling profit seekers to support primary care deserve attention. In particular, we must ask if their keen interest in profit can be compatible with value-based primary care that improves the lives of patients.

Optum Health

The best place to start is Optum. It is a subsidiary of the United-Health Group, which also owns UnitedHealthcare, the largest of the commercial health insurers. Optum is an assembly of companies that its parent (which I will simply refer to as United) has put together over a 20-year period to supplement and complement United's health insurance function. Over time, the number of its member businesses—as well as its revenue—has grown, so Optum is now a huge part of the overall United company. It is certainly the part that shareholders look to for growth.

This story begins back in the late 1990s, when United aggregated several of its assets into an independent data analytics company called Ingenix.[7] Over the course of the next decade, United added banking assets (to deal with health savings accounts) and a pharmacy benefits management company called Prescription Solutions (acquired as part of a deal to buy the health insurer Pacificare). Ingenix grew, and United began to buy medical groups, notably the San Antonio–based WellMed, in 2011. At that point, United announced that its master brand would be Optum, with three pillars: (1) data analytics, (2) care delivery, and (3) pharmacy benefits management. These are now known as Optum Insight, Optum Health, and Optum Rx. Over time, Optum has added revenue cycle management (billing and collection), and broader care delivery (encompassing urgent care, surgical centers, and home care).

In many ways, the admirable (from a capitalist viewpoint) part of Optum's strategy has been the synergy it creates among its three parts and between Optum and UnitedHealthcare, the huge health care insurer. Having a company that sells revenue cycle management programs (overseeing all the billing and follow-ups) and owns primary care practices creates an internal market demand. Closely integrating a pharmacy benefits manager with a health insurer creates opportunities for new care management strategies and improvements in the quality of care. A brilliant corporate strategy like this, admired throughout the for-profit health care field, can also bring concerns about vertical integration and unfair competition. Thus far, even with the increasingly watchful Federal Trade Commission, Optum and UnitedHealth Group have not had to disgorge any assets.

Optum's scope is enormous. At the company's investor conference in 2022, the Optum team revealed that it served 101 million unique customers, had clinical and claims data information on 285 million Americans, and adjudicated more than $120 billion in prescription drug claims.[8] They provided services for 80% of all health insurance plans, 90% of the Fortune 100 companies, and over 100 global life-science firms. Optum regularly adds new assets, like long-term care management and home care. Optum's strategy is widely admired by the investor community, feared and envied by competitors, and reviled by those who are worried about corporate influences in health care.

In contrast, hatred of insurers by many (providers, patients, and beneficiaries) continues to grow, focusing on their efforts to cut costs.

The cold-blooded murder of the UnitedHealthcare CEO in New York in late 2024 is evidence enough.

Optum Health, United's health care delivery arm, is what I will discuss in this chapter. It was headed by Wyatt Decker until recently, when he moved up a level of management, and was replaced by Amar Desai. Both men are doctors with extensive experience in managing physicians' groups. By a recent count, Optum Health employs more than 70,000 physicians.[9] Although United has not disclosed the number of its primary care doctors, it must be at least 40,000. This makes Optum Health the largest employer of physicians in general, and primary care doctors in particular, in the United States. In 2022 alone, Optum Health bought the Kelsey-Seybold Clinic in Houston, Healthcare Associates of Texas in Dallas, and the Atrius Health medical group in Massachusetts.[10] The pace is extraordinary, as Optum Health has doubled in size since 2018. (Not all these physicians work directly for Optum. Depending on state law, many are employees of physician organizations that are in turn controlled by Optum.)

Why would a health insurer buy up so many medical groups? From a managed care point of view, the business strategy is clear. It follows the playbook defined by Kaiser Permanente over the past 40 years. I have argued that the best way to reduce costs and improve the quality of care—that is, to promote value-based care—is to imbue physicians, and their decision-making, with the right incentives. The critical place to do that is a primary care doctor's office, where patients initiate their health care and maintain their medical base of operations. If a primary care clinician chooses diagnostic and therapeutic interventions wisely, emphasizing parsimony yet maintaining excellent quality in the care being rendered and anticipating patients' needs, then costs *can* be reduced. That is clearly Optum Health's view, so a long-term strategy of owning primary care practices makes great sense.

Others have countered that Optum might be interested in vertical integration simply because it can take advantage of medical loss ratio (MLR) regulation by compensating certain aspects of care more generously when it owns the provider. This profit-laden compensation for its own entity contributes to the MLR, satisfying the government's expectation of a "sufficient" portion of the premium dollar going to medical care. And it contributes to Optum's bottom line. Referred to appropriately as taking advantage of transfer pricing, and more colorfully known as "provider fracking," it can offer a potential explanation beyond medical management for vertical integration.[11] But no one has quantified this hypothesis, and Optum's push to own physicians even predates the MLR regulations. The potential for transfer pricing nonetheless bears further consideration.

Optum Health has not taken its control of primary care to Kaiser Permanente's level of integration. The former does not own hospitals and employs relatively few specialists, although it does own urgent care and ambulatory surgery centers, some of which are affiliated with hospitals. Optum also employs a sizable number of specialists, although few surgical specialists, which they make up for by having an expansive network of contracted surgical specialists. UnitedHealth Group's strategy on the hospital side is to partner with hospitalists and hospital-based specialists so as to offer accessible and appropriate care in the hospital. Optum does not and likely will not own hospitals.

Optum Health practices tend to have as many of their commercial health insurance contracts as possible in alternative payment mechanisms. (To be clear, Optum Health contracts with many insurers, not just their affiliated UnitedHealthcare insurer.) As has been done with commercial health insurance contracts in California for years, so long as the commercial insurer uses a health maintenance organization (HMO) plan design with a requirement for a beneficiary to identify a primary care clinician, then Optum Health's groups can negotiate with commercial health insurers for a percentage of the premiums—that is, capitated payment. Reliant, discussed in chapter 3, is a good example, attempting to negotiate for capitation. Other groups, like the Optum Health physician groups in the New York City region, are not yet steeped in capitated payment and managed care, but the idea is to move in that direction.

Optum Health, like other primary care practices, likes to contract with Medicare Advantage insurers for risk. Medicare Advantage, the wing of Medicare that is administered through private insurers, lends itself to alternative payment, as it was always intended to entail managed care. This is unlike traditional Medicare, which has always been fee-for-service payment by the government. The Medicare Advantage insurers mimic commercial health insurance, including use of prior authorization, pharmaceutical formularies, and negotiations with providers over reimbursement. I have reviewed the long history and peregrinations of Medicare Advantage elsewhere,[12] but suffice it to say here that more than half of all Medicare beneficiaries now have Medicare Advantage policies.

Medicare Advantage, long a stolid part of our health insurance universe, has become more controversial as it has steadily grown over the past decade. Part of this is based on the view of many experts in health policy who do not think the government should rely on private corporations to provide a public benefit. A subset of them has sharper concerns. They advocate for replacing commercial health insurance with a single payer—Medicare. Having a significant part of Medicare being administered by private health insurers frustrates that goal.

But the arguments made by those opposed to, or even concerned about, Medicare Advantage are not based solely on ideological grounds. They contend that, all else being equal, the federal government spends more money on a Medicare Advantage beneficiary than it does on a person enrolled in the traditional Medicare program. This represents a subsidy for private corporations that our country can ill afford. There is plenty of support for this argument from a wide range of economists and health policy analysts.[13]

Historically, the Centers for Medicare and Medicaid Services (CMS) has attempted to ensure fair but not overly generous payments for Medicare Advantage, correcting its methodology if it appears the private side of Medicare is being overpaid. As corrections occur, such as after the passage of the Affordable Care Act, Medicare Advantage (MA) spending is trimmed, and studies suggest that MA beneficiaries' costs are similar to those of traditional Medicare (TM). But now, over the past decade, it appears that MA is again overcompensated.

Advocates on both sides spend plenty of time and effort trying to demonstrate quality-of-care differences between the two programs, but this argument is currently a draw.[14] The quality-of-care battle, however, pales in comparison with the one about overpayment.

The overpayment issue today revolves around coding. I have already discussed the basic rules for identifying the severity of an illness and the delegation of patients to specific primary care practices in the overview of Medicaid in chapter 4. For capitation to work, an individual must be assigned to a financial risk–bearing organization, typically through a link to the primary care clinician. The payer then knows who to pay. This basic element, known as attribution, is what ties together so many of the discussions on primary care and capitation/managed care. Attribution to a primary care practice makes sense, as patients and primary care doctors are meant to have continuous relationships. Attribution is necessary to link payment to an individual, the per head payment or capitation.

Once a patient is assigned to a primary care practice, the payer must then know *how much* to pay, which cannot be a uniform amount. If a capitated health care group managed to attract nothing but healthy patients, a uniform sum would overpay them, while sicker patients would generate underpayments. In any arrangement involving capitated payments, a risk score must be calculated for each patient, with the payment for that person adjusted accordingly. For Medicare, the federal government has long employed a specific risk-adjustment tool, which is based on a regression analysis called a CMS-HCC model.[15] The model predicts future costs based on demographic data and hierarchical condition categories (HCCs). These make use of diagnosis codes assigned by the clinicians who are evaluating and treating a patient.

Let me take a somewhat personal example to illustrate how this program works. While writing this book, I had stepped up my exercise routine to nearly two hours a day and increased its intensity. I was swimming one morning, got an odd pain in my chest, and ended up at Massachusetts General Hospital. The diagnosis was cardiac ischemia (reduced blood flow in the coronary artery), so I got a stent (a tiny tube inserted into a blocked passageway to keep it open). I had no medical history of heart problems, so my Medicare Advantage insurer was getting a base amount for financing my health care. Now I have codes for my new history of cardiac ischemia, with a higher HCC weight. Next year, when my health insurer (Aetna) sees the code Massachusetts General Hospital entered for my treatment there, the annual payments from Medicare to Aetna for my health care coverage will increase substantially. (On the health care costs side, for my 23 hours in Massachusetts General, the hospital and its cardiology unit charged $87,000, Aetna paid $18,000, and my share was $335 in out-of-pocket expenses.)

Any provider organization with capitated risk wants to be sure it is adequately paid, according to the severity of a patient's illness, so coding is crucial. Any organization, especially one that wants to create a profit in patient care, will make every effort to ensure that each diagnostic code applying to a patient is documented. An emphasis on coding has not pervaded the Medicaid program to the same extent, largely because it has no single system for judging the severity of an illness. But the increasingly huge amounts spent on Medicare Advantage (now approaching half a trillion dollars) and its use of one methodology (CMS-HCC) for coding means that for a Medicare Advantage program to be profitable for health care providers, they must code carefully.

The fierce debate today is that coding is now seen as simply a means of gaming the system. If clinicians, or their health care organization, can find new codes to attach to patient records sent to the Centers for Medicare and Medicaid Services, they will get paid more. There is no doubt that this is the case,[16] although details about the extent of this overcoding are debated. The even-handed Medicare Payment Advisory Committee (MedPAC) has, however, been very clear about the extent of overcoding.

To the concerns about coding, MedPAC has now added *favorable selection*, or a bias toward sicker patients avoiding Medicare Advantage.[17] This makes some sense: Medicare Advantage plans will manage utilization, including through narrow provider networks and prior authorization. Sick people may want to avoid this. While not previously a centerpiece of the debate, MedPAC now says that selection bias could be leading to a 9% overpayment to Medicare Advantage plans. Moreover, the commission's estimates of the impact of coding continue to rise, to the 13% to 14% range. The result is an estimate that Medicare Advantage may be overpaid by $88 billion in 2024. Major insurers still posit that there is no overpayment in Medicare Advantage and pay actuarial firms to demonstrate this.[18]

While the politics of Medicare Advantage are complicated, reasonable people would agree this overpayment cannot stand because it is too much of a fill-up to private insurers (and providers). What action will be taken? Regarding coding, for much of the past five years, MedPAC has enumerated specific steps that CMS could take. Two specific reforms are now going into place.[19] First, CMS will change its methodology for conducting audits of risk adjustment, specifically the Risk Adjustment Data Validation (RADV) rule. The rule is much more stringent than past renditions,[20] following the reasoning of a careful decision by the District of Columbia Circuit Court of Appeals that suggested there was no need to adjust the auditing to account for parsimonious coding in traditional Medicare.[21]

Even more impactful will be the switch in risk-adjustment models from Model V24 to Model V28.[22] The new model increases the number of HCCs and changes how diagnoses are mapped to HCC codes. Some diagnoses are removed entirely, out of concerns they were too subjective and abused by providers or insurers. These changes should reduce the overpayments to Medicare Advantage firms and their at-risk providers, but likely additional adjustments will be necessary. They must occur if the TM/MA playing field is to be somewhat level.

What is often overlooked today is that this is the history of Medicare Advantage: swings in government reimbursement that at times match what traditional Medicare is being paid, and other times where the government appears to overpay. The changes occurring in 2023–24 should drive a downslope in that sinusoidal curve, with fiscal pressure in place to reduce over-payments.

Stepping back somewhat, I should note seven points about coding in primary care practices at risk for the costs of care that are missed in the heated health policy debate. First, coding all a patient's medical problems has long been seen as a proper and conscientious thing to do, just like careful history and physical. Moreover, as new algorithms are developed to assist clinicians with diagnosis and treatment, coding of diagnoses is essential. In the debate about overcoding, few are accusing clinicians or medical groups of fraud. Rather, it is a matter about how driven or conscientious a practice is. There is no doubt that groups at risk are adding more codes, but that can be seen as both driving revenue and the right thing to do. As well, the comparator is fee-for-service, where there is no incentive to code because it takes time away from jamming the next visit through.

Second, coding is an issue for all practices at risk, whether that be a for-profit group just caring for Medicare Advantage, or a federally qualified health center (FQHC) with a largely at-risk Medicaid population. As we move to risk throughout the insurance universe and move away from fee-for-service, coding will be an ongoing complication. Third, clinicians generally like to avoid the whole discussion of coding. This reluctance applies to every walk of primary care life, from the for-profit group to the rural FQHC. Clinicians I interviewed recognize coding is tied to generating revenue, even if they see it as an embarrassing necessity. Many practices have teams that help identify codes, then query the clinician as to whether the codes are appropriate. In no setting I visited did clinician reimbursement depend on coding volume. But it is sensitive for everyone. Many avoid the term "coding" altogether, using the much more neutral term, *documentation*.

Fourth, overcoding can be corrected simply by changing the weights of codes, especially those that might be somewhat subjective or show huge variation when comparing MA to TM, for example. MedPAC has recommended this solution for years. Indeed, that is the guts of the proposed changes that CMS has put in place for 2024.

Fifth, since no one is saying codes are being made up, just that all applicable codes for patients are slowly being identified, the coding problem should be asymptotic, that is, self-limited. One caveat on this presumption of innocence of fraud. A recent analysis by the *Wall Street Journal* has shown that when for-profit corporations use home visits to identify new codes, a substantial portion of people so identified are not being treated for their coded ailment. For example, nearly 80% of those identified with HIV infection are not being treated. These kinds of results raise real questions about profit-inducing fraud.[23] Even if not fraudulent, recent research suggests that health risk assessments, typically done in the home, contribute $12 billion per year to risk-adjustment payments.[24] (My Medicare Advantage insurer, Aetna, has assiduously contacted me to set up a home visit, and I have resisted.)

Sixth, the comparison of MA to TM made sense when MA was a fraction of TM. But as it grows, one must question the whole effort of basing risk assessment on TM. Finding a new foundation for the MA program is a huge step, one that CMS has conspicuously failed to even acknowledge. Many academic experts have pointed to this as a critical problem.

Seventh and most importantly, those committed to capitation payment realize that coding is an adjunct to the real and difficult job of managing a patient's care in a cost-effective way and eliminating waste. That is the long-term play for primary care. There is evidence that primary care doctors in Medicare Advantage provided less expensive care.[25] A recent Commonwealth study had a headline stating there was little difference in the way primary care practices who cared mainly for traditional Medicare patients compared to those who cared mainly for Medicare Advantage patients.[26] But close examination shows trends in Medicare Advantage practices consistent with anticipation of problems and closer follow-up. That, not better coding, has to be the key motivation for at risk primary care.

In any case, the current controversy about coding and overpayment, and the changes it will spawn in the Medicare Advantage capitation strategies, represents a crucible of sorts for primary care value-based care. Will the practices I visited in 2022–23 continue to thrive in capitation if easy dollars from documentation are foregone? I spoke to Christopher Crow in the summer of 2024, wondering if he and Catalyst had had to change course. His reply was emphatically no. None of the other leaders I spoke to in late 2024 were experiencing any shift in the momentum toward value-based care as a result of coding changes by CMS. Nonetheless, coding is a big question hanging over capitation-centered, value-based primary care.

Returning to the theme of large insurers getting into primary care provision, I have already discussed my visits to some of the Optum groups: the Reliant Medical Group (see chapter 3) and Atrius Health (see chapter 1), both in Massachusetts. Clinicians there did not really notice United/Optum Health's new ownership (although their white coats and a big sign out front blared this information). These clinicians were continuing to practice the way they always had: managing care, referring patients to specialists only when necessary, and following their hospitalized patients closely. But Optum Health was certainly involved in their payer negotiations, their choices of new technologies, and their strategies vis-à-vis hospitals. I got a much more extended view of Optum Health in action in Southern California.

Optum Southern California: HealthCare Partners

The United/Optum Health game plan for primary care is perhaps best illustrated by Optum of Southern California. Its leaders could not have been more accommodating. I got in touch with Amar Desai, who at that time was running the West Coast operations for Optum Health. (He subsequently took a job as president of health care delivery at CVS Health, and then left there to come back as the new president of Optum Health, with Wyatt Decker moving up to become executive vice president and chief physician for UnitedHealth Group.) Desai invited me out to Los Angeles, where Optum Health's core is made up of what was formerly HealthCare Partners.

HealthCare Partners was a storied medical group in the Los Angeles area. Lawrence Casalino and James Robinson have written about the history of medical groups that sprang up throughout California to compete with Kaiser Permanente.[27] Some of them were developed by existing health insurers, others by hospital groups. Over time, each of them moved from capitation for physicians' services to full, or global, capitation, and they increasingly adopted measures that would allow them to control health care costs. Their growth gained momentum as employers, organized by the Pacific Business Group on Health, and the California Public Employees' Retirement System (CalPERS) advocated for the use of capitated physician groups.

The details on the growth of HealthCare Partners Medical Group are fascinating. Robert Margolis, who became the longtime CEO of Health-Care Partners, was one of its founders. I spoke with Margolis, who is now retired and supports the new and effective Margolis Center for Health Policy at Duke University.[28] He recalled the early days fondly. Like a lot of the National Institutes of Health's clinical fellows, he was moonlighting in the emergency department—in his case, at the California Hospital. He found that he had no one to turn to for referrals of patients who needed follow-ups. He and some associates convinced the hospital to give them a couple of rooms in the basement for a clinic. This was the beginning of California Primary Physicians.

Their practice grew and the leaders looked for other similar-minded physician groups with whom to collaborate. Eventually, HealthCare Partners was the product of the merger of California Primary Physicians, the Huntington Medical Group, and the Bay Shores Medical Group that occurred over several years in the early 1990s.

According to Casalino and Robinson, HealthCare Partners stood out among the other large physicians' groups in Southern California by growing slowly and carefully, while not getting into debt.[29] Unlike its competitors, HealthCare Partners thrived and survived into the twenty-first century. Margolis maintained that the company's goal was to provide great health care—particularly primary care—supported by capitation. Over time, HealthCare Partners increased the proportion of its physicians who were practicing primary care, downsized its specialists' practices, and never got involved with hospital ownership. Instead, it focused on reducing the number of patients' hospital days per 1,000 commercial members, going from 218 in 1990 to 149 in 1994.[30] (At the same time, those numbers were 383 and 324 for Massachusetts.) Similar progress was made with Medicare beneficiaries when HMOs began to penetrate this federal program.

As many other independent physicians' groups disappeared or merged with hospitals or health care organizations, HealthCare Partners persisted and continued to grow, staying the course by taking capitation (in the form of a percentage of the premiums from health insurers) for patients assigned to them and managing their care.

Margolis remained as their CEO and spurned purchase offers from a variety of organizations through 2012. By then, HealthCare Partners had over 650,000 patients in managed care and over 700 physicians. On the financial side, revenues totaled more than $2 billion, and profits were nearly $500 million. In 2012, however, HealthCare Partners announced that it was selling to DaVita, long one of two leading dialysis clinic chains in the country. The purchase price was $4.42 billion.[31]

A big driver for this merger was the desire of DaVita's CEO, Kent Thiry, to diversify his business, believing that his company's management of dialysis centers and nephrologists (doctors who diagnose, treat, and manage kidney diseases and conditions) could be extended to incorporate managed care by primary care teams, but this did not work out. In 2018, DaVita sold its HealthCare Partners assets to Optum Health for $4.3 billion.[32] As Margolis saw it, and put it diplomatically, although HealthCare Partners did their due diligence, DaVita never really understood managed care. Most in the health policy community saw it as Optum Health getting a bargain.

I spent two days with Optum Health's Southern California team in November 2022 under sparkling blue skies and a temperature of 70°F. Optum Health's headquarters in Manhattan Beach was also sparkling. It featured carefully selected colorful but cool pastels, with slim-profile furniture and polished floors. More than one person referred to the decor as a leftover from the DaVita days.

Deborah King, the senior director of clinical transformation, was my host.[33] She had been a lawyer, joined DaVita, and then went to Optum Health. She was my first interview of the day, and I was surprised that her focus was on physician burnout, with a full-throated push for better engagement with the clinicians. As she explained, Optum Health believes that the antidote to burnout is professional fulfillment. The leadership team in Southern California was promoting its Wellness Institute, a two-day training program designed to empower their clinicians. They focus on terms like "lean" and "engagement" and "culture." At individual sites, they undertake "mini-Kaizen" brainstorming sessions. I was impressed, but also somewhat overwhelmed.

King then introduced me to Tyler Denstad, and I was immediately returned to earth.[34] Denstad, Optum Health's director of recruiting, is a longtime human resources recruitment expert. He has responsibility for retaining and replacing (as needed) the approximately 1,500 clinicians (including physicians, nurse practitioners, and advance practice clinicians) Optum Health employs in Southern California. The employed doctors, in turn, are surrounded by a larger independent practice association. The total numbers are impressive. The HealthCare Partners division of Optum Health has 1.7 million members, consisting of 501,000 risk-based members, 110,000 accountable care organization (ACO) members, and 1.13 million fee-for-service lives. There are nearly 8,000 physicians caring for these patients, with approximately 2,000 primary care doctors. In addition, there are more than 1,000 advanced practice clinicians in primary care.

HealthCare Partners is not the only Optum Health medical group in Southern California. North American Medical Management in the Inland Empire metropolitan area has more than 500,000 lives, with 77,000 Medicare Advantage recipients who are cared for by 3,100 physicians, 890 of whom specialize in primary care. Monarch HealthCare in Orange County brings in another 377,000 lives, with 41,000 of them in the Medicare Advantage program. Monarch has nearly 900 primary care doctors among its total of 3,700 physicians. AppleCare Medical Group, in a different part of Orange County, is about half the size of Monarch. Optum Health California has also expanded further in the Inland Empire with Beaver Medical Group and Pinnacle Medical Group, together caring for more than 200,000 patients, with over 200 primary care physicians. Optum also recently moved into Northern California, purchasing the Physicians Medical Group of San Jose and adding another 145,000 lives and a primary care network of 900 physicians. This regional view gives a good sense of Optum Health's immense operation.

It keeps Denstad busy, as there is a lot of competition for physicians. He told me that from his viewpoint, there are almost no internists going into primary care anymore. Internists account for only 3% to 5% of the participants in his new clinician training programs. So, he focuses on family practice. Within that pool, he was looking for people who wanted a rigorous primary care practice, spoke Spanish, and were culturally competent. It is not easy finding such people. To add to a nearly perfect storm, the average age of Optum Health's independent practice association (IPA) doctors is over 60, and many of them will soon retire. The plan is to replace these retirees with full-time employees. But many new doctors do not want a five-days-per-week practice; they are interested in virtual jobs with digital health companies. Optum Health is competing for physicians with Kaiser Permanente as well as with Providence Health and Services and others. Denstad believed that Kaiser Permanente could pay more than Optum Health does.

Denstad has kept moving against these headwinds. He hired 150 doctors in 2022, all of them working more than 30 hours per week. The majority practice five days a week, with 38 hours of patient care per week. The average doctor sees 16–18 patients a day. The pay for Optum Health physicians is around $270,000 to $280,000 per year, with a chance for a bonus of 20% to 30% based on quality/Stars measures, proper documentation, patient experience, utilization, medical management, and access to care. He compared this with the $300,000 per year new doctors at Kaiser Permanente earn. Optum Health also has a student loan forgiveness program, as do all the major physician employers.

Optum Health is gaining a reputation, or at least an identity, and the company plans to slowly unify the various practices into a single brand. The first part of this plan primarily involves marketing. But the Optum Health primary care practices will soon shift to a common business platform, starting with human resources functions and then moving to revenue cycle management and electronic medical records. I heard the same thing at the Reliant Medical Group's practice in Leominster, Massachusetts, a few months later (see chapter 3). At Reliant, the doctors had "Optum" lettered on their white coats, and a big Optum sign dominated the parking lot. At the HealthCare Partners practices, the Optum white coats had not yet arrived, but the signs had.

The driving force for Optum Health's Southern California practices is the Medicare Advantage program, supported by the combination of a strong primary care base and percentage-of-premium health insurance contracts. The practices I visited only take beneficiaries with Medi-Cal (California Medicaid) when their patients are qualified for both Medicare *and* Medicaid. Some of the other HealthCare Partners regions take Medi-Cal and commercial insurance as well. Most of the rest of the Optum groups in Southern California are all-payer as well.

I went from Manhattan Beach to the Division 3 flagship medical center called Del Amo in Torrance, California. Cathy Liu was my welcoming host at the Del Amo facility, a large office building in a busy corner of Los Angeles.[35] She had gone to the University of California, Los Angeles, and then to dental school, but she sustained a wrist injury that would not allow her to continue in dentistry. So, she moved into health care administration. She was first employed at a series of dental clinics, got a position at HealthCare Partners, and has worked her way up its organizational chart. When we toured the facility, she said hello to everyone we passed in a consistently cheerful fashion, asking them if they needed help but not sounding solicitous.

The facility itself is at least 20 years old and exemplifies the siloed approach of twentieth-century ambulatory care. There is little room for team interactions or interdisciplinary care. The big HealthCare Partners centers, like Del Amo, have colocated their specialty practices, but they are a curious group: pulmonary specialists, but no cardiology; neurology, but no orthopedics. As in all HealthCare Partners practices, there is a small pediatrics group—not much of one, but enough to serve the commercial health insurance plans. Obstetrics and gynecology are contracted out. Much of the other care is delegated to specialty physicians' groups on sub-capitation contracts, a method that is still practiced in Los Angeles but not in many other places.

Del Amo is a huge center, but it only has six primary care doctors, all of whom are trained in family medicine. Each of them works with two medical assistants. One of the assistants brings patients into the exam room, while the other one makes outbound telephone calls and coordinates with the incoming call center. One aspect of care that is not good, according to the clinicians, is the center's phone system (a complaint I found consistently across value-based primary care clinics).

The medical assistants take care of any follow-ups and are assiduous about paying attention to Star measures, particularly preventive clinical interventions. They ensure that these are well documented, especially as the year progresses. The clinicians have a strong personal connection with the medical assistants, and the physicians report that they have great support. There is not much else in terms of team care on-site.

Although much of Del Amo's health care support had transitioned to off-site during the pandemic, some of it has now returned to the health center. Inpatient care managers have returned to the physical site as well, while care management teams have adopted a hybrid structure. Some behavioral health specialists work in the clinic, but most of the clinicians' behavioral health support comes from a central office, whose staff members occasionally make visits to the clinic. There are few nurse practitioners at the practices I visited, although I was told that they are more common elsewhere in HealthCare Partners. As a physician's panel grows past 600 Medicare Advantage patients, HealthCare Partner's central administration then assigns an advanced practice clinician to help with the workload.

There is a strong emphasis on maintaining a cohesive patient panel, and doctors proactively reach out to their patients on a variety of issues, including social ones. The key measures of clinician performance are panel size, the panel's Medicare risk-adjustment factor score, utilization, and quality of care.

The quality of care the teams currently provide has been excellent. Information is coming in all the time, both to guide patient care and to allow comparisons between the various health care providers. (This is something Robert Margolis took real pride in.) Transparency in performance is a critical part of the ethos at HealthCare Partners. While I did not see Del Amo's statistics publicly displayed, comparative data were prominent at the second center I visited, Downtown Los Angeles.

I met with several clinicians at the HealthCare Partners–Del Amo practice, including Dr. Sean Rogers, an internist, who is the regional medical director for South Bay.[36] Rogers trained at the University of California, San Diego. He went into private practice in San Diego; moved to Bend, Oregon, for a while; completed an MBA; then worked for Polyclinic (a group of health care facilities in Seattle); and finally joined HealthCare Partners and DaVita. (Interestingly, the physicians I met with at HealthCare Partners were on average 25–30 years older than the Kaiser Permanente doctors I interviewed.) Rogers recalled the "old days" of managed care, which he saw as simply inserting a doctor between a health insurance plan and the patients. At that time, in his view, the only value in managed care was in taking dollars out. As a result, managed care disappeared most places, but not in Los Angeles.

Rogers believed that, in contrast to this generic form of managed care, Robert Margolis and William Chin (one of HealthCare Partners' other founders) had a better vision regarding value-based care, with the triple aim of good care, patient satisfaction, and reduced spending. They built a crew of like-minded physicians and started by forming an independent practice association. Margolis was in downtown Los Angeles, while Chin was near Pasadena, and they built out from there. Torrance and the surrounding South Bay area formed Region 3 (after Downtown Los Angeles and Pasadena), and it is still known as such by the old-timers.

According to Rogers, it was clear early on that DaVita did not know what it had gotten into with HealthCare Partners. DaVita had brought efficiencies into the dialysis industry, but primary care did not readily lend itself to that kind of industrial-quality improvement. Rogers's group did not really notice the corporate transitions, as the Los Angeles operation was profitable. Clinics in other regions were only borderline profitable, and DaVita's management created tumult there.

Rogers noted that the overall mechanics of his job as regional medical director are simple. There is one revenue driver: proper documentation. And there is one cost driver: inpatient hospitalization. As long as he concentrated on these, South Bay should be in reasonable financial shape as a managed care operation, especially in terms of their Medicare Advantage contracts. Rogers realized that change was coming. Over time, CMS would adapt codes to remove subjectivity and ensure fair payment. (Indeed, that is exactly what happened about three months after we spoke.) As codes change, the medical teams react rapidly. For example, the CMS had recently allowed a set of codes for secondary immune deficiency syndrome (acquired, rather than genetic, deficiencies in a person's immune system)—setting off a "mad scramble" to get this condition documented.

Beyond this concise description of the fundamentals, Rogers added thoughts on a variety of subjects. For example, regarding the debate about whether it is better to bring in behavioral health as part of a clinic's operations or to rely on the vendor, behavioral health is outsourced in Torrance's and South Bay's clinics. Another issue was Region 3's IPA structure. An IPA dominates, with a roster of 250 primary care doctors, compared with only 25 who are directly employed. But the average age of their IPA doctors is as noted quite high. Getting to a fully employed model will be a long haul. Tyler Denstad has his work cut out for him.

Rogers recognized that recruiting is critical in going forward. As one of the doctors in the independent practice association retires, Optum Health can shift that person's patients to another IPA doctor. Or they can do a "tuck-in," where the IPA doctor becomes employed by Optum Health for a period before retiring. Optum Health can then directly shift that physician's patients over to one of their other employed doctors. In addition, over 80% of the physicians in the IPA are either exclusive with HealthCare Partners or semi-exclusive (serving just one other contractor), so Optum Health can guarantee some focus in their primary care practices. The bottom line, however, is that Optum/HealthCare Partners needs more primary care clinicians. So, the company has started working with local residency programs to nail down recruits early.

Rogers's administrative responsibilities as regional medical director for Torrance and South Bay are:

1. Proper documentation
2. Quality (performance on the CMS's basic Star measures)
3. Utilization (focusing on hospital admissions and readmissions, as well as the use of skilled nursing facilities and emergency departments)

4. Membership growth and retention
5. Patient experience and access to care
6. Clinician satisfaction

Utilization of hospitals, as noted, gets special interest. Rogers makes use of site-based reviews (SBRs) to address hospital admissions. At an SBR, a team can spend an entire hour discussing a particular case and utilization prevention strategies for it.

When I asked about the big challenges the company faces, Rogers was direct, succinct, and on target.

- The corporate changes have been tough, and the whole organization could feel shaky to physicians. But this situation is stabilizing under Optum Health.
- COVID was devastating, but they survived. Telemedicine visits are now back down to 1% to 2% of total patient visits.
- It is imperative to keep growing, a process in which the support of Optum Health has been superb. This contrasts with Kaiser Permanente, which Rogers believed had not been growing and could not pull off its care model outside of California.
- They must keep on recruiting doctors. New doctors like Optum Health's vision statement, which is gratifying.

Rogers believed that Optum Health is adopting HealthCare Partners' playbook and has begun working it into other geographic areas. Some parts of the operation, however, cannot be exported. For example, New Mexico has no sub-capitation contracts for specialists, a feature of the Los Angeles health care ecosystem. The other key differentiating factor, from Rogers's viewpoint, is that patients in Los Angeles understand the managed care model, which makes a huge difference. This view was widely held by Torrance's and South Bay's clinicians, so it must have some basis in reality. But wandering through the patient flow in the Del Amo and Downtown Los Angeles clinics, it was difficult for me to believe that patients have any clue about utilization meetings and risk-adjustment factors.

I asked Rogers about Optum Health's role as a subsidiary of UnitedHealth Group and its huge national insurer, UnitedHealthcare. I was interested in whether the medical group could increase the enrollment in United's Medicare Advantage plans by recommending it to patients, a process known as steerage. Rogers was clear that Optum Health's clinicians are not allowed to mention specific insurers; they are quite agnostic to the source of insurance for the patient. In fact, HealthCare Partners/Optum Health has good contracts with other health insurers, including SCAN.

The other big issue with Optum's ownership of HealthCare Partners is that it is bringing together several huge medical groups: Monarch HealthCare, AppleCare Medical Group, North American Medical Management, and HealthCare Partners. They will have one referral system, one revenue cycle, one electronic medical record system, and one care management/utilization management system. This will be a big change, but the clinicians are looking forward to it as an opportunity for growth. In talking with Rogers, I got a sense of an experienced managed care clinician who is excited about the future with Optum Health.

Dr. Matthew Lombard is another practicing physician at Del Amo.[37] He trained at the Harbor–University of California, Los Angeles Medical Center after attending medical school at Cornell University, and then practiced family medicine at Harbor for 20 years, teaching residents in an ambulatory setting. He came to HealthCare Partners about nine years ago, as he wanted to concentrate on taking care of patients, and that was getting harder to do at Harbor.

Lombard had a "just-the-facts" style that reminded me of first Los Angeleno I ever saw, Jack Webb in the television series *Dragnet*. Lombard was comfortable practicing managed care. The pay was better at Optum Health than it had been at Harbor, and his salary had increased in the last few years. He could get a bonus—up to 15% of his base salary—by paying attention to his individual performance metrics. (The majority of primary clinicians get about a 10% bonus.) At HealthCare Partners, a clinician's panel size is tracked, and the base panel size must be reached before incentives kick in. Lombard's patients were quite sick, and most of them had Medicare Advantage insurance.

So, his weighted panel size was 2,000, consisting of about 1,300 individuals, which met the threshold necessary for incentives.

Lombard had patients scheduled from 8:00 a.m. to 5:00 p.m. He got to the clinic a half hour early, and after seeing his last patient, he remained there for another 45–60 minutes to do his charting. He worked through lunch. He saw 16–18 patients a day. There was nothing fancy about their charting; he did not use electronic or digital shortcuts. Everyone at Del Amo was on an Allscripts EMR platform, and no one used a medical scribe. The EMR provided a lot of information on gaps in care for his patients. Lombard also got a set of paper prompts that came in daily from a central team, including advice about prevention and care management for specific patients, as well as documentation prompts. Twice a month, his health care team met to discuss hospitalizations. They focused on ambulatory-care-sensitive admissions and tried to understand where care management might have intervened.

Overall, Lombard loved his patients and the team at Del Amo. He was pleased that they had few phone calls from patients at night or on weekends. Hospitalists handled all that. But, like almost everywhere else in my travels, he was plagued by the burden of information overload. His patients were always asking questions on the clinic's patient portal, and it was difficult for him to keep up with all the laboratory orders and medications. This was compounded by the bureaucratic tasks involved in complying with the various performance metrics. For Lombard, some improvements would include a better phone system, as the current one is overly centralized; higher pay for and a larger number of medical assistants; and more clinical support in the primary care practice. While he "never has a bad day, [he] can have a long day." What sustained him was the knowledge that "patients appreciate your service."

Dr. Minesh Mehta is a community medical director, reporting to Sean Rogers.[38] He was trained as a general practitioner in Ontario, Canada, and then did a family medicine residency in Brooklyn at the State University of New York's Downstate Medical Center. After that, he came to Los Angeles and worked for Friendly Hills, another IPA that imploded with the state's big physician consolidation effort in the mid to late 1990s. He found refuge with the Bayshore Medical Group, which was the IPA acquisition that formed Region 3 for HealthCare Partners.

I asked, What has changed? Mehta jumped right into a difficult set of issues surrounding risk scoring. He noted that since Optum Health is now publicly traded, he senses a mercantile ambition under some of what they do, focusing on the efforts surrounding Medicare's risk-adjustment factor. While it is important to document and address all of a patient's health issues, to him it is clear that doing so is also a revenue play. Mehta stated this not as a person informed by the current health policy debate, but as an everyday practitioner in managed care.

The connection between risk scoring and revenue made Mehta uncomfortable in some ways, something I sensed in many other conversations with clinicians. His bottom line was, however, firm. Optum Health does have an ethical business model: to promote good health and lower health care costs. The company's priority is to keep patients healthy by offering convenient access to high-quality care—proper documentation is a byproduct of this. Listening closely, my sense was that this view was informed by Mehta's care for his patients, not by his being a company man. Proper documentation brought proper revenue for a Medicare beneficiary.

There is no doubt that this double effect surrounding documentation pervades practices relying on capitation, and that the clinicians struggle with it. To me, it is a healthy sign, one that creates an appropriate tension. As well, the contrast with fee-for-service is striking. I have never heard a fee-for-service-based doctor probe the ethics of overtreatment, which is a clear incentive in that reimbursement method.

No one with whom I spoke at the various Optum practices I visited suggested that there was pressure from administrators to overcode. In the summer of 2024, the investigative team at Stat revealed they had found "dozens" of doctors at Optum practices who "became enmeshed in UnitedHealth's strategy to make their patients seem as sick as possible."[39] Surely some of the tens of thousands of physicians who work for Optum today are dissatisfied with any oversight of coding. Stat investigators have every incentive to find them. But I suspect Mehta's nuanced view is much closer to the view of most clinicians. Nonetheless, any primary care practice owner is careful about the signals that they send their teams on coding, and the Stat revelations will contribute to that in a good way.

Mehta also discussed HealthCare Partners' approach to managed care. He noted that while their commercial health insurance contracts include both health maintenance organization and preferred provider organization plans, HMOs are a better fit with their organization's philosophy of care. Nonetheless, he asserted that Optum Health was still able to manage care for patients who had a PPO plan, including their care by specialists. (This HMO/PPO distinction has hampered care management for years.)

Mehta was pleased that his team was increasingly traveling to the homes of patients on Medicare Advantage plans to address health care issues and modify medications. Another major bonus from managed care is the pharmacy support center, which monitors certain drugs (like the blood thinner warfarin), refills prescriptions, checks on patients' adherence to their medication regimes, and monitors any changes in medications after a hospital stay.

Overall, Mehta's practice is nearly the opposite of a traditional physician in a fee-for-service system. He is surrounded by a cluster of organizations that help him keep his patients healthy and avoid unnecessary and expensive care. He and his other clinicians have a better perception of their patients, seeing them as individual people coping with illness over time, and emphasizing continuity of care. He is proud that Optum Health is using HealthCare Partners' approach and philosophy as a model. The clinicians with Reliant Medical Group in Massachusetts had the same pride. Optum Health's position is enviable, with so many primary care practices acting as laboratories to understand the best approaches to keeping people healthy.

The view from the administrators at HealthCare Partners is highly resonant with the clinical perception. Lindsay Hess oversees four sites associated with Del Amo: Western San Pedro, Torrance Lomita, East Carson, and West Carson.[40] The practices range in size from four doctors to only one physician. Hess was a nurse, liked supervising, got into ambulatory care, and has been promoted from within. She has now been with HealthCare Partners for 15 years. Given that the sites I visited were imposing, I did not realize that HealthCare Partners had other, smaller sites, but that makes sense, given their IPA structure. Hess also made the point that many people like a smaller office, since they feel overwhelmed in a huge practice setting, such as at Kaiser Permanente.

Hess's problems mirror the tectonic changes that I found everywhere in primary care. She experienced much less turnover in physicians than in medical assistants. The starting pay for medical assistants at HealthCare Partners is $19 an hour, going up to $25, but that might not be enough, as local competitors are offering $5 to $10 more per hour. Her other problem was language skills. She had a large Filipino population at one of her Carson sites, so it needed a clinician who spoke Tagalog. A primary care person with this linguistic range has not been easy to find.

Hess's performance is based on two scores. First is the overall satisfaction of her teammates, which is assessed twice a year. Second, there are the ubiquitous site goals: proper documentation, hospitalizations, and Star measures. The prevalence of these three sets of statistics throughout the organization is an impressive accomplishment. Everyone is focused on a finite set of measures.

Hess's challenges are not surprising. The first was to get all four of her sites fully staffed again after COVID. The second is the shift to Optum One, a new comprehensive integrated delivery system business platform. Hess now uses Work Day, a new human resources system. The next move will be adapting to a new revenue cycle system. She did not believe that these infrastructural changes will affect HealthCare Partners' culture, which has survived intact over the past 15 years: "Everyone is a team player; everyone is striving for the best patient care."

She had other struggles as well. First, Hess echoed her clinicians' views that the current telephone system is too centralized. Second, she often has difficulty explaining to PPO patients how underinsurance works. If a beneficiary receives care from a doctor within the PPO's network, the health insurance company provides the highest level of coverage, with the lowest out-of-pocket cost. If that person gets medical care from a provider outside the network, those services are covered at a much smaller percentage of their overall cost. Hess believed that it is the responsibility of their patients, not the HealthCare Partners team, to understand the ins and outs of the health insurance program they signed up for.

Optum Care: Downtown Los Angeles

I went from Del Amo to the Downtown Los Angeles (DTLA) clinic, somewhat blown away by the Los Angeles freeways and the city's sprawl. When Margolis and those who formed the earliest HealthCare Partners team left their jobs at California Hospital, they stayed committed to their rundown neighborhood near Los Angeles's downtown area. They bought an old building, and as commercial real estate demand in that part of the city grew over time, they were able to sell it for a tremendous profit, creating a financial bonanza. They invested the profits in the new DTLA site, which is located about a mile from downtown and serves the same community.

DTLA's clinicians and administrators designed the facility themselves, and it is impressive, reminiscent of the brand-new site in Frisco, Texas, that the Catalyst Health team had just developed. Both building designs suggest where future primary care practices are heading. The patients are in an onstage area, with the clinicians being offstage. Each exam room has two sliding doors: one opening to the patients' waiting area, the other to the clinician's office. They have completely gotten rid of drapes, creating a sense of openness that also facilitates team meetings. There is a sharp contrast between the DTLA and Del Amo sites.

I met with Dr. Jaime Ramos, Geronie Dougé, and Nicole Rubio as a group to get oriented to the center.[41] Ramos was a local, having gone to UCLA for medical school and then to Harbor–UCLA Medical Center to train. He worked in a homeless shelter for years before coming to

HealthCare Partners so he could earn more to support his growing family. He did not have to travel far when he shifted jobs, as there is a huge downtown Los Angeles homeless encampment less than a mile from where we met at DTLA. Ramos has worked his way up in HealthCare Partners' administrative structure and is now the community medical director for the LA North Region.

Nicole Rubio did not go to college. She came up through the administrative ranks in various hospitals, moved to HealthCare Partners, and is now the site administrator for the DTLA site. Geronie Dougé was a medical assistant, got her certification as a licensed vocational nurse, and started working in urgent care. She then joined HealthCare Partners, and by dint of hard work and competence, took on successively important roles. Dougé now oversees the downtown Los Angeles region as a group operations director. They displayed great pride as we toured their clinical home.

The weather could not have been more brilliant, and the conference room where we met offered tremendous views of the downtown Los Angeles megapolis. The team oriented me to the neighborhood from which their patient population is drawn: an arc circling from downtown over to the southwest, toward the University of Southern California campus. The clinic's patients are generally impoverished, Hispanic, and have Medicare Advantage health insurance plans. (The site also has some commercial insurance contracts.) The typical patient graduates from FQHC care to HealthCare Partners as they reach Medicare age or have disabilities that qualify them for this coverage. At age 65, the resources the government is willing to spend on health care increase tremendously, for at least some people.

DTLA has the same basic clinician model as Del Amo, with each physician having two medical assistants. At DTLA, however, as physicians' patient panels enlarge, they are teamed with an advanced practice clinician (usually an NP). These clinicians then begin to develop their own panels. The DTLA team also talked more about digital support. HealthCare Partners originally did not have great digital capabilities, but DaVita improved them, and this strategy is growing under Optum Health's banner.

DTLA primarily uses California Hospital (now a part of Dignity Health), located close to downtown. DTLA's downtown location is a specialty desert, although the clinic has some specialty practices on-site: optometry/ophthalmology, rheumatology, endocrinology, and orthopedics. DTLA also has sub-capitated agreements with specialists in oncology and pain management who will come on-site. But the clinic must also rely on contracts with health care providers somewhat distant from DTLA, which makes for difficult travel for their patients.

As was the case at Del Amo, family medicine forms DTLA's core, with nine physicians and three advanced practice clinicians. Ramos reiterated that almost no internists are going into primary care, which has largely ceded its place to family medicine. In the future, DTLA will probably use more NPs, according to this administrative team. Given the clinic's focus on their Medicare patient population, its family medicine doctors do not offer pediatric or obstetric care. Instead, they must be skilled in geriatric medicine. DTLA's use of advanced practice clinicians has the same issue I saw elsewhere. These caregivers are novices when first coming out of training, and they need time to come up to speed. DTLA also has trouble recruiting personnel, as this is not an attractive zip code for most clinicians. Their staff members live far away, at least in travel time. Ramos's commute is 90 minutes each way; for Dougé and Rubio, it is close to 2 hours each way!

All three impressed on me that DTLA's community is not composed of worried but generally well people. Instead, their patients are impoverished and sick. The average panel for clinicians has 600 Medicare Advantage patients, plus 300 with commercial health insurance. DTLA's family medicine practice starts to struggle when it hits a threshold of 500 Medicare Advantage patients, as the clinicians then need more support. Hence their advanced practice clinician strategy.

Burnout continues to be an issue, even after COVID. New doctors want to work from 9:00 a.m. to 3:00 p.m., for only a few days each week. But primary care is based on relationships with patients, so clinicians must be available more often. Still, the doctors leave at 5:00 p.m. At that point, patients with questions get their health care via telephone, virtual consultation, or a conversation with the clinician (a hospitalist) on duty. The primary care clinicians can monitor and ultimately manage patients electronically. So, while face-to-face interactions decrease somewhat, virtual patient supervision increases substantially. This is the remarkably different reality for primary care in the twenty-first century.

One other observation deserves mention. The DTLA is concerned about the clinic's ability to address social determinants of health (SDOH) for their patients, and there is a great deal of emphasis on diversity (including within their own staff), inclusion, and equity. But DTLA does not offer health care for Medicaid patients, which does not seem to enter its administrators' realm of consciousness. Other sites in the Optum system do care for Medicaid, but the contrast here at DTLA was striking, given the way they strive to support poor people over the age of 65.

The looming issue for Optum Health is its independent practice association. At DTLA, the youngest IPA doctor is 47 years old. The demise of IPAs has been long predicted, but it has not yet occurred. Still, few doctors today, after completing their training, want to own their own practices. There are some hardy IPAs out there that are still largely composed of private practice physicians, such as the Heritage of Northridge medical group in Northridge, California. Nonetheless, in Southern California, private primary care practices in IPAs seem doomed, just like small practices almost everywhere. (This contrasts sharply with Dallas–Fort Worth and Catalyst Health.)

Overall, Optum Health's strategy of vertical integration in health care is impressive. The company has a learning laboratory where it can try out new tactics yet not lose the experience gained from years spent in managing care. Optum Health is battling the headwinds in primary care, particularly in recruiting and in making life within a primary care practice livable. But over time, it can incorporate improved technologies and organizational innovations into its clinics. HealthCare Partners has not yet made much use of advanced technology, particularly innovations like ambient listening and note generation, as well as artificial intelligence (AI)–based programs for follow-ups on Healthcare Effectiveness Data and Information Set (HEDIS) measures and gaps in patient care. Such changes could make their primary care practices more efficient in the future.

HealthCare Partners follows a Medicare Advantage–based strategy. Some will say this is a fatally flawed direction, remaining viable only as long as the federal government does not fix the inappropriately high reimbursement rates that come with overcoding. That may be true, but as a relatively impartial observer, I had the sense that managing care—taking care of the whole person while ensuring efficient care—is the real driver in an organization like HealthCare Partners. Its doctors seem as committed to their patients, while facing some of the same stresses, as their colleagues at FQHCs. If anything, every primary care clinician should have the resources that come with Medicare Advantage, although future resources must come from rooting out unnecessary care, not through exuberant code documentation.

Humana and Managed Care

Other large national commercial health insurers are following the same path, but they are miles behind Optum in terms of the sheer numbers of their affiliated practices. Humana is the closest competition. Humana started in the 1960s as a nursing home chain, led by David Jones Sr. and Wendell Cherry. By the early 1970s, their strategy shifted to owning hospitals. The company, renamed Humana, prospered, but after a dustup with an insurer in Arizona, Humana decided it should also offer its own health insurance plans. In the early 1990s, Humana's shift toward health insurance became complete when Jones sold its hospital chain to the larger Hospital Corporation of America. From that point on, Humana was solely a health insurer. In the late 1990s, UnitedHealth Group attempted to purchase Humana but bungled the process.

Under Michael McCallister, who replaced Jones as Humana's CEO, the company saw the opportunities created by the Medicare Modernization Act's refurbishment of Medicare Advantage, and it shifted its growth strategy heavily toward Medicare. Since that time, Humana has invested in programs to promote health care for seniors and has championed physician-based financial risk, especially for Medicare

Advantage. This evolution culminated in a decision to completely exit the employer-based commercial group health insurance business in early 2023.[42]

Humana has clearly staked its corporate future on value-based health care—rooted in primary care—in the Medicare Advantage market. A 2021 report, reviewing 2020 data, provides good background on their progress.[43] At that time, more than two-thirds of their 3.96 million Medicare Advantage members were seeing primary care doctors who had value-based agreements with Humana. Nearly 800,000 of those members were in arrangements where a primary care team took on a global budget, with its accompanying financial risk, for all aspects of Medicare Part A (hospitalization), Part B (physician and outpatient care), and Part D (drugs). Another 165,000 were in arrangements where the primary care practices assumed responsibility for all of the Part B costs. Those patients whose doctors were in such financial risk arrangements received better care. The overall HEDIS scores for these at-risk primary care practices were higher, as was their patients' adherence to medication regimens. Managed patients had a lower probability of being admitted to a hospital or visiting an emergency department. And they were substantially more satisfied with their health care.

A good deal of this value-based financial risk is founded on Humana's contracts with independent physicians' groups. But Humana also operates a model where it employs primary care physicians, similar to what Optum does. Over time, Humana had bought some of the IPAs that were in a global capitation arrangement, forming them into a subsidiary, Conviva, in Florida and Texas. Humana had also started hiring primary care doctors for its own clinics, under the CenterWell brand. The two subsidiaries have now been brought together under one leadership team and have a common EMR system and data warehouse.[44] In June 2023, CenterWell opened its 250th clinic and plans to open between 30 and 50 more clinics a year over the next three years.[45] These centers accept payments from all health insurers, but their core is the Humana Medicare Advantage program. Vivek Garg, the chief medical officer (CMO) for Humana's primary care operation, put me in touch with his Conviva and CenterWell teams.

I visited with Dr. William Russell at a Conviva practice in West Palm Beach, Florida.[46] Russell brought an extraordinary background in geriatrics to his work with value-based care. He also has a unique approach: informed, opinionated, yet curious and analytic.

Russell grew up in New York City, in the Bronx, and he has not lost the direct (and at times barbed) friendliness that characterizes this borough. He went to Georgetown University for medical school, then trained at the Johns Hopkins University School of Medicine. Russell remained in Baltimore to pay off his National Health Services Corps scholarship, working at a senior living program in West Baltimore, which he loved. He subsequently did a geriatrics fellowship and then was employed by the Daughters of Charity to revitalize a huge skilled nursing facility they operated in the city.

The rest of Russell's career consisted of a series of eclectic stops: working with John Erickson on the design of retirement communities; doing medical informatics, with a focus on EMRs, at the Office of the National Coordinator for Health Information Technology (the federal governmental agency that oversees the nationwide electronic communication of patient data); developing primary care practices with the entrepreneurial Chen family; and then participating in a number of primary care practice settings in Florida. He landed at Conviva two years ago and is now its CMO for the Palm Beach region.

Conviva has five regional operations in Florida: in Dade County, Broward County, Palm Beach County, Orlando, and Jacksonville. The Palm Beach region includes 36 primary care practices and more than 120 physicians. Russell noted that Humana has oscillated in its strategy regarding its primary care practice assets, and Conviva is no exception. Humana had owned Conviva, spun it out, and then reacquired the entire asset. Everything will apparently be consolidated into Humana's CenterWell brand, but for now the Conviva practices have some autonomy. Like Optum Health, these primary care practices nearly exclusively serve patients with Medicare Advantage health insurance. Humana is aggressively purchasing more practices as it signs up more Medicare Advantage and ACO REACH (Realizing Equity, Access, and Community Health) beneficiaries.

Practice purchases used to be a somewhat fraught proposition, as it was never clear exactly what you were buying. Independent primary care doctors could quit a practice like Conviva and start anew on their own. I have experience, having spent time buying primary care practices in Boston in the 1990s to get into managed care, then paying these practices to leave when we shifted strategies. Nor is there anything new in this situation. In *Middlemarch*, Rosamond Vincy tried to reassure her father about the finances of her betrothed, Dr. Tertius Lydgate, by asserting that he had bought Mr. Peacock's practice. The flinty and pragmatic Mr. Vincy quickly retorted, "Stuff and nonsense. What's buying a practice? He might as well buy next year's swallows. It'll all slip through his fingers."[47] Today, physicians are less likely to leave an IPA or other organization to reenter private practice—the economics for small independent practices is just too tough. Purchasing primary care practices is much more the norm, and this is unlikely to be the same as buying next year's swallows.

All the practices doing value-based care in this book has someone like Russell who thinks through the best strategies for providing complete and parsimonious health care for their patients. He focuses on hospitalizations, reading a plethora of discharge summaries that come from a good local health information exchange in Florida. The Conviva team has its own hospitalist service, with care managers on the ground at the local hospitals. But given that the two main incentives for hospitals are to keep their beds full and to reduce the length of patient stays, the financial risks for the plans of patients being treated there is extraordinary. The Conviva team does everything it can to keep their patients out of the hospital. Russell cited an example. If a patient with a damaged heart valve is counseled by a specialist who magnifies the benefits of minimally invasive valve replacement surgery and discounts its risks, that person's primary care doctor needs to step in on behalf of the patient.

From a care management perspective, Russel saw Conviva's primary care practice as being based on the mnemonic five M's. This is a play on the four M's of Dr. Mary Tinetti, a famous geriatrician who cited four key factors that someone taking care of the elderly must observe:

what Matters to the patient, Medication, Mentation (mental activity), and Mobility. Russell added a fifth M: Multiple conditions/complexities arising from social determinants of health. He reiterates these factors whenever he visits Conviva's other facilities in the region. Russell's practices in the Palm Beach region have 8 geriatricians peppered throughout his team of 120 clinicians. Their clinical advice is crucial, and he believed that value-based care has saved geriatrics in many ways. In my travels for this book, Russell was the only person I met who relied on geriatrics-trained doctors in Medicare Advantage situations. As Professor Jerry Gurwitz has pointed out, it is odd that value-based care under Medicare has not engendered a renaissance for geriatrics as a medical specialty.[48] At least in Russell's practices, it has.

Otherwise, a lot of what Conviva does is similar to what happens at an Optum Health or Kaiser Permanente clinic. Their EMR software is eClinicalWorks. Russell had firm views about the EMR universe, preferring Athena or Elation platforms. SalesForce Health provides the backbone for Conviva's care management teams. In office settings, clinicians are paired one-on-one with medical assistants, but there are only two behavioral health specialists and one pharmacist for the entire region, so the support team within a clinic is not broad. Conviva also has a five-person team making home visits. And Russell expects his primary care team to address patients' behavioral health problems, avoiding overmedication. To do this properly, clinicians must talk with their patients, something he feared many specialists—including psychiatrists—do not do.

Conviva's physician incentives are comparable to those in other value-based practices: patient engagement; compliance with clinical pathways; and adherence to various measures, such as net promoter score (indicating patient loyalty and satisfaction), hospital admission rates, and emergency department visits. One prominent issue for Conviva is conducting chart reviews. Russell was remarkably interested in the clinical details of what was happening in the various practices. His motto is "think hard and care."

Russell did not judge every practice in the same way. Those situated in the impoverished part of Palm Beach County are not going to look as good on paper regarding performance measurements, as such measures fail to capture how sick these patients are and how advanced their diseases can be. As he argued, "West Palm needs a good dose of primary care!" Statistics for the Conviva practice that is near a large hospital (run by the for-profit Hospital Corporation of America) are going to show higher utilization, reflecting selection bias by patients who choose this clinic combined with the tug of the incentives of the specialists and the hospital. While Russell's style was direct to the point of being outspoken, these observations by a clinical leader seemed astute and wise.

Russell was also cognizant of the corporate structure in which he practiced. He shrugged off the lack of team resources, noting that publicly traded companies can sometimes fail to see long-term benefits. (I agree generally with that assessment, but what Optum Health and Humana are doing in primary care does appear to be farsighted.) He was also skeptical of private equity investments in health care, concerned that these investors do not have a full understanding of medical care and may be too profit oriented (widely held beliefs, as we will see).

This plays into the risk-adjustment factor conundrum. Conviva does not give bonuses to doctors based on their patients' risk scores. Other practices have made risk adjustment into a science, using analytics and comprehensive audits of patients' charts. Viewed positively, this kind of "mining" of diagnoses may be nothing more than anticipating problems through the use of appropriate data analyses, thus heading off medical conditions before they deteriorate. Russell called it good medicine, since "you are trying to spot problems in the distance and address them." But some practices might overdo it, and Russell believes that CMS is going to catch up with them. So, Russell has concluded that it is best to leave the main responsibility for coding with primary care clinicians and then complement that with analytics and chart reviews. There is no getting around the value of good coding, however, both in terms of anticipating problems and generating revenue.

Given the chance to talk about what he liked and disliked about how primary care is being practiced today, Russell's responses were telling—and ironic. He greatly admires Dr. Bruce Leff at the Johns Hopkins

University School of Medicine. Leff has advocated for providing real care within a patient's home, not just making home visits that are little more than gathering diagnoses for coding purposes. He also extolled the virtues of Dr. James Chen, who started the ChenMed dynasty (see chapter 8). According to Russell, Chen had an unparalleled ability to identify the right thing to do in each clinical situation. In contrast, Russell found other venture capital–backed primary care companies to be nothing more than veneers wrapped around their coding-revenue profit margins. He hated EMRs generally: "They steal the relationship with the patient. If they do not make you more present when seeing the patient, how can they be a good thing? Plus overdocumentation and cloning of other people's notes are rampant."

Russell believed that his regional practices, plus Conviva and Humana in general, were doing the right thing for patients, and that value-based care, with full financial risks, must be part of primary care's future. His clinicians understand this. They knew they were getting into global capitation arrangements, with the attendant financial risk, when they joined the practice. He believed that Medicare would eventually find ways to cut risk-based reimbursement, and the winners would be those who kept their patients healthy and reduced overall medical costs. "Then practices will have to walk the walk."

Other For-Profit Corporations

Among the other major health insurers, Centene and Molina are focused on Medicaid and have not been buying medical practices. A good deal of their clinical base is in federally qualified health centers, and they must remain independent to get payments from Medicaid. For-profit Elevance Health—formed through a merger of Anthem and WellPoint Health Networks and affiliated with formerly nonprofit Blue Cross Blue Shield plans—and Cigna tend to rely on ACOs. They let their integrated delivery systems organize themselves and offer a variety of value-based health insurance contracts. In 2024, however, Elevance announced plans to work with Clayton, Dubiler &

Rice, a venture capital firm, to develop primary care practices under the name of Mosaic Health.

CVS Health has a lot of pharmacies (almost 9,000 in 2023) and 1,100 retail clinics. But in contrast to what Timothy Hoff might say in his 2018 book,[49] the pharmacies and urgent care clinics were never intended to provide primary care (nor were they capable of doing so). In 2023, CVS Health finally jumped into the primary care game by purchasing Oak Street Health (see chapter 7). Walgreens, the other huge retail pharmacy chain, has been involved with primary care for some time.

Like CVS Health, Walgreens was once in the retail health care clinic business, but apparently it could not get the formula correct because its clinics lost money. Eventually, Walgreens looked for integrated delivery systems that might be willing to operate the clinics, taking on the financial risk in return for reduced rent. Today, Walgreens has fewer than 150 retail health clinics, compared with 1,000 in CVS retail pharmacies.[50] Although the hospital industry and organized medicine fear that these retail clinics might become full-service primary care facilities, they are ill fitted to do so. Retail care clinics, typically operating with a single nurse practitioner, are oriented toward low-severity urgent conditions, especially coughs and colds.

Realizing that operating retail clinics was not a way to become an integral part of the US health care system, Walgreens turned to primary care several years ago. In mid-2020, the pharmacy chain announced that it would work with VillageMD, a chain of primary care practices, to put doctor- and advanced practice clinician–based clinics in 500–700 of its stores over the ensuing five years. The company signaled that it was moving from episodic care for minor but acute (temporary) conditions toward care for those with continuous, chronic diseases.[51]

VillageMD had expanded rapidly from its founding in 2013, going from a base of 13 physicians to more than 2,800 in nine markets by 2021.[52] This remarkable growth occurred independently of Walgreens, but then the organizations became tightly linked, with Walgreens owning 63% of the primary care company at one time.[53] Building clinics in Walgreens' retail pharmacies made sense for VillageMD, since the pharmacy chain could select its locations based on ease of access and plenty of foot traffic. In addition, VillageMD was positioned to have Walgreens' pharmacists address the issues of patient adherence to medication regimes and cost-effective drug selection. For Walgreens, patient traffic in the VillageMD clinics was intended to increase their own pharmacy business. In many stores, their huge retail "front end" is a money loser, so bringing in new tenants is profitable. Unlike Optum or Humana (or CVS Health), however, Walgreens is not in the health insurance business and lacks the synergy of the *flywheel effect*, a continuous cycle of growth through a combination of better primary care, lower medical costs, lower premiums, and thus more health insurance business. To address this limitation, Walgreens planned to start offering Medicare Advantage health insurance plans by 2024.[54]

I visited with VillageMD in 2023. Clive Fields, its cofounder, put me in touch with Dr. Viresh Patel, one of the physicians at a Walgreens-based VillageMD practice in Houston.[55] Patel had trained at Louisiana State University in internal medicine/pediatrics, but he returned home to Houston to practice. He took a job with the Tenet hospital chain, which was building a primary care infrastructure. Tenet then sold their hospitals to the Hospital Corporation of America, and HCA was not interested in the strategy of growing physicians' primary care practices. VillageMD ended up hiring most of the doctors formerly employed by Tenet, including Patel.

Patel worked in the sixth of the Houston area's remodeled Walgreens stores. The clinic took up about half the space of what was formerly the front of the store. He stated that having access to the store's pharmacists was a huge advantage. The teams from the two entities met weekly to discuss mutual issues. VillageMD patients got fast pharmacy service, and Walgreens' pharmacists could get help with required prior authorizations and physicians' instructions. VillageMD also had its own central pharmacist team that helped patients, and their doctors, with adherence issues and questions about medications.

This VillageMD clinic had all the same issues as other primary care practices that were also trying to offer value-based health care but seemed a bit less mature. Walgreens was not as focused on financial risk arrangements, taking all forms of insurance (except Medicaid) and using a reimbursement structure for the providers in which half of the payments were still based on relative value units. Patel noted that the clinic was moving toward an empaneled approach, and he was able to spend a great deal more time with his patients than he did when working for Tenet. The clinical team consisted of a couple of people working the phones and greeting people up front, and a physician who was paired with a medical assistant (an additional medical assistant was available if volume thresholds were hit).

Patel praised his Athena EMR platform, which VillageMD also used for its revenue cycle management. He thought the Athena EMR system had a great managed care program, although VillageMD had its own population health management program, called docOS, that ran alongside the EMRs. At Tenet, he felt a tug to get patients into one of their hospitals. At VillageMD it was the opposite, which accorded with his belief that hospitals are best avoided until absolutely necessary. He was also a big booster of VillageMD's Village at Home program, which sends advanced practice clinicians to a patient's home.

This VillageMD practice in Houston had many of the same problems that one finds elsewhere in primary care. Patel saw about 20 patients a day, which, he allowed, is a lot. He wrote all his own patient notes. He had no medical scribes, but a good transcription service was available. The Houston clinic stayed open late to avoid having patients use urgent care facilities. The clinicians did have Medicare Advantage patients, and they were instructed about the importance of annual wellness visits. But overall, Patel did not seem hassled and instead felt rather refreshed. In his interactions with VillageMD's corporate team, he was dealing with clinicians who understood value-based care. Tenet was overseen by administrators who lacked an appreciation for clinical issues and focused on volume. Moreover, Patel enjoyed the sense of being on the cutting edge of what medicine should be.

The future for VillageMD practices like Patel's is now no longer clear, as over the course of a year, Walgreens has completely backed away from bricks and mortar primary care. Trying to find a new way forward, Walgreens parted ways with CEO Rosalind Brewer, who championed the primary care model. Tim Wentworth, a longtime pharmacy benefit manager (PBM) executive, replaced her and decided the company could not tolerate the losses at primary care clinics. Closures began almost immediately, affecting about 160 of the more than 600 clinics.[56]

Walgreens had a controlling interest in VillageMD and is now planning to give that up. The Walgreens rationale for rapid expansion in primary care had always been a bit odd, given that it did not have an insurance entity that could profit from value-based care. The pharmacy retailer had discussed relationships with Medicare Advantage insurers, but it is not clear that any of these came to fruition. Moreover, it was not clear how robust the management model was at VillageMD, as the company had grown quickly.

Amid this tumult, I spoke with Tim Barry, who heads VillageMD and was one of the founders.[57] Barry was appropriately guarded in his comments, but he was clearly pained by the closures, especially since many clinics had been growing well and according to plan. I got the impression that financial difficulties in the overall corporation made ongoing losses at primary care intolerable. I also had the sense that the Brewer administration had pushed for establishment of *de novo* clinics, those without an existing patient base (as opposed to purchase or affiliation with an existing practice). These new clinics obviously take longer to fill. Nonetheless, Barry was optimistic, and convinced their management model could lower costs. However, in November 2024, Barry left Walgreens and VillageMD.

As these changes occurred at Walgreens in the spring of 2024, Walmart gave up on its somewhat quixotic journey through primary care. The huge retailer had employed at least five different strategies in primary care, starting more than a decade ago.[58] The most recent was establishing large clinics that would be a one-stop shop for an array of health services, including primary, dental, and vision care. The scale was enormous, up to 4,000 clinics by 2029. Then in early June came the announcement that all 51 existing clinics would close immediately, following losses of nearly a quarter of a billion dollars.[59]

Even more so than Walgreens, Walmart seemed to be betting on profitable fee-for-service, which always seems a poor bet for primary care. There was much discussion of a relationship with UnitedHealthcare in Medicare Advantage, but that never led to many patient visits. One might presume that with the dimmer prospects for Medicare Advantage profitability as risk-adjustment changes take place, the top management just lost interest in a failing asset. As the *Wall Street Journal* put it, the change in perception about the role of retailers in primary care was dramatic: "Just a few years ago, it looked as though national retail chains were going to be your doctor, too. Now they are medical-school dropouts."[60]

Similar to traditional retailers, the huge online retailer Amazon has dipped into primary care as well. Amazon, like Walmart, is feared by the big commercial health insurers, pharmacy retailers, and hospital chains. When Amazon comes into a service area, existing companies are generally overwhelmed and go out of business within a few years, a fate that the health care players hope to avoid.

But health care is a bit different. During my years spent in the health care business, I had heard thinly veiled threats from different tech executives that their new initiatives were going to replace what those of us in the more traditional (to them, hidebound) companies were doing. Some quiet satisfaction resulted as those threats came and went. Nonetheless, a statement from a consultant familiar with Amazon remains with me: "What is easier, for Amazon to learn pharmacy, or a chain like CVS to learn tech?" Good point, I thought, and one likely applicable to primary care.

Its reputation well earned, Amazon nonetheless has not conquered, yet, in health care. Instead, its approach smacks of the same haphazard approach originally taken by Walmart. In 2019, the company's initial step was a virtual health care program for employers, called Amazon Care. Soon thereafter, Amazon bought PillPack, an online pharmacy firm that started in New Hampshire, and stock prices for retail pharmacy chains dropped. Within a year, PillPack changed its branding from "PillPack, an Amazon company" to "PillPack by Amazon Pharmacy." But it did not rapidly gain market share. Amazon Care expanded, albeit slowly, throughout 2021. Amazon Web Services (AWS) began to offer AWS for Health, a computer platform explicitly designed for hospitals and clinics. The capabilities of Amazon's Alexa app were extended to hospitals for use in ambient documentation and home monitoring.

But by 2022, Amazon Care was shut down and replaced by Amazon Clinic, which is a type of clearinghouse for other virtual health care providers. In 2023, AWS unveiled HealthScribe, which was meant to take electronic health care documentation to a new level, relying only on ambient recordings and a big dose of AI. This latter product will compete with similar ones from other big technology firms, particularly Microsoft, Apple, and Google. The new emphasis appeared to be on virtual and digital products.

At the same time, Amazon bought One Medical, a primary care chain, which struck many as veering toward bricks and mortar. (Another Amazon purchase was Whole Foods, and my Whole Foods paper bags now have advertisements for One Medical, so there is some synergy there.) One Medical was originally founded by Dr. Tom Lee, a serial entrepreneur who had started one of the first mobile medical reference devices, Epocrates. Lee thought that medicine lacked a "high-touch" approach to primary care, involving personal attention and service, and that high-quality service could be affordable. He averred that he could provide ten times the primary care service at one-third the price, simply through better management.[61]

The model he developed had certain aspects of what has been called concierge medicine's personalized approach. It is not a true concierge practice in that patients with all insurance are accepted. If a patient wants to step up to additional services, they are charged a yearly membership fee, which today stands at $199. For that additional money, participants get on-demand care, by video, on a 24/7 basis.[62] Patients also have access to an app called "Treat Me Now" that allows them to get care for common concerns like colds and flu, skin issues, allergies, urinary tract infections, and more at no extra costs. There are no copays for any of these services. This program is available at all 240 offices.

It is a distinctive approach. In most concierge practices, the annual fees are much higher, and the concierge physicians would typically trim the number of their patients back from, say, 2,000 to 500, allowing more leisurely appointments and greater access. One Medical does this less expensively through better management and better technology. Their mantra is that patients should be able rely on their One Medical app for all their medical needs. It fits with digital commerce: buy-ups for extra services are part of many people's daily lives.

Lee left the company in 2017 and was replaced by Amir Dan Rubin, whose background included running Stanford Medical Center and working as an executive at Optum Health. One Medical had been promoted as a better health care option to employers who might be willing to offer their employees higher-quality primary care, with a promise that their health care costs would be lower. It also began to partner with academic medical centers in developing primary care practices for them. But it did not have a hand in Medicare Advantage.

That deficiency was solved in late 2021 with the purchase of Iora Health for $1.4 billion.[63] Iora was founded a decade earlier by Dr. Rushika Fernandopulle, its longtime CEO, and Christopher McKown, its executive chairman. They, too, were looking for a better way to provide primary care services, and for years they attempted to work with employers. Eventually, though, they settled on a Medicare model, taking a percentage of the total premiums to manage Medicare Advantage plans on a full-risk basis. Their "secret sauce" included much smaller patient panels, careful assessments of financial risk, and health coaches who maintained tight relationships with patients. At the time of its acquisition by One Medical, Iora Health had about 39,000 members (mostly on Medicare Advantage plans), with revenues of $318 million, whereas One Medical had 621,000 members but proportionately smaller revenues (about $480 million), since it mostly had commercial health insurance beneficiaries.[64]

It will be interesting to see where One Medical heads. The original program, with an emphasis on digital care and a series of high-touch virtual services for a relatively small fee, was based largely in fee-for-service. Iora had a long history in employer-based programs but eventually arrived at a risk-based Medicare Advantage model. The coevolution of the two stands to be fascinating. High-touch, virtual-assisted care does seem like a great fit with the attention each Medicare Advantage patient needs. The average member at One Medical interacted with clinical care ten times per year, two physically and eight digitally. This could lead to great member engagement, while still being efficient.

Why did Amazon pay $3.9 billion for One Medical?[65] Perhaps it wanted to fine-tune its other new products. One Medical gives Amazon a health care relationship with employers, plus more than 200 clinics that can complement its virtual services. Amazon Web Services' HealthScribe product, which is designed to integrate voice recognition, AI, and machine learning in order to improve medical office practices, would probably be perfected in One Medical primary care facilities.[66] This does seem like the kind of solution that primary care clinicians are looking for—something that allows them to escape writing patient notes and focus on being with their patients. The same technology combination would presumably be efficient in finding gaps in patients' health care, encouraging preventive steps, identifying at-risk patients, and even suggesting diagnostic codes.

In February 2023, One Medical's corporate team announced the results for both its fourth quarter and the full 2022 year. For the latter, revenues were $1.046 billion. But their net loss was $144.1 million, so they were a long way from profitability.[67] Meanwhile, membership continues to grow. At the end of 2022, One Medical had 876,000 members. But the big question is, Can the model persist once there are expectations of profitability by Amazon? Whether One Medical becomes profitable or whether questions remain about its model, there is still money to be made by investors and executives. For example, in October 2022, Amir Dan Rubin sold some of his One Medical stock, worth almost $100 million.[68]

How does all this work out for the primary care clinicians at these practices? Dr. Fernandopulle introduced me to the One Medical and One Medical Seniors (the new name for Iora) practices in Arizona, which I visited on a surprisingly cool week in January.

First, I went to Gilbert (southeast of Phoenix), through what seemed like 100 miles of parched desert that was covered in housing tracts, and arrived at the rather new SanTan Village Mall. As was explained to me that cold morning, it is an outdoor mall, so people cannot easily go there in the heat of the summer, even though its broad walkways are covered with generous overhanging roofs. The mall had stores selling all the latest fashions and other businesses, although at nine o'clock in the morning, barricades indicated that the mall was still closed.

The One Medical office was in a corner—small, but just as beautifully sleek as the rest of the mall. One nicely appointed waiting area led to a central hallway with examining rooms on each side, so it did not have an onstage/offstage design. A decision had been made to have this facility be in the high-rent district but occupy a rather small square footage.

The first person I met was Zachary Ortiz, a cheerful and engaging family medicine doctor.[69] He received a joint MD/MPH (master of public health) degree from the University of Arizona and then trained at Banner–University Medical Center in Phoenix. He came to One Medical right after completing his residency, having been impressed by a presentation given by One Medical's executive team at a job fair. Ortiz had reached the conclusion that his residency training was too rushed, and he was intrigued by the slower pace at One Medical. He also disliked the NextGen EMR system used at Banner–University Medical Center, so One Medical's emphasis on an alternative approach to EMRs interested him. Ortiz signed up with One Medical a few days after attending that job fair, and several years later, he still had no regrets.

At other potential employers, Ortiz was looking at a schedule of 20–25 patient visits a day, while at One Medical, he never saw more than 16 patients. One Medical has a $199 annual fee, but Ortiz and others at the clinic recoiled at a characterization of this approach as concierge medicine, much preferring to see it as a "member-driven organization." There are also family memberships and a variety of discounts, so the One Medical primary care practices are not concerned about excluding people because of this annual fee.

When Ortiz began working at the Gilbert facility three years ago, One Medical had four primary care practices in Arizona. Over time that number has grown, and just as importantly, the clinics have developed a relationship with Dignity Health to provide a primary care base for Dignity's medical centers. This has enabled One Medical's primary care clinicians to become familiar with Dignity's specialists and work closely with them on integrating managed care into what they do. One Medical's clinicians are not restricted to Dignity Health's facilities for hospitalizations, but over time, as these relationships grew, it seemed natural to use Dignity's specialists and facilities. These are close ties. For example, on Wednesday afternoons, One Medical's clinicians have joint hospital rounds with Dignity Health specialists, and the clinicians can get continuing medical education credit from this arrangement. Both sides enjoy the give-and-take in their discussions about clinical cases—which focus on hospitalizations, as might be expected.

One Medical's goal is to change the fabric of primary care, and Ortiz has bought in to this. He saw patients four days per week, and some of those visits were still virtual. He is able to get most (at least 90%) of his charting done during the day. Devotion is not too strong a word for Ortiz's attitude toward One Medical's EMR system, 1Life. The company has invested heavily in this platform, as it wants to simplify its primary care clinicians' workflow and make information available in a well-tailored manner. Ortiz spent half a day per week working with the technology team on changes in that clinical flow.

Ortiz was fascinated by, and openly speculated on, One Medical's leadership changes. From his point of view, Tom Lee had great energy, but perhaps the business got too big. Lee had the vision, but Ortiz felt that Amir Dan Rubin was better suited to run a company of this size. Such speculation reflects a real sense of team ownership of the company (although the real owner now is Amazon, Dan Rubin having departed in 2023).

Ortiz went into some detail on the development of One Medical's 1Life EMR system. Everything is based on an ever larger series of application programming interfaces (APIs), which support connections to other digital interventions. He recalled an exciting day when the clinicians could start accessing information from CVS Health on vaccinations. One senses that the open nature of this EMR, combined with Amazon's aspirations for AI and large language models, made One Medical a good fit for Amazon.

Some of the other details on the in-person time Ortiz spent with his patients did seem to offer a picture of the future of primary care. He does charting for a patient while he is seeing that person. As he charts, he can enter a "help out" request that will pull up information on that patient and provide it to Ortiz within minutes. This service will even download data from the local health information exchange. The 1Life program includes many keyboard shortcuts that speed up charting, and it edits out unhelpful information, such as well-known interactions between drugs. These are the kinds of things other primary care clinicians desire but cannot get with their off-the-shelf EMR systems. In addition, patients frequently use the One Medical app, which interacts directly with 1Life's EMR records. The entire experience for One Medical's physicians and their patient seems facilitated by digital communications, not beset by them.

One Medical has delinked its clinician reimbursement from fee-for-service payment, which contributes to this sense of continuity in a patient's primary care. RVUs are not part of One Medical's compensation scheme. Ortiz saw 20% to 30% fewer patients per day at One Medical than he would have had he stayed at Banner–University Medical Center. Rather than evaluate its clinicians on the number of patient visits, One Medical scrutinizes patient feedback, relying on a net promoter score and the completion of preventive medicine tasks. Ortiz also receives a 360-degree evaluation from his team, meaning that everyone he works with is engaged in judging his work. The rewards are company based. Ortiz received stock in One Medical when he hit "First Star" status and got even more stock after seven years with the clinic, when he reached "Second Star" status.

Everyone in the Gilbert facility emphasized One Medical's team-based approach. The physicians and advanced practice clinicians work closely together. Arizona allows nurse practitioners to provide care without physician oversight, so there is a lot of curbsiding, as well as a six-month mentorship program for advanced practice provider (APPs). A member support specialist answers telephone calls and does pharmacy-related tasks. All their clinics have labs on-site, and a lab support specialist does blood draws. One Medical's facilities in Arizona do not have care managers or pharmacists, but the company is starting to add these professionals centrally. At present, most of the Gilbert primary care practice's patients have commercial health insurance plans, so there is less need for care management. One Medical, however, has developed a program called Mindset by One Medical for mental health services. Another program, Impact, provides access to a multidisciplinary team that creates a personalized wellness plans for patients with chronic diseases. Patients can also join group visits, which have proven to be successful.

All of this works well for Ortiz. He loves his primary care practice, as it provides "authentic interactions with people," "really values him," and "buffers against burnout." He asserted that One Medical readily recruits staff from other clinical organizations that simply "burn and churn." On top of One Medical's commitment to its clinicians, staff members get perks like family medical leave, a sabbatical every five years, and competitive salaries.

I also got a chance to talk to an office manager in Gilbert, Diana Vinh.[70] She came from the retail clothing business and retains the same customer relations qualities she learned there. At One Medical, Diana worked up from a position as an office support specialist (the front desk), to shift leader (providing direct supervision to shift-based employees), to office manager. She loved her work, both in managing the clinicians and in directing many of its complex operations. Describing her work at the front desk, she noted, "You have the first and the last impression with the customer, so you have to make the most of it." Demand is high in their primary care clinic, and her team must handle many duties. In a typical medical office, the only responsibilities for the front office person are to ask for a patient's name, date of birth, and health insurance information. Not at One Medical. Every patient gets a warm greeting, feels at home, and is told how long the waiting time at the clinic will be. Each patient also receives a post-visit survey, and their responses are tied directly into staff bonuses (everyone, including the doctors, is on a salary). Diana had "eight hours a day to be kind and empathetic."

The last person I met at the Gilbert clinic was Rakesh "Rocky" Patel.[71] He grew up in suburban Detroit, went to the University of Michigan and then to Wayne State University for medical school, and trained at Oakwood Hospital and Medical Center in Dearborn, Michigan. He then moved west and went into private practice in Gilbert, working first for the Desert Samaritan Medical Center's hospital for seven years. From 2005 to 2016, he put out his own shingle, did all his own inpatient work, and made rounds at three hospitals. That must have been exhausting. He did some family medicine cross-coverage (being the covering doctor for other physicians, such as at night or on weekends), and that primary care organization eventually transitioned first into an IPA and then into an ACO in the Medicare Shared Savings Program. The IPA had 120 clinicians and they did well, getting money back through the Medicare Shared Savings Program.

Patel's work/life balance finally got the better of him. He came to One Medical in 2016 and has taken the lead on several initiatives, particularly on lipid management and cardiovascular medicine. (Among all the rest of his activities, he was at one point the owner of a clinic for cardiometabolic health, which are issues related to diabetes, heart diseases, and strokes.) One Medical does not buy physicians' practices, so Patel had to convert his patients over to One Medical's primary care practice. He had 4,000–5,000 patients when he joined One Medical, working with one physician assistant and a half-time nurse practitioner. Not all his patients signed up with One Medical, but many did. Patel was surprised—in some ways stunned—at how much he liked working in the new environment.

Since January 2022, Patel has been the market medical director for Phoenix and works with a strategic population health management team. The population management team strives to have the clinicians consider the total medical expenses for their patients, their own performance on quality-of-care measures, and how to network with specialists. Not surprisingly, given their ubiquity elsewhere in primary care for seniors, coding and hospitalizations get a lot of attention.

Patel's energy and ambition shone through in our conversation. He clarified that the One Medical Seniors teams are taking advantage of the tools developed at Iora Primary Care: health care navigators, coaches, and case management. It does need fine-tuning, though. Patel noted that primary care has not yet cracked the code on behavioral health or on cardiometabolic health. But he believes One Medical has the curiosity, and the commitment, to develop a platform that offers extraordinary primary care. I found that to be an extremely well-put statement—something that would make me happy if I owned One Medical stock.

Yet based on my visit to a clinic in Glendale, Arizona, there is work to do at the One Medical Seniors practices. Throughout this book I have tried to keep judgments on specific primary care practices to a minimum. These are not scientific samples, but observations at just one clinic, where a number of factors could come into play. The day I visited could be different from the next day. The people who approved my visit had a lot of control over who and what I saw. And even my mood on a given day could affect my conclusions.

Compared with Gilbert, everything seemed tired in Glendale (about nine miles northwest of Phoenix), even the mall. This mall, like many others, seemed to be marching toward extinction. In the middle of the day, the parking lot was empty. That theme continued into the clinic, which was largely empty and worn. I saw few patients while I was there, but I did see staff members waiting around patiently.

Jacob Coleman started his career as a radiology technician and worked his way up in administrative positions at medical centers, finally overseeing a range of urgent care clinics.[72] But he always thought that long-term relationships were the key to good health care, so he kept an eye on Iora Primary Care as it developed, then jumped at the chance to work for them. Coleman is now their director of operations, but when we spoke, he was a market operations leader, overseeing seven clinics in the West Valley area of Phoenix. In this position, he shared the supervisory role in a tightly linked "dyad" with the medical directors.

Iora Primary Care / One Medical Seniors has now been in Arizona for seven years. In the past, it provided employer-based health care, but it has now evolved to serve only Medicare Advantage beneficiaries. At the time I visited, there had not been much change after One Medical purchased Iora, although there are plans to shift over to a single EMR system. The One Medical Seniors primary care model entails three to at most five primary care clinicians per site. Its distinguishing characteristic is that a health coach is present during all patient visits. One Medical Seniors also has medical assistants, behavioral health support, lab assistants, and care management nurses, but the health coaches (usually two of these per clinician) stand out as an innovation. They maintain close contact with the patients and guide medical decisions.

The average patient panel size for doctors is 600, 300 for health coaches. A typical full-time clinician spends eight-hour days in the clinic, four days a week. Each visit is long: 60 minutes for a new patient and 30 minutes for follow-ups. The Glendale team was vague about the compensation model at One Medical Seniors. It appears to be based on patient satisfaction and some utilization measures, but staff members were coy, perhaps signaling a reluctance to disclose too much about Iora Primary Care's integration plan with One Medical. With a bit more persistence, it became clear that medical expenditures and data from HEDIS performance measurements on managed care loomed large as compensation measures. But the staff, led by Coleman, reiterated that their guiding ambition was to develop the best primary care experience for their patients.

Notably, the patient population at One Medical Seniors is not just composed of Medicare Advantage beneficiaries but all those in Medicare, including its traditional fee-for-service plans. The clinicians and other staff members at Glendale were also careful to say that the clinic's doctors are not chasing after billing codes to boost revenues, but there is a team that helps with coding. This mix of traditional, fee-for-service Medicare enrollees and Medicare Advantage ones is unique. Almost all similar types of primary care practices prefer patients with Medicare Advantage plans because they want to manage care and get paid for it. Iora Primary Care / One Medical Seniors apparently had never endorsed such specialization.

Jacob Coleman was soon joined by Kurt Neeley, who is One Medical Seniors' market operations director for the entire Phoenix metropolitan area.[73] We talked a lot about recruiting, but this was not of great concern, since One Medical Seniors had had a great deal of success recruiting both physicians and advanced practice clinicians. At Glendale, all the clinicians were nurse practitioners.

Kena Carter heads the primary care practice in Glendale.[74] She attended Grand Canyon University and earned a doctorate of nursing practice. She has been at Glendale for a year, having previously worked at the Veterans Health Administration in Phoenix and in urgent care for Optum. Carter enjoyed the flexibility of the One Medical Seniors practice and was not pushed to see an ever larger number of patients. Her panel consisted of 400–500 patients, whereas at the VA, it was more than 1,000. At One Medical Seniors, she could rely on the health coach to make sure her patients understood their care plans, as well as to help with documentation. Carter rates Iora Primary Care's EMR system, CHIRP, as excellent, although the clinic will probably move to One Medical's platform.

Like the other clinicians I talked with, Carter believed a health coach's intimacy with individual patients was the key difference between One Medical Seniors and other primary care practices. The nature of this intimacy was not entirely clear, and I did not meet a health coach, but the coaches seemed to be in frequent contact with patients by telephone and even do home visits. Carter's assigned health coach worked with her throughout the day, seeing 12 and perhaps as many as 14 patients.

Joshua Perkins, a nurse practitioner, is another One Medical Seniors clinician who trained at Grand Canyon University.[75] He had worked in emergency departments and at urgent care facilities for years, and he was eager to understand what happened to patients after those visits. So, he answered a recruiting call from the Glendale clinic. When I asked him for an example of the kinds of cases he found interesting, he mentioned one where the patient needed to have an incision and then drainage of the affected area. Seemingly, his interests have not completely changed.

Perkins had 482 patients, all of them elderly, and he did not differentiate between those on Medicare Advantage plans and those using traditional Medicare. The Glendale practice was more fulfilling for him than his previous jobs, for many reasons. First, he found the CHIRP EMRs to be user-friendly, compared with the Cerner program he had at Banner–University Medical Center. Second, he was not rushed, seeing only 11–14 patients a day. Third, he was on salary. Fourth, the health coaches made caring for patients much easier. Perkins told me the coaches' responsibilities include (1) preparing patient notes ahead of time and then writing part of them; (2) reconciling medications; (3) putting together discharge notes for hospitalized patients; (4) explaining matters to the patients; (5) communicating with clinicians on follow-up issues, like lab reports; and (6) documenting patient care in the EMRs. The clinicians also have a supportive telephone triage service. A call gets answered by the member service's health care specialist, but it can be passed on to the nursing staff, who then talk with the advanced practice clinician on call.

One Medical Seniors encourages immediate access for its patients, so their medical problems can be addressed promptly. Yet Perkins rarely took work home. He got in at 7:45 a.m., joined the team huddle at 8:00 a.m., and then began seeing patients at 8:30 a.m. He went to lunch from noon to 1:00 p.m., saw more patients from 1:00 to 4:30 p.m., and left at 5:00 p.m. Compared with the situation for the clinicians with whom I spoke in other primary care practices, it sounded almost too good be true.

I was still trying to spot patients as I left, but there was no one in any of the exam rooms I strolled through. When I stepped out into the cold afternoon, a wheelchair-accessible van rolled up and deposited an elderly woman onto the curb in a none-too-gentle fashion. She slowly rolled her wheelchair up to the front door, which I helped her open, and she proffered effusive thanks. The waiting room was empty, which was good for her, I thought.

Dr. Natasha Bhuyan is another University of Arizona Wildcat. She attended medical school in Tucson and did her residency in family medicine at Banner–University Medical Center.[76] When she finished in

2015, she explored several primary care practice options and found a lot of burned-out people. One Medical was different—almost too good to be true. Her view at the time, which continues today, is that standard primary care is unsustainable. At One Medical, in contrast, the clinicians are on a lasting journey with their patients.

Almost as soon as Bhuyan started practicing, management opportunities began to present themselves. Over time, she became the office, then the district, then the regional, and now a national medical director for One Medical. It is a young organization, and it extensively uses emerging leader programs. Today, Bhuyan has a panel of 900 patients and spends 12 hours a week in a One Medical family medicine practice in Phoenix, while also undertaking a broadening job for the company.

As national medical director, Bhuyan's job is to support the in-office care teams, particularly by standardizing the work process. She also has responsibility for recruiting, retaining, and providing workload support for One Medical's clinicians. We talked about her recruiting advantages, as the workload and practice experience at One Medical clinics seem appealing to many doctors coming out of training.

Bhuyan also provided a glimpse into One Medical's headquarters in San Francisco. When we talked in January 2023, there were more than 200 health care practices in the company, including a home-based primary care team (PeakMed) and One Medical Seniors (formerly Iora Primary Care). The central office is busy trying to create one model for the future, combining the best of One Medical Seniors and the programs for the commercial health insurance plans. For example, Iora Primary Care had long championed the use of health coaches. From Bhuyan's viewpoint, health coaches know their community, so that aspect will remain. But One Medical realizes that it must incorporate more video evaluations, as opposed to home visits, in its primary care practices, as there is great expense for home-visiting teams.

As One Medical surveys the primary care horizon, its main concern is the clinician workforce. Bhuyan is working with the American Academy of Family Physicians to get the number of graduating students interested in primary care up to 15% (it is 11% today). The top of the funnel is insufficiently wide. But the good news for Bhuyan is that today's medical students are looking for the ability to spend time with patients, a reasonable work/life balance, and tech enablement, all of which One Medical can support.

A crown jewel for One Medical is its virtual medical team. It now operates 24/7 and is made up of physician assistants and nurse practitioners. They refill prescriptions, do triage, and hand off lab reports to the patients' physicians. Their work offloads tasks that would otherwise be done at the end of the day by the primary care clinicians and decreases the load in primary care inboxes by hundreds of messages. Tom Lee was the architect for the digital infrastructure at One Medical, but now its digital team is using AI-based technology to make its overall primary care system seamless.

Bhuyan also contrasted Iora Primary Care's legacy in One Medical Seniors and the approach by One Medical. In both One Medical and One Medical Seniors, teams huddle every morning, but the session for One Medical Seniors' clinicians lasts longer (approximately half an hour) as they discuss patients' difficult problems in some detail, especially those who are hospitalized. The One Medical teams gather for closer to 15 minutes, discussing key issues and using a lean format. They focus on patient access and net promoter scores while deemphasizing coding issues, since One Medical wants its clinicians to concentrate on caring for patients. There is a central team, called Bird's Eye, that helps with coding.

Summarizing the organization, Bhuyan said that when One Medical's clinicians compare themselves with others, they ask, What does your leadership team prioritize? And her teams assert that "the clinician's voice is heard; she is not a cog in the wheel."

I was impressed by the One Medical approach. But its absorption into Amazon was new when I visited, and someone with a sense of for-profit corporations, and their accommodation with purchased start-ups, had to suspect that there was another shoe to drop. Specifically, one had to wonder how long losses would be tolerated and a high-touch approach be preserved. By early 2024, there were public reports of layoffs occurring in the Amazon health business, particularly front desk staff, health coaches, and behavioral health specialists. Losses at One Medical were reported to be in the $500 million range. Former Iora employees loudly complained that resources were being stripped out of the clinics.[77] Just how much change has occurred in clinical practice is not clear, but the trend seems similar, if not quite as draconian, as other retailers.

Corporations and Primary Care

What should we think when big, national, for-profit companies start buying up primary care practices? A few things seem clear. First, these companies have developed a business plan where managed primary care plays a crucial role: reducing health care costs and enhancing its quality. They have endorsed the proposition that managed care—centered on primary care—can work. This is especially true for health insurance companies like Humana or Optum/UnitedHealth Group, which are generally focused on Medicare Advantage plans. Alternatively, companies that supply a variety of other health care goods, such as Amazon, can find new markets for those products when primary care is included in the mix. Moreover, having clinics as testing laboratories is a crucial way to assess the results. In all instances, there is a credible business plant that is fixed on profit for the parent.

Second, the connection to value-based managed care is critical. Profit is based on saving money by reducing unnecessary medical costs, and by being paid reasonably under risk adjustment. The changes in reimbursement, especially for Medicare Advantage-oriented organizations, will test the resolve of the insurers who have invested in primary care based on this calculus. But for retailers without a direct stake in the overall costs of care, the reductions in reimbursement appear to have greatly reduced their interest in primary care as a line of business.

Ultimately, the only measure that counts for these corporations is profitability. And that profitability is not assured. Much of corporate investment focuses on Medicare Advantage. Savvy doctors and nurses in leadership roles in big insurers and retail health companies acknowledge that there may be overpayments from the federal government today, and that this will eventually end. Changes in the financial structure of Medicare Advantage could and should turn the management from a coding strategy to one of managing care to eliminate waste. Insurers believe that this is possible, since they see so much financial waste in a fee-for-service reimbursement system, but they are cautious. In this regard, the retreat by Walmart and Walgreens is not that surprising. What would be more striking would be for Optum or Humana to change their overall strategy.

The big question is, in an endeavor intended to reduce human suffering, which is what health care is about, how much profit is tolerable? Will insurers and other big corporations have the wisdom to weight profitability against patient welfare? That question will loom even larger as I examine the next set of funders and leaders in primary care development: venture capital.

CHAPTER SEVEN

The Role of Private Equity

INSURERS AND HEALTH CARE COMPANIES are not alone in their interest in investing in primary care today. Private investors are pouring capital into entrepreneurial practices and physicians' groups to organize and deliver value-based care. In the health policy literature, these investments are known as venture capital (VC) or private equity (PE). They are viewed somewhat dimly in health care policy discourses, betraying a suspicion of their profit motives. This is not to say such suspicion—and even opposition to unchecked profits—is completely unwarranted.

Venture capital and private equity are distinct entities. Venture capital typically is money provided by private groups or individuals to help new companies get started. Private equity refers more generally to large investments made by any type of investor in what is usually (but not exclusively) a non–publicly traded firm, often with an eye to when that company might give an initial public offering (IPO) of its stock.

The differences between private equity and venture capital can be subtle, but private equity tends to focus on companies that are reasonably well established but often financially distressed.[1] A private equity investor may be attracted by that latter aspect and believe the situation could be remedied by bringing in new management, thus turning the company around. Usually, the investor will gain control of the company into which funds were infused, often owning 100%. A venture capital investor, in contrast, usually believes in a company's current management and, along with others of a similar ilk, takes a minority share of the company's stock. Private equity investments are typically much larger than individual venture capital investments. But both PE and VC are founded on the profit motive, looking for opportunities to gain returns.

In health care, much of the policy literature focuses on private equity. Not much good is said about it, although the actual data are not quite as negative as the rhetoric. Private investment has occurred throughout the health care ecosystem—in hospitals, nursing homes, and physicians' groups of various stripes. The general fear is that the new owners will thin out staff in an effort to cut costs and improve profitability, thereby endangering patients. In addition, private equity investors are accused of playing hardball with commercial health insurers, forcing them to pump up their reimbursement rates, thus making health care more expensive.

Many of the private equity deals that have gained notoriety involve takeovers of hospital or skilled nursing facility chains. But private equity has had a great deal of interest in physicians' groups. Private equity investors most often buy specialty practice groups, such as dermatologists or gastroenterologists, creating an effective monopoly in specific geographic regions and then using this leverage to gain better reimbursement rates from insurers—thus increasing health care costs. Another private equity approach is to target hospital-based specialties, like emergency department care, and create leverage for better fees. This can be complemented by systematic surprise billing—where patients must pay unforeseen and often exorbitant bills—a ploy that is lucrative for the private equity owners. Underneath all this is the assumption that private equity investors are only interested in financial returns, not patient welfare.

A June 2023 meta-analysis of studies on private equity acquisitions—looking across nursing homes, hospitals, and various medical specialty groups—concluded that new PE ownership was associated with higher costs.[2] The data were less conclusive, however, regarding the quality of care. In May 2023, the assessment in an annotated review of the literature by the National Institute for Health Care Management (NIHCM) was also mixed.[3] The article examined several studies of hospitals that showed an increase in total per day charges, particularly by specialists like anesthesiologists. But another study demonstrated that acquired hospitals had reductions in their costs per discharged patient. The NIHCM report did suggest that private equity investors clearly attempt to consolidate specialists, creating leverage for higher fees. Private equity was also associated with increased utilization of services in a fee-for-service reimbursement setting.

On the quality front, the NIHCM report cited articles showing improvements in outcomes—including reduced inpatient mortality—for hospitals purchased by private equity investors. In addition, broader quality-of-care measurements appeared to improve, although much of this effect may have been attributable to facilities operated by the Hospital Corporation of America, which might not be considered "typical" private equity–owned institutions. Other studies have shown deteriorating patient experiences in hospitals owned by PE firms. In late 2023, another study of quality in hospitals with private equity ownership demonstrated several poor outcomes regarding patient safety, specifically intravenous line infections.[4] In this study, however, there was significantly lower inpatient mortality at investor-owned hospitals.

NIHCM also cited health policy experts Dr. Jane Zhu and Dr. Zirui Song, who warned that acquired hospitals shuttered unprofitable services—ones that could have been important to the local community. Moreover, most acquisitions by private equity have no regulatory oversight—over 90% are exempt from federal review—so there are often little data on the local effects of this new ownership.

In a widely read article, Dr. Christopher Cai and Dr. Zirui Song advocated for better oversight of PE in health care.[5] They worried that the short-term focus on profits and leveraged buyouts, which create a huge debt for the entity that is acquired—especially hospitals and nursing homes—leads to an enhanced risk of bankruptcy. In such instances, ceasing operations may be an intelligent and legitimate option for the private equity team, but it could be a disaster for the local community. Cai and Song suggested that (1) states should become more involved in the oversight of private equity purchases, (2) increased transparency is necessary, and (3) a ban on leveraged buyouts should be considered. A team writing in the *Harvard Business Review* had two additional suggestions.[6] First, segregate the types of entities that are purchased, as the issues are different for hospitals and nursing homes or physicians' groups. Second, rather than eliminating private equity altogether, align incentives and penalties so private capital can still be invested in health care.

All these proposed reforms are reasonable but will probably come about slowly, depending on how offensive private equity buyouts continue to appear. Meanwhile, more bad press accumulates. An *American Prospect* article on Medical Properties Trust (a real estate investment trust) and its interactions with Steward Health Care portrayed the worst kind of behavior, with maximum profits being generated while hospitals serving low-income populations closed their doors.[7] These kinds of stories are what will eventually bring regulations to bear. It is perhaps for this reason that 2022 saw less private equity investment in health care.[8] As Dr. Robert Pearl, the former CEO of the Permanente Medical Group, suggests, the most prominent private equity investments tend to be in hospitals and in hospital-based specialty groups.[9] Notably, the business plans underlying these purchases all feature fee-for-service reimbursement and suggest overutilization as a business plan.

What about primary care? Dr. Zirui Song and colleagues have been cataloging investments in primary care by venture capital and private equity.[10] They stated that from 2010 to 2020, the number of deals between primary care groups and either venture capital or private equity investors increased from 2 to 46. The total capital raised went from $15 million to $3.83 billion. In the first half of 2021 alone, that amount totaled $8.4 billion. In the early 2010s, most investments were by venture capital or even angel investors (individuals who fund start-ups in exchange for equity or royalties), but larger investment firms have gotten involved recently. Nonetheless, primary care ownership by private equity is miniscule compared to other specialties: a recent report pegged PE ownership of gastroenterology practices at 14%, primary care at 2%.[11]

Song and colleagues noted primary care groups taking advantage of this money benefited just as others getting such investment would. They were able to experiment with new health care models without having to sustain financial losses for their organizations. They also got advice (particularly financial advice) from their investment partners, as well as some useful lessons in organizational management. Having contact with the venture capitalists' other investments also provided new insights for these primary care groups.

Song's team also proffered some advice for primary care groups. First, work with people who understood the group's mission, especially when that mission is to provide better, less expensive overall care for patients. Second, even with great agreement between the parties at the outset, anticipate that there could be misaligned objectives. Therefore, right from the start, put clear parameters in place about who has what decision rights. Third, emphasize transparency. Given the various types of private equity investments and the size range of the primary care practices involved, this seems like excellent advice.

Song and his colleagues went into some detail to differentiate venture capital from private equity, but for my purposes in understanding this type of funding in primary care, it is sufficient to note that venture capital usually arrives early, makes a lot of bets, and expects returns in the 5–10 times range. Private equity investments come after those by venture capital, when companies mature and prepare to go public through an IPO. Private equity will also invest in public firms and return them to private status. Their return expectations are in the 2–3 times range.

In primary care, there are two paths followed by the entrepreneurs who are developing companies and the investors who are betting on them. The first is simple: doctors and care managers decide to start hiring clinicians, set up clinics, and develop a chain of primary care facilities. These new health care businesses eventually go public, remain independent, or are bought by larger corporations. But their start has been fueled by venture capital and supplemented by private equity. One Medical is a good example of this journey. It started with venture capital, then had an IPO, and was later bought by Amazon (see chapter 6). To this point, there are few if any systematic studies comparing the quality or cost of care delivered by these new entrepreneurial, venture-funded, primary care groups compared to conventional ones.

In addition to One Medical, I visited with several other primary care firms that were nurtured by investors. Oak Street Health's history is like One Medical's.[12] It was originally funded by venture capital before receiving $40 million in investments in 2016 from Quantum Strategic Partners, Oxeon Partners, and Harbour Point Capital. General Atlantic came in a year later, and after an IPO, Silicon Valley Bank and Hercules Capital provided $300 million in return for stock in the company. In May 2023, CVS Health purchased Oak Street Health and its 169 clinics for $10.6 billion, creating a great return for all of the investors.[13] Cityblock Health (in many ways similar to Oak Street Health but focused on Medicaid beneficiaries) is still private, having decided not to make an IPO yet, but it is continuing to raise large amounts of money in late-stage funding, the most recent infusion being $400 million from a consortium led by SoftBank.[14]

A second path into primary care for venture capital is to support facilitators who help individual, independent organizations (usually primary care facilities with 4–20 clinicians) undertake value-based care, especially that based on financial risk contracts with health insurers. Several firms do this today, most notably Privia Health Group, Evolent Health, agilon health, and Aledade. Privia Health Group, Evolent Health, and agilon health are all now publicly traded, while Aledade remains private.

I visited agilon health's and Aledade's primary care practices. Their investment history is representative of what has been happening in primary care. The private equity firm Clayton, Dubilier and Rice started agilon health in 2016 specifically to "accelerate the conversion to value-based care in the United States."[15] It subsequently successfully completed an IPO in 2021. Aledade has built itself up through a series of investment rounds by venture capital and, increasingly, what might be seen as private equity. Its most recent series of investments, totaling $260 million, was led by Lightspeed Venture Partners, Venrock, Avidity Partners, OMERS Growth Equity, and Fidelity Management and Research Company.[16]

These are some of the big players in venture capital and private equity—the ones that many in health care policy fear and loathe. But the primary care practices they have established, or ones they have relationships with, are not much different than many other progressive practices that I visited elsewhere. They all have the same incentives and challenges. In fact, the practices that received private equity investment seemed generally happier and driven by their mission in value-based care.

Perhaps this is because the clinical leaders at companies owned by or supported by private equity have carefully followed Song's advice about ensuring transparency and identifying mission. Or perhaps it is wrong to frame private equity in a unidimensional fashion, as if it is all simply a matter of real estate investment trusts bilking small hospitals, or management teams that promote surprise billing in emergency departments. There is at least some evidence that primary care supported by private equity is different than other parts of health care so supported. My visits to practices affiliated with private equity suggested that the investments were engendering a vibrant brand of primary care dedicated to value-based care.

Central Ohio Primary Care

The headquarters for Central Ohio Primary Care, known as COPC, is located in a vast expanse of corporate buildings in Westerville, north of Columbus, Ohio. On the way there, I passed a large JPMorgan Chase installation that has over 10,000 employees. Columbus has become one of the resurgent cities in Middle America, like Indianapolis and Nashville, something most would not have predicted 30 years ago. Corporate America likes Columbus.

COPC's headquarters does not really suggest a typical primary care facility. The building is brand new, clean, and decorated with many of COPC's business slogans—as corporate in appearance as any of the JPMorgan Chase buildings I saw. There was a flat screen TV in the lobby, playing a video loop extolling the virtues of primary care at COPC. All that was missing to make this a classic corporate ad was a small window at the bottom of the screen, showing the current stock price. The headquarters for many nonprofit hospital systems would have the same amenities, but the sheen was still a bit shocking, and as I found, out of place given all the grounded and humble people working at COPC.

COPC has a long-term affiliation agreement with agilon. As outlined above, agilon was birthed by the PE firm Clayton, Dubilier and Rice (CDR), working with a couple of other industry experts, including Ron Williams, the former CEO of Aetna. (Williams was my boss at Aetna.) In 2021, agilon went public. Ravi Sachdev at CDR is widely seen as a savvy and influential health care investor, and he has championed agilon health.[17] He outlined their strategy for me.

agilon is an enabler, intending to help primary care groups move toward financial risk–based, value-based care. It does not *buy* health care practices but helps them thrive through a value-based care format. On financial risk contracts, agilon takes on all the downside risk and 50% of the upside risk. It signs a 20-year exclusive relationship deal with physicians' groups, ensuring a long-term return for agilon's shareholders. agilon relies on an analytic engine that is fed by data from health insurance claims. This information helps primary care clinicians identify at-risk patients and address their needs before unnecessary medical treatments, referrals to specialists, and hospital or emergency department visits occur. The program is aimed directly at Medicare Advantage beneficiaries, but it can be used with other forms of health insurance plans as well.

The company continues to expand its capabilities in that regard as it develops long-term contracts with various primary care groups, similar to what it has done with COPC. For example, CDR bought Vera

Whole Health, which has a network of primary care clinics that are often located in proximity to workspaces. CDR will coordinate between agilon practices and the Vera network. Among Vera's other assets is Castlight Health, a company that aggregates health data from a variety of sources, which Vera bought in 2022. Aggregated data are analyzed and provide information for clinicians caring for patients, particularly to anticipate care for incipient problems.

agilon health seems to have found a successful formula. The company is working with physicians' groups in 17 markets in 2022, expanding to 23 in 2024.[18] Some are small, but others are quite large, such as the ones with over 30,000 Medicare Advantage beneficiaries in primary care groups in Michigan and Wisconsin. agilon has also recruited the 700-bed Maine Medical Center. In late 2023, the company had a roster of more than 500,000 patients, just under 400,000 with Medicare Advantage plans and nearly 100,000 in the ACO Realizing Equity, Access, and Community Health (REACH) Program of the Centers for Medicare and Medicaid Services. Their loss for the last quarter of 2023 was $17 million, on revenues of over $1 billion (strikingly better than One Medical, for example.)

Sachdev is considered one of the masterminds of the agilon model. He struck me as levelheaded and reflective, hardly the stereotypical grasping, brash venture capitalist. I asked him directly if he thought financial risk bearing in primary care could be the fulcrum for a cost-effective health care system. He said that when agilon health got started in 2016, his answer would be no, but now it is yes. In October 2017, agilon had a global risk arrangement with only one health care insurer, and most insurers were refusing to consider this path. Now agilon is in 25 markets, with global risk contracts across the spectrum of health insurers. Moreover, the ACO REACH program enables the agilon groups to attract fee-for-service traditional Medicare beneficiaries.

The other driver for agilon's growth is its taste in partners. Groups like COPC have done well, and that enables agilon health to attract new ones. As Sachdev saw it, the participating doctors are making money, their managed care approach is saving the government money, and their quality-of-care scores are excellent. agilon is also developing new clinical mechanisms, such as better ways to coordinate patient care, as well as establishing relationships with national health services firms (like the big dialysis companies) and forming closer ties with specialist groups. He saw this as a great role for venture capital—providing the tools to manage financial risk across diverse markets.

Sachdev realizes that some of the venture capital and private equity players are looking for quick wins and do not consider patient welfare. But there is a broad spectrum of private equity investors, and Sachdev and his colleagues are in it for the long haul. They know that if they are going to make profits, they must insist on a better quality of health care, lower costs, and excellent patient experiences. All that said, Wall Street has not treated the public company agilon well. A few months after its initial public offering in 2021, the stock was trading above $43. At the end of 2024, it had fallen to $2.

Companies like agilon health or Aledade are providing the tools that primary care clinicians need if they are going to succeed in moving toward capitation, instead of remaining in a fee-for-service mindset. They believe that physicians, like farmers, need advice on best practices. Experts in the American Farm Bureau Federation have long played that role in agriculture, introducing new technologies and approaches to increase yields. agilon does the same in health care, although it keeps a portion of the profits. Moreover, the company's willingness to absorb financial losses helps overcome typical physicians' reticence in gambling with their income source.

I met with Dr. William Wulf, who is now retired after a long tenure as leader of COPC.[19] The setting was corporate, but Wulf hardly fits that bill. He is a careful listener, thoughtful and measured in his comments, and self-effacing. He always has an eye turned toward patient welfare and a keen understanding of medical practices, based on his 30 years as a physician and primary care practice leader. Wulf, like many of his coworkers at COPC, trained in internal medicine at Riverside Methodist Hospital, which was the original member of an integrated delivery system, Ohio Health. Ohio Health now dominates in central Ohio, overshadowing Ohio State University's Wexner Medical Center.

In 1996, Wulf's small primary care practice joined with 11 others to form a single physicians' group. Changes in funding for graduate medical education and new rules regarding work hours meant that Riverside Methodist Hospital no longer had enough doctors-in-training to cover its inpatients full-time. It sounded to Wulf like the time had come for these 12 primary care practices to free themselves from the hospital. The new physicians' group (1) developed a hospitalist program for their practices; (2) hired new professional administrators, focusing on better billing; (3) put systems in place to employ the providers of their ancillary services and make a profit from that; (4) began to negotiate for new payer contracts (with 33 doctors, they could go toe-to-toe with health insurers); and (5) moved to a single EMR system. Their newly negotiated contracts and ownership of ancillary services contributed substantially to their bottom line. Additional small practices looking for other options began to join, and by 2005 their physicians' group included 200 doctors.

By 2007, Wulf had graduated from masterminding the ancillary lab program to being the group's medical director. He started to accumulate quality-of-care information on his clinicians, with new insights becoming available through the EMR data. Historically, Wulf and most other physicians thought that the way to judge physicians' quality of care for their patients was to determine if they were "busy," meaning that people wanted to see those doctors. His quality-of-care data, however, revealed that the busiest doctors were not the best ones. The best were those who took their time during patient visits and followed up with them afterward. They complied with practice guidelines and had fewer patients making emergency department visits or needing hospital readmissions. Plus, their patients were happier. These doctors were practicing value-based care.

Wulf and his leadership team took several steps to begin to prepare for a value-based primary care future. First, he concentrated on what was needed to acquire medical home status, and all their practices became patient-centered medical home (PCMHs), accredited by the National Committee for Quality Assurance. He did not intend for their group practice to continue to be accredited as a PCMH. Rather, he used the accreditation data to legitimize his own data collection initiative. Next, he went to the health insurance companies and negotiated value-based contracts, established on outcome measures. (There was no broad capitation, or even capitation for primary care clinicians, available in the health care market at that time in Ohio.) He used the good performance results from doctors in his data set to build new educational programs for both clinicians and patients, such as for smoking cessation. These initiatives were all intended to prepare the group's primary care practice for capitation.

Growth continued through the 2010s, with COPC approaching its present size of 500 doctors, including 200 adult primary care clinicians, 100 hospitalists, 100 pediatricians, and a smattering of specialists for noninvasive treatments. The group added new capabilities—such as building its own urgent care centers and observation units—to avoid the substantial costs of hospital care.

Nonetheless, the COPC team realized that if they were serious about taking on financial risk, they needed outside help. They learned a lot about this from Essa Health, a leading health maintenance plan in St. Louis, Missouri, which eventually spawned Lumeris, another firm working with primary care practices interested in value-based care. (COPC maintains a good relationship with Lumeris.) They increasingly got into upside financial risk deals, but they realized that they did not have the insurers' actuarial data and worried about experiencing adverse financial risk, given their attention to sick as well as healthy patients. They did join the Center for Medicare and Medicaid Innovation's Comprehensive Primary Care Plus (CPC+) program, and that worked out well for them, but they did not join an accountable care organization and stayed out of the Medicare Shared Saving Program.

Wulf and COPC then decided to find a partner. They talked to Health-Care Partners, Lumeris, and Accretive Health. Then Stuart Levine, a well-known physician-investor, introduced them to Ravi Sachdev at Clayton, Dubilier and Rice. According to Wulf, Sachdev and CDR had recently bought the coding program MDX, which was the first investment in what was to become agilon.

As agilon incubated under CDR, Sachdev made a great case to COPC and Wulf. The proposal from agilon to COPC was, as noted, that all the downside financial risk would be absorbed by agilon, with agilon also taking a 50% share of any upside risk. COPC and agilon remained independent, but they created a risk-bearing entity (RBE) as a joint venture. The RBE/joint venture would hold the financial risk health insurance contracts, and the relationship would be in place for 20 years. In addition, the RBE was only delegated to provide health care, so no insurance license was necessary, as it carried no insurance risk, only contractual risk.

agilon would bring an enhanced set of care management tools to the relationship:

1. Burden-of-illness documentation tools (helping with patients' risk scores).
2. Expertise in contracting with health insurance payers.
3. Better data analysis on utilization.
4. Risk stratification and predictive analytics.
5. Attribution models.
6. Data on the value of various specialists.
7. Ideas about the most effective forms of managed health care.

All this information is processed through a separate electronic dashboard used by clinicians that is not integrated with the EMR (although there are plans for an integrated model).

In its mature form, COPC wants to enter full-risk contracts with all health insurers. Its medical team is almost entirely made up of primary care clinicians. The organization has 50 specialists, but they all work on providing care for their chronically ill patients. When I visited in August 2022, COPC had 75,000 senior lives, 40,000 Medicare Advantage enrollees, and 35,000 in ACO REACH. They provided care for a total of approximately 450,000 patients. With Medicare Advantage insurers, they negotiate a division of the financial responsibility, which usually means receipt of a percentage of the premiums, typically 85%. COPC receives payments prospectively, based on the previous year's set of assigned patients and their health care results, with adjustments made over time as incurred-but-not-reported claims come through. This means that bonus payments to clinicians are made without a 6- to 12-month delay. The same set of arrangements apply to their ACO REACH contracts.

Wulf's focus in on the quality of the clinical care. He was clear about the trade-offs between a managed care approach and staying in a fee-for-service system. Fee-for-service is clearer in terms of its financial incentives—see more patients, get paid more. But providing medical care on a treadmill cannot be good. It creates burnout for doctors and likely prevents the establishment of a genuine relationship with their patients. The managed care approach means that measures other than financial ones also matter. For example, COPC's doctors receive bonuses based on the number of patients attributed to a clinician, activities that medicine considers "good citizenship,"[20] quality-of-care measures, patients having annual wellness visits, and patient reviews. They are also attentive to total cost of care: no bonus dollars unless there is profit.

In central Ohio, hospital systems are busy trying to buy up physicians, but there are not many left in established practices. COPC must compete with them for new residency program graduates. COPC is competitive in terms of salary—a primary care clinician can make $325,000 to $350,000—so it has been able to hire and grow. Wulf also argued that working for his value-based primary care practice was more professionally satisfying. COPC is down to 153 hospital admissions per 1,000 patients in their Medicare population (in 2021, the Ohio average was 225),[21] and their readmission rate is 10% to 11% (in 2018, the national average was 16.9%). That indicates good primary care for patients, and it resonates throughout the COPC group. Wulf commented, "Eliminating waste eliminates patient suffering." Wulf is sold on this approach to primary care. He has now retired as the head of COPC but is on agilon health's board of directors. So, it is not surprising that he is a booster.

I was curious about how COPC's rank-and-file might see things. I met with Dr. Maria Varveris at a COPC practice in Columbus, Ohio.[22] Varveris struck me as a no-nonsense, serious person, but she was also compassionate when talking about her patients. She made me a bit nervous, as I had the vague impression that I might be wasting her time, which I probably was. But her mood was not readable. In that regard, she reminded me of a quality attributed to Tertius Lydgate in *Middlemarch*: "Mr. Lydgate had the medical accomplishment of looking perfectly grave, no matter what nonsense was talked to him."[23]

Varveris did her residency in 1998 at Riverside Methodist Hospital, in the same program as William Wulf. She joined COPC in 2001, at a time when the practice had 100 doctors. Primary care at COPC was mostly in a fee-for-service setting then, but Varveris has experienced the gradual evolution to value-based care over the past decade. This evolution entailed the addition of numerous managed care programs, all made possible by taking on more financial risk. For example, COPC has incorporated more care coordinators, including social workers and nurse managers. This makes it a much safer primary care practice, as fragile patients can have home visits and appropriate attention to their needs. Vaveris had a high regard for the team care concept: "There are substantial benefits of having others' eyes on one's patient."

Varveris receives a lot of electronic reminders in her EMRs, and she feels that they prompt her to do appropriate screenings and apply preventive care measures for her patients. Varveris also gets information on risk scores, but she does not look at these too closely. She might add a suggested code every so often, but it is not a major part of her practice. The bottom line was that she felt COPC had a much better primary care program for patients, and her work was gratifying.

Varveris gave an example of COPC's benefits for elderly patients. One individual was beginning to forget things and was having difficulty driving home, losing her way. Vaveris was able to line up a comprehensive neurological assessment and social evaluation. The team inspected the patient's home and evaluated her risk for falls. They were able to arrange appropriate support and made some modifications in her living situation. All this was beneficial for the patient, including a reduced risk of hospitalization for a serious medical condition, which would have been costly for Medicare—and the COPC clinic. This assiduous type of care is not as likely to occur in a fee-for-service setting.

In terms of staff morale, Varveris acknowledged that all COPC's primary care clinicians were tired after the COVID pandemic. For her, COPC's EMR system was difficult to use, requiring far too many clicks to document patient care. She was excited about COPC's new Epic EMR program, which would provide access to information from the Ohio State University's Wexner Medical Center, as well as all the OhioHealth and Trinity hospitals, because they all use Epic EMRs. But learning a new system would no doubt be tough, she thought. (Bill Wulf subsequently told me that the 2023 rollout of Epic was not smooth, and much more costly than anticipated.)

Be this as it may, Varveris was convinced that COPC was providing wonderful care for its patients. Its leadership is excellent, and a patient-first attitude suffuses the entire organization. She was excited about the recent addition of behavioral health experts to their practice. This integration is more prevalent in pediatrics today than it is in internal medicine, but COPC is looking to add this to their health care repertoire.

In terms of compensation, Varveris was satisfied that she was well paid. She believed that everyone got an increase over their former rate of pay when they first started with agilon, but that was no longer true in 2021. Wulf had explained to me that COPC's team received bonuses during 2020, as patients' utilization of specialists, hospitals, and emergency departments decreased, but when this picked back up in 2021, the additional costs meant no increase in the bonuses.

Varveris saw 50–70 patients per week, which she found manageable. She had started to use a virtual medical scribe, which helped reduce her workload, as she no longer had to write notes about her patients at the end of the day. She believed that she performed well on the quality-of-care measures that COPC's administrative staff compiles, which are transparent within the practice. She attended monthly office meetings, where she got feedback and clinical data from the organization's central headquarters. She also participated in pod meetings, where her fellow clinicians went into some detail on medical issues, particularly emergency department visits and hospital admissions. She found these gatherings to be beneficial. As part of her citizenship bonus requirement, she must attend two meetings a year with the clinic's entire staff.

If Varveris were able to put her finger on the key difference between COPC's past fee-for-service foundation and today's emphasis on value-based care, it would be seeing fewer patients and providing better care for them. She was doing better financially, but the real change was being able to see her patients in a more sophisticated light, understanding their social issues better. That is truly fulfilling for her as a professional.

Varveris was not alone in that assessment. Dr. James Dorado has been a COPC physician since 2000.[24] He trained at Wright State University in a combined medicine/pediatrics program, but his practice today is almost all in adult medicine. Dorado is on COPC's board of directors, so he is well informed about the company's strategies and history. His first job was at a Cigna HMO, where all the physicians were on salary. Cigna pulled out suddenly, however, which created a big crisis. The group of doctors left high and dry by this HMO pulled together, and within a year they were the eighth primary care office associated with COPC. There are now more than 80 affiliated practices.

Dorado outlined the big changes he has seen over time. The key issue for him was that his work life had improved. A fee-for-service system—based on an "eat what you kill" approach—meant that he had to see four patients an hour. That, he thought, is a horrible treadmill and cannot be consistent with good care. Now, with COPC's emphasis on value-based medicine, he could see as few as two patients per hour. Another significant change was that Dorado had a lot of flexibility within his practice. For example, he now worked with a nurse practitioner who saw one patient per hour and managed phone calls. The NP performed general examinations and annual wellness physicals, while he saw the sick patients. But the design of how his practice is conducted is up to him, since he no longer must follow the simplistic logic of a fee-for-service framework.

This flexibility and creativity were made possible by the prospective payments Dorado gets from managed care for his 120 Medicare Advantage patients, which allowed him to underwrite these different kinds of practice arrangements. He was also considering using an electronic scribe. Parenthetically, COPC has appointed Robert Strohl as its director of physician satisfaction, charged with overseeing physician wellness. Strohl is evaluating a much broader use of virtual scribes, an effort closely watched by COPC's board of directors.

Dorado believed that his satisfaction with COPC's new approach to a primary care practice was widespread within the organization. He estimated that 80% of the doctors at COPC understand its value-based incentives and thrive on them, with the other 20% still encumbered by fee-for-service thinking. Asked about the chart review process for his Medicare Advantage patients, he sometimes added new diagnoses. But Dorado didn't think this was gaming the system. He saw it as a beneficial process, with two equal parts: providing better care for patients by anticipating potential problems and increasing overall revenue.

In enumerating the benefits of managed care, Dorado raised some similar points to those made by Varveris. First, some of his patients had behavioral health issues intertwined with their medical ailments. He can take care of a patient's medical issues in a relatively short period. But unless he understands what else is going on in that person's life, his care can be ineffective. Moreover, a patient in emotional turmoil really cannot hear a clinician's diagnosis or recommendations, so it's important for Dorado to be able to adapt his approach to his patient's mental state. This takes time, which he did not have in a fee-for-service primary care practice. In COPC's value-based environment, it is time well spent.

Providing a second example, Dorado recently had an elderly patient, a retired radiologist, who was evaluated in their transitional care unit (COPC's version of an urgent care facility, used to avoid hospitalizations or unnecessary emergency department visits). A care coordinator sat with the patient the entire time, explaining everything that was occurring while he received intravenous fluids and careful monitoring. The retired radiologist was impressed by this extra care and was pleased to avoid the hospital. The process also helped reduce costs that would have been paid by his Medicare Advantage plan.

I asked Dorado where he thought things were headed in the future. First, COPC must keep its same leadership ethos, even if its leaders are changing. Second, the organization must incorporate more advanced practice nurses. Third, COPC must ensure that its medical assistants work to the top of their license. Fourth, COPC must move value-based care into its commercial health insurance contracts, which are currently all fee-for-service arrangements. Fifth, and most importantly, COPC must maintain its commitment to the good of the patients.

There are 80 COPC offices now, making a uniform approach more difficult. But each office has one person participating in COPC's Physician Advisory Committee, which advises the board on issues surrounding patient welfare. As Dorado stated with some pride, COPC is still a doctor-oriented practice, meaning that there is appropriate clinical oversight of its business issues. Dorado was also proud of the COPC Foundation, which is focused on supporting free clinics, food banks, and shelters. He thought this was exactly the kind of thing that a good medical practice should be doing. Paraphrasing Wulf, Dorado said, "If you do good, the money will follow and then you can do more good."

Donald Deep (the new CEO at COPC) leads his organization with a good sense of balance.[25] Like numerous others at COPC, he trained in internal medicine at Riverside Methodist Hospital from 1994 to 1997. Joining COPC, he did two weeks of medical office practice and hated it. As a result, he was given the responsibility of developing COPC's hospitalist program. In 1997, the hospitalist movement was young, having only been named in 1996 by Dr. Robert Wachter and Dr. Lee Goldman. Nor was the notion of doctors making rounds full-time in a hospital widely accepted. The COPC organization had come into being because of a loss of covering house staff at Riverside Methodist Hospital. COPC started with two hospitalists, and now they have more than 90 doctors serving as full-time hospitalists. Deep was COPC's medical director from the beginning of its hospitalist program until January 1, 2023, when he became the organization's CEO.

Hospitalists' responsibilities are complex. They maintain firm ties with COPC's primary care doctors, but they also work closely with non-COPC specialists. They make decisions about which specialist teams are the most efficient and the most responsive. This development of specialist relationships, necessary in caring for at-risk patients, is crucial for any medical group as it grows.

The progress of COPC as a whole, in terms of managing care, can be traced through Deep's additional responsibilities over time. In 2017, Wulf made Deep the head of acute care services. He retained his responsibility for the hospitalists while overseeing a new program for urgent care and same-day care centers. COPC now has three of these, which are meant to be used in place of visits to an emergency department. The following year, Deep set up a post–acute care program for visiting discharged hospital or emergency department patients at home. COPC clinicians also began making rounds at a handful of the 70 skilled nursing facilities in the Columbus area. They now concentrate on about a dozen of these facilities, but they also gather information from the others. Most recently, Deep developed COPC's Comprehensive Home and Palliative Care Program, which is made up of what he saw as two equal parts: palliative care and complex internal medicine treatments.

Deep has not pursued a hospital-at-home program. He had extensive discussions with many of the vendors that led him to think the average hospital-at-home scheme was a revenue ploy. For acute-care hospital inpatient stays under Medicare Part A, each case is assigned to a diagnosis-related group (DRG). Every DRG has a payment weight assigned to it, based on the average cost of resources used to treat Medicare patients in that DRG.[26] So hospital-at-home providers were getting an inpatient DRG reimbursement for what should only have been a stay in an observation unit. That didn't seem right to Deep, nor does such a program help with COPC's managed care approach.

Deep wrestled with the merits of a homegrown hospital-at-home program, relying on his clinical training in contemplating its design. The program he wants to develop is tricky because many of these patients are quite sick, creating a stressful situation in their home settings. He pointed out that providing hospital-level care at home required an experienced doctor steeped in acute care. He mentioned one example: a patient with both chronic obstructive pulmonary disease (COPD) and diabetes who needed steroid therapy—a situation that demands blood sugar management as well as pulmonary monitoring. All of this can be done at home, but it must be supervised by a good acute-care physician, as it involves intense labor on the part of the care team to ensure the patient's safety. I was impressed by Deep's consideration of all the factors involved, addressed from the point of view of the patient.

Deep faces a series of strategic and tactical issues as he begins to head up COPC. Like many of the other leaders of primary care organizations with whom I met, he was worried about the supply of trained medical assistants and COPC's ability to pay them a competitive wage. He wants to get his staff back into the office, in order to maintain their sense of purpose. COPC's primary care practices still have many fee-for-service contracts, which interferes with the organization's value-based mindset. Finally, COPC now has 2,000 employees, and they need to be imprinted with the commitment to patient welfare that is the organization's touchstone. This last aspect, Deep believes, is a crucial part of being COPC's chief executive officer. Imbuing clinicians with a commitment to patient welfare was also the best protection against burnout, he reasoned. When I spoke with him in August 2022, COPC was bringing in 25 new physicians, and the entire organization was excited about this growth.

COPC is pleased with its partnership with agilon. Deep and Wulf are aware of the reputation private equity has, but they think agilon understands COPC's need to center all of its actions on care for their patients. In addition, both men appreciate some of the financial discipline PE investors bring to a partnership, plus the various contracting and care management playbooks they offer.

I was surprised by what I learned when visiting COPC's primary care practice. It was taking real steps toward value-based care, and growing as it did so. COPC's leaders were clearly making the decisions, but they had a lot of help, and a good business partner, in the agilon health team. agilon, while public today, is a product of private equity culture, having carefully assessed a business opportunity and taken steps to make its capital work for its investors and now its shareholders. Yet there was little sense of the "evil capitalism" that pervades reports of private equity's involvement in health care. With regard to agilon's relationship with COPC, it would be hard to conclude anything other than that patients were getting better care—at least in terms of spending more thoughtful time with their primary care physicians. In addition, the doctors seemed much happier in their work than the average primary clinician.

I was impressed with how little discussion dwelt on risk adjustment or documentation. As was the case with every practice I visited, I saw a selected sample of clinicians. COPC could have been careful in its choice of the people with whom I spoke, although I discount that. Perhaps COPC's risk-adjustment effort might have been something that its clinicians were somewhat ashamed of and thus avoided discussing it. But in any case, risk adjustment did not pervade the conversation. Patient welfare did.

It is not all sunny, though, at least from the agilon perspective. As noted, the stock price decreased from a high of $43 in early 2022 to just over $2 in late 2024. At an earnings call for the fourth quarter of 2023, agilon shared that many of their Medicare Advantage plans were doing poorly, with earnings dropping.[27] A competitor, Privia, indicated at much the same time it was abandoning capitated payment. The fallout from tightened Medicare Advantage reimbursements continues to play out in the value-based primary care sector.

Stone Creek Family Physicians

COPC would be more remarkable if it was an outlier. But I encountered many of the same aspects of value-based care in Manhattan, Kansas, at a much smaller primary care practice. Manhattan is a city of about 60,000 people, just north of the state's starkly beautiful Flint Hills and the Tallgrass Prairie National Preserve. It is also the home of Kansas State University. That probably explains the distinctive commercial aspect of the city's downtown area. I have never seen such a concentration of bars and clubs, and it was easy for me to imagine what a Saturday night in the fall must be like after a Wildcat home football game. Otherwise, the town seemed typical of Middle America, not necessarily a place where one would expect to find cutting-edge, value-based care.

I was introduced to Manhattan, and the Stone Creek Family Physicians' practice, by Aledade, another company that provides convenor services—bringing groups together to address a problem or an opportunity—for primary care practices that are attempting to undertake value-based care. It was difficult to get in touch with Aledade and arrange a visit to one of their practices. Their leadership is well known nationally. Dr. Farzad Mostashari and Matt Kendall head the organization, as its CEO and president, respectively. Dr. Mandy Cohen had joined Aledade to lead their health care services unit before leaving to become the director of the Centers for Disease Control and Prevention. John Doyle, the former CEO of Castlight Health, is their chief financial officer. Yet I could not get anyone to return a phone call or an email, which was surprising to me in the somewhat chummy world of health policy and health care services. Being the suspicious sort, I guessed they had little interest in an impartial observer visiting their practices. Finally, however, I found a contact who put me in touch with Dr. Ryan Knopp, who was welcoming and gracious.

On paper, Aledade is a brilliant business concept. Their public statements outline that they act as a facilitator, helping physicians' practices and federally qualified health centers (FQHCs) that participate in Medicare ACOs and the Medicare Shared Savings Program. Of note, the physician-based accountable care organizations have performed much better in the MSSP than the hospital-based ACOs have. The Aledade playbook is similar to that of agilon. Aledade downloads information from their clients' revenue cycle systems and their EMRs to help identify at-risk patients and opportunities to address gaps in care. It offers tips for improvements on quality-of-care measures and new risk-adjustment codes. The company also assists in negotiations with private health insurers and organizes its own multi-practice accountable care organizations in the MSSP.

This latter service distinguishes them from agilon, among others. agilon is focused on Medicare Advantage and, recently, on ACO REACH. Aledade gets physicians' practices started in the Medicare

Shared Savings Program and moves on from there. It also works with FQHCs.[28] (The practices I visited in Oregon had an Aledade contract.) Aledade continues to raise money from venture capital. In 2023 it received another $260 million from a consortium led by Lightspeed Venture Partners. Aledade is not publicly traded. It recently became a public benefit corporation, which means it must consider not just investors, but also stakeholders (their primary care clinician collaborators) in their decision-making. As CEO Mostashari states, this change should better align the company with its clinician clients and with their patients.[29]

Aledade's scope is impressive. Started in 2014, the company now has more than 2 million patients under its management, working with 1,500 practices in 45 states. Aledade claims that in eight years, it has saved more than $1.2 billion in unnecessary medical spending.[30] Given all this, I thought the organization would be eager to talk about its approach to primary care and its strategies, but all I could get was, "Call Ryan Knopp in Manhattan, Kansas."

Knopp and his team could not have been more welcoming. The Stone Creek practice is in the western part of town, perhaps its more affluent side. It sits in a prototypical suburban office building that has tripled in size over the past decade as the practice has grown. Stone Creek Family Physicians now has 12 doctors and 3 physician assistants. They do their own laboratory work and extremity radiology, with interpretation by their doctors. Thus they can cover a lot of urgent care situations where an injured person might otherwise go to an emergency department.

Jennifer Thelwell leads their administrative team.[31] She works for the practice's professional corporation, Stone Creek Family Physicians LLP, which is controlled by its 10 physician partners. (A professional corporation—in this instance, a limited liability partnership or LLP— is the historical and sturdy organizational format for most small physicians' practices.) She has been with the practice since 1988 and has led it through several expansions. Rachel Bittle, their nursing supervisor, has been at Stone Creek for five and a half years.[32] Bittle oversees 11 full-time nurses and 3 part-time ones, as well as 19 medical assistants. This seems to me like a lot of staff for a fee-for-service practice with 10 physicians—but that is because they are slowly turning away from fee-for-service reimbursement to value-based care. The clinicians see around 250 patients a day, with a total of about 25,000 patients in their panels. Stone Creek is still growing, and they will be adding 2 more physicians. (Doctors come in as employees for two years and then can become partners.)

Thelwell and Bittle described the practice for me. Like much of the rest of primary care in late 2022 and early 2023, they are getting back on their feet after staggering through the COVID pandemic. Using their eClinicalWorks EMR system, they were able to switch to virtual patient visits in a hurry. They did drive-thru COVID testing and provided vaccinations for 18 months. Stone Creek Family Physicians retained all their staff through the pandemic, which the partners saw as a testament to the practice's organizational integrity. But they still cite burnout as their number one problem. This applies to all the staff: medical assistants, nurses, advanced practice clinicians, and physicians.

The practice is organized into five pods, each consisting of two doctors, two nurses, and two medical assistants. The nurses are engaged in phoning patients with their test results, following up with the labs, and triaging referrals, as well as arranging prior authorizations. The nurses also do a lot of patient education. The five pods work as a team, but doctors see their own set of patients. The Stone Creek practice does not have its own pharmacists, but it is considering adding them.

The rest of Manhattan's primary care practices are independent groups who are not involved in managing care. Nor are the local hospitals or specialists. Stormont Vail Health is a large hospital and integrated system in nearby Topeka, and it has specialists in Manhattan. These physicians do not provide value-based care, nor are they likely to do so soon. Stormont Vail has not shown a strong interest in buying up primary care practices, and neither has the local Ascension Via Christi Hospital. Stone Creek Family Physicians has not tried to develop organic relationships with these organizations, although that might be a next step for the practice. For now, Stone Creek is an isolated purveyor of value-based care in Manhattan.

Stone Creek Family Physicians' history with Aledade is fascinating. As a group, the practice had decided that it needed to start providing value-based care, using contracts based on financial risk. The local hospital, Ascension Via Christi, was participating as an ACO in the Medicare Shared Savings Program, and the Stone Creek group decided to join. That turned out to be a mistake, according to the Stone Creek team. The practice received no data, no feedback, and no advice. At a loss for what to do next, it was pure serendipity that they found Aledade. A solo-practice doctor Knopp knew in rural Kansas had been recruited into a clinical group that was using Aledade, and that led to an introduction to the company.

Aledade is active in Kansas. The company works with 31 primary care practices including 8 FQHCs, and it has a Kansas ACO that is part of its national ACO network. Knopp serves on the board of the Aledade/Kansas ACO. The Stone Creek team is justifiably proud of their practice; they are generally one of the top performers in the Kansas ACO, and for Aledade nationally. (Maybe that is why Aledade suggested I travel to Manhattan.)

I asked them how things had changed once they started working with Aledade, and the answers were admirably quick and crisp. Three categories were cited as being the most important.

1. They did a lot more screening and preventive testing, focusing on high-prevalence Healthcare Effectiveness Data and Information Set (HEDIS) measures—colon and breast cancer screening, hemoglobin A1c tests, and blood pressure readings—and ensured that they were applied to their entire population of patients. This involved a new emphasis by the whole team on quick follow-ups and consistency.
2. They emphasized that patients must have an annual wellness visit. The practice is reimbursed for these visits (with no out-of-pocket costs to the patients), and the completion of such visits is an important quality-of-care measure for Medicare. Today, about 90% of their Medicare patients schedule an annual wellness visit, and most of these exams are done by the physician assistants.

3. Their patient visits have nearly doubled. There is much more outreach to encourage patients to come in more frequently, and the practice is proactive, rather than reactive.

Aledade's main role is to use data from the EMRs (Aledade works closely with eClinicalWorks) and from the patients' health care insurers' claims reservoir to identify actionable items and gaps in care. All of this comes through on the Aledade app. Using this app entailed a two-year learning curve, but now almost all of the clinicians and nurses use both the app and the EMRs.

Stone Creek Family Physicians also has full-time care coordinators, employed by the Stone Creek practice but trained by Aledade. These individuals are in touch with as many as five hospitals and primarily use the app to help coordinate hospital discharges and keep track of people who have gone to an emergency department. The practice also has outreach to the hospitals and skilled nursing facilities in the area, attempting to avoid unnecessary admissions.

Aledade handles the practice's arrangements with health insurers. Stone Creek's financial risk contracts include their ACO's Sunflower Health Plan (an MSSP coordinated through Aledade), KanCare (the state Medicaid organization), and Blue Cross Blue Shield of Kansas (an affiliate of Elevance Health). This constitutes about 60% of their practice: 30% to 40% of their patients are insured through Blue Cross Blue Shield, 20% are on Medicare, and 3% to 4% on Medicaid. The rest are covered through commercial health insurance plans, which are not offering value-based contracts. Stone Creek tends to treat their commercially insured patients like the others, but these individuals do not show up in the Aledade app. It is remarkable that a primary care practice like this, in the middle of a state that is not considered a hotbed of managed care, can be so focused on value-based care.

Knopp spent some time taking me through Stone Creek's financial relationship with Aledade, focusing on the practice's total cost-of-care component. At the outset, Aledade charged a $1 per member, per month fee. Now, all their Aledade contracts have downside and upside risk, and the split is 50/50 with Aledade. Like agilon, Aledade has no withholding mechanism. Estimated payments are made monthly, an important feature to doctors who are being recruited from fee-for-service systems.

But unlike agilon, Aledade's financial payments are not based solely on capitated performance. The Kansas ACO has a board made up of the doctors in Aledade's affiliated practices. They decide on the relevant outcome measures and their percentage weights. The key ones include the number of (1) emergency department visits per thousand patients, (2) hospital admissions per thousand, (3) annual wellness visits per thousand, and (4) follow-ups on hospital admissions. They also use typical quality-of-care parameters, including monitoring care for patients with hypertension and diabetes, and treatment outcomes. These seem to emulate Aledade's contracts with health insurers, which are outcome based, rather than percentage-of-premium amounts. There is, of course, no bonus to distribute if there is no upside in the risk contracts, so the base is still total cost of care.

Knopp's perception of Aledade is that the company is a coach, an advisor, and a resource manager. For example, he outlined how Aledade emphasized advance planning for care transitions, the use of standard wellness and quality-of-care measures, and—increasingly—the incorporation of behavioral health into primary care practices. Recently, Aledade put Stone Creek in touch with Iris Healthcare, a contractor that assists patients with end-of-life planning, which is not a resource the practice could have easily found on its own. Aledade also helps with coding, making suggestions that come to clinicians via the Aledade app or a daily printout. Knopp believes Stone Creek is financially conservative with regard to coding, and the practice has an independent audit each year, on which they do very well.

The future for Stone Creek Family Physicians is based on its growth in all aspects of value-based care. Specifically, Knopp outlined three major next steps, all of which are related: (1) obtain more value-based commercial contracts, (2) raise the percentage of dollars coming into the practice from value-based care from 10% to 50%, and (3) move to revenue based on a percentage of premiums, rather than payments arising from calculations of outcome measures.

When Stone Creek Family Physicians started this journey with Aledade in 2017, Knopp was not sure where things were headed. In late 2022, he felt like the train had left the station. Knopp cited Aledade's growth curve, which is tremendous. He believes that Aledade gives independent primary care practices a chance to thrive. Speaking to him again in the summer of 2024, he still saw steady progress toward a value-based future.

Although I tried to get some specific financial numbers to piece together the profitability of the practice, Stone Creek's administrative team did not have clearance to go into any detail with me. Jennifer Thelwell did comment that their current overhead (the costs for everything but the doctors'/partners' salaries) was 73%, and that the practice roughly has a 3% to 4% profit margin. She was adamant that the value-based payments from Aledade are incredibly important to Stone Creek's overall financial health. Their fee-for-service revenues are not increasing, and income from their labs and other ancillary facilities is going down. The practice's value-based payments are largely derived from doing well on quality-of-care and performance measurements, not the total cost of the care they provide. The team at Stone Creek does not focus much on the latter, although they realize that if they adhere to follow-ups for their patients, in the long run, their patients are healthier, and the health care costs for them decrease. That has become an important part of the practice's internal culture.

I was interested in how Dr. Knopp became such an advocate for value-based care.[33] He grew up in Chapman, Kansas, and attended the University of Kansas for his undergraduate degree and medical school. (Jayhawk banners and paraphernalia are prominent in his office, although the town is deep in Kansas State University territory.) He trained in family medicine at Kansas University Medical Center and came to Manhattan in 2003, right out of training. Knopp soon became a partner in Stone Creek Family Physicians and has enjoyed his professional life.

But he was not satisfied that the practice's fee-for-service foundation was viable for the long haul, so he cast about for value-based care options. Their ACO venture with Ascension Via Christi Hospital was a toe-in-the-water event that offered no real benefits to the practice. Knopp called it "an exercise in futility," echoing what I heard from his administrative team. Stone Creek continued to look for alternatives, prompted by ongoing signals from the American Academy of Family Practice, which advocated for physician-led, value-based care.[34] The practice's relationship with Aledade was almost accidental. As Knopp commented, "It fell into our lap." Now Stone Creek Family Physicians is "making a bet for a decade from now."

The primary care practice's embrace of value-based care has not been uncontroversial. Knopp champions it, and he has three or four partners who agree with him. Three or four of the other partners sit in the middle, and a couple remain skeptical. Knopp admitted that value-based care is more work and results in increased overhead costs. But, as he put it, the numbers currently speak for themselves, and what future is there in a fee-for-service system, really? Stone Creek has always endorsed incurring more overhead than a typical medical practice, as the partners believed this was part of their commitment to their patients. Other primary care practices in Manhattan, receiving only fee-for-service reimbursements, remain quite lean. There are few solo practitioners in the area now, but a number of three- to four-person practices still exist.

According to Knopp, Stone Creek has a hybrid financial structure, with both value-based payments and fee-for-service reimbursements. The practice expects its clinicians to see 18–25 patients a day, although some see less than 17, and others see more than 30. Clinicians receive productivity bonuses, based on relative value unit (RVUs), and the practice's overhead costs are apportioned among the individual doctors. In 2017, they began to add a value-based component, and in 2020, during the COVID pandemic, this became significant as their RVU volume dropped by nearly 50%. (Knopp estimated that in a steady-state situation, not disrupted by a pandemic, the value-based component of the practice's budget could be $1.5 million out of a base of $15 million.) These funds enable the practice to hire new people, give raises, and provide bonuses.

The plan today is to expand Stone Creek Family Physicians, adding new doctors (two of them were hired in 2022–23). Newcomers join the practice for a year or two and decide to stay if they like how it operates. Knopp believes Stone Creek's approach is not for everyone, as any new doctor must be a team player and committed to hard work. The newcomers, who are not yet partners, also get a smaller paycheck, probably around $200,000 for the first couple of years. That is below the going market rate in Manhattan. But once they become a partner, their pay increases.

Stone Creek's transition to entirely value-based primary care entails incremental steps. Their major new component is the care coordinators. Knopp and his team have now hired three of them, who reconcile medications, mediate all patient transitions to other care facilities, and undertake follow-ups after emergency department visits. Stone Creek has not yet begun to integrate behavioral health into its primary care practice, but one of their care coordinators is a social worker. The partners would like to hire a new family medicine physician who had psychiatric training, which indicates how important mental health care expertise is to the primary care practice.

I also spoke with Dr. Amy Cunningham, who had joined Stone Creek Family Physicians three years earlier.[35] She went to osteopathic medical school in Kansas City, then trained at the University of Minnesota in family medicine. She set up a practice in southeastern Kansas with some friends from her training but eventually ended up in solo practice. That exhausted her—not so much the amount of work, but the need to make every financial decision by herself. She had heard about Aledade, met Knopp, and eventually moved to Manhattan to join Stone Creek.

I was curious about Cunningham's prior career, since being a woman in a rural, solo practice seemed unique to me. She matter-of-factly explained that, to her, it wasn't anything out of the ordinary; it was just where she ended up. In her solo practice, she always had two or three medical assistants and a nurse, so she was used to working with a team. Aledade does business with a number of solo medical practices, she explained, which was not something I would have anticipated.

Cunningham believes most of the practices in the Aledade's Kansas ACO are small, with Stone Creek being the largest.

Cunningham found her daily routine manageable. She and half of the other doctors at Stone Creek used medical scribes. She said it allowed her to concentrate on her patients and get through the day quicker. Cunningham usually finished her charting by the end of the day. While there might be three or four patients who would need additional charting, she did not spend a lot of time doing this at home. The practice's doctors rotate who is on call at night and on weekends. They only make rounds in the hospital's nursery, relying on local hospitalists for adult care.

Aledade comes into play every day in the clinic. Cunningham prints out information on the patients she needs to discuss at the practice's daily huddle, a subset of her daily 20 patients. Her printouts consist of messages from the Aledade app, which in turn are derived from background analytics on EMR and insurance claims data. She works through these messages with her team, wanting to know if issues regarding diagnoses were resolved, prescribed medications were taken, whether a patient need a vaccine, and if a patient's high-cost medications should be changed. She also gets a full list of potential gaps in care: missed annual wellness visits, delinquent mammograms, and blood pressure control reminders. She consults with the care coordinator to get information on patients in transition to other health care facilities and other problems the Aledade app has identified.

Cunningham was a big supporter of value-based care. She thought it provided a better quality of care and was pleased that the practice had value-based contracts for some of its patients: "Getting off FFS [fee-for-service] means you can get paid for doing care well." She and Knopp would like to get more of their health care insurance contracts into this format, even though she considered herself one of the people in the middle in terms of the partners' commitment to value-based care. Cunningham thought that fee-for-service payments would persist, and she enjoyed doing procedures that were based on this reimbursement format. Nonetheless, Cunningham realized in retrospect that her old practice resembled a cattle call, and she was now partially off that treadmill. She mentioned that there are about 55,000 people in Manhattan, and the Stone Creek practice is providing nearly half of their primary care. From her viewpoint, Stone Creek is on the right track. They are crowded to the point of bursting, so the future is bright.

These are the kinds of statements I would expect to hear in California, or even in long-term managed care clinics in places like Boston. But to have them expressed in a 10- to 12-person professional corporation, in a small city in the absolute center of the country, is striking. It gave me a real appreciation not only for the kind of work Aledade is doing, but also—more importantly—for how value-based care is penetrating throughout the American health care system. Of note, leaders in primary care have suggested that the government finance a primary care extension program modeled on the Department of Agriculture program.[36] Aledade and agilon are already doing this, to my view.

Cityblock Health

Cityblock Health, a health care provider for lower-income communities, offers the same lesson. The company has more than 100,000 members and approximately 1,100 employees. Like Aledade, it is based on venture capital and private equity funding—to the tune of over $900 million.[37] Its investors include SoftBank, Tiger Global Management, General Catalyst, and Maverick Ventures, among others. After the last round of investments, Cityblock was valued at $5.7 billion. Given this list of investors, and the amount of money involved, those concerned about private equity's influence on the concept of high-quality treatment for all in health care might find Cityblock to be a useful case study.

Cityblock's website has a bold statement in its "Our Story" section, worth quoting at length.[38]

> We see healthcare as a basic human right. Not luck of the draw. Not based on where you were born. Or the way you look. The way we see it, healthcare should be available to you no matter your circumstance. But not healthcare as it exists now. Something different. Radically different. An approach that puts you first, knowing that everything

affects your health. So you will no longer feel neglected and ignored by a healthcare system that does not include everyone. Or be judged before being diagnosed. We believe in caring for you. In looking you in the eye and asking how you're really doing. Because we listen to you, we understand you, simply put—we see you. **Be seen. Be heard. Be healthy.**

Cityblock is clearly committed to individuals who previously have not had access to care, and it is fundamentally aimed at primary care within the community. Its strategy is resonating with investors. The federal government, and state governments, spend a great deal of money on beneficiaries in Medicaid's programs, but a large portion of that goes for acute care—dealing with problems occurring at the end of a health care episode, not with its root causes. Cityblock is attempting to address these root causes through better primary care and community outreach, with a heavy emphasis on behavioral health for the sickest— and often the most impoverished—patients.

Cityblock seems to be taking two approaches to its stated mission. One is constructing a layer of community outreach and health care management that works with existing primary care organizations, often focusing on their sickest patient populations. The other is a standard primary care clinic strategy, probably best illustrated in North Carolina, where Cityblock has several brick-and-mortar practices.

Conversations with the Cityblock Health team in our nation's capital demonstrate that the organization lives up to the principles enunciated on its website. Phyllis (Cityblock preferred that I use only first names for employees who are not public facing) is a community health worker for Cityblock's High-Risk Behavioral Health Program in Washington, DC, where they have a contract to address behavioral health problems among Medicaid recipients.[39] She suffered a personal tragedy over 30 years ago, became depressed as a result of posttraumatic stress disorder, and began abusing drugs. After 12 years, she finally got help and got clean. She now has had no recurrences for 21 years. All this took place in the southeastern part of DC, where she still lives and now works.

Phyllis's team consisted of nine people, including four licensed social workers. She is one of two community health workers who visit individuals in their homes and get to know their patients more intimately. Her caseload consisted of roughly 60 patients, almost all of them people of color. They ranged from moderately to critically ill individuals, including some who had been diagnosed with schizophrenia. There was also a good deal of substance abuse in her patient group.

Phyllis's own experiences drive her work. She believes that her patients could get healthy again, like she did, but often it takes baby steps to get back on the right path. For example, she visits one patient weekly to look for evidence of regression (like poor personal hygiene) and provide advice on small steps toward better living. Every patient is different, and every patient's mental health disorder is different. But, working closely with the social workers, Pendleton felt like she could make a real difference, especially by getting people to stay on their medication regimes.

This is not the kind of care that normally comes to mind when people think of venture capital or private equity investments in health care, particularly in primary care. Cityblock's investors are obviously interested in making money. Cityblock provides careful attention to small problems, believing this can help prevent further breakdowns for people with behavioral health issues. For these individuals' health insurers, prevention saves them money by eliminating unnecessary care, and that creates profits. So, the link between an investor, who has never visited a neighborhood like the one Phyllis Pendleton works and lives in, and what Pendleton does for her patients, is clear. The private equity investors are funding innovation that lowers cost, which in this case consists of close and carefully considered attention by one community health worker for one patient.

As mentioned, Cityblock has two paths. One is full primary care. The company has five health care centers in North Carolina: Charlotte, Fayetteville, Greensboro, High Point, and Winston-Salem. Greensboro has Cityblock's largest clinic in the state, with three-and-a-half full-time clinicians. Cityblock is a strong believer in the advanced practice provider model, aiming for one physician for every four APPs.

Cityblock only contracts with one health insurer in North Carolina. (They asked me not to identify the insurer.) The contract is unique. The patients assigned to Cityblock are those who have not had a primary care visit in the last year. The insurer sends contact information for these people to Cityblock, and Cityblock searches for them. Eighteen months into the contract, the organization has found about one-third of their potential members. This sleuthing process is enabled by data from health insurance claims, admission/discharge/transfer (ADT) notifications in electronic medical records, and information from the North Carolina Health Information Exchange.

There are plenty of big hospital systems in North Carolina, but Cityblock has not yet developed relationships with them, although their care coordinators are finding some of their target patients in the hospitals, and there will likely be many synergies as the relationships evolve. Currently, the North Carolina clinics have the feel of being solo primary care centers, with few of the care network relationships that a typical FQHC would have with its neighboring hospitals and surrounding medical community. That will change.

I visited the Cityblock primary care clinic in Greensboro, North Carolina, located in a sunny but worn strip mall next door to a Dollar General store. The building had what I have come to appreciate as the modern primary care design: a large central work area divided into cubicles surrounded by exam rooms. (The newest design, like the one at Catalyst Health in Dallas, or Reliant Medical Group in Massachusetts, has a separate access for patients, so they do not see the offstage area where the clinicians work and consult with each other.)

My host was Dorthya "Dodie" Robinson, who was the definition of a "straight shooting," no-nonsense person.[40] She apprised me of the structure of the clinic. There is a virtual huddle every morning with care managers, community health workers, behavioral health specialists, medical assistants, and clinicians. The team talks about at-risk patients and task lists for the coming day. They rely on their EMR for most of the information and are in the process of moving to an athenahealth system, but they did not purchase the athenahealth revenue cycle program. They are not really submitting insurance claims, as their contract is completely based on risk-adjusted capitation. Nor will they use athenahealth's population health management tool, which is valued by other health care groups with financial risk contracts.

The teams work sedulously outside the clinic, with an intense focus on reducing preventable hospital admissions. The care managers have created a cohesive transition-of-care program, with great follow-up at home by the community health workers. They also have a mobile integrated care team consisting of community care clinicians, emergency medicine technicians (EMTs), and paramedics who address health care problems in people's homes, all with the oversight of a doctor. The information from this community care goes into a homegrown database called Commons, which the clinicians can use to coordinate patient care. As might be expected, social determinants of health play a huge role in the Commons database.

Still, the practice has the feel of a start-up. Robinson is a veteran, having worked at the University of North Carolina Medical Center, and then for DaVita, running dialysis clinics. At DaVita, she had the data she needed to run things tightly, but here teams are still working to ensure they have basic utilization and quality-of-care data, although other more mature Cityblock markets have established this foundation. They are also working to improve information on clinicians' productivity, as well as the ability to define which interventions are working effectively. Robinson had a sense that Cityblock's central administration is taking all the right steps to address these problems.

Another issue was that the clinic was providing a lot more pediatric care than they expected, and the value-based care model for pediatrics was not well defined. Again, this is an area of development for them, as they are focused on a maternal health model in which they have risk for both mothers and babies. Finally, they are constantly seeking improvements in their sharing of data with the insurer, so they can get better alignment across key metrics, and map progress against shared goals. Robinson is patient, though, and sees progress being made weekly. Cityblock wants to grow, take on more patients, and potentially open more clinics.

I spoke with a number of the clinicians, and one, Angel, stands out.[41] She is a physician assistant who has worked in primary care practice for more than 20 years. She was recruited by a Cityblock employee who assured her that Cityblock's approach was the way medicine was meant to be practiced, and she has not been disappointed. Jones loved the team-based aspect of managed care, as well as the interventions she could provide. One of her patients had end-stage congestive heart failure and was constantly bouncing in and out of the hospital. Jones tried to get a palliative care team involved, but neither the patient nor that person's family were interested in such a discussion. So, now she has the paramedic team visiting that person three days a week, ensuring that all prescribed medications are being taken and evaluating any new symptoms. The patient is happy and is staying out of the hospital. And Cityblock is saving money, some of which will eventually return to its investors.

This alternative approach to medical care—one that is oriented around primary care and based in community care—is heartening. One cannot help but hope that Cityblock will thrive. I did find it odd, however, while spending one morning at the clinic, I never saw a patient.

In other cities, Cityblock is taking the second path, working hand in hand with the health plan's existing provider network to extend care coordination beyond the doctor's office and meet member's clinical and nonclinical needs. Their Boston team brought me up to speed on how they operate this community "wraparound" program. Dr. Dhruva Kothari leads Cityblock's medical operations in Massachusetts.[42] He has an extensive background in managed care and Medicaid programs. After going to Columbia University for medical school and receiving internal medicine training at Yale University, he worked for the Commonwealth Care Alliance, a groundbreaking managed care plan in Massachusetts. Kothari was getting restless there, and Cityblock's commitment to intensive health care management for the sickest patients appealed to him.

Kothari and his team are usually not the primary care clinicians for the patients. Their main contract is with one of the large nonprofit insurers in Massachusetts. The contract focuses on *dual eligible beneficiaries*—low-income patients who qualify for Medicaid and also have Medicare insurance coverage due to a disability. Three-quarters of their patients have mental health problems. Cityblock's program basically supplements the work of primary care clinicians, using advanced data analytics to anticipate breakdowns in care and then intervene quickly. Kothari stated that just giving a patient a prescription to solve a health care problem was not enough. The Cityblock team must ensure that it gets into the patient's mouth. Or a hospital might treat a patient's acute medical problem, but its doctors will not take the time to understand how this happened in the first place. Cityblock needs to go the extra mile to get that information.

Cityblock's staff do provide primary care for a subset of patients, however, visiting the patients at home. Their clinicians schedule 30- to 90-minute visits and have access to EMT-type services, like the North Carolina team does. Given that Cityblock's clinicians can make four to five of these home visits a day, their data analytics—and the targeting information it produces—must be precise, focusing on the sickest patients. Cityblock earns a return if they keep the total medical expenses below a preset budget.

For the majority of patients who also have non-Cityblock primary care clinicians, reactions to this joint relationship can vary. Some of these clinicians are happy to have Cityblock involved: its people have sharper eyes and ears, as well as the ability to visit patients at home. Others are concerned about the loss of direct contact, wanting to maintain their own close relationships with their patients. Both sides worry about a lack of coordination, as the various EMR systems do not necessarily communicate with each other. At least 10–12 primary care practices in Boston have more than 100 patients that Cityblock is following, and relationships with those practices appear to be cordial and smooth, as the primary care clinicians get comfortable with Cityblock.

Kothari's operation, with a patient population of 3,600, involves eight physicians, eight behavioral health specialists, and many paramedics, nurses, and community health workers. The health plan was spending over $100 million a year on these patients, and their bet with Cityblock was that wraparound health care services could lower costs. The exciting part of this wraparound program is that the patients it serves are exactly the people to whom the message on Cityblock's website is sent. Cityblock seems to be walking the walk, instead of just talking the talk.

Cityblock's emphasis on behavioral health is striking, and it is absolutely essential, given the type of patients they serve. Dr. Michael Tang, who heads Cityblock's mental health team in Massachusetts, offered some interesting perspectives.[43] Tang went to medical school at Harvard University and then trained in pediatrics at Boston Children's Hospital. By the time he finished there, he had become so certain that behavioral health was at the core of medical care for children that he went back for a separate residency in psychiatry. He subsequently worked at the Dimock Community Health Center, an FQHC in Boston, before joining Cityblock.

The integration of behavioral health and primary care has only taken place slowly and haltingly, even in a progressive state like Massachusetts. So, when Cityblock approached Tang with a position in a primary care program that was paid a capitated sum rather than relying on a fee-for-service system, he jumped at this chance to help bring about what he saw as a needed change in health care. He was a strong critic of fee-for-service reimbursements, arguing that they do not allow clinicians to address social determinants of health and overlooked many of the sickest patients: "I can only bill for the patients who show up in my office; sometimes the sicker patients, the one who really need care, are no-shows." Capitation allows clinicians to creatively go after those patients.

Echoing others at Cityblock, Tang stated that data analytics is foundational, allowing them to find the right patients at right time. The Cityblock team continues to push the envelope in that regard. Another part of this mindset is to "get out of the box" in their mental health care approach, being far more proactive than reactive, such as addressing substance use disorders with medication-assisted therapy expeditiously, rather than having one of their patients be in the emergency department, suffering severe withdrawal symptoms. A third aspect is trust, emphasized from Cityblock's executives on down to the trenches. Here the organization's community health workers—people from within their patients' own neighborhoods—are crucial. As Tang put it, his behavioral health team provides backup for the community health workers.

Dr. Kameron Matthews is Cityblock's widely admired chief health officer.[44] Talking with her brought to life the path from an established group to a newly created start-up organization. While she enjoyed working at the Veterans Health Administration (VA), which has a formidable bureaucracy, the opportunity for more autonomy and innovation at Cityblock impressed her. It surprised me, however, that she thought Cityblock would do well by adopting some of the structure she had at the VA. When she started at Cityblock, she concentrated on updating policies, developing flexible job descriptions, establishing a proper flow of data, and bringing more uniformity between markets.

The benefits of a start-up culture were clear to her from the outset. She loved how the organization could turn on dime, which the VA certainly could not. But Cityblock did need to build clinical pathways and strengthen its health information management, just as she had to do at the VA.

I pushed Matthews to comment on the contrasts between these two organizations, but, tellingly, she found similarities. Both focus on the whole patient, integrate care, and have a strong sense of mission. Such critical thinking, combined with excellent leadership, has brought Cityblock hundreds of millions of dollars in private equity investments, and it seems to be leading the way with creative ideas for providing health care to people who have not had any (or little) in the past. Supporting companies like Cityblock, and bringing care to patients who have not had any, is not something that private equity gets credit for, but it is occurring. Perhaps this means that health policy should have a more nuanced view of private investment.

But this is where Ravi Schdev's point about the long haul comes into focus. All the people I talked to at Cityblock seemed extraordinarily committed to care for the impoverished and unempowered. They were also devoted to their model and wanted to show success, committed but also patient. Their investors are ultimately interested in profitable return, however. On behalf of their fiduciaries, investors are constantly assessing market conditions and interest rates, thinking about the best time to step out of an investment like Cityblock. For Cityblock leaders, this must create some cognitive dissonance, and certainly some unease. It will be interesting to see how this plays out for companies like Cityblock.

Oak Street Health

I did not spend any time with the leadership teams at Aledade, agilon health, or Cityblock Health, so I cannot comment on their views of the future of their companies or the health care market. Certainly, though, one possible future is to sell to a larger health care company that is convinced of the value being created at a start-up. As I was researching this book, One Medical purchased Iora Health, and then One Medical was bought by Amazon. Just a bit later, as I was arranging a visit to Oak Street Health, it was bought by CVS Health (my employer for over a decade). It was informative to arrive at Oak Street Health just after this purchase occurred.

Oak Street Health is another chain of primary care clinics, specializing in serving Medicare beneficiaries, particularly those with Medicare Advantage plans. It was founded in 2012 by Michael Pykosz, Griffin Myers, and Geoff Price, who became, respectively, its chief executive officer, chief medical officer, and chief operating officer. The company grew over time, and as of May 2023, it had over 170 clinics in 21 states. After venture and private equity investment rounds, Oak Street Health went public in late 2020, with a stock price that then varied between $15 and $65 a share.[45] In March 2023, CVS Health bought the company at $39 per share, for a total of $10.6 billion.

CVS Health had long been promising its shareholders it would be serious about entering the primary care business, and Oak Street Health was in a good position to provide that for them. Oak Street's investors did well by this purchase. So did the founders. Pykosz and Myers had shares worth approximately $320 million and $189 million, respectively.

This is the return from being entrepreneurial, building a great business, and demonstrating that better primary care can improve outcomes and reduce costs. Some might nonetheless see it as excessive.

I found the Oak Street methods and approaches to care to be refined and thoughtful. Oak Street teams tell new doctors that their days will be as hectic as those in any primary care practice, but the focus is on far fewer patients, so caring for them is much more rewarding. The use of an electronic medical scribe is ubiquitous, which allows the clinicians to spend time with their patients. They toggle between what was their old EMR system, Greenway, and their new homegrown data system, Canopy. Some refer mostly to Canopy EMRs as their source of patient information, but typical primary care documentation goes into Greenway.

Oak Street Health is growing, and some of its staff feel that growth pressure. Recruiting is a big problem. This is mostly done through a central team, but everyone takes advantage of their contacts. Oak Street's clinicians, like everyone else, increasingly rely on advanced practice providers, and they encounter the same set of issues around training and precepting. The APPs each have their own patient panel, though.

Oak Street Health has followed a specific recipe for managing care. The company locates their practices in impoverished or working-class areas; only accepts patients with Medicare insurance, particularly those having Medicare Advantage plans; makes percentage-of-premium deals with health insurance companies; carefully codes their clinicians' encounters with patients; and pays attention to their patients' utilization of specialists, emergency departments, and hospitals. Oak Street Health's goal is to improve their patients' lives—and to make a profit, at least eventually. At the end of 2022, with 159,000 at-risk patients out of a total of 224,000 patients, Oak Street Health's revenues stood at $2.16 billion, almost all from capitated payments.[46] Their net loss was $500 million for the year, which is largely attributed to rapid growth—as new clinics open, they lose money until they recruit a sufficient number of patients.

I visited several Oak Street Health clinics in the Chicago area. Although primary care doctors are generally seen as being unhappy and burned out, in the year I spent interviewing clinicians, they almost universally exhibited a lot of joy, were interested in talking about their jobs, and expressed excitement when discussing clinical issues. In addition, I persistently encountered the somewhat earthy sense of humor one finds throughout health care. Oak Street Health, in contrast, seemed somewhat muted.

Part of this might be explained by decisions made by management that structured my visit. Before showing up, I was sent an extensive list of things I could not talk about. In retrospect, somewhat surprisingly, no other sites I visited were as directive. As well, I only met with senior management. I had the sense they were not eager to go into much depth about the practice.

I arrived at the Oak Street practice in Bronzeville—a historically African American neighborhood on Chicago's South Side, just down the road from Comiskey Park (the Chicago White Sox's baseball field)—on a cold but sunny April morning. The clinic was on South State Street, a wide and busy thoroughfare, but it was the only real business establishment in sight. There were no other stores, gas stations, or homes. Looking far down the street, I spotted what perhaps were some warehouses. Across from me, an elderly man pushed a wheelbarrow, full of what appeared to be rags, across a rut-strewn lot. It was the picture of urban poverty.

The center itself was lively. Outside, I saw some impressively lime green cars, with "Oak Street" emblazoned on the sides, used to shuttle patients to and from the clinic. The large building had approximately 45 people working there, similar in size to the Stone Creek Family Physicians' practice in Manhattan, Kansas. To put the recent purchase in perspective, CVS Health had just paid approximately $69 million apiece for this clinic and another 160 like it.

The geography inside the facility was similar to other new practices I visited: the clinical teams are all centrally located, with exam rooms on the periphery. The Bronzeville site had a waiting room, staffed with friendly "welcome coordinators," but no community room. (The other Oak Street Health primary care practices I visited had community rooms, but they were not being used, at least when I visited.) The health care team consisted of a clinician (either an MD or an APP), a scribe, and a medical assistant, and there were several teams at Bronzeville. The various teams all shared a nurse, a social worker, and a care manager. The clinicians have panels of about 500 patients. I was not authorized to talk with staff members about their form of reimbursement, but apparently it is determined by their risk-adjusted panel sizes. The clinic was jumping, busy with patients and clinicians moving fast and directed.

Dr. Julie Blankemeier met me in Bronzeville.[47] Her warmth and engaging nature marked her as someone who was likely a great primary care doctor. Blankemeier is a regional medical director, with oversight for much of Chicago's South Side. She was trained in family medicine at Advocate Lutheran General Hospital (located in a Chicago suburb) and has always practiced in places where patients have not had much access to health care. I asked what was different about Oak Street Health, and she responded quickly with a reason that speaks to why she became a physician. Blankemeier wanted not only to care for those in need, but also to take *great* care of them, and Oak Street offered her the resources to do so. Giving an example, she noted she did not have to double-book patients. And she had time to phone her patients, including on the weekend, to see how they were doing. That level of health care pays off in terms of better patient outcomes.

Blankemeier showed me their Canopy EMR system, which can range from aggregated data across the whole organization to information on individual patients. She used it to manage the six clinics she oversees, as well as to review data on her patients scheduled to visit that day in her morning huddle with her medical assistant, a medical scribe, and, often, a care manager or a social worker. Once a week, in a bigger huddle, a much larger team—including all the clinic's social workers, care managers, and community health workers, as well as the clinicians—gathers to discuss their sickest patients. I came to realize these team huddles are the best marker of a medical group taking care management seriously.

Blankemeier maintained that the ethos of the organization had not changed as they have grown. She used to see Oak Street's CEO, Michael

Pykosz, frequently, but not anymore (he left CVS Health in late 2024). And there are a lot of new faces on the clinical teams. But the overall culture remains. "Being Oaky" means assuming everyone has good intentions—having pride in "ownership" of the practice, maintaining a positive energy level, and exhibiting relentless determination on behalf of the patients. Like most value-based primary care clinicians, Blankemeier was proactive, asking, "What can I do to make this patient's life better?"

At Bronzeville, all the patients and a large part of the staff are African American, and the district is impoverished. Oak Street Health's Brighton Park practice, located on the southwestern side of Chicago, is in a neighborhood that is largely Hispanic: 95% are of Mexican descent, and the rest are from Central America. Everyone in the clinic speaks Spanish, and Dr. Francina Peralta-Machado, the regional medical supervisor I met with, was no exception.[48] She went to medical school and trained in the Dominican Republic, then did internal medicine training at Advocate Illinois Masonic (in the Chicago metropolitan area), followed by a geriatric fellowship at Loyola University. She has been with Oak Street Health for five years. Over that period, the organization transitioned from a mix of patients covered under traditional Medicare and Medicare Advantage plans to today's set of patients, limited solely to those with Medicare Advantage and ACO REACH plans.

Dr. Peralta-Machado clearly wanted to be elsewhere rather than talking with me. I could not blame her, as her day was a busy one. She made some good points during our brief visit, however. One was that the Brighton Park clinic provides great care for their patients, care that otherwise would not be available to them. So, their impact in this neighborhood—located between Midway Airport and the warehouses lining I-55—was positive. They had as many patients as they could handle, mostly coming to them through self-referral. I saw this a testament to the positive impact that Oak Street was having in its community. Indeed, Ali Khan, the chief medical officer for their value-based strategy, pointed out that Oak Street is not seeking locations in wealthy suburbs. "We go where the problems are hardest, we dig in proactively, and the work of restoring trust therein is frankly some of the most challenging work of our careers. It is deeply meaningful, but it is hard."[49]

Peralta-Machado had seen Oak Street Health's Canopy EMR system improve over time, becoming ever more useful. And she mentioned the Rubicon system—a virtual specialty consultation program that her teams use a great deal—that Oak Street Health had bought for $100 million last year. These themes, more data analytics to better understand patients' needs, and increased use of low-cost virtual interventions, will no doubt play an ever larger role in primary care.

The next day, I went up to the Edgewater clinic, a lakefront community on Chicago's North Side, taking one small step up in average area income levels. Oak Street Health has been following that trend. Originally, most of their practices were in neighborhoods like Bronzeville, where they could concentrate on patients turning 65 who were graduating from the hectic forms of health care under Medicaid to the high-touch health services in Medicare Advantage plans. In Edgewater, they would be getting more patients who had previously been covered by health insurance through their employers, or perhaps shifting to Medicare Advantage from traditional Medicare.

Dr. Andrea Khosropour met with me.[50] She went to the David Geffen School of Medicine at the University of California, Los Angeles, trained in family medicine at West Suburban Medical Center in Oak Park (a Chicago suburb), spent some time at Chicago's Cook County Hospital, and came to Oak Street eight years ago. At that time, it was a smaller organization, and everyone there knew everyone else. She used to see Oak Street Health's cofounders frequently. The organization was more spry, and medical directors used to be able to make their own decisions and get things done right away, but that has now changed. Other aspects of the organization have not changed. A clinician/scribe/medical assistant team has been a sturdy triad throughout her time with Oak Street, as has the Greenway EMR.

Khosropour was frank about numerous issues. In discussing physicians' workloads, Oak Street's clinics have no patient portal, so no messages from patients come directly to their doctors. The Greenway system formerly had a portal, but it was shut down. She reasoned that the clinic's patients are older, low income, and would not be likely to use it. Khosropour's team was using Rubicon a good deal, but referrals to live specialists were generally difficult. The referral system is centralized and slow, so it is difficult to arrange visits using it. (I had heard this complaint at a number of managed care sites and began to wonder if centralizing referrals was a corporate strategy.) Nor does Oak Street have tight relationships with hospitalists, so clinicians rely on their care coordinators to follow up on their hospitalized patients.

One thing that impressed me at Oak Street Health was that all the clinical managers spend a good deal of time overseeing quality-of-care measures. Canopy has some helpful metrics, but Khosropour emphasized that she read a lot of charts in Greenway, as this helped her understand the pulse of her clinics. Chart review itself is quite "old school," but it is impressive in that it suggests a real commitment to ensuring a high quality of care for patients. She also related that Oak Street's doctors and APPs have a formal mentoring/collaboration relationship, which all parties take seriously.

I asked Dr. Khosropour about some of the other techniques that practices use to manage care. She was not as enthusiastic about reviewing reports on hospital admissions, as she was not certain that there was much to learn from them. But in their huddles, the teams do go over the hospital stays, and she thought that kind of discussion provided some focus on prevention. Mentioning coding and documentation brought an initial eye roll, but, as she admitted, being careful about documentation was part of the job.

Khosropour, like her Oak Street Health colleagues, was bullish on the business. She has opened several new clinics, and they fill up quickly. Patients love the attention they get, and the doctors appreciate being able to concentrate on a relatively small number of patients. Somehow, though, she and the other physicians I met at the Oak Street health clinics lacked the joy I found elsewhere. They were grateful to be able to treat patients who had not previously had the attention they deserved, and they deeply appreciated that value-based care was getting them off the fee-for-service merry-go-round. I hoped I had caught them on bad days, or at the end of a long Chicago winter. More to the point,

I hoped that purchase by a large corporation had not changed the sense of purpose at Oak Street Health. Their transition will no doubt be the future for other start-ups, so it bears close watching.

Venture Capital, Corporate Ownership, and Primary Care

I came away surprised by the role of private-equity-financed organizations in primary care. I was prepared to find a patina of cynical support for patient welfare that covered over constant pressure for quick profit. Following private equity's history in hospitals and with specialist physicians, taking advantage of fee-for-service in abusive ways, my hunch was not unwarranted. But that is not what I found. The clinicians in practices owned by private equity, or supported in their efforts to provide value-based care by PE-owned or PE-spawned companies, seemed every bit as devoted to their patients as those I found in other primary care practices. Furthermore, their commitment to value-based care, and to moving away from reactive fee-for-service to proactive managed care, was sharp and genuine. In this regard, the influence of private equity seemed to complement efforts by the federal and state governments, as well as insurers, to move primary care to a better future at the center of a cost-effective health care system.

One must acknowledge there are little data that can be used to assess how such practices are performing compared to the typical primary care practice. But in the clinic, at the level of care delivery, an Aledade-advised practice, or a Cityblock care management team, sees many of the same challenges, has a similar toolbox of solutions, and has the same belief in value-based primary care as Optum or the FQHC that is managing care. Across the board, the clinicians are speaking the same language and have the same beliefs. To me, this seems like good news.

The only question is the ephemeral nature of investor capital. Venture capitalists are almost definitionally short-termers: they take a lot of shots, knowing that some will fail but others will be home runs. Finding the right exit at the right time is perhaps the critical talent for a venture capitalist. Private equity is not much better. In its worst form, it disrupts the enterprise and sells off partis. In its best, it boosts a firm to a successful IPO or new set of owners. No matter what, though, private equity will not persist—they move on.

This means that the firms we discussed in this chapter are headed toward change. Some, like agilon, have already made the move from venture-backed to corporate independence. Others might follow that path. But the more likely outcome, especially for care providers like Cityblock, is that they will be bought, as happened to One Medical and to Oak Street. Then the question is, How will they do as part of a vertically integrated corporation?

The accepted logic is that this change in control is usually not a great thing, with a spry and agile start-up placed into a heavily bureaucratic organization, especially one with expectations of returns on investment that are in many ways more durable and concrete than what the original private equity owners expected. Oak Street Health was running a $500 million loss on $2 billion worth of business.[51] Its investors did well, knowing they could tolerate loss in the hope a sale would come.

CVS Health could not and would not tolerate such huge losses in one of its operating entities. But Optum appears to be rather easily integrating large primary care practices, pursuing what appears to be a durable strategy over the past 15 years. There is a strong business case for an insurer to cultivate primary care, developing a value-based foundation for care for its beneficiaries. This may be a viable pathway for replacing fee-for-service.

As value-based care grows and deepens, we will likely reach a steady state with less opportunity for venture investment. There will be large independent primary care groups, like COPC or Catalyst in Texas, that will rely to some extent on help from convenors like agilon or Aledade. The convenors themselves will likely become publicly traded companies. Other practices will decide it is better to go with vertical integration and be bought by Humana, Optum, or CVS Health, to name a few. Either path suggests the spread of value-based care, which the health care system needs. Either path also entails a primary care enterprise that is valued and placed at the center of the health care system, anticipating patient needs, promoting health, and eliminating unnecessary costs. At this point, private investors appear to be contributing to that brighter future.

Of course, there is the possibility that much of this promise is built on bloated returns from Medicare Advantage, in turn based on inappropriate risk coding. As the government addresses this, and it will, the question is, Will large corporations persist in their interest in value-based care? And will groups like Catalyst and COPC continue to grow and prosper? The next decade will provide critical answers.

CHAPTER EIGHT

The Future of Primary Care

WHERE IS PRIMARY CARE in the American health care system headed? One reasonable conclusion, based on most of what is written about primary care today, is that this field of medicine will slowly fade away as fewer doctors and nurses select it as their vocation. Many others who already work in the primary care arena will leave, ground down by a constant bombardment with patient issues that these clinicians are ill equipped to address. Nurse practitioners and physician assistants may continue to choose primary care, but will they not ultimately be worn out as well? Patients will find their way to specialists on their own, using retail health facilities for minor problems.

This future presumes a fee-for-service system, with little oversight on the costs of care or its quality, and a great deal of provider-induced demand. A specialty-dominated future also entails the expenses associated with a lot of what would otherwise be preventable diseases—sizeable sums that could have been foregone had appropriate preventive care been delivered, and chronic diseases like diabetes and hypertension been treated.

To my eyes, this future seems untenable, simply because of the costs involved. Any rational individual, armed with the data we have on the efficacy of primary care, would surmise that health care authorities cannot allow primary care to deteriorate further. We already have a health care system we cannot afford, and to let it sink further into a specialty- and hospital-dominated fee-for-service system is neither acceptable or nor viable. But in a world where the wealthy control an increasing share of the national income,[1] it may be that the most powerful individuals will still be able to afford great medical care, and their satisfaction will drain the political will of others to maintain a system that works for all.

But stepping back from this pessimistic, perhaps even cynical precipice, let us presume that our government is rational, and the effort to develop primary care-based alternatives to fee-for-service medical care is earnest and bearing fruit. The reports from the field in the previous chapters suggest that this is happening. The federal and state governments, health insurers, health care corporations, and venture capitalists are all taking steps to promote value-based primary care because it is in their own interests to do so. Payers need more cost-effective health care, and providers can make a profit if they produce it. Many of the primary care practices I visited demonstrated a firm commitment to managing care in a value-based fashion, utilizing the prism of delivering health care for the whole person.

Though burnout is real, it rarely was the controlling or driving force in the primary care practices I visited. Even those clinicians who seemed most overwhelmed by the volume of work they faced nonetheless spoke in cheerful and glowing terms about interactions with their patients. Part of this is due to their empathy, a predilection which must be part of their decision to go into primary care in the first place. Another is the application of their craft—clinical problem-solving—which can be so satisfying after spending years in training. My travels suggest that the core of primary care—commitment to patients and the skillful use of medical expertise—is in good shape. What is needed is for that core to find the right health care structure that allows these clinicians to thrive. One more example makes that point.

ChenMed's Vision for Primary Care

The most impressive such health care structure I have seen is in ChenMed's primary care practices. Stephen Greene, the chief administrative officer at ChenMed, told me that there are three types of primary care: traditional, advanced, and transformational.[2] (Not too dissimilar to Paul Keckley's Primary Care 1.0, 2.0, and 3.0.) Traditional is the fee-for-service-based practice. Advanced primary care will accept some financial accountability, up to and including full financial risk. Its background structure, however, is based on a management services organization or independent practice association arrangement. These organizations tend to stitch together the means to deal with full risk, generally through various types of contracts with health insurers. But insurers still call the shots on how costs are controlled. In contrast, transformational primary care relies on a primary care physician to coordinate and lead the health care team. The teams have specific outcomes that they are trying to obtain, and they do this by establishing trusting relationships between patients and their physicians. As a result, they reduce unnecessary care. This is what ChenMed does.[3]

The company's founder, Dr. Jen-Ling James Chen, began a private primary care practice in the mid-1970s in Miami Gardens, Florida. According to Greene, Chen's competitors, mostly Cuban American primary care practices, were involved in financial risk contracts. Chen followed suit and embraced full financial risk, emphasizing close supervision of sick patients and preventive approaches to disease. But he could not do this and keep a foot in fee-for-service. He therefore accepted only full-risk contracts, not a mix of capitation and fee-for-service payments As a result, his practice was unique.

A further chapter in the family story occurred when Dr. Chen was diagnosed with cancer in 2003. As the ChenMed website notes, "He and his family experienced firsthand the frustrations of navigating the healthcare system where profits, not patients, are the focus. While Dr. Chen fought for his life, he and his family fought for access and coordinated care. After his recovery, Dr. Chen was determined to revolutionize the healthcare delivery system. He created ChenMed to provide accountable, compassionate, and coordinated physician-led, family-oriented primary care."[4]

This privately held company now operates 125 clinics in 15 states. The Chen family had occupied much of the C-suite of the company until 2023, when they tapped Steve Nelson from UnitedHealthcare to be the president of ChenMed. The family's history is carefully captured by James's sons Christopher and Gordon in *The Calling: A Memoir of Family, Faith, and the Future of Healthcare*.[5] A family-owned business, run by the family, starting from a single primary care practice. Their own family autobiography. All of this is unique.

I should note that some of the story I can tell based on my visit in early 2023 might already be changing. When I traveled to Miami, the Chen family still dominated the executive positions. But since that time, leadership changed, with Nelson bringing in a new team. Then, in the summer of 2024, Nelson stepped down and Christopher Chen resumed as CEO. What I present here is a snapshot in early 2023 of what the family produced. I found it a fascinating example of what primary could be.

I was aware, at least in outline form, of the Chen model of care before I visited. First, the practices are solely geared toward care of patients with Medicare Advantage. They contract with Medicare Advantage firms for a percentage of premium. The clinician-led teams have small panels, and they ensure that all preventive measures are taken and that all health care utilization is appropriately scrutinized. They also make sure they document diagnoses carefully. If it sounds like some of other practices reviewed in this book, it is. The difference is that ChenMed wrote much of the script that others are emulating.

The Chens were direct about the patient population they intended to serve: elderly people, many of whom have not had great access to health care. This is admirable, although I wondered why they have focused solely on Medicare Advantage plan beneficiaries instead of also including the uninsured or those with Medicaid. Their answer: We know our niche, and we are working to get better and better at providing the care they need.

A visit to ChenMed's headquarters in Miami Gardens, Florida, provided me with a much richer perspective on the company. Approaching primary care practices or companies, I usually asked to visit particular primary care practices, but I found that at the most open and most successful practices I visited—ChenMed and Optum/HealthCare Partners—the leaders (respectively, Chris Chen and Amar Desai), wanted me to visit their administrative office as well. The first person I met with at ChenMed was Jamey Lutz, the managing director of brand and service excellence.[6] He "curates the clinic experience for the patient." His background includes stints with various employers, including Ritz-Carlton, Atlantic Capital, HomeBanc Mortgage Corporation, and the Orlando Magic NBA basketball team.

While his presentation was somewhat steeped in marketing jargon, Lutz's efforts seemed to be founded on common sense and human insight. He believes in consistency of delivery, so the company can avoid heroic efforts to fix patients' problems. For example, ChenMed's bigger health care centers have longer wait times, so they rely on electronic notification systems to alert patients about any delay. As long as patients understand an issue, he reasoned, they are going to be satisfied.

All of Lutz's work is based on a culture of fine service for ChenMed's "customers"—the patients. As Lutz described it, patients need world-class, VIP service, and his job is to make it easier to provide that experience. This culture was in place when Lutz arrived. But what he does is harvest survey data from patients, examine that information, and find areas for improvement. Currently he uses Qualtrix, which is based on texting. For some seniors who do not text, he installed stand-up kiosks in the clinics' offices and uses them to solicit information. He has found that the big driver of patients' satisfaction is how effectively their clinicians listen to them. Based on this metric, Lutz's team analyzes verbatim statements and assesses the amount of eye contact that is made, providing coaching opportunities for individual clinicians. I noticed the results of this in the way ChenMed's doctors position themselves vis-à-vis a patient in the exam room. They sit quite close, facing the patient, with their EMR screen to the side and out of reach. And they repeat back what they hear from their patients.

Lutz is also constantly probing. He worried that the organization was not good at understanding how patients' experiences change over time, so he was tracking longitudinal data. For example, he had statistics on disenrollment but had not yet found good predictors. Surprisingly, net promoter scores did not correlate with patients leaving a ChenMed primary care practice. He was also trying to understand how clinician/team engagement works, as he did not have good data there. He was certain, however, that the key component of the ChenMed brand is the physicians' relationships with their patients, and the degree of trust that relationship engenders. (Trust is crucial everywhere, but it is an issue that comes up much more frequently among clinicians who are taking care of underserved communities.) Lutz's analytical approach seems like something you would find in any corporate setting, but it is all designed to prompt a specific behavior on the part of the clinical teams—one that says to patients, "We have your back."

Stephen Greene, ChenMed's chief administrative officer, was affable and welcoming, but when talking about the company, his tone was businesslike and analytic. In citing the key issues that determine new expansion sites for ChenMed primary care clinics, he used crisp bullet points.

- Density of seniors.
- Ecology of insurers, especially their willingness to pay a high percentage of the premiums.
- Areas with lower-than-average incomes and a high percentage of people of color.

These issues can be supplemented with a variety of statistics: area deprivation index, opportunity zone status, medically underserved status, and health professional shortage area status. Then, in keeping with ChenMed's quirky combination of commercial insight and family intuition, Mary Chen, the family's matriarch, traditionally made the final decisions on clinic locations. (One aspect that likely changes as the Chen family drops back.) Once a site is selected, the focus shifts to that area's senior citizens and their health insurance brokers.

Stephen Greene previously worked at Kaiser Permanente, and the contrast he drew between that organization and ChenMed is notable. Their philosophy is the same: use only one payment system, capitation. But Kaiser Permanente, at least in California, was a closed system, with the insurance company, doctors and nurses, and hospitals in one package. ChenMed is totally dependent on primary care. And, Greene noted, the relationships between ChenMed and health insurers are not like what happens in California, where utilization management, explanations of benefits, and the like are delegated to the medical groups. In some ways, if ChenMed's approach works, it should be exportable to much of the rest of the country in a way that Kaiser is not.

Like Kaiser Permanente, ChenMed manages specialty care, but the difference is that ChenMed does not employ its own specialists. There is a ChenMed comprehensive provider list (CCPL) for most of Florida's metropolitan areas, which is a curated group of specialists who understand managed care. Their CCPLs are drawn up by looking at quality-of-care measures and costs—similar to what insurers do in putting together their favored networks of health care providers. ChenMed also maintains a series of experts who can be consulted by telephone.

Recruiting is finally honed. ChenMed needs clinicians who are interested in the company's stated mission and will concentrate on serving their patients. They also must be able to lead a team, incorporate behavioral health into patient care, and be agile learners. ChenMed executives spend a lot of time talking with individuals training in primary care residencies. Once clinicians sign on, they get "black-belt training" in primary care to learn ChenMed's systems and methodology. New hires must be willing to be coached, and some do not make the grade. The turnover rate is around 15% in the first year. All of this is similar to what happens at other primary care practices attempting to take on capitation, but ChenMed's process is better conceptualized, with real programs built around clinicians' successful execution of ChenMed's policies.

With regard to health care insurers, Greene recognized that the momentum in Medicare Advantage plans is shifting away from health maintenance organizations (HMOs) toward preferred provider organization (PPOs), which makes it more difficult to police patient self-referrals. As a result, ChenMed must depend even more on their doctor–patient relationships, particularly in ensuring that patients follow their doctor's advice. With the PPO plans, ChenMed tries to get another percentage point or two from the premiums. They also bargain on stop-loss policies, designed to limit downside risk. Sometimes they must buy these from the health insurer, and sometimes they must buy it themselves. For a long time, some health insurers, like Humana, have been receptive to financial risk flowing to a health care group. Others, such as Aetna, stayed on the sidelines, hesitating to issue percentage-of-premium contracts. Slowly, all insurers are coming around.

ChenMed's management team also fully understands the controversy surrounding documentation and coding in Medicare Advantage plans. ChenMed patients are being seen at least monthly, so any health issues are quickly identified, and gaps in care are soon closed. For them, this is just good patient care: "You cannot manage what you do not detect." Their documentation is robust as a result of this high-touch care, not because of an insurer-like search for possible additional codes. There is no goal-setting for patient risk-adjustment factors, but there is one for clinicians' closing gaps in care. ChenMed has a team that looks over patient charts and makes suggestions, but the primary care clinicians make all documentation decisions. (This appears to be the model developing throughout value-based primary care, from federally qualified health centers to corporate-owned practices.) The bonus plan for doctors is based on patient satisfaction, hospitalization utilization, and to some extent on the Centers for Medicare and Medicaid Services' Star measures (or a similar set of metrics, given the CMS's latency in making changes to its Star criteria).

All of this takes thought—and ample resources. But as Greene pointed out, ChenMed has never accepted venture capital or private equity investments. The company is entirely self-funded. At times they have received development dollars from health insurers (Humana in particular) to have a presence in certain metropolitan areas, but this is then paid back by reducing their percentage of premium in risk contracts. ChenMed also worked with Turner Impact Capital, a social-impact investment firm, but again, this was to allow the company to develop primary care practices in underserved areas of additional cities. Once these new clinics were up and running, ChenMed then returned the full amount of Turner Impact's investment. Greene could not, or would not, share any details on the closely held family business's financial data. The general view in Florida's primary care and venture capital worlds is that the Chen family has made a great deal of money, but they clearly are not beholden to any venture capital or private equity firms. The local experts respect the fact that Chen family members have done it all themselves.

Greene did speak about the mission of the company, however. Their job, as they see it, is to deliver high-quality care to seniors in underserved urban areas. And they hope other health care companies will make it their mission to serve Medicaid patients or work in rural areas. ChenMed knows its area of expertise—one honed by James Chen—and it plans to stay there. They want to become "America's leading provider of primary care, transforming care of the neediest population."

I found their training for clinicians to be especially thoughtful. Other primary care practices I visited rely on individual doctors quizzing candidates about certain issues, such as health care for an impoverished person with diabetes, or on informal mentoring roles. ChenMed does this programmatically. Dr. Daniel McCarter is an example of the primary care expertise the Chens are bringing in.[7] He joined the company roughly five years ago, after a long career at the University of Virginia, helping to establish and lead a family medicine program. He then was in charge of developing the university's ambulatory clinic, and subsequently became the leader of their nascent ACO. Now he attracts, trains, and retains doctors for ChenMed. To give some sense of these tasks, in 2019, ChenMed hired 60 doctors; in 2022, they hired 300, half of them coming straight out of residency training.

McCarter noted that most of their new doctors had an excellent knowledge base, as well as the humility to recognize their deficiencies. But they did not have to be accountable for outcomes when they were in training. Nor did they have to consider the costs of medical care. They just had positional leadership—you are the doctor, so you write the orders. At ChenMed clinics, the clinicians need to be able to lead through personal relationships, both with patients and with their teams. Leadership, accountability, and team orientation are crucial elements of their training at ChenMed. So, too, is understanding their patients.

McCarter also proffered information on ChenMed's retention program, where he has worked closely with Dr. Jessica Chen. The new doctors get mentoring and precepting help, as well as training in ChenMed's various systems and ways of doing things. The company invests in them. ChenMed encourages clinician wellness: they get a "wellness afternoon" (time off from work) four to eight times a year. And they can become partners in ChenMed after two to three years, a step that comes with more pay and greater influence in how the company develops. All of this is designed to have clinicians become invested in the company and its mission.

I asked McCarter how working at ChenMed differed from the years he spent at the University of Virginia. His response was quick: its clinicians are not chained to relative value units (RVUs), and prospective payment is so different from the fee-for-service world. Payment through capitation creates a window, allowing clinicians to pay attention to the needs of their patient and to preventive measures.

In ChenMed's Miami Gardens headquarters, I met the two Chen brothers, Gordon and Christopher. Gordon Chen is soft spoken and chooses his words carefully.[8] *The Calling: A Memoir of Family, Faith, and the Future of Healthcare* dwells on the boys' scrapes with other kids in Miami Gardens, where they grew up, as well as their wrestling and football successes. But Gordon's gentle and courteous demeanor suggests no ferocity, just the opposite. He was thoughtful and scholarly in our discussion.

For example, I expressed surprise that the clinical teams were doing echocardiograms when a patient first arrived, a practice I had not seen in the preventive medicine literature. (I also suspected it might have been a way to identify new codes for patients and increase revenue.)

He responded mildly that I was mistaken, that there was good evidence for doing them. By the end of the day, a team member brought me reprints of four papers the Chen team has published on the cost-effectiveness of echocardiograms in a primary care setting, two of them coauthored by Gordon Chen.

When I visited, Gordon was responsible for the clinical integrity of the ChenMed centers. (At the time of this writing in late 2024, Gordon is no longer on the executive team.) Their medical directors reported into him, while the business managers reported to the company's president. ChenMed maintained this clinical/administrative duality throughout the organization. Others who reported to Gordon include the company's chief clinical officer (at the time, Gordon's wife Jessica was the chief clinical officer, but she left the leadership team as well), who oversaw the recruitment and development of new clinicians; the chief medical information officer, who worked with the Curity technology team; the recruiting and retention teams; and the transformation team, which came up with new clinical interventions.

The management of the ChenMed health care centers turns on nearly constant evaluation of data and trial runs of new approaches. Gordon Chen noted that the teams must be standardized to ensure the best patient outcomes. But new programs go into place constantly and then are evaluated, combining creativity with probing. For example, in late 2022, they had just rolled out a program called InTouch Health, which relied on increasing digital interactions with seniors, particularly text messaging. Another innovation was the development of congestive heart failure clinics in the centers, so patients can get their medications titrated weekly.

Some of the questions ChenMed is asking are fundamental. How often should I see a patient? The initial data on this question suggest that ChenMed's more aggressive centers, which see their patients more often, seem to get better results. These results are then shared throughout the organization, in the various huddles they attend.

ChenMed focuses on low-income patients, using this as a criterion for choosing clinic sites. When I asked Gordon about this, his first response was family oriented. Patients at his father's original primary care practice in Miami Gardens were nearly all low-income African Americans. So, providing health care for the impoverished became their mission. ChenMed still avoids situating clinics in wealthy communities.

Pushed further, he cited clear business rationales. First, their sense of mission creates connectedness among staff members, and that creates cohesion. Second, many people in these communities do not already have a firm connection with a primary care clinician, so moving to ChenMed is facile. Third, ChenMed has greater opportunity for making an impact on patient outcomes in underserved communities, especially with regard to improvements on quality-of-care measures.

Gordon introduced me to the Curity information technology team, which is now a separate corporation with over 300 employees. The cornerstone is its homegrown EMR, based on rapid and easy delivery of data on interventions to clinicians, who tend to chart during patient visits. With the Curity system, there is little to do after a visit is finished. Curity's EMR does not need long notes by the clinicians, and their "need follow-up action" items are clear. The clinicians transmit feedback to the Curity team continuously, and since the entire computer program is in the cloud, new enhancements go out as often as twice a week. As for recommendations that come back to the clinicians, they must explicitly opt out if they choose not to follow them. Questioned about whether they could continue to fund its development, the Curity team had a comprehensive and convincing analysis of their internal costs versus the costs of a purchased system, such as Epic.

My final visit at ChenMed's headquarters was with Christopher Chen, who had been the company's CEO for the past decade (and is again in mid-2024).[9] He has a bit more swagger than his younger brother, but like Gordon he evinces a real curiosity about how to improve medical care. He picked up, for example, on my mentioning their computer team's contrast between a Curity EMR and an Epic EMR. The latter, he asserted, is designed to increase the volume of health care services for a patient, as well as demonstrate the severity of that patient's illness. The prototypical EMR note in Epic is five pages long, ample evidence of this complexity. At ChenMed's clinics, patients are seen frequently, and the Curity EMR notes can be specific, without a need for redocumentation. Moreover, the notes have built-in workflows for preventive interventions and alerts about gaps in care. Curity is purpose driven. (I am not sure Epic would agree, but it is probably true that the EMR needs of a capitated primary care practice are different from those of specialists or a hospital.)

Christopher exuded confidence. He was bullish about Medicare Advantage. He was convinced that the ACOs associated with hospital are doomed, but physicians' groups forming ACOs will eventually get around to value-based care. That said, hospitals were becoming more interested in ChenMed. The company recently entered an arrangement with the nonprofit OhioHealth system, but their real future he felt was in physician/clinician-based primary care. Christopher reminded me that ChenMed has never accepted any outside capital. Their growth was based on their own revenues. He was proud of this, but he wondered how ChenMed could grow faster and still maintain its culture and its brand. Bringing in a new president with a long history at UnitedHealthcare was part of the answer—quite a move in this family-driven enterprise. (Albeit a strategy that worked for only about 18 months.)

I left the headquarters to visit some clinics. By way of background, some general facts and statistics are helpful. The ChenMed teams are not large. Each practice has four or five clinicians, with about 400–450 Medicare Advantage patients per doctor. The doctors are joined by 20–25 other staff members: care facilitators, care promoters, a care coordinator, a pharmacy technician, and several layers of managers. The clinicians do as much primary care on-site as possible—labs, radiology, wound care, counseling. The typical clinic also has a behavioral health specialist who is shared with another clinic. The various clinicians all work together, and the energy level is palpable compared with other practices I visited. According to Gordon Chen, the primary care clinicians are the quarterbacks. They are generally supported 1:1 by a care promoter (a medical assistant), and 2:1 by a care facilitator and a care coordinator.

Primary care clinicians are responsible for their patients' welfare. Each patient has their primary care clinician's cell phone number. There is an answering service, so the clinicians are not on call 24/7. Nor do the clinicians make hospital rounds. Most area hospitals do not have ChenMed hospitalists. But the transition-of-care coordinators (case managers) are checking on ChenMed's hospitalized patients every day, and the doctors in the clinics tend to talk on the phone to hospitalized patients or their families several times a day. The team works hard to keep patients out of the hospital, and once a patient is admitted, strives to quickly get them out and back home again.

In the primary care practices, there is a focus on social determinants of health (SDOH) and ways to keep patients healthy, instead of concentrating on RVUs. There is also a strong emphasis on expansion, with ChenMed's membership growth consultants going to senior centers, local pharmacies, and neighborhood centers to set up booths and talk to potential patients. The growth consultants also work with local insurance brokers, but they carefully follow ChenMed's rules about acceptable marketing efforts.

The primary care teams have a morning huddle each morning, with additional meetings throughout the day. A super-huddle has the doctors and the transition-of-care team talking about patients in the hospital. Each doctor also has meetings with key team members about their "top 40" patients—those most at risk. A ChenMed team relies heavily on analytics to identify these fragile patients, but in the end, the primary care clinicians make the decision about who should be included as a top 40 patient. The teams were hesitant to share performance data with me, a reticence I also noted when I visited ChenMed's headquarters. Within the teams themselves, however, there seems to be complete transparency on performance data.

The multicultural mix of clinicians is striking. Outside of ChenMed headquarters, over 70% of their workforce consists of women of color, and that is apparent at both practices I visited. Moreover, people genuinely enjoy their jobs. The sense that they are serving their community is reiterated in many of my conversations with them. The ChenMed primary care practices feel like a cheerful, high-energy, committed FQHC, only with more investment in their locations and analytics.

A number of people I talked with in venture capital, having done their research, thought the ChenMed primary care practices were the most impressively efficient ones they had seen. I was interested in visiting their operation, expecting at least some of the hype to be just that.

I started at the 95th Street Center in the West Little River section of Miami. The day begins with the entire practice joining in a huddle. The first order of business is for one of the employees to read the ChenMed mission statement, which seems a bit hokey, but its premise is sincere and emphasizes the need to serve patients who have not had access to health care in the past. The team then focuses on a large-screen TV that displays a series of metrics, listed under three headings: (1) deliver VIP service, (2) detect and manage high-risk diseases, and (3) reduce hospital sick days. The data are updated daily, and the team drills down on specific issues.

The meeting is led by the clinic's medical director, Dr. Tameka Joseph, and its manager (in ChenMed speak, the center director), Ozzie Drago. Drago had a long career in urgent care before coming to ChenMed. Joseph trained at the University of Miami in internal medicine.[10] She had heard a talk by Gordon Chen, who emphasized the accountability aspect of care for the underserved, which really appealed to her. She comes from South Florida and speaks Creole, which is a key asset in this community. She has been with ChenMed for six years and has not seen the mission fade. Dr. Joseph found the sincere commitment to equity and the use of data to guide the practice to be unique. So, too, is the emphasis on the team—everyone participates. Drago and Joseph are also responsible for the financial performance of the clinic, and key to that is patient recruitment, growth, and then careful oversight for each patient.

Joseph personally felt lucky to be working at ChenMed. Compared with her friends at other primary care practices, she has much better tools and data, enabling her to stay focused on the patients she wants to serve. She relished ChenMed's emphasis on keeping people healthy, which allowed her to spend time on social issues as well as medical ones. Joseph was also experiencing great professional growth as a member of the clinic's management staff, with 50% of her time now being spent as the clinic's medical director. She has the back part of the office, and Drago has the front part—although that is clearly a permeable membrane, and the two of them often confer. The architecture of the 95th Street practice is like that of other cutting-edge primary care clinics, with the exception of the community room, which is lively in the ChenMed practices. The central collaboration area for the clinicians is a hub of various conversations, and the team spends time in both the front and back of the clinic with the patients.

Joseph also works with the talent acquisition team, which searches for primary care clinicians to add to ChenMed's various sites. As Gordon Chen described the situation to me, 20 years ago the Chens thought only a trained internist could do the kind of managed care work they expected, but then they brought in family practice physicians and, later, nurse practitioners.[11] The critical issue for primary care clinicians, they found, was not necessarily their training, but their orientation and commitment.

Dr. Joseph has found that recruiting goes well, slowed only by the fact that not many medical students want to go into primary care. Once they are recruited, however, the doctors tend to stay. The management team has been focused on clinicians' wellness, and the company has started programs to identify new clinicians. The pay at ChenMed's clinics is competitive with other primary care practices, and bonuses can be 10% to 30% of the base salary, depending on the center and the physicians' individual performances.

Joseph also introduced me to their Curity computer system. Every program that the ChenMed teams touch is developed and owned by Curity—all the scheduling and care management information, pharmacy and utilization data, labs, and EMRs. Joseph claimed that this system is logical, and that she had access to all the information she needed, obtained smoothly and with high integrity. Other health care organizations have tried to emulate this structure by developing their own personalized EMR systems, but as is the case at Oak Street Health, their clinicians usually fall back on the old EMR program. ChenMed's drive to own and adapt their computer systems to their clinical practices is unmatched.

I next went to meet with Matthew Kaminske and Dr. Yahaida Rimola-Dejesus at the Chen Senior Medical Care Center on South State Road 7 in Hollywood, Florida. Next door to the center, the Miramar Cuban Bakery is a cheerful place serving breakfast, lunch, and dinner. A wide line forms in its big lobby, where patrons gather. Tables are placed haphazardly on one side of the lobby, where people sit and talk and eat. The same thing happens on its front porch. The bakery is in an old mall, with a thrift shop on the other side. On a pleasant day in mid-December when I visited, there were plenty of people socializing. The vibe is one of community and engagement.

The ChenMed primary care practice next door has the same feel. There is an expansive waiting room in the front, facing a phalanx of front desk personnel. (As part of their constant efforts to improve, the ChenMed team told me that in the future, they might reduce the number of people in the clinic and have more people at a central location.) The Chen team, which has a new name for every position, calls the front desk people *care facilitators*. Various members of the Chen team were circulating through the waiting room and talking with the patients, including the care promoters (medical assistants) and care coordinators (who work on referrals), as well as the pharmacy technician. Membership growth consultants were also chatting with the patients and their families, as well as conducting a holiday ham giveaway program. Everyone was highly engaged. The waiting room contained a table with brochures introducing people to yoga classes, and another offered opportunities to participate in cooking classes. The atmosphere was congenial, energized, fun, and totally unlike any other waiting room I visited.

The clinic's location reflects ChenMed's mission to provide health care for the underserved. (It also supporting the company's savvy business interests.) Hollywood is a relatively low-income community, with large Hispanic and Haitian populations. This clinic, like all the other ChenMed primary care practices, only accepts Medicare Advantage beneficiaries as patients, including those who also qualify for Medicaid, known as duals (dual eligible). Kaminske told me that the mall was underused, so they can have health fairs in the parking lot, cordoning off a large portion of the space and setting up tents.[12] They also hold bingo events. Hollywood is a leading ChenMed practice (the practices are rated as launching, learning, or leading). So, other practices come to Hollywood to see how things are done.

Dr. Yahaida Rimola-Dejesus was a wonderfully extroverted and friendly doctor.[13] She trained in Lawrence, Massachusetts, at the family practice residency that trained most of the doctors at the Lynn Community Health Center. She had recently been recruited by ChenMed after practicing in North Andover, Massachusetts, for nearly 15 years. Her former practice was owned by the Beth Israel Lahey Health system, and she felt as though she had no opportunity for advancement—once you were a primary care clinician, you were stuck there. She also hated the RVU-based approach in Massachusetts, and the fee-for-service economy in general.

ChenMed gave Rimola-Dejesus the chance for leadership, and she seized it. She was everywhere in the clinic, talking to everyone, but also managing to see 11 patients during the morning when I was there. She marveled at the difference between her old practice and her current situation. In Massachusetts, she would have had to see 20 patients, write long notes, and deal with all sorts of technical issues with the EMRs—leading to two to four hours of work after leaving the clinic. Here, Rimola-Dejesus conferred closely with each patient, eliciting symptoms and documenting them discretely, without diverting attention to her EMR screen. Her notes were comparably minimal, so she finished her work by 5:00 p.m. and could go home. She found ChenMed's EMR program to be much friendlier than her old system.

As noted, the ChenMed clinicians do not make hospital rounds. The hospital and continuity team does that and keeps the clinicians informed about their patients there. (The big player in the area, Memorial Healthcare System, with four hospitals, is somewhat at loggerheads with ChenMed. It maintains its own primary care physicians, and there is competition in South Florida for Medicare Advantage enrollees with capitated plans.) Rimola-Dejesus's immediate team (and that of every clinician) consists of a care facilitator, a care promoter, and a care coordinator. They gather each morning, and then meet again later in a super-huddle with the transition-of-care coordinators to go over their hospitalized patients. The super-huddle features impressive details on both the medical and the social situations of these patients. The latter is not a mere nod to SDOH, but instead is seen as an integral part of addressing a patient's health care and recovery, as well as having an impact on the costs of that care. This brand of managed care creates incentives to integrate social needs with medical ones.

While at the Hollywood clinic, I began to wonder about the financial picture of a ChenMed center. The staff did not and would not provide any details, but back-of-the-envelope calculations have long been my financial specialty. In the simplest terms, this center has around 30 employees, 20 of whom are paid at close to or just above minimum wage. There are 4 doctors and perhaps 3 other professionals, including a pharmacist, and 3 managers. At an estimated $3.5 million in salaries, plus rent and supplies, one might estimate it would cost $4 to $4.5 million annually to run the center. Each doctor has 450 patients, so 4 doctors have a total of 1,800 patients. The Medicare per-member, per-month payments to insurers might run to nearly $1,000. Depending on the risk-adjustment factor scores and the percentage of capitation they get from the patients' health insurers, ChenMed, or a center like this, might get annual revenues of $16 to $20 million. Out of this, the clinic must pay for all the health care costs of the center's patients, plus any hospitalizations and medications, and a portion of the expenses for patients in long-term care. That is the calculus any similar clinic—and any clinic specializing in Medicare Advantage capitation—is up against. Any steps the clinicians can take to prevent worsening medical conditions for their patients, and thus reduce unnecessary hospitalizations and emergency department visits, help turn a profit. This is the challenge—and the promise—of capitated primary care.

This same basic math applies to many of the advanced primary care practices I visited. The federal government through the Centers for Medicare and Medicaid Services as well as many state governments and private payers are all encouraging the use of value-based care through alternative payment models. For many years, the Health Care Payment

Learning and Action Network (HCPLAN) has defined the framework for alternative payment methods, with fee-for-service being category 1, and population-based payment as category 4 (defined as a *global budget*, or a full percent-of-premium payment).[14] The HCPLAN board has set a goal to have 100% of Medicare payments by 2030 be in category 3b (which calls for shared savings with downside risk for providers) or category 4, as well as 50% of Medicaid and commercial health insurance payments. Health care organizations like Kaiser Permanente, Oak Street Health, or ChenMed are thus in the vanguard of what most health policy experts are recommending.

Perhaps more importantly, advanced primary care practices (ChenMed in particular) seem to be bucking the general rule, which is that primary care clinicians are worn out and despondent. With the possible exception of Kaiser Permanente, in my limited sample, primary care practices taking on financial risk through capitation were more optimistic about the future and more outspoken about patient advocacy. ChenMed in particular demonstrated the joy of practice in which you have enough time to consider the needs of your patient as a person and think about how to promote health. A reasonable conclusion is that primary care makes the best sense when it is capitated (i.e., population based). Those stuck in fee-for-service arrangements are just that—stuck.

Polar Alternative Solutions for Primary Care: Unions and Concierge Care

I intended this research project to answer one compelling question. Is there sufficient political and financial will for a future in which primary care is central to, and thriving in, a health care system based on managed competition that produces value-based care? I have argued elsewhere that that is the only rational future for the American health care system,[15] and so have many others. But we might all be wasting our time if primary care is close to being finished: poorly paid, undervalued, and abandoned by clinicians who are utterly disappointed by the context for the care. Given what is published today about clinician shortages and caregiver burnout, the demise of primary care seems more likely than a primary care renaissance.

Dejected primary care practitioners can readily be found. In this book I discussed one instance, at the University of Alabama at Birmingham Medical Center, where that seemed to be the case for at least some of the older physicians. But I could have (and did) identify many other similar primary care clinics and clinicians suggesting despair, especially the health care employees at integrated delivery systems and academic medical centers. UAB is not an outlier. Rather, it represents the norm for what primary care is like in many practices today: hardworking people who are trying to do the right thing for their patients, but without sufficient professional satisfaction and with huge demands on their time.

The remaining primary care practices I have discussed in this book are a selected sample. I asked many people in primary care, Who is doing it right? Which groups or organizations are providing good models about how primary care can be delivered? I also sought diversity in the types of practices I visited—urban and rural; primarily Medicaid and predominantly commercial health insurance beneficiaries; those steeped in managed care and those dipping their toes in value-based programs. So, while attempting to identify a cross-section of primary care practices, my choices were not completely random, and I fully admit to there being selection bias.

But what I was searching for was the existence of blooming flowers amid an otherwise parched landscape—ones that represented hope for the future. Even so, I was not convinced that I would come away with a sunny prognosis for primary care. I reasoned that if the practices that experts recommended were not looking toward a successful value-based future, then what hope was there?

There is hope. One could see companies like Catalyst Health slowly shifting their work to value-based, risk-based primary care, producing better results and lower costs along with clinicians who are excited, engaged, and satisfied in their work. For a senior population, ChenMed offers a seemingly viable alternative. Again, the striking difference with fee-for-service primary care is the energy in the practice and the resonance of anticipatory, value-based care with the key primary care attributes of continuity and whole-person care. The same is found in Anchorage, Alaska, where South Central Foundation provides paradigmatic team-based care on federal revenues.

But that hope is tempered. Even over the time I have been researching this book, some momentum seems to have come out of the value-based primary care movement. There is more than a suggestion that high-touch clinics like ChenMed or Optum Health have been built on inappropriately high revenues, chiefly derived from inappropriate documentation of patient diagnoses, making patients appear at higher risk than they are. Only two years ago the enthusiasm was real, with large retailers appearing to champion valued-based primary care. But today Walmart and Walgreens have dropped out, and no one can predict what Amazon might do. Those worried about the power of large insurers are now calling for laws that prohibit insurers from owning providers. What this means for Kaiser, let along Optum, is not clear.

All this suggests that perhaps a value-based future is just too distant and too difficult to organize, not a potent enough alternative to overcome dominant fee-for-service. If that is the case, then the only answer is better pay for primary care doctors. One way to do that is the focus for the primary care advocacy organizations, that is, to change the RVU system and modify the evaluation and management codes that are the mainstay of primary care reimbursement. As noted previously, prominent and insightful health policy voices, led by Bob Berenson, have suggested that RVU reform could be combined with value-based reimbursement in an effective manner. But given zero-sum physician reimbursement, the relative power of the specialists, and their alliance with the hospitals, it is difficult to see reform of the RVS Update Committee as a high probability.

Another alternative, one not discussed to this point, is for primary care doctors to force their employers to reassess the contribution of primary care and to provide better pay and lower volume expectations, making the fee-for-service environment more conducive to patient-centered primary care. One could not viably propose these changes 20 years ago, or even 10 years ago, as too much of primary care was still in smaller physician practices that billed insurers directly. Today, however, most primary care clinicians are employed by hospitals, FQHCs, or even by insurers. Together, primary care clinicians could advocate for better pay and better conditions for patient care, and their employers might find their arguments persuasive. But paying them more means having to pay others less, or do fewer things, and in most situations, the others and other things in fee-for-service (cardiologists and catheterization labs, for example) are more profitable. Most primary groups simply do not have the power to demand change.

But with employment has come the ability to unionize. For years, physician unionization was nearly nonexistent in American health care. Some residency programs have long been formally organized and represented by unions, but most doctors were not employees. That has obviously changed, rapidly over the past decade, with estimates ranging as high as 77% of physicians now employees at hospitals or corporations.[16] As employees, doctors have every right to take advantage of the National Labor Relations Act and to form collective bargaining units.

The American Medical Association has documented the growth in union membership among doctors. In 1998, the AMA estimated there were at most 20,000 union doctors, mostly employed by public systems in states that allowed public employees to unionize. By 2014, the number had grown to 47,000 doctors, and five years later to 67,000, or about 7.2% of practicing physicians. From 2021 to 2024, the number of unionized residents nearly doubled, to 32,000.

Several large unions have turned their attention to physicians. The Service Employees International Union (SEIU) supports the Doctor's Council, which represents all the physicians in the New York City Health and Hospital Corporation. The Union of American Physicians and Dentists (UAPD) is affiliated with the American Federation of State, County, and Municipal Employees (AFSCME), and is perhaps the largest player today, based originally in California. Both provide resources for physicians interested in pursuing a collective bargaining unit, and there are many today, including in primary care.

In 2024, the highest-profile unionization effort involved primary care and hospitalist doctors at Allina Health Care in Minneapolis. They worked with the Doctor's Council and brought more than 500 physicians, physicians assistants, and nurse practitioners into a single bargaining unit that spanned more than 60 facilities.[17] There are similar conversations at many medical centers, as clinicians see that they have lost control of their professional lives and practice grows more difficult.

The UAPD put me in touch with clinicians who have recently formed a collective bargaining unit at Unity Health in Washington, DC. Unity is a large FQHC with at least eight health centers spread across the District. I made numerous attempts to contact both the clinical (Dr. Ryan Buchholz) and business (Dr. Jessica Henderson Boyd) leadership of the organization, without success.

The physicians who led the union effort were open about their motives to establish a more viable practice for primary care. Dr. Danielle Fincher was a medical student at UAB and did her family medicine residency at the University of California, Davis.[18] While she was there, the residents organized into a union. She had a National Health Services Corp scholarship, which required her to work in an underserved area, and she found a job at Unity.

She and many of her colleagues were frustrated with their work conditions and the perceived large gulf between themselves and the administration. The patient schedule was central to the dissatisfaction. The administration thought that more patients needed to be seen (fee-for-service incentives), so they put in a place a "wave" schedule that placed another person in the slot of any patient who failed so show up for their appointment ("no-shows"). The patients were generally high acuity, and there did not seem to be enough time to do a thorough job.

As well, at least from the point of view of the doctors I talked to, the administration used the notion of "mission-driven" care as a cudgel. The administration valued access, but access for them was any patient contact. For the clinicians, access meant having enough time to understand the patient's needs. The situation worsened over 2022.

In June 2023, Fincher and another resident began to talk to the various physician unions, include Doctor's Council and UAPD. They were most impressed with the latter. They were required by National Labor Relations rules to have a broad collective bargaining unit that included all physicians, nurse practitioners, physician assistants, and mental health providers, but the dissatisfaction with the work conditions was deep, so recruiting was not difficult. By August, they were able to file with the National Labor Relations Board and voted overwhelmingly to unionize in November. The administration opposed them at every step and hired the renowned law firm of Little Mendelson to develop the anti-union campaign. The negotiations for a new contract have gone slowly, with the bargaining unit seeking reduced patient targets, more administrative time, and a cost-of-living increase. Morale has continued to flag, according to Dr. Fincher.

James Tracy is a family nurse practitioner who sees many of the same issues, but he was more optimistic.[19] He had been an emergency room nurse, went back to nurse practitioner school, and has done family practice for nearly a dozen years at Unity. He works at their flagship Columbia Heights practice, where the overwhelming proportion of their patients are Hispanic. Many are undocumented, but fortunately DC has a program called Alliance that provides some coverage for this population, including prescriptions and specialty care. Tracy figured that with Medicaid and Alliance, Unity should be well positioned to succeed.

Tracy had been happy for years, but the pandemic changed things. Everyone felt like they made sacrifices to keep the clinic afloat, but there was a lack of appreciation for these efforts on the part of the administration. (It is hard to overstate the malignant effect that the COVID pandemic had on much of primary care.) Then the wave schedule forced more patients into everyone's day, often creating chaos as these inserted patients usually had no previous relationship with the clinician. The union movement was swift, but both Fincher and Tracy emphasized that clinicians continue to leave Unity.

Both were also surprised that the administration had not embraced value-based care; instead the clinic is pure fee-for-service. As a result, there is no real team taking care of patients, although most clinicians have access to a medical assistant during sessions. James Tracy has long been interested in prospective payment and the anticipatory care it can bring. He hopes things can turn around at Unity, and he is now the clinician representative for UAPD as they start real negotiation.

I also spoke with Drs. Alison Rigel[20] and Natasha Khawaja.[21] Both trained at Unity in the Teaching Health Center residency, which each thought was a great way to train. Most of their training time was in ambulatory care, although they did rotate through Howard University Hospital. Both were disillusioned with the administration at Unity, finding it ironic that they would hire a union-busting law firm at a FQHC. Rigel noted that their only choice was to unionize, something they probably would not have considered three years ago. Both gave numerous examples of Unity's missteps, all of which resonated with a unidimensional view of succeeding in fee-for-service. What they signed up for was a practice where they knew their patients and could help them cope with the SDOH stacked against them. Both found they were trying to keep their heads above water as they saw 75% new patients every session, exacerbated as clinicians left for other FQHCs in the District. All their points were trenchant, and in many ways tragic.

It is possible these clinicians are outliers at Unity, and most are supportive of the administration. But the vote to unionize was overwhelming. This seems like a course of action that will occur at many unhappy primary care practices, where the clinicians feel like cogs in a machine that just generates fee-for-service. It could lead to re-empowerment, or better pay, or just better conditions in which the clinicians can care for their patients. Given the tremendous momentum behind physician employment, there could be equal momentum in labor activism. That is certainly the view of the union organizers I talked to.

Nonetheless, unionization of primary care clinicians strikes me as only a partial solution. The real solution must move to value-based care. But perhaps that is where the unions/clinicians will lead administrators in health care.

There seems to be one other potential future for primary care. Continuation of a fee-for-service regime will no doubt lead to greater clinician dissatisfaction, and eventually to clinician shortages. Maybe unionization can forestall this, but if not, and value-based care cannot catch on, then the future for primary care—that is, for primary care patients—looks bleak. I have already cited all the statistics about difficulty in getting a primary care appointment and overwhelmed clinicians. Underneath the statistics, a grim reality has percolated into conversations with clinicians and patients about access. Since the pandemic, the situation has worsened dramatically, with no end in sight.

But pressure to fix primary care would wane, given certain political realities. Looking to the future of policy change, one is always most comfortable when long-term evolution is clear. Demographics usually provides some certainty. There is no doubt that China is in for tumultuous change as its population halves over the course of the next 80 years, Japan even more so. There seems to be little that can prevent that.

For my purposes in this book, the irresistible force is the aggregation of wealth in the upper 25% of the American population. Thomas Piketty and colleagues have been documenting this concentration in many Western countries, finding that income equality grew from 1915 to 1975, when it began to decrease rapidly.[22] Today in the United States, somewhere between 71% and 85% of total wealth is held by upper 20% of the income bracket.[23] The top 1% command a sizable proportion of that. The same is true in many other countries. With the second Trump administration about to begin as I write, there is little doubt wealth inequality will deepen.

Regarding health policy and primary care, there is always going to be a certain market, made up of powerful, wealthy people, who will be able to access care. They can cover huge-out-of-pocket expenses that insurance does not cover. Restrictions on access that apply to other people will not matter to them because their health care will still work. Certain costly therapies will be available only to those who can afford them, sold outside of an insurance context.

Primary care is slowly adapting to this reality, providing a solution for higher-income people called concierge care, or direct primary care.

The idea is rather simple. A clinician, more often a physician, offers to continue care for his or her patients only if they will pay a monthly or annual out-of-pocket fee. Many will not, so the physician narrows the practice to a much smaller size while earning a reasonable income from the concierge fee.

When concierge practices began to take shape over 30 years ago, insurers at first threatened not to pay the bills submitted by concierge doctors for the evaluation and management codes they did. But this type of prohibition proved to be short-lived as concierge practices could point to additional services they offered, like wellness counseling. By 2005, when I wrote an editorial critical of the concierge movement based on fears that it could cause substantial inequity in access to care, concierge practices were few, less than 200 practices.[24]

Unfortunately, those with concerns about concierge care could not counter the concentration of wealth, and today many people are willing to pay a monthly fee to see their primary care doctors. The Direct Primary Care Coalition estimated in 2022 that 300,000 patients were being cared for at 1,600 direct primary care practices. Most analysts expect great growth over the course of the next decade. The typical practice charges patients membership fees of a few hundred to several thousand dollars per year. The reader might recall that the One Medical team resisted being referred to as a concierge practice, rather referring to the clinic as a membership organization. Some companies, like MDVIP, will help doctors establish concierge practices and then supply marketing help. But even large and prestigious medical centers like the Massachusetts General Hospital have now gotten into the concierge business, seeing it as an approach some of their patients may prefer.[25]

I spoke with Dr. Jeff Bass, an internist in Newton, Massachusetts, who started a concierge practice in 2007. Dr. Bass had long been a partner in a storied practice with Dr. Martin Solomon in Brookline, Massachusetts. Bass and Solomon were widely recognized as among the busiest and most popular primary care doctors in Boston. I knew them when I was an executive at the physicians' organization at the

Brigham and Women's Hospital, and we recruited them away from the Beth Israel Hospital.

Bass estimates that he had as many as 4,500 patients himself. He would get to the hospital to round by about 5:30 a.m., work in the office until 6:30 p.m., then do paperwork until 10:00 p.m., and repeat the next day. On the weekends, he would work for 12 hours on Saturday and 6 on Sunday. He had three children ages 9–15, and he felt like life was passing him by. He had seen another concierge practice started by other Harvard-trained doctors, and he began to explore what was necessary to start one of his own. With Solomon's blessing, he left and started PersonalMDs.

He wrote to his 4,500 patients, and 800 were willing to come with him and pay an annual fee of $3,600. He hired another doctor and kept about 450 of his patients. In the beginning, there were plenty of insurance company requirements that he provide additional services, so he hired nutrition and wellness counselors. Today, however, there is little insurer oversight, although the additional services the practice offers have expanded to include yoga, personal training, and Pilates. The fee is now up to $5,200 per year.

Jeff Bass has hired five associates over time. Between the six of them, they have about 2,600 patients. Notwithstanding the much smaller patient base, Bass still struggles with work/life balance. A complete physical and history used to take 20–30 minutes; now it can be 90–120 minutes. He does, however, have time to talk with his patients and to understand what is going in their lives. If the patient needs to see a specialist, he creates a list of issues the specialist must address. With only 10–12 patients per day, he relies less on "reflex" medicine, instead trying to anticipate issues. The bedrock of primary care, for him, has always been enjoyment of relationships with patients. He can actually do that today.

There are many other benefits. Bass has no trouble recruiting doctors—the practice is deciding whether to add another now, as they have a wait list of 200 patients. He can spend some of the administrative fee on an ombudsman who can work with patients who are stymied by aspects of their insurance. He remains on the Mass General Brigham EMR, and he works closely with the hospital staff there.

I spoke with two of his associates, Dr. Tania Bandak and Dr. Rachel Haims. Dr. Bandak noted that when she trained in the 1990s, most of the primary care doctors she came into contact with were members of small practices. She admired how well they knew their patients, combining familiarity with caring. This sense of intimacy, she felt, was also supported by the fact that different types of patients could choose primary care doctors that fit their expectations. Over time, though, she saw that primary care practices were becoming anonymized and homogenized. Administrators also began to play a bigger role, stifling the clinician's efforts to customize the practice in ways that suited her patients.

All of these problems have been addressed in her concierge practice. She can flex her practice in ways that support patient care. Her staff is stable (and the practice is able to pay them more than other practices can). A lot more of her work is on email and the phone, which she considers appropriate. No longer is her attention frayed by having to drive more patients through.

The only problem, she realizes, is the cost. She wishes the system did not work like this, and that all patients could access good primary care. Dr. Haims had the same view. She had at first resisted recruitment from PersonalMDs, not wanting to endorse what might be perceived as two-tier care. But just before the pandemic, she joined. She's happy she did, as she feels like she can always be an "A+" doctor. In the concierge practice, she can do a great job for her patients.

At PersonalMDs, Haims worries that sometimes she is dealing more with anxiety than medical problems, but she has grown more interested in mind/body problems. She has time to explore such issues even though the practice is still demanding. The other upside is that she earns "multiples" of what she did in regular primary care. It seems hard to believe that this combination of better pay and better job satisfaction might not eventually appeal to more primary care clinicians.

The doctors at PersonalMD are able to practice primary care in a manner consistent with their professional ideals. They have time to spend with patients and anticipate their needs. They can make available wellness programs and preventive approaches to care. And they are doing so in fee-for-service environment. But what enables these things is the over $13 million in fees that patients are paying upfront for the six-person practice. The majority of Americans cannot afford the membership cost, and so it is not a viable solution for all.

But it is viable for the people in the upper 20%, or maybe 10%, in terms of income level. It is also these people who donate to politicians and exercise a reasonable amount of control over the political process. Over time, the majority of Americans might become totally dissatisfied with an overly expensive fee-for-service-based health care system. They will be unable to access good primary care services. But will that matter if the wealthiest quintile in the United States is satisfied with their care in concierge practices?

Could concierge practice spread more widely? It might if employers begin to endorse it. There have long been employers that offer primary care services on-site, with the belief that better primary care offered by the company will lower overall medical costs. On-site primary care is still relatively rare, except where it is mostly an adjunct to occupational health. Tech companies have endorsed it as a benefit in a competitive labor market. But generally, over the past two decades, there has been little growth in utilization of such services.[26]

One interesting firm, Marathon Health, is growing. Based in Indianapolis, Marathon offers primary care for employees of corporations. The clinics are generally not on-site but are instead located in accessible suburban areas, presumably near where employees live. Marathon also has some on-site clinics and a nationwide virtual care program.

Marathon is the product of recent consolidation in the on-site/employer primary care space. In February 2024, the two large players, Marathon and Everside, merged, and the Marathon management, headed by Jeff Wells, largely took over the operation. The company today emphasizes its model as direct primary care and advanced primary care.[27] Direct primary care eliminates the insurance company, instead relying on a PEPM (per employee, per month) fee, much the same as a concierge practice. This means more attention, as each clinician has fewer patients. The advanced primary care part adds advanced analytics to develop a deep population health focus with data-driven engagement. In many ways, it is concierge medicine plus value-based care, pitched to the ultimate payer: the employer.

I visited with the Marathon health leadership team in an impressive office tower in downtown Indianapolis on a boiling day in late August 2024. They had sufficiently absorbed the merger with Everside to be able to talk about next steps. The company still has about 500 clinics on business campuses, guided by the need to have about 1,000 employees on-site to make it work. To serve employers with smaller worksites, they are pivoting to network or neighborhood sites. These are primary care offices but they are not open to the public, only to the firms that have contracted with Marathon for primary care services.

It's not correct to refer to this arrangement as direct primary care. These clinics do not bill insurance at all, and the patient pays no additional fee, so Marathon is not a two-tier system. The self-insured employer is paying Marathon for primary care instead of paying for conventional primary care. Marathon gets its reimbursement through a per employee, per month charge rather than a fee-for-service bill.

Perhaps just as important, Marathon is totally value based in its approach. It earns a bonus from the employer whenever it can reduce the total of cost of care. So, like other value-based programs centered on capitation, the Marathon team sees fewer patients, anticipates their needs, emphasizes prevention, and carefully plans treatment courses. Wells, whom I found to be extremely insightful, emphasized that time was the most valuable element in health care. The traditional fee-for-service system does not value clinician time, so patients get jammed through and clinicians are rushed. In this rushed state, they are overly cautious, schedule too many tests, and do not think enough about what to do, which creates bad care. This sentiment was strikingly similar to that expressed by the CEO of the North Central program in Anchorage, and it resonates.

I toured the Marathon clinic in downtown Indianapolis, and it shared all the characteristics of a value-based practice. The site had one family medicine doctor, one nurse practitioner, two medical assistants, a nurse, a behavioral health specialist, and a health coach. Some practices share the health coaches and behavioral health specialists, and some offer physical therapy. They are on an athena platform, but they have developed their own population health module. A central team working on a sophisticated data infrastructure does all referrals, identifying the best specialists in each region. This team also follows up on the referrals, keeping clinicians apprised. The clinicians are pleased with their work, finding relief from fee-for-service and able to serve patients, the one similarity to concierge practice.

Slim and wearing jeans, Wells is youthful in appearance, the picture of an entrepreneurial CEO. He has great backing from the very best venture capital firms, allowing Marathon to grow organically. Wells asserts he can open new facilities at a fraction of the cost of an Oak Street or ChenMed, as he has a waiting group of employees to whom he can market, with the employer creating incentives for employees to see the Marathon clinicians. Yet he speaks with wisdom, having spent five years earlier in his career running Medicaid for the state of Indiana. And he understands fee-for-service. His sale to employers is the confidence to remove the 25% waste from health care that fee-for-service produces. It is a great model, perhaps a better example of value-based care than of direct primary care. Time will tell how it does in the employer sector.

Considering the Future of Primary Care

So, what is the future for primary care? It could stay firmly in the fee-for-service domain. Hospitals and many specialists appear to be content there, and primary care does not have the political clout to create change in comparison. But that prospect is depressing, as it is hard to see how primary care flourishes. The wealthiest people will have access to concierge primary care. But most will find their options dwindling as fewer and fewer clinicians go into the field and access diminishes. Given the hardiness of fee-for-service and the forces supporting it, this must be the most likely future, although I have argued elsewhere that it is difficult to see employer-sponsored insurance persisting in these conditions.[28]

There is a chance, in a fee-for-service-dominated commercial sector, that government payors move to value-based primary care. This is especially true of Medicaid, which increasingly is segregated in the health care system. Much of the care for Medicaid recipients and certainly for the uninsured occurs at community health centers, many of them federally qualified. Given the limited payment available for Medicaid programs (the outstanding equity issue in the American health care system), there may be no choice other than to endorse the efficiency of value-based care. Thus the best approaches to primary care, and the health of patients, may paradoxically be in programs dependent on Medicaid.

Medicare is different in that it is much larger in terms of funds flow, and more mainstreamed than Medicaid. While some hospitals have recently made headlines by ending contracts with Medicare Advantage firms, the reality is hospitals are dependent on Medicare, at least until some forms of concierge hospital care start to take shape. This means that the forcing pressure that the Centers for Medicare and Medicaid Services and the Center for Medicare and Medicaid Innovation (CMMI) continue to generate will be vital. The federal government has been remarkably committed to value-based care, although all bets might be off with the second Trump administration.

So, the future as usual is uncertain. Nonetheless, most people I have spoken with over the past three years about primary care remain bullish on the prospects for value-based care. Not all. Some venture capitalists have backed off, fearful of government changes in Medicare Advantage reimbursement. Retailers without access to insurance risk are going, nearly gone. The average clinician or administrator in predominantly fee-for-service practices remain despondent, though some with hope surrounding unionization. But the believers—people like Bill Wulf, or Ashley Thurow, or Tom Borys—remain committed to and see promise and progress in value-based care. For them, as well as for the average patient who should prefer value-based primary care, what can one reasonably conclude today? Ten observations frame my answer to that question.

Number One: Capitated Primary Care Produces Better-Value Care, but We Must Be Patient

Perhaps the most foundational question in health policy today is, Does capitated primary care, designed to deliver value-based care, produce better outcomes and better patient experiences, at a lower price? Much of the empirical literature suggests this is the case, but it is not definitive. The federal government, many state governments, health insurers of various stripes, large health care corporations, and venture capitalists think so. They all want a health care system where value-based care is overseen through a primary care relationship. Can they all be wrong? Perhaps.

Not all states or commercial health insurers are convinced that capitation is the future, and many of them are not seeking ways to facilitate a transition to value-based care. As well, at least some of the companies and practices engaged in primary care management of health today are not making money—in fact, most do not. The proposition that they can eliminate enough health care waste to profit from capitation remains somewhat debatable. Furthermore, the vast majority of hospitals and specialists remain committed to a fee-for-service system, which still dominates health care financing in the United States.

Much of the commitment to fee-for-service is a matter, at least from my perspective, of profit and lethargy. In particular, most hospitals have never seen any other future, and a minority of them do reasonably well in fee-for-service. The hospital/well-paid specialist axis has been a dependable model for 50 years. Many insurers are mired in that frame of mind as well. They have negotiated network rates based on fee-for-service and returned reasonable profits, or fund balance, depending on their respective for-profit or not-for-profit status. A move to a capitated future would require huge system changes, and a lot of network noise.

Why change? The current path leads to misery for many. Primary care is being extinguished. The bottom third of hospitals, especially those in rural areas, do not look like they can survive. For insurers and their clients, costs continue to go up, now once again surpassing the rate of inflation. The government sees a deteriorating base for care of the middle class, and especially for those in the bottom quartile of income. Without a primary care base, the foundation for public health interventions is lost.

The alternative is in front of us. The medical literature has found that a primary care system that offers continuity, remains focused on prevention, and runs on teams with attributed patients has better outcomes. After visiting many practices engaged in managing value-based care, I saw a strong connection between a rigorous oversight of care that comes with taking on full financial risk and the welfare of patients. The old perception that scared many about managed care in the 1990s—primary care doctors would simply stint on care to make a profit—has faded. Instead, clinicians committed to value-based care see the relationship with their patients in anticipatory terms. They must know their patients well enough to be prepared for potential problems and, more importantly, prevent them from occurring. That requires proactive, not passive, care, and it needs to be continuous. This kind of longitudinal care requires continuity of funding; it is not possible with à la carte fee-for-service. During my interviews, these sentiments were expressed uniformly, from Alaska to Florida, from concierge practices to federally qualified health centers.

An anticipatory attitude also promotes a better understanding of the social determinants of health, as well as of the problems people face because of persistent inequity and bias. Clinicians must be cognizant of a patient's entire social situation to be able to offer that person the most cost-effective health care. Thus lower costs and better care are inextricably entwined with social justice.

But we cannot expect to flip a switch from fee-for-service to managed, value-based anticipatory primary care. Many primary care practitioners are not ready for, or know enough about, value-based care.[29] That is why the range of practices one finds around the country are so exciting: there are numerous experiments underway that can promote value-based care, all with a recognition that change will take time.

One of the best examples, which I have referred to only in passing, is the CMS's Making Care Primary (MCP) model, which was taking shape in eight states.[30] MCP was to operate operate using Medicare and Medicaid funds but was assiduously seeking an all-payer approach. Under MCP, smaller practices were to be paid more to undertake care management and care integration, as well as to connect patients to social supports. There was no downside to start, and practices could sign up for one of three tracks, with the first intended for those new to value-based care. In the first track, practices stayed in fee-for-service; in track 2, payment went to 50/50 fee-for-service and prospective; and in track 3, it was fully prospective. The program was set for a 10-year term, giving practices plenty of time to learn. In some ways, Making Care Primary recognized there was too much, too fast, in the Primary Care First model. Different parts of the health care system will evolve at different paces, and the idea was to nurture these practices. No wonder that a well-informed observer like Patrick Gordon was so excited about Making Care Primary. The cautionary end of the story: Trump 2.0 canceled MCP.

The nascent value-based primary care practices indicate that at least there is an alternative to a system fracturing under fee-for-service. Most telling, there does not seem to be another path to a better health care system. Disjointed specialist-dominated care cannot be the answer. A rejuvenated primary care is the only way to go, and that involves prospective payment supporting value-based care.

Number Two: Promotion for Primary Care Is Occurring Across the Health Care System

The most heartening and exciting thing about surveying primary care reform is the multiplicity of sources of impetus for change. The federal government's efforts, particularly through the CMMI and the Medicare Shared Savings Program (MSSP), are slowly shifting assumptions about the future away from fee-for-service reimbursements and toward risk that prompts value-based care. Recently, CMMI's leaders acknowledged that they are in it for the long haul.[31] As noted above, the cancellation of Making Care Primary demonstrates, however, the peril of relying solely on government, as policies can change in a dramatic fashion with a new administration.

Many states are in the same situation. Their role as stewards of Medicaid creates the platform for reform. Fee-for-service is not working for lower-income people. Thus many states are working with CMS on waiver programs that can remodel reimbursement and promote prospective payment and anticipatory care. The FQHCs are their natural allies and operatives, and in those states where reform has begun, it appears the FQHCs have a sense of hope and even success. It is not easy, and it is not smooth, and many clinicians will burn out trying to care for uninsured people with limited resources, but the sense of change in Oregon, or Massachusetts, or at SouthCentral Foundation in Alaska, is bracing.

Private health care is also lending its support toward the same set of goals. State and national health insurers are creating programs designed to cultivate managed care, up to and including ownership (through direct employment) of their primary care base. Private investors are betting on specific primary care chains, as well as on facilitators who will help independent primary care practices transition toward value-based care. All these public and private sources of financial support, and their creative ideas for improving health care, are having the same effect. They are creating momentum for committed clinicians to holistically care for sick people, striving to prevent illness and its complications.

Number Three: For-Profit Entities in the Health Care Market Could Have a Role to Play

As I have mentioned, many primary care clinicians with whom I have spoken over the past couple of years endorse greater government involvement in health care, in many cases advocating for a single government payer. This is understandable for settings where a significant proportion of patients cannot access medications or specialty care because of an inability to pay for the services or lack of insurance. But it is not just physicians caring for the uninsured who advocate for government-based solutions. Many policy experts argue that government intervention to create a single payer is the only way to save primary care. Promotion of primary care and promotion of a single payer tend to be highly aligned.

Here my views are somewhat contrary to the primary care mainstream. What I found, and somewhat to my surprise, is that market forces can be primary care's friend, if not savior. Venture capital and private equity have made significant investments in companies that are developing primary care practices or primary care management, such as Oak Street Health and Cityblock Health. They have also invested in firms like agilon and Aledade, which are supporting primary care practices that are on the road toward value-based care. Many of these new companies will remain independent, earning expected profits for their investors or shareholders. But some may be bought by larger for-profit health care companies looking to create vertical integration. Optum has bought many primary care practices. CVS Health purchased Oak Street Health in early 2023.[32] In early 2024, rumor had it that Walmart would buy ChenMed,[33] but then Walmart dropped out of health care altogether. What they (excluding Walmart now) have in common is that all these companies want to move from fee-for-service to value-based care, their profit incentives aligned with the better outcomes that capitated primary care can bring.

It is probably instructive to segment the large corporation participation in primary care between those that can benefit from doing better on insurance risk and those that cannot. For Walgreens and Walmart, there was never a risk-bearing entity. Both announced at one time or another that they were working with UnitedHealthcare on risk contracts, but not much came of that. Doing primary care in retail locations to lure business to the retailer has never had strong empirical support as a profit driver. Even at the big pharmacy chains, CVS Health and Walgreens, the "front store" always operated rather independently from pharmacy. A strong pharmacy business did not guarantee retail success. Thus it is not surprising to see Walmart drop out of health care completely, and to see Walgreens downsizing, especially its "in-store" primary care centers.[34]

The large insurers now doing primary care are different. United HealthGroup and Humana have been at it for years. Providing value-based care at their clinics should lower costs and improve quality, thus making their insurance products more attractive and more profitable. While publications like *Stat* have recently found some doctors unhappy with United HealthGroup ownership, my sense after spending time at their centers is that the situation is stable, with many doctors and nurses saying that Optum leaves them alone and can provide capital for expansion.

This experiment with vertical integration, especially primary care ownership by large health insurers and retailers, is relatively new. Therefore it is too early to judge its durability. But the critique leveled by some academics and analysts—that corporate ownership is inimical to good primary care—is at best speculative. From what I have seen, excellent primary care is occurring in practices owned and operated by for-profit companies. Why would this not be the case? Corporations understand what they are buying: the ability to provide high-quality and cost-effective managed care.

One word of warning, though. For-profit managers must carefully gauge their expectations, as the pursuit of ever greater returns cannot be sustained in primary care. Time will tell how this dynamic plays out. In the meantime, some supporters of primary care will continue to argue that insurers should not own primary care.

This discussion of the role of the market in promoting viable primary care resonates with a similar debate concerning the foundation of Medicare. Medicare is split today between traditional Medicare (based on fee-for-service payments, with governmental control of reimbursement fees) and Medicare Advantage (operated by private health insurance companies making capitated payments). As Medicare Advantage continues to grow, advocates see it as the wave of the future. Detractors argue that this growth is simply a matter of overpayment by the federal government. Proponents of a single-payer program would like to build that on a traditional Medicare structure, with no corporate involvement.[35] They worry that having private health insurers involved in a public program will corrode it. This rift between public and private forms of Medicare parallels the one about the involvement of private investors in primary care.

I have argued elsewhere that the acceptance of private enterprise in health care will depend on corporations' ability to control greed, understand the civic mindedness that is central to health care, and promote programs that put patient welfare first.[36] All the corporate players can talk that talk, but time will tell whether they can walk the walk. For now, with the growth of Medicare Advantage and the expansion (in many ways rational) of vertical integration, the corporate model has momentum. And that momentum pulls primary care into their solutions: capitated Medicare Advantage is the best fuel for value-based primary care. So, for now, the market incentives surrounding capitated payment, especially from the government, could be a tailwind for primary care. But the next decade will determine whether this is durable. In particular, the next oscillation of government support for Medicare Advantage will put pressure on at risk practices to show that they can eliminate waste.

All that said, strong sentiment against profit by health insurers has been captured by the assassination of the president of UnitedHealthcare in late 2024. The public response to this act was that the executive, and by extension everyone working at for-profit health insurers, had it coming. This clearly indicates that the profit motive in health insurance will continue to be controversial, something that could be addressed by a single-payer system. But that sentiment is juxtaposed in midcentury against a Trump administration that supports privatization of Medicare, reflecting just how uncertain the current health care policy prospects are. Presumably, many of the same people justifying murder of a health care executive are also people who voted for Trump.

Number Four: Fixing Fee-for-Service Reimbursement for Primary Care

Staying on the prosaic issue of payment, my fourth point is that the efforts to solve the primary care dilemma by simply boosting fee-for-service payments are unlikely to succeed. The most aggressive of such arguments revolve around nationalization of the Relative Value Scale Update Committee (RUC) at the American Medical Association. Anyone visiting from another country would be perplexed about why the United States allows the AMA, dominated by specialists, to determine what fees should be paid for individual services, especially when our primary care system is failing. This does not make any sense, and a 2021 report on primary care issued by the National Academies of Science, Engineering, and Medicine (an organization that is never radical) said as much.[37] So NASEM and others have asked, Why not have Medicare take over the payment system and let the Centers for Medicare and Medicaid Services make the decisions, treating the RUC like an advisor. Recent estimates suggest that if Medicare increased the amount of spending on primary care by 4%, primary care supply would increase by 1%. In short, more primary care dollars could alleviate some primary care clinician shortages.[38]

The problem with this approach is that it is both politically infeasible and treading the wrong path. No one in the AMA is considering a better home for the RUC, which at this point serves the AMA's interests. They would strongly oppose any change of the status quo. Nor is the CMS prepared to assert leadership on this issue. Well-heeled specialty organizations would not allow it. Restructuring the RUC would likely require federal legislation, and the votes are not there. The specialists' lobby, supported by the hospitals, is too strong. Personally, I am not opposed, from a policy point of view, to the government making these reimbursement decisions. It just seems unlikely in the absence of other sweeping legislation, such as an act that created a single-payer system.

Even if such a change were possible, the re-platforming of the RUC keeps primary care on the fee-for-service hamster wheel. Better pay per patient evaluation would help a lot of primary care practices, but it does not change their basic incentive to see as many patients as possible in a given day. This cannot be good for the practices' health, their patients' health, or public health. In many ways, the RUC's abstemious attitude toward primary care creates an incentive to move toward value-based care, founded on financial risk contracts. After two years of visiting many of practices, the population health management orientation for risk-contracted primary care doctors seems to me to be even more compellingly beneficial for patients in real time than it was in theory. And there appears to be some momentum developing on many fronts. Our health care system risks losing this momentum by spending time and lobbying efforts on a RUC "fix."

This is not, however, meant to dismiss an incremental approach. As noted previously, sage voices like that of Robert Berenson have argued that changes in codes within the RUC architecture can help move toward value-based care, such as explicit care management codes and payment for bundled services. CMS is listening. As Andy Slavitt and Andie Steinberg point out, the Calendar Year 2025 Medicare Physician Fee Schedule proposed rule has at least three proposals that move clinicians toward value-based care.[39] First, there are advanced primary care management (APCM) codes that can be used when billing for care of patients with chronic diseases. Second, for those in ACOs, there are prepaid quarterly shared savings payments and health equity benefit adjustments. Third, CMS is proposing new telehealth definitions that include audio only. These payments together can be substantial, and all push practices toward the kind of anticipatory care that is the hallmark of value-based primary care.

Insertion of these types of value-based payment into the coding manual can help drive toward value-based care. Perhaps it is an important incremental step; one can see companies like Aledade and agilon working with their practices to take advantage of new codes. But I think it would be a mistake to believe we can fix primary care solely through adjustments to fee-for-service.

Related to the issue of primary care physicians being better paid under a fee-for-service arrangement, as discussed above, disgruntled doctors are now turning to trade unions to negotiate better reimbursement for their work within integrated delivery systems. In late 2023, the physicians, nurse practitioners, and physician assistants at Allina Health in Minneapolis voted to form a union, garnering a certain amount of press.[40]

This may be an important and salutary development, especially for primary care. But hopefully it will not turn health care's attention away from a more important move—toward value-based contracts. Just because physicians are members of a union does not change the dynamics of a fee-for-service payment system, nor does it increase the amount that their employer will be able to collect for each patent visit. Increasing the financial return for primary care depends on improving care through continuity relationships, thereby eliminating health care waste. A transformed RUC does not do that. A physicians' union could help, but only insofar as it promotes value-based care.

A much better approach than rate enhancement is the recently proposed ACO PC Flex. For smaller ACOs in the MSSP program (typically all physician groups, not hospitals) CMS is combining greater efficiency in Medicare with higher rates of reimbursement for primary care.[41] For the first time in the MSSP, CMS will pay ACO PC Flex participants monthly population-based payments, adjusted for clinical and social risk. There are also start-up funds available to prepare a practice for prospective management of care. These kind of programs, to build capacity for value-based managed care, may be at risk; time will tell where Trump 2.0 CMS heads.

Number Five: Train More Primary Care Clinicians

Any discussion of the future of primary care must dwell on training, as the current number of primary care clinicians is insufficient for tomorrow's needs. One relatively inexpensive way for the federal government to address this shortage of physicians is to fund more training slots for primary care, especially in underserved and rural areas. There are some programs that already promote this goal, including the Health Resources and Services Administration's Teaching Health Center Graduate Medical Education (GME) Program, although it is dependent on periodic congressional approval.[42] Making more primary care slots available could lead to the opening of new medical schools, especially osteopathic and offshore medical ones. These medical education facilities are currently somewhat constrained by the availability of openings for primary care training. Importantly, federal support for medical training is a relatively cheap intervention in our $4 trillion health care system. For short money on the federal scale, the government could create incentives for medical school graduates to go into primary care.

On the nursing side, funding is again the issue. While the supply of nurse practitioners is exploding, students and their families are footing the bill for their education. In addition, more than 75,000 qualified applicants were turned away from nursing programs in 2022 due to lack of teaching faculty and clinical sites.[43] Increasing the number of positions in nurse practitioner programs—and especially funding for clinical preceptor slots in community settings—is both a need and comparatively inexpensive. The same arguments apply for behavioral health professionals and community health workers. Primary care in the future requires this team approach. Even modest federal funding can solve the problem of primary care clinician shortages. Those shortages are real, and they are retarding the further development of value-based care in nearly every practice I visited. Congress appears increasingly willing to take up the challenge of training more primary care doctors in community settings.[44] This cannot happen soon enough.

The other key point on training is that its segregation does not fit the future. That future is fewer physicians, more nurse practitioners, and a team concept where multiple professionals work together. Yet current training occurs in silos, except for some prominent joint training programs operated within the Veterans Health Administration. Such training should not be the exception but the rule. Many facilities are taking a piecemeal approach to team training; for example, nurse practitioners are finding more informal residency programs in practices. But with an addition of slots for prospective primary care clinicians should come interdisciplinary programs.

Just to reiterate, training programs are inexpensive compared to other health policy interventions. As well, the current GME funds are poorly spent in hospitals. It will be difficult to pry them away from hospitals, but there should be some impetus in that regard as Congress and administrations look to primary care reform.

Number Six: The Primary Care Team

Primary care as a team sport is the sixth insight from my study of best practices. When I was a medical student (many years ago), George Silver, a professor at Yale University's School of Public Health, gave me a copy of John Berger's *A Fortunate Man: The Story of a Country Doctor*.[45] The book features John Sassall, a general practitioner in rural Gloucestershire, and his work there. Sassall (the name is a pseudonym) knew his patients and the county they lived in well, being aware of all their social determinants of health long before that term was coined. He worked long hours, struggling to care for all his patients, and characterized a doctor as "a man who was all knowing but looking haggard."[46] (The book betrays the sexism extant at the time. It is likely still just as extant, but not as blunt.) Berger writes beautifully, with resplendent descriptions of doctoring and hard work. I have always remembered the last sentence: "I can only end by quoting the logic by which he [Sassall] himself has to work, a logic which for all its stoicism has in it the seed of a great affirmative vision: 'Whenever I am reminded of death—and it happens every day—I think of my own and that makes me work harder.'"[47]

Sassall was alone in his medical practice, except for some aides in his surgery (the British term for a medical office). That isolation seemed unremarkable nearly 50 years ago, when I first read the book. But today it is preposterous. Primary care in the United States can no longer be one doctor caring for patients. Primary care needs multiplayer teams, composed of clinicians who are doctors, nurse practitioners, physician associates, medical assistants, care managers, and pharmacists. They should also work closely with community health workers, behavioral health experts, care managers, pharmacists, nurses, and medical assistants. They must be bound together by an EMR system that they all use. Above all, they should be devoted to their patients, but they should not be expected to become exhausted and haggard because of their jobs.

Teamwork and an understanding of team dynamics are skills that are crucial to their patients' welfare. Solitary labor on behalf of a patient, like that of the "fortunate man," is simply anachronistic. In many ways, this is a critical sea change in the medical profession, especially in primary care, compared with what things were like the twentieth century. Good teams should also go a long way to making primary care clinicians work manageable, along the lines that Christine Sinsky has so carefully outlined over the past decade.[48]

The team concept brings us back to training. Not only should advance practice practitioners and doctors train together, but so too should the entire team. Again, that calls for explicit reform in graduate medical education.

Number Seven: Data and Analytics Knit the Team

Decidedly related to the above, a primary care team is dependent on an encompassing information system. Without a shared digital record, teamwork on behalf of a patient is not possible. It is ironic in that the current rendition of electronic medical records has become the bane of many a primary care doctor's existence. EMRs show too many results, contain too many clinical messages, and have too many questions for clinicians coming through patient portals. But it is an absolute necessity in providing team-based care for patients.

One of the most exciting prospects for clinicians, especially primary care ones, is the role of artificial intelligence in automating health care.[49] The big EMR companies are rapidly gearing up for AI to assume a larger role in health care. For example, I spoke with Epic's development team, which is working closely with Microsoft using GPT-4 (commonly known as Chat GPT).[50] Their primary focus is to reduce clinician burnout by automating administrative tasks and eliminating keyboard time.

In the not-so-distant future, ambient listening and note generation could be the norm. EMR devices will listen in on clinicians' conversations with their patients and compose the necessary note, delivered seconds after the visit.[51] AI could be used to draft responses to patients who ask questions on a patient portal, obviating a great deal of work by primary care clinicians. Clinicians will talk to the charting device, rather than having to enter data using thousands of keystrokes a day. AI will also help all clinicians practice at the top of their license.

Informed judgments, careful listening, and empathy will be the hallmarks of primary care practice as doctors' and nurses' knowledge is supplemented and complemented by information that is resident in their computer systems. Using this technology, anticipating a patient's needs will be much easier.

Such predictions may be too rosy, but the potential seems to be there. Of course, this prospect depends on making EMRs, claims data, and insurance information available for the algorithms to do their work, but again we are on the cusp of interoperability that enables such reach. Steady government pressure over the past 15 years finally has opened closed systems and made data-sharing possible. The kind of real-time data-driven huddle that ChenMed uses with its extended clinical team will and should become the norm for dealing with a panel of chronically ill patients.

Watching primary care clinicians, and discussing with them their work life, there seems to be no better prospect for improving their lot than alleviation of the burdens of documentation and integration of information from various sources. AI is primed to help with both, and one can foresee a brilliant future.[52] Of course, concerns about how well programs are trained and guards against confabulation are important.[53] The technology is not there yet, but most informatics experts I have spoken with are quietly confident.

Number Eight: Documentation and Coding

The current conundrum surrounding documentation and coding must be addressed. The best primary care practices producing value-based care and promoting population health management rely exclusively on risk patients, particularly Medicare Advantage beneficiaries. To take the best care of their patients, they must identify all their patients' problems and ensure any medical issues are appropriately entered into the information systems that their teams use and will over time feed their algorithms. Documentation is critical. Recall Dr. Gettinger at the University of Alabama at Birmingham, a conscientious and traditional primary care physician. He wanted all his patient's ailments documented so that anyone else taking care of the patient could understand the issues. In a world dependent on data analysis, documentation as careful coding is part of the same impulse.

Skeptics and detractors see things differently. They would say that some primary care practices are able to turn a profit simply because they use as many codes as possible, to build as much risk-based payment as possible, and the federal government allows that. They have a point—which is what makes this such a conundrum. Not all practices overcode; data from the Medicare Payment Advisory Commission (MedPAC) show tremendous variation between practices in coding intensity. But there are abuses, no doubt.

This argument has been ongoing since the beginning of the twenty-first century. CMS has shown that it can modify coding weights, and tighten up reimbursement rates, so payments from Medicare Advantage plans are not unfairly higher compared with those from traditional Medicare.[54] Further effort is needed today. Nearly every impartial observer, particularly the MedPAC, is calling for well-defined adjustments to rein in abuses caused by overcoding, and as discussed, CMS is taking the next steps to do so.[55] Risk adjustments must be continuously recalibrated in order to ensure fair payment. But practices also must continue to document properly to ensure patients receive the best care.

Primary care practices that are advised by agilon or Aledade, and chains of primary care clinics operated by Oak Street Health or ChenMed, will have to demonstrate their continued financial viability as the rules change. They will have to call the bluff of skeptics who charge that they are overly dependent on careful coding. The clinicians at these practices believe they provide better and more efficient care by keeping people healthy and paying close attention when patients are sick, thereby thriving when their capitation payments are based on typical care. With new CMS regulations on coding coming into place, the business model for value-based primary care will be tested. Talking to leaders at these practices from 2022 to 2024, as tougher restrictions on coding came into play, I was heartened to find little reduction in their enthusiasm for risk or for value-based care.

I believe the practices that emphasize proactive outreach and continuity of care will continue to succeed. More importantly, their progress will filter into other primary care groups or organizations taking capitated payments, whether they are FQHCs in a state that is paying capitation on primary care, or academic medical centers with new commercial health insurance contracts containing a value-based component.

The alternative future is that overcoding alone is making Medicare Advantage–based primary care viable, and without inappropriate coding, it is not viable. This is certainly a possibility, one that drives the system back to market-based fee-for-service (a disastrous alternative), or toward a single payer.

Number Nine: Primary Care Is a Lens on Our Inequitable Health Care Structure

Visiting primary care practices reveals our starkly inequitable system of financing health care. To my eyes, one of the most ironic phenomena in health care is the migration of patients from uninsured status or Medicaid to Medicare Advantage at places like HealthCare Partners/Optum Health or ChenMed. The primary care organizations that provide great care to Medicaid beneficiaries and the uninsured, like many of the FQHCs, are a testament to what is good in our health care system. But many of those on Medicaid, or those who have limited resources available to them, or uninsured individuals, do not get great care. As we have seen, primary care providers must develop "workarounds" for uninsured patients who cannot afford specialty care, or they lose track of patients when they are admitted to city hospitals. Yet once a citizen turns 65 and qualifies for Medicare, the health care doors literally open. A person who is 64 and 364 days old cannot get care at ChenMed, but the next day they can, with a primary clinician devoted to their health. There is every reason to believe they receive much more attentive and holistic care than they have gotten in the past.

These doors open because the federal government made an arbitrary decision to begin paying for health care when people reach age 65. Given the high cost and inefficiency of commercial health insurance, it seems inevitable to me that government-sponsored health insurance will replace the former over time. The most important financial fact in our health care system is that the federal government pays less than commercial health insurers for every service that our health care system delivers. As fee-for-service commercial insurance grows too expensive, employers will be open to using government programs for health insurance, if they are allowed access. Once a federal payment program is in place, hospitals and specialists looking to maintain their financial well-being will have to learn how to profit from removing unnecessary health care waste. And they will depend on primary care for that.

But more importantly, to have a well-functioning primary care system, the inadequate payments from Medicaid, and the lack of health insurance for many, must be addressed. Much has been written about inequity in health care, but the fundamental problem centers on lower rates of payment for care for low-income people (or no payments for the uninsured). It is hard to see primary care "fixed" without a move to universal, government-sponsored health insurance that treats everyone as equals and uses the same rates of payment as what is paid for Medicare beneficiaries. This kind of commitment to equitable rates of payment, and the system changes it entails, seems to me to be inescapable in any policy discussion of primary care.

Number Ten: Caring for Patients

Primary care is really not about EMRs and coding issues and payment structures. It is about *people*, with certain individuals (clinicians) serving others (patients) in their time of need and remaining committed to them over time. Although I was a bit doubtful when I started this book, I was surprised and gratified to find that everywhere I went, primary care clinicians were devoted to their patients and were there for them when needed. Even the most harassed and harried people I talked with, fatigued by the "Gatling gun" of a patient portal and unable to keep up with their clinical notes, brightened when talking about their patients and describing the joy they got from patient care. Patients were grateful for the clinicians' work and their generosity with their time, and that in turn inspired the caregivers.

I was reminded of Polly Morland's excellent book, *A Fortunate Woman*.[56] Morland had tracked down the former practice of "Dr. John Sassall" and found that today it was run by a woman general practitioner (largely unidentified by Morland). The nature of the "fortunate woman's" practice was different from that of Berger's "fortunate man's," but not wholly so. At its heart was still a strong commitment to the patients, and a willingness to accept the rigors associated with the profession. One passage in that regard is memorable.[57]

> The doctor worked hard to keep personal and professional in some kind of equilibrium, in part for herself and her family, but also for her patients. It is equilibrium that that makes the work sustainable, its pressures possible to withstand, and if you get the balance right, it's what brings the richest rewards of the job. For being there, available most days for your patients, is one of the key elements of building relationships, and strong rooted relationships don't just help the patients. They help the doctor.

Above and beyond the current technological changes in the practice of medicine, no matter how powerful they are, sick people will always need someone they can depend on, someone who can guide them through illness and counsel them about the future. They need a healing relationship. That is really the role of the primary care clinicians—doctors, nurses, physician assistants, and others on a health care team—and it is an irreplaceable role. The gratitude that comes from that relationship is uplifting. Today it does sustain many doctors, even while other aspects of their practice pull them down.

When one sees the practice of the future, it is one funded by prospective payment so that the fundamental financial incentive is aligned with the fundamental therapeutic incentive: keeping the patient healthy. The primary care clinician of the future will have fewer patients, keep close watch on their medical problems, and work with a team of other clinicians who can help. The relationships with patients will thus be durable and meaningful, which along with appropriate work/life balance sustains the clinicians. This is the kind of practice I saw at ChenMed, for example, and its contrast with a fee-for-service mill could not have been greater, for patient or for clinician.

In summary, we can change our system of financing health care to make it more cost-effective and produce higher-quality care. In so doing, the practice of primary care will become much more conducive to the kind of whole-person care that clinicians want to deliver, and that patients need. These changes will be good for primary care clinicians, making their job not just possible, but more enjoyable—there will be the equilibrium they need to do their difficult job. A changed health care system, one that is value based, will also be good for all of us who are patients, and who need that healing relationship with their clinician.

NOTES

Preface

1. Troyen A. Brennan, *The Transformation of American Health Insurance: On the Path to Medicare for All* (Baltimore: Johns Hopkins University Press, 2024).

2. "Primary Care," American Academy of Family Physicians, accessed April 13, 2023, https://www.aafp.org/about/policies/all/primary-care.html.

3. Molla S. Donaldson, Karl D. Yordy, Kathleen N. Lohr, and Neal A. Vanselow, eds., *Primary Care: America's Health in a New Era* (Washington, DC: National Academy Press, 1996).

4. Linda McCauley, Robert L. Phillips, Marc Meisnere, and Sarah K. Robinson, eds., *Implementing High-Quality Primary Care: Rebuilding the Foundation of Health Care* (Washington, DC: National Academies Press, May 2021).

5. Dolores Yanagihara and Ann Hwang, *Investing in Primary Care: Why It Matters for People with Commercial Insurance* (Oakland: California Health Care Foundation, April 2022), https://www.chcf.org/wp-content/uploads/2022/04/InvestingPrimaryCareWhyItMattersCommercialCoverage.pdf.

6. Mark W. Friedberg, Peter S. Hussey, and Eric C. Schneider, "Primary Care: A Critical Review of the Evidence on Quality and Costs of Health Care," *Health Affairs* 29, no. 5 (2010): 766–72.

7. Sanjay Basu, Seth A. Berkowitz, Robert L. Phillips, et al., "Association of Primary Care Physician Supply with Population Mortality in the United States, 2005–2015," *JAMA Internal Medicine* 179, no. 4 (2019): 506–14, https://jamanetwork.com/journals/jamainternalmedicine/fullarticle/2724393.

8. Sara Schaefer, Shukri Dualeh, Nicholas Kunnath, John Scott, and Andrew Ibrahim, "Higher Rates of Emergency Surgery, Serious Complications, and Readmissions in Primary Care Shortage Areas, 2015–2019," *Health Affairs* 43, no. 3 (2024): 363–71.

9. James C. Robinson, "Theory and Practice in the Design of Physician Payment Incentives," *Milbank Quarterly* 79, no. 2 (2001): 149–80, https://www.jstor.org/stable/3350546?read-now=1&seq=1#page_scan_tab_contents.

10. Yalda Jabbarpour, Stephen Petterson, Anuradha Jetty, and Hoon Byun, *The Health of US Primary Care: A Baseline Scorecard Tracking Support for High-Quality Primary Care* (New York: Milbank Memorial Fund, February 2023), https://www.milbank.org/wp-content/uploads/2023/02/Milbank-Baseline-Scorecard_final_V2.pdf.

11. Debora Cohen, Annette Totten, Robert Phillips, et al., "Measuring Primary Care Spending in the US by State," *JAMA Health Forum* 5, no. 5 (2024): e240913.

12. Evan Gumas, Corinne Lewis, Celli Horstman, and Munira Gunja, *Finger on the Pulse: The State of Primary Care and Nine Other Countries* (Issue Brief) (New York: Commonwealth Fund, March 28, 2024).

13. Milbank Memorial Fund, *The Health of US Primary Care: 2024 Scorecard Report—No One Can See You Now* (New York: Milbank Memorial Fund, February 28, 2024).

14. McCauley et al., *Implementing High-Quality Primary Care*, 3.

15. McCauley et al., *Implementing High-Quality Primary Care*, 283.

16. Michael Liu and Rishi K. Wadhera, "Primary Care Supply by County-Level Characteristics, 2010–2019," *JAMA* 328, no. 19 (2022): 1974–75, https://jamanetwork.com/journals/jama/fullarticle/2798415.

17. Joanne Finnegan, "A Startling 79% of Primary Care Physicians Are Burned Out, New Report Finds," Fierce Healthcare, August 6, 2019, https://www.fiercehealthcare.com/practices/a-startling-79-primary-care-physicians-are-burned-out-new-report-finds/.

18. Victoria Knight, "American Medical Students Less Likely to Choose to Become Primary Care Doctors," *Kaiser Family Foundation Health News*, July 3, 2019, https://kffhealthnews.org/news/american-medical-students-less-likely-to-choose-to-become-primary-care-doctors/.

19. John E. Snyder, Rachel D. Upton, Thomas C. Hassett, et al., "Black Representation in the Primary Care Physician Workforce and Its Association with Population Life Expectancy and Mortality Rates in the US," *JAMA Network Open* 6, no. 4 (2023): e236687, https://jamanetwork.com/journals/jamanetworkopen/fullarticle/2803898?utm_source=silverchair&utm_medium=email&utm_campaign=article_alert-jamanetworkopen&utm_content=wklyforyou&utm_term=041423.

20. Vladimir Lenin, *What Is to Be Done? Burning Questions of Our Movement* (London: Wishart, 1956).

21. Kevin O'Leary, "The Library: A 2019 View on Primary Care Disruption," Health Tech Nerds, May 9, 2024, https://www.healthtechnerds.com/p/library-2019-view-primary-care-disruption.

22. Timothy Hoff, *Next in Line: Lowered Expectations in the Age of Retail- and Value-Based Health* (New York: Oxford University Press, 2018), xi.

23. Brennan, *Transformation of American Health Insurance*.

24. Interview with Dr. Trevor Huber, private practice, November 3, 2022.

25. Interview with Venita Owens, president, Baylor Scott & White Health and Wellness Center, November 3, 2022.

26. Interview with Dr. Andrea Harris, Baylor Scott & White Health and Wellness Center, November 3, 2022.

27. Donald Wesson, Heather Kitzman, Kenneth H. Halloran, and Kristen Tecson, "Innovative Population Health Model Associated with Reduced Emergency

Department Use and Inpatient Hospitalizations," *Health Affairs* 37, no. 4 (2018): 543–49, https://www.healthaffairs.org/doi/full/10.1377/hlthaff.2017.1099.

28. Interview with Dr. Lydia Best, Craft Health and Wellness Center, November 3, 2022.

29. Interview with Dr. Elizabeth Quinn, Lynn Community Health Center, December 5, 2022.

Chapter 1. The Somewhat Recent History of Primary Care

1. Rosemary A. Stevens, "The Americanization of Family Medicine: Contradictions, Challenges, and Change, 1969–2000," *Family Medicine* 33, no. 4 (2001): 232–52, https://fammedarchives.blob.core.windows.net/imagesandpdfs/fmhub/fm2001/apr01/PDFS/2001-33-4-232-243.pdf.

2. Timothy Hoff, *Searching for the Family Doctor: Primary Care on the Brink* (Baltimore: Johns Hopkins University Press, 2022), chap. 4.

3. American Academy of Family Physicians, *The History and Evolution of Family Medicine* (Leawood, KS: AAFP, March 2013).

4. Katrina Armstrong, Nancy L. Keating, Michael Landry, et al., "Academic General Internal Medicine: A Mission for the Future," *Journal of General Internal Medicine* 28, no. 6 (2013): 845–51, https://www.ncbi.nlm.nih.gov/pmc/articles/PMC3663942/pdf/11606_2013_Article_2334.pdf.

5. Linda McCauley, Robert L. Phillips, Marc Meisnere, and Sarah K. Robinson, eds., *Implementing High-Quality Primary Care: Rebuilding the Foundation of Health Care* (Washington, DC: National Academies Press, May 2021), 1.

6. John McPhee, *Heirs of General Practice* (New York: Farrar, Straus, Giroux, 1984).

7. Interview with Dr. Donna Conkling, private practice, March 7, 2023.

8. Barbara Starfield, *Primary Care: Concept, Evaluation and Policy* (New York: Oxford University Press, 1992).

9. Starfield, *Primary Care*, 9.

10. Abraham Verghese, *Cutting for Stone* (New York: Vintage Books, 2009).

11. McCauley et al., *Implementing High-Quality Primary Care*, 46.

12. Dennis McIntyre, Lisa Rogers, and Ellen Jo Heier, "Overview, History, and Objectives of Performance Measurement," *Health Care Financing Review* 22, no. 3 (2001): 7–21, https://www.ncbi.nlm.nih.gov/pmc/articles/PMC4194707.

13. Michel Foucault, *Discipline and Punish: The Birth of the Prison*, trans. Alan Sheridan (London: Penguin, 1975).

14. Troyen Brennan, *The Transformation of American Health Insurance: On the Path to Medicare for All* (Baltimore: Johns Hopkins University Press, 2024), chap. 6.

15. Alain C. Enthoven, "The History and Principles of Managed Competition," *Health Affairs* 12, suppl. (1993): 24–48, https://pubmed.ncbi.nlm.nih.gov/8477935.

16. William Shrank, Teresa Rogstad, and Natasha Parekh, "Waste in the US Health Care System: Estimated Costs and Potential Savings," *JAMA* 322, no. 15 (2019): 1501–9, https://jamanetwork.com/journals/jama/fullarticle/2752664.

17. Troyen A. Brennan, *Just Doctoring: Medical Ethics in the Liberal State* (Berkeley: University of California Press, 1991).

18. Starfield, *Primary Care*, 85.

19. Eric J. Cassell, *Doctoring: The Nature of Primary Care Practice* (New York: Oxford University Press, 1997).

20. David M. Studdert and Troyen A. Brennan, "The Problems with Punitive Damages in Lawsuits against Managed Care Organizations," *New England Journal of Medicine* 342, no. 23 (2000): 280–84, https://www.nejm.org/doi/full/10.1056/NEJM200001273420411.

21. Brennan, *Transformation of American Health Insurance*, chap. 3.

22. Starfield, *Primary Care*, 28.

23. Anna D. Sinaiko, Vilsa E. Curto, Katherine Ianni, Mark Soto, and Meredith B. Rosenthal, "Utilization, Steering, and Spending in Vertical Relationships between Physicians and Health Systems," *JAMA Health Forum* 4, no. 9 (2023): e232875, https://jamanetwork.com/journals/jama-health-forum/fullarticle/2808890.

24. Timothy Hoff, *Next in Line: Lowered Expectations in the Age of Retail- and Value-Based Health* (New York: Oxford University Press, 2018).

25. "RVS Update Committee (RUC)," American Medical Association, updated October 18, 2023, https://www.ama-assn.org/about/rvs-update-committee-ruc/rvs-update-committee-ruc/.

26. William Weinfeld, *Income of Physicians, 1929–49* (St. Louis: Federal Reserve Bank, July 1951), https://fraser.stlouisfed.org/files/docs/publications/SCB/pages/1950-1954/4374_1950-1954.pdf.

27. John Langenbrunner, Deborah Williams, and Sherry Terrell, "Physician Incomes and Work Patterns Across Specialties: 1975 and 1983–4," *Health Care Financing Review* 10, no. 1 (1988): 17–25, https://www.cms.gov/Research-Statistics-Data-and-Systems/Research/HealthCareFinancingReview/Downloads/CMS1191016dl.pdf.

28. Starfield, *Primary Care*, 105.

29. S. E. Peterson and A. E. Rodin, "GMENAC Report on U.S. Physician Manpower Policies," *Health Policy and Education* 3, no. 4 (1983): 337–49, https://pubmed.ncbi.nlm.nih.gov/10299011/.

30. Marie C. Reed and Paul B. Ginsburg, "Behind the Times: Physician Income, 1995–99," Center for Studying Health System Changes, *Data Bulletin* 24 (March 2003): http://www.hschange.org/CONTENT/544.

31. Reed Abelson, "Doctors; Average Pay Fell 7% in 8 Years, Report Says," *New York Times*, June 22, 2006.

32. "The Doctors Paid the Most (and the Least), Charted," Advisory Board, updated March 18, 2023, https://www.advisory.com/daily-briefing/2022/04/19/physician-compensation#:~:text=Overall%20compensation%20increases&text=On%20average%2C%20primary%20care%20physicians,2021%20and%20%24346%2C000%20in%202020.

33. McCauley et al., *Implementing High-Quality Primary Care*, 286.

34. Yalda Jabbarpour, Stephen Petterson, Anuradha Jetty, and Hoon Byun, *The Health of US Primary Care: A Baseline Scorecard Tracking Support for High-Quality Primary Care* (New York: Milbank Memorial Fund, February 2023), https://www.milbank.org/wp-content/uploads/2023/02/Milbank-Baseline-Scorecard_final_V2.pdf.

35. Commonwealth Fund, *Overworked and UnderValued: Unmasking Primary Care Physicians' Dissatisfaction in 10 High Income Countries* (New York: Commonwealth Fund, August 16, 2023).

36. Laurence F. McMahon Jr., Kim Rize, NiJuanna Irby-Johnson, and Vineet Chopra, "Designed to Fail? The Future of Primary Care," *Journal of General Internal Medicine* 36, no. 2 (2020): 515–17, https://www.ncbi.nlm.nih.gov/pmc/articles/PMC7390445/pdf/11606_2020_Article_6077.pdf.

37. Brian Schilling, *The Federal Government Has Put Billions into Promoting Electronic Health Record Use: How is It Going?* (New York: Commonwealth Fund, April 2023), https://www.commonwealthfund.org/publications/newsletter-article/federal-government-has-put-billions-promoting-electronic-health/.

38. Andrew Auerbach and David W. Bates, "Introduction: Improvement and Measurement in the Era of Electronic Health Records," *Annals of Internal Medicine* 172, suppl. (2020): S69–S72, https://www.acpjournals.org/doi/10.7326/M19-0870.

39. McMahon et al., "Designed to Fail."

40. McMahon et al., "Designed to Fail," 516.

41. John W. Ayers, Adam Poliak, Mark Dredze, et al., "Comparing Physician and Artificial Intelligence Chatbot Responses to Patient Questions Posted to a Public Social Media Forum," *JAMA Internal Medicine* 183, no. 6 (2023): 589–96, https://jamanetwork.com/journals/jamainternalmedicine/fullarticle/2804309?&utm_source=BulletinHealthCare&utm_medium=email&utm_term=050123&utm_content=NON-MEMBER&utm_campaign=article_alert-morning_rounds_daily&utm_uid=1909450&utm_effort=MRNRD0.

42. "Table 4: Selected Practice Characteristics of Active AAFP Members," American Academy of Family Physicians, December 31, 2020, https://www.aafp.org/about/dive-into-family-medicine/family-medicine-facts/table4.html.

43. Edward Levine, Rupal Malani, Andrew Odden, and John Schultz, "Ensuring the Financial Sustainability of Academic Medical Centers," McKinsey and Company, April 4, 2024, https://www.mckinsey.com/industries/healthcare/our-insights/ensuring-the-financial-sustainability-of-academic-medical-centers.

44. Interview with Dr. Stuart Cohen, medical director, Prime Care, UAB Hospital, December 3, 2022.

45. Interview with Dr. Jay Herndon, retired, UAB Hospital, December 3, 2022.

46. Interview with Dr. David Gettinger, retired, UAB Hospital, December 3, 2022.

47. Interview with Dr. Alan Gruman, UAB Hospital, December 3, 2022.

48. Bradley M. Gray, Jonathan L. Vandergrift, Jennifer P. Stevens, and Bruce E. Landon, "Evolving Practice Choices by Newly Certified and More Senior General Internists: A Cross-Sectional and Panel Comparison," *Annals of Internal Medicine* 175, no. 7 (2022): 1022–27, https://www.acpjournals.org/doi/epdf/10.7326/M21-4636.

49. "Advance Data Tables: 2023 Main Residency Match," National Residency Matching Program, March 17, 2023, https://www.nrmp.org/wp-content/uploads/2023/04/Advance-Data-Tables-2023_FINAL-2.pdf.

50. Matthew Desmond, *Poverty, by America* (New York: Crown, 2023).

51. David Brady, Ulrich Kohler, and Hui Zheng, "Novel Estimates of Mortality Associated with Poverty in the United States," *JAMA Internal Medicine* 183, no. 6 (2023): 618–19, https://jamanetwork.com/journals/jamainternalmedicine/article-abstract/2804032.

52. Interview with Dr. Mirza Baig, Atrius Health, February 3, 2023.

53. Hoff, *Searching for the Family Doctor*.

Chapter 2. Signs of a New Deal for Primary Care?

1. Stefan Larsson, Jennifer Clawson, and Josh Kellar, *The Patient Priority: Solve Health Care's Value Crisis by Measuring and Delivering Outcomes That Matter to Patients* (New York: McGraw-Hill, 2023).

2. Asaf Bitton and Katherine Rouleau, "Primary Care Is Essential and Under Siege," *NEJM Catalyst, Innovations in Care Delivery* 4, no. 7 (July 2023): doi:10.1056/CAT.23.0175.

3. Interview with Dr. Christopher Crow, November 1, 2022.

4. Interviews with Beth Martinez, executive vice president for operations, and Jenna Hemingway, senior vice president of network strategy and operations, Catalyst Health, November 1, 2022.

5. Interview with Dr. Matt Weyenberg, chief medical officer, Catalyst Health, November 1, 2022.

6. Interview with Christopher Abbott, vice president of payer relations, Catalyst Health, November 1, 2022.

7. Interview with Dr. Jamison "Jamie" Albrecht, Village Health Partners, November 1, 2022.

8. Robert Baillieu, Michael Kidd, Robert Phillips, et al., "The Primary Care Spend Model: A Systems Approach to Measuring Investment in Primary Care," Practice, *BMJ Global Health* 4, no. 4 (2019): e001601, https://gh.bmj.com/content/4/4/e001601.

9. Ann Kempski and Ann Greiner, *Primary Care Spending: High Stakes, Low Investment* (Washington DC: Primary Care Collaborative, December 2020), https://www.pcpcc.org/sites/default/files/resources/PCC_Primary_Care_Spending_2020.pdf.

10. Sanjay Basu, Russell S. Phillips, Zirui Song, Asaf Bitton, and Bruce E. Landon, "High Levels of Capitation Payments Needed to Shift Primary Care toward Proactive Team and Nonvisit Care," *Health Affairs* 36, no. 9 (2017): 1599–605, https://www.healthaffairs.org/doi/full/10.1377/hlthaff.2017.0367.

11. Michael L. O'Dell, "What Is a Patient-Centered Medical Home?," *Missouri Medicine* 113, no. 4 (2016): 301–4, https://www.ncbi.nlm.nih.gov/pmc/articles/PMC6139911.

12. Institute of Medicine, *Primary Care: America's Health in a New Era* (Washington, DC: National Academies Press, 1996).

13. "The Chronic Care Model," Accelerating Care Transformation Center, accessed December 15, 2023, https://www.act-center.org/application/files/1616/3511/6445/Model_Chronic_Care.pdf.

14. "The Future of Patient-Centered Medical Homes: Foundation for a Better Health Care System," National Committee for Quality Assurance, accessed December 15, 2023, https://www.johnahartford.org/images/uploads/reports/The_Future_of_PCMH-NCQA_White_Paper.pdf.

15. Richard J. Baron, "Not All (Medical) Homes Are Built Alike: Some Work Better Than Others," *JAMA Internal Medicine* 174, no. 8 (2014): 1358–59, https://pubmed.ncbi.nlm.nih.gov/24958281.

16. Christine A. Sinsky, Rachel Willard-Grace, Andrew M. Schutzbank, et al., "In Search of Joy in Practice: A Report of 23 High-Functioning Primary Care Practices," *Annals of Family Medicine* 11, no. 3 (2013): 272–78, https://pubmed.ncbi.nlm.nih.gov/23690328.

17. Zhigang Xie, Sandhya Yadav, Samantha A. Larson, Arch G. Mainous III, and Young-Rock Hong, "Associations of Patient-Centered Medical Home with Quality of Care, Patient Experience, and Health Expenditures," *Medicine* 100, no. 21 (2021): e26119, https://www.ncbi.nlm.nih.gov/pmc/articles/PMC8154504/pdf/medi-100-e26119.pdf.

18. Anna D. Sinaiko, Mary Beth Landrum, David J. Meyers, et al., "Synthesis of Research on Patient-Centered Medical Homes Brings Systematic Differences into Relief," *Health Affairs* 36, no. 3 (2017): 500–508, https://www.healthaffairs.org/doi/epdf/10.1377/hlthaff.2016.1235.

19. Karen Appold, "Patient-Centered Medical Homes: Were They Built to Last?," *Managed Healthcare Executive* 31, no. 5 (2021), 26–28, https://www.managedhealthcareexecutive.com/view/patient-centered-medical-homes-were-they-built-to-last-/.

20. "Workforce Projections," Health Resources and Services Administration, accessed December 15, 2023, https://data.hrsa.gov/topics/health-workforce/workforce-projections/.

21. Primary Care Collaborative, *Health Is Primary: Charting a Path to Equity and Sustainability* (Washington, DC: Primary Care Collaborative, October 2023).

22. David I. Auerback, Peter L. Buerhaus, and Douglas O. Staiger, "Implications of the Rapid Growth of the Nurse Practitioner Work Force in the US," *Health Affairs* 39, no. 2 (2020): 273–79, https://www.healthaffairs.org/doi/10.1377/hlthaff.2019.00686.

23. Joanne Pohl, Patricia Pittman, Marcy Anslie, Mary Beth Bigley, and Taynin Kopanos, "A Decade of Data: And Update on the Primary Care and Mental Health Nurse Practitioner and Physician Workforce," *Health Affairs Forefront*, September 30, 2023.

24. Linda McCauley, Robert L. Phillips, Marc Meisnere, and Sarah K. Robinson, eds., *Implementing High-Quality Primary Care: Rebuilding the Foundation of Health Care* (Washington, DC: National Academies Press, May 2021).

25. Anna L. Goldman and Michael L. Barnett, "Changes in Physician Work Hours and Implications for Workforce Capacity and Work-Life Balance, 2001–2021,"

JAMA Internal Medicine 183, no. 2 (2023): 106–14, https://jamanetwork.com/journals/jamainternalmedicine/article-abstract/2799541.

26. McCauley et al., *Implementing High-Quality Primary Care.*

27. Diane M. Wohler and Winston Liaw, *Team-Based Primary Care: Opportunities and Challenges* (Washington, DC: Robert Graham Center, 2017), https://www.graham-center.org/content/dam/rgc/documents/publications-reports/reports/Starfield Summit_Report_TeamBasedPrimaryCare.pdf.

28. American Osteopathic Association, *Osteopathic Medical Profession Report* (Chicago: American Osteopathic Association, 2023), https://osteopathic.org/index.php?aam-media=/wp-content/uploads/2023-OMP-Report.pdf.

29. "How IMGs Have Changed the Face of American Medicine," American Medical Association, October 19, 2021, https://www.ama-assn.org/education/international-medical-education/how-imgs-have-changed-face-american-medicine/.

30. Jordan Everson, Nathaniel Hendrix, Robert Phillips, et al. "Primary Care Physicians' Satisfaction with Interoperable Health Information Technology," *JAMA Network Open* 7, no. 3 (2024): e243793, https://jamanetwork.com/journals/jamanetworkopen/fullarticle/2816741.

31. OneCommunity Health Center interviews, May 17, 2023.

32. Discussion with Alan Hutchison, Ryan Foley, and Garrett Adams, primary care team, Epic Systems Corporation, June 12, 2023.

33. Sam Eaquinto, *2023 Best in KLAS Awards: Software and Services* (Pleasant Grove, UT: Klas Research, 2023), https://klasresearch.com/report/2023-best-in-klas-awards-software-and-services/3037.

34. "History of Federal Qualified Health Centers (FQHCs)," *Visualutions*, accessed December 12, 2023, https://www.visualutions.com/blog/the-history-of-federally-qualified-health-centers/.

35. Anna Erickson, "A Policy History of the Community Health Centers Programs: 1965–2022," University of Michigan, Ann Arbor, Michigan, accessed December 12, 2023, http://www-personal.umich.edu/~baileymj/CHC_history.pdf.

36. Sara Rosenbaum, Peter Shin, Jessica Shirac, and Colleen Bedenbaugh, "Community Health Centers and Medicaid: A Deeper Dive into FQHC Alternative Payment Reform," *Health Affairs Forefront*, January 27, 2023, https://www.healthaffairs.org/content/forefront/community-health-centers-and-medicaid-deeper-dive-into-fqhc-alternative-payment-reform.

37. Letter from HPNEC [Health Professions and Nursing Education] to Rosa DeLauro, chair, and Tom Cole, ranking member, House Appropriations Subcommittee on Labor, Health and Human Services, Education, and Related Agencies, and Patty Murray, chair, and Roy Blunt, ranking member, Senate Appropriations Subcommittee on Labor, Health and Human Services, Education, and Related Agencies, March 31, 2021, http://uat.apha.org/-/media/Files/PDF/advocacy/letters/2021/210331_Title_VII_and_VIII_Appropriations.ashx.

38. Ying Xue, Elizabeth Greener, Viji Kannan, et al., "Federally Qualified Health Centers Reduce the Primary Care Provider Gap in Health Professional Shortage

Counties," *Nursing Outlook* 66, no. 3 (2018): 263–72, https://www.nursingoutlook.org/article/S0029-6554(17)30605-X/fulltext/.

39. Caroline Behr, Peter Hull, John Hsu, Joseph P. Newhouse, and Vicki Fung, "Geographic Access to Federally Qualified Health Centers before and after the Affordable Care Act," *BMC Health Services Research* 22, art. 385 (2022): https://bmchealthservres.biomedcentral.com/articles/10.1186/s12913-022-07685-0.

40. "An Overview of Federal Health Center Funding," National Association of Community Health Centers, accessed December 15, 2023, https://www.nachc.org/focus-areas/policy-matters/health-center-funding/federal-grant-funding/.

41. Sara Rosenbaum, Jessica Sharac, Peter Shin, and Jennifer Tolbert, "Community Health Center Financing: The Role of Medicaid and Section 330 Funding Explained," Kaiser Family Foundation, March 26, 2019, https://www.kff.org/medicaid/issue-brief/community-health-center-financing-the-role-of-medicaid-and-section-330-grant-funding-explained/.

42. National Association of Community Health Centers, *Community Health Center Chartbook, 2020* (Bethesda, MD: National Association of Community Health Centers, January 2020), https://www.nachc.org/wp-content/uploads/2020/01/Chartbook-2020-Final.pdf.

43. Martha Hostetter and Sarah Klein, *The Perils and Payoffs of Alternative Payment Models for Community Health Centers* (New York: Commonwealth Fund, January 2022), https://www.commonwealthfund.org/publications/2022/jan/perils-and-payoffs-alternate-payment-models-community-health-centers/.

44. See Troyen A. Brennan, *The Transformation of American Health Insurance: On the Path to Medicare for All* (Baltimore, Johns Hopkins University Press, 2024).

45. Interview with Dr. Alejandro "Alex" Esparza, chief executive officer, Holyoke Health Center, December 3, 2022.

46. Interview with Dr. Monica Liao, chief medical officer, Holyoke Health Center, December 3, 2022.

47. Interview with Dr. Stephanie Billings, Holyoke Health Center, December 3, 2022.

48. Interview with Lisa Connors, chief operating officer, Holyoke Health Center, December 3, 2022.

49. Barbara Starfield, *Primary Care: Concept, Evaluation and Policy* (New York: Oxford University Press, 1992).

50. Thomas Bodenheimer, Amireh Ghorob, Rachel Willard-Grace, and Kevin Grumbach, "The 10 Building Blocks of High-Performing Primary Care," *Annals of Family Medicine* 12, no. 2 (2014): 166–71, https://www.annfammed.org/content/annalsfm/12/2/166.full.pdf.

Chapter 3. What Can the Federal Government Do to Promote Primary Care?

1. Troyen A. Brennan, *The Transformation of American Health Insurance: On the Path to Medicare for All* (Baltimore: Johns Hopkins University Press, 2024).

2. "Workforce Projections," Health Resources and Services Administration, accessed December 14, 2023, https://data.hrsa.gov/topics/health-workforce/workforce-projections/.

3. Ruth Jessen Hickman, "PCP Shortage Affects Hospitalists: What Are the Options?," *The Hospitalist*, August 1, 2023, https://www.the-hospitalist.org/hospitalist/article/35220/practice-management/pcp-shortage-affects-hospitalists-what-are-the-options/.

4. Jim Kinsey, "New Patients Wait Average 205 Days to Get Doctor's Appointment in Franklin County, Topping Massachusetts Survey," *Mass Live*, August 9, 2012, https://www.masslive.com/business-news/2012/08/franklin_county_tops_physician_wait_time.html.

5. Marco A. Villagrana, *Medicare Graduate Medical Education Payments: An Overview*, IF10960 (Washington, DC: Congressional Research Service, updated September 29, 2022), https://crsreports.congress.gov/product/pdf/IF/IF10960.

6. Villagrana, *Medicare Graduate Medical Education Payments*.

7. Medicare Payment Advisory Committee (MedPAC), *Report to the Congress: Aligning Incentives in Medicare* (Washington, DC: MedPAC, June 2010), https://www.medpac.gov/wp-content/uploads/import_data/scrape_files/docs/default-source/reports/Jun10_EntireReport.pdf.

8. Justin A. Grischkan, Ari B. Friedman, and Amitabh Chandra, "Moving the Financing of Graduate Medical Education into the 21st Century," *JAMA* 324, no. 11 (2020): 1035–36, https://jamanetwork.com/journals/jama/fullarticle/2770076.

9. Robert Orr, "Federal Policy Misallocates American Doctors," Niskanen Center, February 1, 2023, https://www.niskanencenter.org/federal-policy-misallocates-american-doctors/.

10. Linda McCauley, Robert L. Phillips, Marc Meisnere, and Sarah K. Robinson, eds., *Implementing High-Quality Primary Care: Rebuilding the Foundation of Health Care* (Washington, DC: National Academies Press, May 2021), 207.

11. Accreditation Council for Graduate Medical Education, *ACGME Program Requirements for Graduate Medical Education in Family Medicine* (Chicago: Accreditation Council for Graduate Medical Education, June 12, 2022), https://www.acgme.org/globalassets/pfassets/programrequirements/120_familymedicine_2022.pdf.

12. "What Hospitals Need to Know about the New Graduate Medical Education Legislation," PYA [formerly Pershing and Yoakley, CPAs], March 9, 2022, https://www.pyapc.com/insights/what-hospitals-need-to-know-about-the-new-graduate-medical-education-legislation/.

13. "CMS Awards 200 New Medicare-Funded Residency Slots to Hospitals Serving Underserved Communities," news release, Centers for Medicare and Medicaid Services, January 9, 2023, https://www.cms.gov/newsroom/press-releases/cms-awards-200-new-medicare-funded-residency-slots-hospitals-serving-underserved-communities/.

14. "H.R. 238—Resident Physician Shortage Reduction Act of 2023," Congress.gov, accessed December 14, 2023, https://www.congress.gov/bill/118th-congress/house-bill/2389?s=1&r=22.

15. "Match by the Numbers," in "2023 Main Residency Match," The Match: National Resident Matching Program, accessed December 23, 2024, https://www.nrmp.org/match-data-analytics/residency-data-reports/.

16. Philip Gruppuso and Eli Adashi, "The Fair Access in Residency (FAIR) Act Takes Aim but Misses Its Mark," *Health Affairs Forefront*, January 31, 2024. https://www.healthaffairs.org/content/forefront/fair-access-residency-fair-act-takes-aim-but-misses-mark?utm_medium=social&utm_source=facebook&utm_campaign=forefront&utm_content=gruppuso.

17. "Quick Facts," American Association of Colleges of Osteopathic Medicine, accessed December 14, 2023, https://www.aacom.org/become-a-doctor/about-osteopathic-medicine/quick-facts/.

18. Atsushi Miyawaki, Anupam B. Jena, Nate Gross, and Yusuke Tsugawa, "Comparison of Hospital Outcomes for Patients Treated by Allopathic versus Osteopathic Hospitalists," *Annals of Internal Medicine* 176, no. 6 (2023): 798–806, https://www.acpjournals.org/doi/10.7326/M22-3723.

19. "Advocacy in Action: Clearing IMGs' Route to Practice," American Medical Association, updated June 7, 2023, https://www.ama-assn.org/education/international-medical-education/advocacy-action-clearing-imgs-route-practice#:~:text=The%20number%20of%20IMGs%20practicing,populated%20specialty%20among%20these%20individuals/.

20. Robbert J. Duvivier, Elizabeth Wiley, and John Boulet, "Supply, Distribution and Characteristics of International Medical Graduates in Family Medicine in the United States: A Cross-Sectional Study," *BMC Family Practice* 20, art. 47 (2019): https://bmcprimcare.biomedcentral.com/articles/10.1186/s12875-019-0933-8/.

21. Yusuke Tsugawa, Anupam B. Jena, E. John Orav, and Ashish K. Jha, "Quality of Care Delivered by General Internists in US Hospitals Who Graduated from Foreign versus US Medical Schools: Observational Study," *British Medical Journal* 356 (2017): j273, https://www.ncbi.nlm.nih.gov/pmc/articles/PMC5415101.

22. "Performance Data," United States Medical Licensure Exam, accessed September 30, 2023, https://www.usmle.org/performance-data.

23. Interview with Dr. Andrew Sussman, chief executive officer, Medforth, June 10, 2023.

24. Tarun Ramesh, Marcela Horvitz-Lennon, and Hao Yu, "Opening the Door Wider to International Medical Graduates—The Significance of a New Tennessee Law," *New England Journal of Medicine* 389, no. 21 (2023): https://www.nejm.org/doi/full/10.1056/NEJMp2310001.

25. Edward S. Salsberg and Candice Chen, "Graduate Medical Education Positions and Physician Supply Continue to Increase: Implications of the 2021 Residency Match," *Health Affairs Forefront*, May 21, 2021, https://www.healthaffairs

.org/content/forefront/graduate-medical-education-positions-and-physician-supply-continue-increase/.

26. US Department of Health and Human Services, *Fiscal Year 2023 Health Resources and Services Administration: Justification of Estimates for Appropriations Committee* (Washington, DC: US Department of Health and Human Services, 2022), https://www.hrsa.gov/sites/default/files/hrsa/about/budget/budget-justification-fy2023.pdf.

27. Robert L. Phillips and Barbara J. Turner, "The Next Phase of Title VII Funding for Training Primary Care Physicians for America's Health Care Needs," *Annals of Family Medicine* 10, no. 2 (2012): 163–68, https://www.ncbi.nlm.nih.gov/pmc/articles/PMC3315144/pdf/0100163.pdf.

28. Institute of Medicine, *Graduate Medical Education That Meets the Nation's Health Needs* (Washington, DC: National Academies Press, July 2014), https://nap.nationalacademies.org/resource/18754/GME-REC.pdf.

29. Caitlin Smith Davis, Tuhin Roy, Lars E. Peterson, and Andrew W. Bazemore, "Evaluating the Teaching Health Center Graduate Medical Education Model at 10 Years: Practice-Based Outcomes and Opportunities," *Journal of Graduate Medical Education* 14, no. 5 (2022): 599–605, https://meridian.allenpress.com/jgme/article/14/5/599/487458/Evaluating-the-Teaching-Health-Center-Graduate/.

30. Health Resources and Services Administration, *Report to Congress: Teaching Health Center Graduate Medical Education Direct and Indirect Training Expenses Report* (Washington, DC: US Department of Health and Human Services, 2019), https://bhw.hrsa.gov/sites/default/files/bureau-health-workforce/about-us/reports-to-congress/report-to-congress-thcgme-2019.pdf.

31. Vinaya Gogineni, Wendy Barr, and Robert Phillips, "Community-Based Primary Care Training Is Threatened by Funding Instability, *Health Affairs Forefront*, April 16, 2024. https://www.healthaffairs.org/content/forefront/future-community-based-primary-care-training-threatened-funding-instability.

32. "Summary of the Bipartisan Primary Care and Health Workforce Act," Office of Senator Bernie Sanders, September 14, 2023, https://www.sanders.senate.gov/wp-content/uploads/Bipartisan-Primary-Care-and-Health-Workforce-Act-Summary_09.14.2023.pdf.

33. Leighton Ku and Sara Rosenbaum, "CBO Score for the Bipartisan Primary Care and Health Workforce Act Recognizes the Value of Primary Care Health Investments," *Health Affairs Forefront*, March 21, 2024, https://www.healthaffairs.org/content/forefront/cbo-score-bipartisan-primary-care-and-health-workforce-act-recognizes-value-primary.

34. US Department of Health and Human Services, *Health Workforce Strategic Plan 2021* (Washington, DC: US Department of Health and Human Services, 2021), https://bhw.hrsa.gov/sites/default/files/bureau-health-workforce/about-us/hhs-health-workforce-strategic-plan-2021.pdf.

35. Institute of Medicine, *Graduate Medical Education*.

36. Sadiq Y. Patel, David Auerbach, Haiden A. Huskamp, et al., "Provision of Evaluation and Management Visits by Nurse Practitioners and Physician Assistants in the USA from 2013 to 2019: Cross-Sectional Time Series Study," *British Medical Journal* 382 (2023): e073933, https://www.bmj.com/content/382/bmj-2022-073933.

37. Chuan-Fen Liu, Paul L. Hebert, Jamie H. Douglas, et al., "Outcomes of Primary Care Delivery by Nurse Practitioners: Utilization, Cost, and Quality of Care," *Health Services Research* 55, no. 2 (2020): 178–89, https://www.ncbi.nlm.nih.gov/pmc/articles/PMC7080399.

38. "Nurse Practitioner Profession Grows to 385,000 Strong," American Association of Nurse Practitioners News, November 13, 2023, https://www.aanp.org/news-feed/nurse-practitioner-profession-grows-to-385-000-strong/.

39. Joanne M. Pohl, Patricia Pittman, Marcy Anslie, Mary Beth Bigley, and Taynin Kopanos, "A Decade of Data: An Update on the Primary Care and Mental Health Nurse Practitioner and Physician Workforce," *Health Affairs Forefront*, September 20, 2023, https://www.healthaffairs.org/content/forefront/decade-data-update-primary-care-and-mental-health-nurse-practitioner-and-physician/.

40. Interview with Dr. John Schneeweiss, medical director, Reliant Medical Group–Leominster, January 9, 2023.

41. Dr. Schneeweiss was clear that being a clinician at Reliant is a challenging job. The patients' needs are complex, as the simple stuff is taken care of by protocols or care teams. For example, for a patient with hypertension, he will send them home with a blood-pressure cuff and titrated medications, based on MyChart exchanges. If he were a full-time clinician (some of his time is devoted to administration), he would be in at five o'clock in the morning and remain there until seven o'clock in the evening. Their EMR system, as it is everywhere, is a blessing and a curse: "It comes at you like a Gatling gun," which in turn leaves clinicians with a reasonable amount of "pajama time" (administrative tasks done after hours or at home). A clinician currently cannot possibly see 20 patients a day, since the easy patients are taken care of by protocols and the sick are very sick.

For someone who decidedly styles himself as "old school," he liked Optum and what they are trying to do. According to Schneeweiss, after Reliant spent $180 million on building construction, they were headed toward bankruptcy. Then Optum stepped in. The buildings are great, and Optum has standardized some administrative functions but has not interfered with patient care. At first it was a hard sell, but Optum has kept its promises. Schneeweiss appreciated that Optum is not buying hospitals: "Hospitals are toxic."

The Reliant doctors have a minimal amount of time being on call and no hospital rounds. Schneeweiss made rounds for 20 years, but now this is all done by hospitalists. He does not miss the unpredictability of having four to eight patients in the hospital.

42. I asked Schneeweiss, "How do we expand primary care?" He responded that an adequate salary for its physicians is necessary but not sufficient in and of itself. Doctors also must undertake lifestyle changes. Similar to most older physicians,

younger people's insistence on having a work/life balance bothered him. But people need help with the rapid fire of a current primary care practice. And policymakers must recognize that primary care deals with a lot of irresolvable issues. Schneeweiss believed that Optum had the right idea, since one-third of today's health care is wasted. So, he argued, get rid of the waste, take some profit, and reform primary care.

I asked him to give me an example of managing health care waste, and he chose a cogent one: an 83-year-old man with chronic lymphocytic leukemia (cancer of the blood and bone marrow), dementia, congestive heart failure, and chronic kidney failure, all of which were severe. An evaluation of this patient's congestive heart failure found that he had a cardiac ejection rate (indicating how well a heart is pumping) of 28%. For an average patient, guidelines would recommend implanting a cardioverter-defibrillator. Schneeweiss's view was that given this patient's overall condition, the procedure did not make sense, but a cardiologist convinced the man's family to go ahead with it. Soon thereafter, the patient died of pneumonia. According to Schneeweiss, "No one was looking at where the train was headed."

Schneeweiss shoots straight, but he is not gruff. He was gratified by his patients: 100 three-generation families, and 10 four-generation families. He recounted that statistic with genuine pride and real joy. Nonetheless, he could not be optimistic about recruiting others to enjoy this kind of practice. Rather, the lack of new doctors was a problem to be worked around, not one that could be solved.

43. Interviews with Kelli Locke, Athena Crowley, and Lauren Katz, nurse practitioners, Reliant Medical Group–Leominster, January 9, 2023.

44. Congressional Budget Office, *Federal Budgetary Effects of the Activities of the Center for Medicare and Medicaid Innovation* (Washington, DC: Congressional Budget Office, September 2023), https://www.cbo.gov/publication/59612.

45. McCauley et al., *Implementing High-Quality Primary Care*, 297.

46. "Independent Evaluation of Comprehensive Primary Care Plus (CPC+): Fourth Annual Report," Mathematica, May 17, 2022, https://www.mathematica.org/publications/independent-evaluation-of-the-comprehensive-primary-care-plus-cpc-fourth-annual-report/.

47. Adam A. Markovitz, Roslyn C. Murray, and Andrew M. Ryan, "Comprehensive Primary Care Plus Did Not Improve Quality or Lower Spending for the Privately Insured," *Health Affairs* 41, no. 9 (2022): 362–68, https://www.healthaffairs.org/doi/abs/10.1377/hlthaff.2021.01982.

48. Praya Singh, Ning Fu, Stacy Dale, et al., "The Comprehensive Primary Care Plus Model and Health Care Spending, Service Use, and Quality," *JAMA* 331, no. 2 (2023): 132-46, https://jamanetwork.com/journals/jama/fullarticle/2813197.

49. McCauley et al., *Implementing High-Quality Primary Care*, 300.

50. "Making Care Primary (MCP) Model," Centers for Medicare and Medicaid Services, June 8, 2023, https://innovation.cms.gov/innovation-models/making-care-primary?utm_source=newsletter&utm_medium=email&utm_campaign=newsletter_axiosvitals&stream=top/.

51. John Ayanian, "Transforming Primary Care through Innovations in Primary Care," *JAMA* 4, no. 12 (2023): e235071, https://jamanetwork.com/journals/jama-health-forum/fullarticle/2813266.

52. Tianna Tu, David Muhlestein, S. Lawrence Kocot, and Ross White, *Origins and Future of Accountable Care Organizations* (Washington, DC: Brookings Institution, May 2015), https://www.brookings.edu/wp-content/uploads/2016/06/impact-of-accountable-careorigins-052015.pdf.

53. William K. Bleser, Frank McStay, David Muhlestein, and Mark B. McClellan, "Accountable Care in 2023: Evolving Terminology, Current State, and Priorities," *Health Affairs Forefront*, February 24, 2023, https://www.healthaffairs.org/content/forefront/accountable-care-2023-evolving-terminology-current-state-and-priorities/.

54. J. Michael McWilliams, Laura A. Hatfield, Bruce E. Landon, Pasha Hamed, and Michael E. Chernew, "Medicare Spending after 3 Years of the Medicare Shared Savings Program," *New England Journal of Medicine* 379, no. 12 (2018): 1139–46, https://www.nejm.org/doi/full/10.1056/nejmsa1803388.

55. Annette Dubard, Joshua Israel, and Farzad Mostashari, "Less Is More: Quality Measurement in Primary Care," *Health Affairs Forefront,* June 15, 2023, https://www.healthaffairs.org/content/forefront/less-more-quality-measurement-primary-care.

56. Robert Phillips and Rebecca Etz, "CMS's Universal Foundation Measures Are Not Universally Good for Primary Care," *Health Affairs Forefront*, May 8, 2023, https://www.healthaffairs.org/content/forefront/cms-s-universal-foundation-measures-not-universally-good-primary-care.

57. Congressional Budget Office, *Medicare Accountable Care Organizations: Past Performance and Future Directions* (Washington, DC: Congressional Budget Office, April 2024), https://www.cbo.gov/publication/59879.

58. Interview with Dr. Jason VanGundy, chairman of the primary care group, SSM Health–Lake St. Louis, October 12, 2022.

59. Interview with Candy Guern, regional clinical manager, SSM Health, October 12, 2022.

60. Interview with Nicole Vetter, nurse practitioner, SSM Health–Nashville October 13, 2022.

61. Interview with Dr. Michael Kirk, SSM Health–Columbia, October 14, 2022.

62. Interview with Jayceen Ensrude, vice president of operations, SSM Health–St. Louis regional headquarters, October 14, 2022.

63. Interview with Dr. Kalyan Katakam, SSM Health–St. Louis regional headquarters, October 14, 2022.

64. Joshua Liao and Amol Navathe, "Distinctive Features in the Making Care Primary Model," *Health Affairs Forefront*, August 21, 2023, https://www.healthaffairs.org/content/forefront/distinctive-features-making-care-primary-model.

65. "Issue Brief: HHS Is Taking Action to Strengthen Primary Care," Department of Health and Human Services, November 7, 2023, https://www.hhs.gov/blog/2023/11/07/us-department-health-and-human-services-taking-action-strengthen-primary-care.html.

66. McCauley et al., *Implementing High-Quality Primary Care*, 302.

67. In the next few paragraphs, I generally follow a review of the history of Medicare's control of physicians' rates of payment. See my *Transformation of American Health Insurance*.

68. William C. Hsiao, Pewter Braun, Nancy L. Kelly, and Edmund R. Becker, "Results, Potential Effects, and Implementation Issues of the Resource-Based Relative Value Scale," *JAMA* 260, no. 16 (1988): 2429–38, https://jamanetwork.com/journals/jama/article-abstract/374679.

69. David C. Chan, Johnny Huynh, and David M. Studdert, "Accuracy of Valuations of Surgical Procedures in the Medicare Fee Schedule," *New England Journal of Medicine* 380, no. 16 (2019): 1546–54, https://www.nejm.org/doi/full/10.1056/NEJMsa1807379.

70. John W. Urwin, Emily Gudbranson, Danielle Graham, et al., "Accuracy of the Relative Value Scale Update Committee's Time Estimates and Physician Fee Schedule for Joint Replacement," *Health Affairs* 38, no. 7 (2019): 1079–86, https://www.healthaffairs.org/doi/abs/10.1377/hlthaff.2018.05456.

71. McCauley et al., *Implementing High-Quality Primary Care*, 286–88.

72. McCauley et al., *Implementing High-Quality Primary Care*, 287.

73. Robert A. Berenson and John D. Goodson, "Finding Value in Unexpected Places—Fixing the Medicare Physician Fee Schedule," *New England Journal of Medicine* 374, no. 14 (2016): 1306–9, https://www.nejm.org/doi/full/10.1056/NEJMp1600999.

74. Maya Goldman, "Fight over Medicare Pay Hinges on Primary Care," Axios, September 18, 2023, https://www.axios.com/2023/09/18/primary-care-medicare-doctor-pay/.

75. "College Joins Fight against Implementation of G2211 Code," *ACS Brief*, August 1, 2023, https://www.facs.org/for-medical-professionals/news-publications/news-and-articles/acs-brief/august-1-2023-issue/college-joins-fight-against-implementation-of-g2211-code/#:~:text=The%20ACS%2C%20with%2018%20other,and%20negatively%20affect%20surgical%20patients/.

76. Stephanie Quinn, "The Simple Truth about Primary Care's Complexity," in "CMS Releases Proposed 2024 Medicare Physician Fee Schedule," *ACP Advocate*, August 11, 2023, https://www.acponline.org/advocacy/acp-advocate/archive/august-11-2023/cms-releases-proposed-2024-medicare-physician-fee-schedule.

77. Hannah T. Neprash, Ezra Golberstein, Ishani Ganjuli, and Michael E. Chernew, "Association of Evaluation and Management Payment Policy Changes with Medicare Payment to Physicians by Specialty," *JAMA* 329, no. 8 (2023): 662–69, https://jamanetwork.com/journals/jama/fullarticle/2801848.

78. Corinne Lewis, Melinda Abrams, Christopher Koller, Hongmai Pham, and Robert Berenson, "How Congress Can Strengthen Primary Care through Payment Reform," *Commonwealth Fund* (blog), March 27, 2023, https://www.commonwealthfund.org/blog/2023/how-congress-can-strengthen-primary-care-through-medicare-payment-reform.

79. Robert Berenson and Kevin Hayes, "The Road to Value Cannot Be Paved with a Broken Medicare Physician Fee Schedule, *Health Affairs* 43, no. 7 (2024): 950–58, https://www.healthaffairs.org/doi/10.1377/hlthaff.2024.00299?url_ver=Z39.88-2003&rfr_id=ori%3Arid%3Acrossref.org&rfr_dat=cr_pub++0pubmed.

80. Laurence McMahon and Zirui Song, "Rebuilding the Relative Value Unit-Based Physician Payment System," *JAMA* 332, no. 5 (2024): 369-70, https://jamanetwork.com/journals/jama/fullarticle/2820915.

81. Indian Self-Determination and Education Assistance Act of 1975, Pub. L. No. 93-638 (1975).

82. Interview with Melissa Merrick, executive vice president for primary care, Southcentral Foundation, October 4, 2022.

83. Interview with David Fenn, health program analyst, and Steve Tierney, chief medical informatics officer, Southcentral Foundation, October 4, 2022.

84. Interview with Jerry Markus, director of operations, Southcentral Foundation, October 5, 2022.

85. Interview with Chelsea Ryan and Rona Johnston, nurses, Southcentral Foundation, October 4, 2022.

86. Interview with April Kyle, chief executive officer, Southcentral Foundation, October 5, 2022.

87. "Evidence for Fentanyl Test Strips," Centers for Disease Control and Prevention, September 13, 2023, https://harmreductionhelp.cdc.gov/s/article/Evidence-for-Fentanyl-Test-Strips/.

88. Interview with Dr. Verlyn Corbett, primary care medical director, Southcentral Foundation, October 5, 2022.

89. Interview with Dr. David Lessers, Southcentral Foundation October 5, 2022.

90. Interview with Dr. Doug Eby, Southcentral Foundation, September 23, 2022.

91. Sanjay Basu, Russell Phillips, Zirui Song, Asaf Bitton, and Bruce Landon, "High Levels of Capitation Payment Needed to Shift Primary Care toward ProActive Team and Nonvisit Care," *Health Affairs* 36, no. 9 (2017): https://www.healthaffairs.org/doi/full/10.1377/hlthaff.2017.0367.

92. Candace Chen, YoonKyung Chung, Stephen Petterson, et al., "Changes and Variation in Medicare Graduate Medical Education Payments, *JAMA Internal Medicine* 180, no. 1 (2020): 148–50, https://jamanetwork.com/journals/jamainternalmedicine/fullarticle/2752363.

93. "New Grant from VA Supports Fresh Look at Primary Care Training," *Medicine@Yale* (March/April 2011): https://medicine.yale.edu/news/medicineatyale/article/new-grant-from-va-supports-a-fresh-look/.

94. Congressional Budget Office, *Federal Budgetary Effects of the Activities of the Center for Medicare & Medicaid Innovation* (Washington, DC: Congressional Budget Office, September 2023), https://www.cbo.gov/system/files/2023-09/59274-CMMI.pdf.

95. Marilena DeGennaro, "CMMI Prioritizes Multi-Payer Alignment in New Models," National Committee for Quality Assurance, October 31, 2023, https://www.ncqa.org/blog/cmmi-prioritizes-multi-payer-alignment-in-new-models/.

96. Daniel Bowling, Barak Richman, and Kevin Schulman, "The Rise and Potential of Physician Unions," *JAMA* 328, no. 7 (2022): 617–18, https://jamanetwork.com/journals/jama/fullarticle/2794951.

97. "ARC Issue Brief: Collective Bargaining for Physicians and Physicians-in-Training," American Medical Association Advocacy Resource Center, accessed December 19, 2023, https://www.ama-assn.org/system/files/advocacy-issue-brief-physician-unions.pdf.

Chapter 4. The States' Role in Primary Care Reform

1. Howard Haft and Craig Jones, *Considerations for Statewide Advanced Primary Care Programs* (New York: Milbank Memorial Fund, March 2024), https://www.milbank.org/publications/considerations-for-statewide-advanced-primary-care-programs/.

2. Julia Paradise, Barbara Lyon, and Diane Rowland, *Medicaid at 50* (Menlo Park, CA: Kaiser Family Foundation, May 2015), https://files.kff.org/attachment/report-medicaid-at-50/.

3. Public Health and Welfare, 42 U.S.C. §1369 (May 29, 2003).

4. Troyen A. Brennan, *The Transformation of American Health Insurance: On the Path to Medicare for All* (Baltimore: Johns Hopkins University Press, 2024); Cindy Mann and Deborah Bachrach, "Medicaid as Health Insurer: Evolution and Implications," *To the Point* (blog), July 23, 2015, https://www.commonwealthfund.org/blog/2015/medicaid-health-insurer-evolution-and-implications/.

5. Anthony Albanese, "The Past, Present, and Future of Section 1115: Learning from History to Improve the Medicaid-Waiver Regime Today," *Yale Law Journal* 128 (2018–19): 827–47, https://www.yalelawjournal.org/forum/the-past-present-and-future-of-section-1115.

6. Benjamin D. Sommers, Lucy Chen, Robert J. Blendon, John Gray, and Arnold M. Epstein, "Medicaid Work Requirements in Arkansas: Two-Year Impacts on Coverage, Employment, and Affordability of Care," *Health Affairs* 39, no. 9 (2020): 1522–30, https://www.healthaffairs.org/doi/full/10.1377/hlthaff.2020.00538.

7. Andy Schneider, "Overview of Medicaid Managed Care Provisions in the Balanced Budget Act of 1997—Report," Kaiser Family Foundation, November 29, 1997, https://www.kff.org/medicaid/report/overview-of-medicaid-managed-care-provisions-in-2/.

8. Sara Rosenbaum, Alexander Somodevilla, Maria Casoni, and MaryBeth Musumeci, "Inside the Administration's Proposed Medicaid Managed Care Rule: Steering a Behemoth," *Health Affairs Forefront* (blog), June 15, 2023, https://www.healthaffairs.org/content/forefront/inside-administration-s-proposed-medicaid-managed-care-rule-steering-behemoth/.

9. Elizabeth Hinton and Jada Raphasel, "10 Things to Know about Medicaid Managed Care," Kaiser Family Foundation, updated March 1, 2023, https://www.kff.org/medicaid/issue-brief/10-things-to-know-about-medicaid-managed-care/.

10. Stephen Zuckerman, Laura Skopec, and Joshua Aarons, "Medicaid Physician Fees Remained Substantially below Fees Paid by Medicare in 2019," *Health Affairs* 40, no. 2 (2021): 343–48, https://www.healthaffairs.org/doi/abs/10.1377/hlthaff.2020.00611.

11. US Government Accountability Office (GAO), *Medicaid Payment: Comparisons of Selected Services under Fee-for-Service, Managed Care, and Private Insurance* (Washington, DC: GAO, July 2014), https://www.gao.gov/assets/670/664782.pdf.

12. Kayla Holgash and Martha Heberlein, "Physician Acceptance of New Medicaid Patients: What Matters and What Doesn't," *Health Affairs Forefront* (blog), April 10, 2019, https://www.healthaffairs.org/do/10.1377/hblog20190401.678690/full/.

13. Rosenbaum et al., "Inside the Administration's Proposed Medicaid."

14. Rajaie Batniji and William H. Shrank, "Value Veneers and How to Enable Value in Medicaid Care Delivery," *Health Affairs Forefront* (blog), June 23, 2023, https://www.healthaffairs.org/content/forefront/value-veneers-and-enable-value-medicaid-care-delivery/.

15. Amy Goldstein, "Why Vermont's Single-Payer Effort Failed and What Democrats Can Learn from It," *Washington Post*, April 29, 2019, https://www.washingtonpost.com/national/health-science/why-vermonts-single-payer-effort-failed-and-what-democrats-can-learn-from-it/2019/04/29/c9789018-3ab8-11e9-a2cd-307b06d0257b_story.html.

16. "History," in "1115 Waiver Documents," State of Vermont, Agency of Human Services, accessed December 12, 2023, https://humanservices.vermont.gov/about-us/medicaid-administration/global-commitment-health-1115-waiver/1115-waiver-documents/.

17. Craig Jones, Karl Finison, Katharine McGraves-Lloyd, et al., "Vermont's Community Oriented All-Payer Medical Home Model Reduces Expenditures and Utilization while Delivering High Quality Care," *Population Health Management* 19, no. 3 (2016): 196–206, https://blueprintforhealth.vermont.gov/sites/bfh/files/Blueprint%20Journal%20Article%20-%20Vermont%27s%20Community-Oriented%20All-Payer%20Medical%20Home%20Model%20Reduces%20Expenditures%20and%20Utilization%20While%20Delivering%20%20High-Quality%20Care.pdf.

18. Interview with Anya Wallach, senior vice president, University of Vermont Health Network, August 30, 2022.

19. "About GMCB," State of Vermont, Green Mountain Care Board, accessed December 12, 2023, https://gmcboard.vermont.gov/board/.

20. Interview with Tom Borys, vice president of finance, OneCare Vermont, October 7, 2022, and April 17, 2023.

21. Discussions with Blueprint for Health staff members: Kathleen "Katie" Bocchino, population health project manager, July 29, 2022; Laura Ruggles, vice president of marketing and community health improvement, August 3, 2022; and Julie Parker, assistant director, August 10, 2022.

22. Discussion by telephone with Dr. Laura Newell, Northeastern Vermont Regional Hospital, August 8, 2022.

23. Discussions with Shawn Tester, chief executive officer, and Michael Rousse, chief medical officer, Northeastern Vermont Regional Hospital, November 11, 2022.

24. John H. Knowles, *Doing Better and Feeling Worse: Health in the United States* (New York: Norton, 1977).

25. Interviews with Dr. Irene Krechetoff and Dr. Thomas Myrter, Kingdom Internal Medicine, November 11, 2022.

26. Discussion with Dr. Reija Rawle, private practice, December 15, 2022.

27. Interview with Dr. Kim Fodor, Southeastern Vermont Medical Center, December 15, 2022.

28. Laura Joszt, "Vermont All-Payer ACO Successfully Drove Down Costs, Acute Care over 4 Years, *American Journal of Managed Care*, August 11, 2023, https://www.ajmc.com/view/vermont-all-payer-aco-successfully-drove-down-costs-acute-care-over-4-years.

29. Sandra L. Decker and Samuel H. Zuvekas, "Primary Care Spending in the United States Population," *JAMA Internal Medicine* 183, no. 8 (2023): 880–81, https://jamanetwork.com/journals/jamainternalmedicine/article-abstract/2805979.

30. Rachel Block, "Rhode Island's Updated Affordability Standards Support Behavioral Health and Alternative Payment Models," *Milbank Memorial Fund*, June 23, 2020, https://www.milbank.org/news/rhode-islands-updated-affordability-standards-to-support-behavioral-health-and-alternative-payment-models/.

31. Aaron Baum, Zirui Song, Bruce E. Landon, Russell S. Phillips, Asaf Bitton, and Sanjay Basu, "Health Care Spending Slowed after Rhode Island Applied Affordability Standards to Commercial Insurers," *Health Affairs* 38, no. 2 (2019): 237–45, https://www.healthaffairs.org/doi/epdf/10.1377/hlthaff.2018.05164.

32. Office of the Health Insurance Commissioner, *Rhode Island Commercial Insurance Enrollment* (Cranston, RI: Office of the Health Insurance Commissioner, September 2013), https://ohic.ri.gov/sites/g/files/xkgbur736/files/documents/Commercial-Insurance-Enrollment-General-Sept-2013.pdf; "Health Insurance Coverage of the Total Population," in "State Health Facts, Timeframe 2022," Kaiser Family Foundation, accessed November 5, 2024, https://www.kff.org/other/state-indicator/total-population/?dataView=0&currentTimeframe=0&sortModel=%7B%22colId%22:%22Location%22,%22sort%22:%22asc%22%7D.

33. Office of the Health Insurance Commissioner, *Primary Care Spending Data Update* (Cranston, RI: Office of the Health Insurance Commissioner, June 2020), https://ohic.ri.gov/sites/g/files/xkgbur736/files/documents/2020/June/Primary-Care-Expenditure-Data-Update-June-2020.pdf.

34. Gorman Actuarial, *Rhode Island Market Summary Based on 2022 Rate Filing Submissions as of October 15, 2021* (Marlborough, MA: Gorman Actuarial, 2021), https://ohic.ri.gov/sites/g/files/xkgbur736/files/2022-05/RI-Market-Summary-from-Rate-Filing-Data-20211015.pdf.

35. Office of the Health Insurance Commissioner, *Primary Care in Rhode Island: Current Status and Policy Recommendations* (Cranston, RI: Office of the Health Insurance Commissioner, December 2023), https://ohic.ri.gov/sites/g/files/xkgbur736/files/2023-12/Primary%20Care%20in%20Rhode%20Island%20-%20Current%20Status%20and%20Policy%20Recommendations%20December%202023.pdf.

36. Interview with Luis Echeverria Jr., practice manager, Coastal Medical, November 4, 2022.

37. Dr. Kristen Hubbard, Coastal Medical, November 4, 2022.

38. Amy Russo, "Finding a Primary Care Doctor in Rhode Island Is Getting More Difficult: Here's Why," *Providence Journal*, February 8, 2023, https://www.providencejournal.com/story/news/healthcare/2023/02/08/primary-care-doctor-shortage-in-ri/69843973007.

39. Christopher Koller, "Improving Primary Care Access When You Cannot Wait for Policy Change," Milbank Memorial Fund, March 22, 2024, https://www.milbank.org/2024/03/improving-primary-care-access-when-you-cant-wait-for-policy-change/.

40. Brennan, *Transformation of American Health Insurance*, chap. 7.

41. Rachel Gershon, Robert Seifert, Rebecca Elliott, and Lisa Braude, *The MassHealth Proposed Demonstration Extension 2022–2027: Building on Success, Focusing on Equity* (Boston: Blue Cross Blue Shield of Massachusetts Foundation, June 2022), https://www.bluecrossmafoundation.org/sites/g/files/csphws2101/files/2022-06/MH_Demonstration_Extenson_Jun22_FINAL_0.pdf.

42. University of Massachusetts Medical School, *Draft Independent Evaluation Interim Report, Massachusetts Medicaid 1115 Demonstration Extension 2017–2022* (Worcester: UMass Medical School, August 2021), https://www.mass.gov/doc/1115-demonstration-interim-evaluation-report/download/.

43. Catherine L. Hersey and Nate Wiecha, "Medicaid ACOs and Managed Care: A Tale of 2 Cities," *American Journal of Accountable Care* 10, no. 3 (2022): 28–33, https://www.ajmc.com/view/medicaid-acos-and-managed-care-a-tale-of-2-states/.

44. Medicaid and CHIP Payment and Access Commission (MACPAC), *Medicaid Managed Care Capitation Rate Setting* (Washington, DC: MACPAC, March 2022), https://www.macpac.gov/wp-content/uploads/2022/03/Managed-care-capitation-issue-brief.pdf.

45. Arlene S. Ash and Eric Mick, *UMass Risk Adjustment Project for MassHealth Payment and Care Delivery Reform: Describing the 2017 Payment Model* (Worcester: UMass Medical School, October 2016), https://www.mass.gov/doc/umass-modeling-sdh-summary-report-3/download/.

46. Amol S. Navathe, Ezekiel J. Emanuel, Amelia Bond, et al., "Association between the Implementation of a Population-Based Primary Care Payment System and Achievement on Quality Measures in Hawaii," *JAMA* 322, no. 1 (2019): 57–68, https://jamanetwork.com/journals/jama/fullarticle/2737174.

47. Erin Taylor, Michael Bailit, and Jennifer Sayles, *Prospective Payment for Primary Care: Lessons for Future Models* (New York: Milbank Memorial Fund,

September 2020), https://www.milbank.org/wp-content/uploads/2020/09/LessonforFutureModels_Bailit_v4.pdf.

48. Sanjay Basu, Russell S. Phillips, Zirui Song, Asaf Bitton, and Bruce E. Landon, "High Levels of Capitation Payments Needed to Shift Primary Care toward Proactive Team and Nonvisit Care," *Health Affairs* 36, no. 9 (2017): 422–32, https://www.healthaffairs.org/doi/10.1377/hlthaff.2017.0367.

49. Justin Markowski, Jacob Wallace, Mark Schlesinger, and Chima Ndumele, "Alternative Payment Models and Performance in Federally Qualified Health Centers," *JAMA Internal Medicine* 184, no. 9 (2024): 1065-73, https://jamanetwork.com/journals/jamainternalmedicine/article-abstract/2821079.

50. Discussion with Dr. Kiame Mahaniah, formerly with Lynn Community Health Center, June 30, 2022.

51. Interview with Dr. Geoffrey Pechinsky, chief medical officer, Lynn Community Health Center, December 2, 2022.

52. Interview with Dr. Clark Van Den Berghe, Lynn Community Health Center, December 2, 2022.

53. Interview with Dr. Brian Faherty, Lynn Community Health Center, December 2, 2022.

54. Wendy Warring, "Integrating Behavioral Health in Primary Care: Overcoming Decades of Challenges," *Health Affairs Forefront* (blog), May 17, 2023, https://www.healthaffairs.org/content/forefront/integrating-behavioral-health-primary-care-overcoming-decades-challenges/.

55. Interview with Dr. Roopa Chari, Lynn Community Health Center, December 3, 2022.

56. Interview with Dr. Elizabeth Quinn, Lynn Community Health Center, December 3, 2022.

57. Interview with Ryan Griffin, advanced practice registered nurse, Lynn Community Health Center, December 3, 2022.

58. Jonathan Oberlander, "Health Reform Interrupted: The Unraveling of the Oregon Health Plan," *Health Affairs* 25, suppl. 1 (2006): w96–105, https://www.healthaffairs.org/doi/epdf/10.1377/hlthaff.26.1.w96.

59. Nicole Rapfogel and Natasha Murphy, *How States' Heath Care Commissions Can Advance Affordability and Equity*, CAP 20 (Washington, DC: Center for American Progress), October 2022), https://www.americanprogress.org/article/how-state-health-care-cost-commissions-can-advance-affordability-and-equity/.

60. Discussion with Chris Demars, director for delivery systems innovation, Oregon Health Authority, December 9, 2022.

61. David Raths, "States Try Different Approaches to Boost Primary Care Spending," Healthcare Innovation, May 20, 2022, https://www.hcinnovationgroup.com/population-health-management/primary-care/article/21268484/states-try-different-approaches-to-boost-primary-care-spending/.

62. Mary Jo Condon, Elizabeth Koonce, Vinayak Sinha, et al., *Investing in Primary Care: Lessons from State-Based Efforts* (Oakland: California Health Care

Foundation, April 2022), https://www.chcf.org/wp-content/uploads/2022/03/Investing PCLessonsStateBasedEfforts.pdf.

63. Diana Crumley and Summer Boslaugh, "National Overview on Primary Care Spending," slide presentation in "Increasing Investment in Primary Care through Medicaid Managed Care," Center for Health Care Strategies, May 12, 2022, https://www.chcs.org/media/05.12.22_webinar_slides.pdf.

64. Oregon Primary Care Association, *Robert Wood Johnson Foundation Payment Reform Evaluation Project: Transforming Payment for Oregon's Community Health Centers through Alternative Payment Methodology* (Portland: Oregon Primary Care Association, August 2015), https://depts.washington.edu/payeval/docs/oregon-report.pdf.

65. K. John McConnell, Stephanie Renfro, Richard Lindrooth, et al., "Oregon's Medicaid Reform and Transition to Global Budgets Were Associated with Reductions in Expenditure," *Health Affairs* 36, no. 3 (2017): 451–59, https://www.healthaffairs.org/doi/epdf/10.1377/hlthaff.2016.1298.

66. "CCO 2.0: The Future of Coordinated Care; OHA Signs Contracts with 15 CCOs," in "Oregon Health Policy Board," Oregon Health Authority, accessed December 13, 2023, https://www.oregon.gov/oha/OHPB/Pages/CCO-2-0.aspx.

67. "What's Changing in the 2022–2027 1115 Demonstration Waiver," in "Medicaid Policy," Oregon Health Authority, accessed December 13, 2023, https://www.oregon.gov/oha/HSD/Medicaid-Policy/Pages/Changes.aspx.

68. Value-Based Payment Compact Workgroup, *Paying for Value in Health Care: A Roadmap for Implementing the Oregon Value-Based Payment Compact* (Portland: Oregon Health Leadership Council, July 2022), https://orhealthleadershipcouncil.org/wp-content/uploads/2022/07/VBP-Compact-Roadmap-1.pdf.

69. "Oregon Value-Based Payment Compact," Oregon Health Leadership Council, accessed December 13, 2023, https://orhealthleadershipcouncil.org/oregon-value-based-payment-compact/.

70. Value-Based Payment Compact Workgroup, *Paying for Value*.

71. Oregon Health Authority, *Recommendations and Policy Considerations for Aligning for Health (A4H): Oregon's Regional Multi-Payer Global Budget Model; House Bill 2010 (2021)* (Salem: Oregon Health Authority, July 2022), https://www.oregon.gov/oha/hpa/hp/docs/HB-2010-Global-Budget.pdf.

72. Visit to One Community Health, Hood River and The Dalles, Oregon, May 16–17, 2023.

73. Interview with Max Janasik, chief executive officer, One Community Health, May 16, 2023.

74. Interview with Dr. Connie Serra, One Community Health–Hood River, May 16, 2023.

75. Interview with Brooke Nicholls, nurse practitioner, One Community Health–Hood River, May 16, 2023.

76. Interview with Harley Davidson, chief operating officer, One Community Health, May 16, 2023.

77. Sachin H. Jain, "'Practicing at the Top of Your License' and the 'Great' American Healthcare Labor Arbitrage," *Forbes*, April 4, 2022, https://www.forbes.com/sites/sachinjain/2022/04/04/the-great-american-healthcare-labor-arbitrage/?sh=3c698f046613.

78. Interviews with Amy Marquez, site director, and Kendahl Caminiti, nursing supervisor, One Community Health–The Dalles, May 17, 2023.

79. Interview with Dr. Jennifer Jehnsen, One Community Health–The Dalles, May 17, 2023.

80. Trisha Ambrose, Jane Montealegre, Susan Parker, et al., "National Breast, Cervical, and Colorectal Cancer Screening Use in Federally Qualified Health Centers," *JAMA Internal Medicine* 184, no. 6 (2024): 671-79, doi:10.1001/jamainternmed.2024.0693.

81. Sungchul Park and Rishi Wadhera, "Use of High- and Low-Value Health Care among US Adults, by Income, 2010–2019," *Health Affairs* 43, no. 7 (2024): 1021–31, https://www.healthaffairs.org/doi/10.1377/hlthaff.2023.00661?url_ver=Z39.88-2003&rfr_id=ori%3Arid%3Acrossref.org&rfr_dat=cr_pub++0pubmed.

Chapter 5. State-Based Health Insurers' Role in Primary Care

1. "Market Share and Enrollment of Largest Three Insurers—Large Group Market," in "State Health Facts, Timeframe 2019," Kaiser Family Foundation, accessed December 12, 2023, https://www.kff.org/other/state-indicator/market-share-and-enrollment-of-largest-three-insurers-large-group-market/?currentTimeframe=0&sortModel=%7B%22colId%22:%22Location%22,%22sort%22:%22asc%22%7D.

2. Troyen Brennan, "The Settlement of the Blue Cross Blue Shield Antitrust Litigation: Creating a New Potential Catalyst for Health Insurance Industry Restructuring," *JAMA Health Forum* 3, no. 12 (2022): e224737, https://pubmed.ncbi.nlm.nih.gov/36525255.

3. Zirui Song, Yunan Ji, Dana G. Safran, and Michael E. Chernew, "Health Care Spending, Utilization, and Quality 8 Years into Global Payment," *New England Journal of Medicine* 381, no. 3 (2019): 242–63, https://www.nejm.org/doi/pdf/10.1056/NEJMsa1813621?articleTools=true/.

4. Song et al., "Health Care Spending."

5. Allison Cuellar, Lorens A. Helmchen, Gilbert Gimm, et al., "The CareFirst Patient-Centered Medical Home Program: Cost and Utilization Effects in Its First Three Years," *Journal of General Internal Medicine* 31, no. 11 (2016): 1382–96, https://www.ncbi.nlm.nih.gov/pmc/articles/PMC5071295.

6. CareFirst, *Patient-Centered Medical Home 2017 Program Performance Report* (Baltimore: CareFirst, 2018), https://individual.carefirst.com/carefirst-resources/pdf/2017-pcmh-program-performance-report.pdf.

7. Interview with Brian Wheeler, senior vice president for health services, CareFirst, March 15, 2023.

8. Kevin G. Volpp, Amol Navathe, Emily Oshima Lee, et al., "Redesigning Provider Payment: Opportunities and Challenges from the Hawaii Experience," *Healthcare* 6, no. 3 (2018); 167–74, https://pubmed.ncbi.nlm.nih.gov/30001958.

9. Amol S. Navathe, Ezekiel J. Emanuel, Amelia Bond, et al., "Association between the Implementation of a Population-Based Primary Care Payment System and Achievement on Quality Measures in Hawaii," *JAMA* 322, no. 1 (2019): 57–68, https://jamanetwork.com/journals/jama/fullarticle/2737174.

10. Discussion with Cary Koike, vice president for strategic network relations, Hawaii Medical Services Association, March 1, 2023.

11. Arlene S. Ash and Randall P. Ellis, "Risk-Adjusted Payment and Performance Assessment for Primary Care," *Medical Care* 50, no. 8 (2012): 463–73, https://www.ncbi.nlm.nih.gov/pmc/articles/PMC3394905.

12. Alliance of Community Health Plans, *Strengthening Primary Care for Patients: Capital District Physicians' Health Plan* (Washington, DC: ACHP, 2013), https://achp.org/wp-content/uploads/CDPHP-ACHP-Strengthening-Primary-Care-Profile.pdf.

13. "Payer-Provider Alignment Spurs Innovation, Drives Value: Enhanced Primary Care 2.0," in *Health Care 2030: ACHP's Road Map to Reform*, Alliance of Community Health Plans (Washington, DC: ACHP, September 2020), https://achp.org/wp-content/uploads/Enhanced-Primary-Care-2.0-ACHP-Case-Study.pdf.

14. Capital District Physicians' Health Plan, *Quality Management Program Evaluation 2022* (New York: CDPHP, January 2023), https://www.cdphp.com/-/media/files/otherpdfs/quality-management-program-evaluation.pdf.

15. Interview with Christopher Bush, senior vice president of network management, Blue Cross Blue Shield of Rhode Island, July 5, 2023.

16. Discussion with Dr. Gary Knaus, private practice, September 27, 2022.

17. George Eliot, *Middlemarch: A Study of Provincial Life* (London: Arcturus Press, 2022; originally published in 1871–72 by William Blackwood & Sons), 166.

18. Discussion with Dave Ressler, chief executive officer, Aspen Valley Hospital, September 27, 2022.

19. Discussions with Ross Brooks, chief executive officer, and Art Fernandez, chief operating officer, Mountain Family Health Centers, September 27, 2022.

20. Interview with Madeleine "Maddie" Nieslanik, physician assistant, Mountain Family Health Centers–Rifle, September 26, 2022.

21. Martha Hofstetter and Sarah Klein, "Integrating Behavioral Health Services into Primary Care: How One Medicaid Care Plan Managed Made It Work," Commonwealth Fund, December 14, 2022. https://www.commonwealthfund.org/publications/case-study/2022/dec/integrating-behavioral-health-services-primary-care.

22. Interviews with Dr. Anneliese Heckert and Dr. Matt Percy, co-chief medical officers, Mountain Family Health Centers–Glenwood Springs, September 27, 2022.

23. Interview with Ashley Thurow, executive director, Monument Health, September 29, 2022.

24. Interview with Marc Lassaux, chief executive officer, Quality Health Network, September 29, 2022.

25. Interview with Dr. Gregory Reicks, SCL Health, September 29, 2022.

26. Interview with Patrick Gordon, chief executive officer, Rocky Mountain Health Plan, September 29, 2022.

27. "Our Impact," in "About Kaiser Permanente," Kaiser Permanente, March 31, 2023, https://about.kaiserpermanente.org/commitments-and-impact/public-policy/our-impact/.

28. "No-Bid Medicaid Contract for Kaiser Permanente Is Now California Law, but Key Details Are Missing," *Medical Net*, July 19, 2022, https://www.news-medical.net/news/20220719/No-bid-Medicaid-contract-for-Kaiser-Permanente-is-now-California-law-but-key-details-are-missing.aspx.

29. Interview with Dr. Marc Todd Philippe, Kaiser Permanente–Redwood City Center, November 22, 2022.

30. Interview with a physician/team leader, Kaiser Permanente–Redwood City Center, November 22, 2022.

31. Interview with Dr. Baonhan Le, Kaiser Permanente–Redwood City Center, November 22, 2022.

32. Interview with Dr. Helen Lin, Kaiser Permanente–Redwood City Center, November 22, 2022.

33. Interview with a senior physician Kaiser Permanente–Redwood City Center, November 22, 2022.

34. Lisa Rosenstein, Richard Gitomer, and Bruce Landon, "Pursuing Gender Equity by Paying for What Matters in Primary Care," *New England Journal of Medicine* 389, no. 3 (2023): 198–200, https://www.nejm.org/doi/full/10.1056/NEJMp2301282.

Chapter 6. The National Health Insurers (and Other Corporations)

1. Troyen A. Brennan and Donald M. Berwick, *New Rules: Regulation, Markets, and the Quality of American Health Care* (San Francisco: Josey-Bass, 1996).

2. Timothy Hoff, *Searching for the Family Doctor: Primary Care on the Brink* (Baltimore: Johns Hopkins University Press, 2022).

3. Gregg Coodley, *Patients in Peril: The Demise of Primary Care in America* (Austin, TX: Atmosphere Press, 2022).

4. Kevin Grumbach, "Forging a Social Movement to Dismantle Entrenched Power and Liberate Primary Care as a Common Good," *Annals of Family Medicine* 21, no. 2 (2023): 180–83, https://www.annfammed.org/content/21/2/180.

5. Troyen A. Brennan, *Transformation of American Health Insurance: On the Path to Medicare for All* (Baltimore: Johns Hopkins University Press, 2024).

6. David Hunter, "At Breaking Point or Already Broken? The National Health Service in the United Kingdom," *New England Journal of Medicine* 389, no. 2 (2023): 100–103, https://www.nejm.org/doi/full/10.1056/NEJMp2301257.

7. Jeff Byers, "Optum a Step Ahead in Vertical Integration Frenzy," Healthcare Dive, April 12, 2018, https://www.healthcaredive.com/news/optum-unitedhealth-vertical-integration-walmart/520410.

8. UnitedHealth Group, *Optum* (Minnetonka, MN: UnitedHealth Group, November 2022), 10–20, https://www.unitedhealthgroup.com/content/dam/UHG/PDF/investors/2022/conference/UHG_IC_22_Optum_Consolidated.pdf.

9. Jakob Emerson, "Meet America's Largest Employer of Physicians: United-Health Group," *Becker's Payer Issues*, February 16, 2023, https://www.beckerspayer.com/payer/meet-americas-largest-employer-of-physicians-unitedhealth-group.html.

10. Patsy Newitt, "Optum's $8B+ Year of Deals: 6 Acquisitions to Know," *Becker's Ambulatory Surgery Centers Review*, December 14, 2022, https://www.beckersasc.com/asc-transactions-and-valuation-issues/optums-8b-year-of-deals-6-acquisitions-to-know.html.

11. Jeff Goldsmith, "Optum: Testing Time for an Invisible Empire," *Health Care Blog*, April 2, 2024, https://thehealthcareblog.com/blog/2024/04/02/optum-testing-time-for-an-invisible-empire/.

12. Brennan, *Transformation of American Health Insurance*.

13. Ryan Crowley, Omar Atiq, and David Hilden, "Financial Profit in Medicine: A Position Paper from the American College of Physicians," *Annals of Internal Medicine* 174, no. 10 (2021): 1447–49, https://www.acpjournals.org/doi/full/10.7326/M21-1178.

14. Robert Otto Valdez, "The 2022 National Healthcare Quality and Disparities Report: We Still Have Much Work to Do," *AHRQ Views* (blog), November 22, 2022, https://www.ahrq.gov/news/blog/ahrqviews/2022-national-healthcare-disparities-report.html.

15. Samuel Young, "Demystifying Medicare Risk Adjustment," Inside Angle, 3M, July 15, 2019, https://insideangle.3m.com/his/blog-post/demystifying-medicare-risk-adjustment/.

16. Richard Gilfillan and Donald M. Berwick, "Medicare Advantage, Direct Contracting, and the Medicare 'Money Machine,' Part 1: The Risk-Score Game," *Health Affairs Forefront*, September 29, 2021, https://www.healthaffairs.org/content/forefront/medicare-advantage-direct-contracting-and-medicare-money-machine-part-1-risk-score-game/.

17. MedPAC, *Medicare Payment Advisory Commission: Public Meeting* (Washington, DC: MedPAC, January 2024), https://www.medpac.gov/meeting/january-11-12-2024/.

18. Ali Heinrich, Sam Smetek, and Brett Swanson, *Value of Medicare Advantage to the Federal Government* (Minnetonka, MN: UnitedHealth Group, April 2024), https://www.milliman.com/-/media/milliman/pdfs/2024-articles/4-29-24_value-of-ma-to-the-federal-government.ashx.

19. Ankur J. Goel, Emily R. Curran, and Kristen O'Brien, *CMS Finalized Risk Adjustment Model in 2024 Rate Announcement for Medicare Advantage and Part D* (Chicago: McDermott Will & Emery, April 5, 2023), https://www.mwe.com/insights/cms-finalizes-risk-adjustment-model-in-2024-rate-announcement-for-medicare-advantage-and-part-d/.

20. "CMS Finalizes Long-Awaited RADV Program Rule," Bass, Berry & Sims, February 6, 2023, https://www.bassberry.com/news/cms-finalizes-medicare-advantage-risk-adjustment-data-validation-program-rule/.

21. UnitedHealthcare Ins. Co. v. Becerra. 16 F.4th 867 (D.C. Cir. 2021), https://casetext.com/case/unitedhealthcare-ins-co-v-becerra.

22. Rosie Brown and Dr. Calum Yacoubian, "Mapping a New Course: Embarking on the Journey from Risk Adjustment Model V24 to V28," IQVIA, October 13, 2023. https://www.iqvia.com/blogs/2023/10/mapping-a-new-course-embarking-on-the-journey-from-risk-adjustment-model-v24-to-v28.

23. Christopher Weaver, Tom McGinty, Anna Wilde Matthews, and Mark Maremont, "Insurers Pocketed $50 Billion from Medicare for Diseases No Doctor Treated," *Wall Street Journal*, July 8, 2024, https://www.wsj.com/health/healthcare/medicare-health-insurance-diagnosis-payments-b4d99a5d.

24. Hannah James, Beth Dana, Momotazur Rahman, et al., "Medicare Advantage Health Risk Assessments Contribute up to $12 Billion per Year to Risk Adjustment Payments," *Health Affairs* 43, no. 5 (2024): 614–24, https://www.healthaffairs.org/doi/10.1377/hlthaff.2023.00787?url_ver=Z39.88-2003&rfr_id=ori%3Arid%3Acrossref.org&rfr_dat=cr_pub++0pubmed.

25. Eran Politzer, Timothy Anderson, John Ayanian, et al., "Primary Care Physicians in Medicare Advantage Were Less Costly, Provided Similar Quality versus Regional Average," *Health Affairs* 43, no. 3 (2024): 372–82, https://www.healthaffairs.org/doi/10.1377/hlthaff.2023.00803?url_ver=Z39.88-2003&rfr_id=ori%3Arid%3Acrossref.org&rfr_dat=cr_pub++0pubmed.

26. Arnav Shah and Gretchen Jacobsen, "Does Medicare Advantage Affect the Way Primary Care Practices Deliver Care?," Commonwealth Fund, March 21, 2024, https://www.commonwealthfund.org/publications/issue-briefs/2024/mar/does-medicare-advantage-affect-primary-care-practices.

27. Lawrence Casalino and James Robinson, *The Evolution of Medical Groups and Capitation in California* (San Francisco: Kaiser Family Foundation, September 1997), https://www.chcf.org/wp-content/uploads/2017/12/PDF-casalino.pdf.

28. Interview with Dr. Robert Margolis, retired chief executive officer, HealthCare Partners, July 23, 2023.

29. Casalino and Robinson, *Evolution of Medical Groups*, 20.

30. Casalino and Robinson, *Evolution of Medical Groups*, 30.

31. "DaVita and HealthCare Partners Announce Merger Agreement," BusinessWire, May 21, 2012, https://www.businesswire.com/news/home/20120521005532/en/DaVita-and-HealthCare-Partners-Announce-Merger-Agreement/.

32. Tina Reed, "DaVita Drops Price of Medical Group to $4.3 Billion in Sale to UnitedHealth," Fierce Healthcare, December 17, 2018, https://www.fiercehealthcare.com/payer/davita-drops-price-medical-group-to-4-3b-sale-to-unitedhealth/.

33. Interview with Rebecca King, senior director of clinical transformation, Optum Health, November 14, 2022.

34. Interview with Tyler Denstad, director of recruiting, Optum Health, November 14, 2022.

35. Interview with Cathy Liu, HealthCare Partners–Del Amo, November 14, 2022.

36. Interview with Dr. Sean Rogers, regional medical director, HealthCare Partners, November 14, 2022.

37. Interview with Dr. Matthew Lombard, HealthCare Partners–Del Amo, November 14, 2022.

38. Interview with Dr. Minesh Mehta, HealthCare Partners–Del Amo, November 14, 2022.

39. Bob Herman, Tara Bonnow, Casey Ross, and Lizzy Lawrence, "Health Care Colossus: How UnitedHealth Harnesses Its Physician Empire to Squeeze Profits Out of Patients," Stat, July 25, 2024, https://www.statnews.com/2024/07/25/united-health-group-medicare-advantage-strategy-doctor-clinic-acquisitions/?utm_campaign=dc_diagnosis&utm_medium=email&_hsenc=p2ANqtz--WHcfJnqVH2EsEiVwAhAHnqgBXD9ELdsXLp249wEQ33gEHFm67uQFqNwBuaZZLBX-enskmNBi1aLZ3nuUu4pNEZM1NkQ&_hsmi=317234362&utm_content=317234362&utm_source=hs_email.

40. Interview with Lindsay Hess, nursing supervisor for four sites, HealthCare Partners, November 14, 2022.

41. Interviews with Dr. Jaime Ramos, regional medical director; Geronie Dougé, director of group operations; and Nicole Rubio, administrative manager, HealthCare Partners–Downtown Los Angeles, November 15, 2022.

42. Humana, "Humana to Exit Employer Group Commercial Medical Products Business," press release, February 23, 2023, https://press.humana.com/news/news-details/2023/Humana-to-Exit-Employer-Group-Commercial-Medical-Products-Business/default.aspx#gsc.tab-0.

43. Humana, *Value-Based Care Report* (Louisville, KY: Humana, April 2021), https://humana.gcs-web.com/static-files/39bb066e-bca5-45ff-aab2-827fe03c92c1.

44. Vivien Ho, "Lessons from Vivek Garg, Chief Medical Officer at Humana, on the Future of Primary Care and Selling Medicare Plans," Pear Healthcare Playbook, January 11, 2023, https://medium.com/pear-healthcare-playbook/lessons-from-vivek-garg-chief-medical-officer-at-humana-on-the-future-of-primary-care-and-4ea6feb5a6f1.

45. Paige Minemyer, "Humana Opens 250th Primary Care Center as It Continues to Focus on Growth," Fierce Healthcare, June 6, 2023, https://www.fiercehealthcare.com/payers/humana-opens-250th-primary-care-center-it-continues-focus-growth/.

46. Interview with Dr. William Russell, chief medical officer for the Palm Beach region, Conviva, January 9, 2023.

47. George Eliot, *Middlemarch: A Study of Provincial Life* (London: Arcturus Press, 2022; originally published in 1871–72 by William Blackwood & Sons), 349.

48. Jerry Gurwitz, "The Paradoxical Decline of Geriatrics Medicine as a Profession," *JAMA Network* 330, no. 8 (2023): 693–94, https://jamanetwork.com/journals/jama/article-abstract/2808221.

49. Timothy Hoff, *Next in Line: Lowered Expectations in the Age of Retail- and Value-Based Health* (New York: Oxford University Press, 2018).

50. "Retail Clinics Target Chronic Care," American Hospital Association, May 30, 2023, https://www.aha.org/aha-center-health-innovation-market-scan/2023-05-30

-retail-clinics-target-chronic-diseases#:~:text=Big%20Retailers%20Dominate%20 the%20Market,and%20Walmart%2C%20Definitive%20Healthcare%20states/.

51. Elise Reuter, "Walgreens Resets Retail Clinic Strategy with Partnership with VillageMD, but Faces Tough Competition Ahead," MedCity News, July 8, 2020, https://medcitynews.com/2020/07/walgreens-resets-retail-clinics-with-villagemd -partnership-but-faces-tough-competition-ahead/.

52. Andrew Donlan, "VillageMD CEO: Life-Changing Primary Care Needs a Home-Centric Approach," Home Health Care News, March 23, 2021, https:// homehealthcarenews.com/2021/03/villagemd-ceo-life-changing-primary-care-needs -a-home-centric-approach/#:~:text=Founded%20in%202013%2C%20the%20 Chicago,than%202%2C800%20across%20nine%20markets/.

53. Rebecca Pifer, "Walgreens-Backed VillageMD Acquires Connecticut Medical Group," HealthCare Dive, March 2, 2023, https://www.healthcaredive.com/news /walgreens-villagemd-acquires-connecticut-medical-group-starling/644143/#:~:text =Walgreens%20first%20invested%20in%20VillageMD,from%2030%25%20to%20 63%25.

54. Paige Minemyer, "Alignment Healthcare, Walgreens Launch Co-Branded Medicare Advantage Plans," Fierce Health Care, October 17, 2023, https://www .fiercehealthcare.com/payers/alignment-healthcare-walgreens-launch-co-branded -medicare-advantage-plans/.

55. Interview with Dr. Viresh Patel, VillageMD clinic in Houston, Texas, April 27, 2023.

56. Rebecca Pifer, "Walgreens to Reduce Stake in VillageMD, Close Stores," Health Care Dive, June 27, 2024, https://www.healthcaredive.com/news/walgreens -to-reduce-villagemd-stake-close-stores/719984/.

57. Discussion with Tim Barry, May 8, 2024.

58. "Walmart Health: Will the Fifth Attempt at Clinics Be the Charm?," ReCon Strategies, February 27, 2021, https://reconstrategy.com/2021/02/walmart-health -will-the-fifth-attempt-at-clinics-be-the-charm/.

59. Shelby Livingstone, "Exclusive: Walmart Shut Down Its Healthcare Clinics after Losses Reached Nearly a Quarter of a Billion Dollars," EndPoint News, June 6, 2024, https://endpts.com/walmart-shut-down-its-healthcare-clinics-after-losses -reached-nearly-a-quarter-of-a-billion-dollars/.

60. David Wainer, "Why the Walmart Model Doesn't Work in Healthcare," *Wall Street Journal*, July 5, 2024, https://www.wsj.com/health/healthcare/why-the -walmart-model-doesnt-work-in-healthcare-c61a5cbc.

61. "From Pandemics to Predictions: Insights from Serial Healthcare Entrepreneur Tom Lee, MD," Cedar, April 22, 2020, https://www.cedar.com/blog/from -pandemics-to-predictions-insights-from-serial-healthcare-entrepreneur-tom-lee -md/.

62. "The One Medical Experience Goes Above and Beyond Your Typical Primary Care Practice," One Medical, accessed November 8, 2024, https://www.onemedical .com/membership/.

63. Laura Lovett, "One Medical Closes Acquisition of Senior-Focused Iora Health," MobiHealth News, September 1, 2021, https://www.mobihealthnews.com/news/hybrid-primary-care-provider-one-medical-closes-acquisition-senior-focused-iora-health#:~:text=In%20terms%20of%20scope%2C%20Boston,members%20and%20Iora's%2039%2C000%20patients/.

64. Lovett, "One Medical Closes Acquisition."

65. Karen Weise, "Amazon to Acquire One Medical Clinics in Latest Push into Health Care," *New York Times*, July 21, 2022, https://www.nytimes.com/2022/07/21/business/amazon-one-medical-deal.html.

66. Sai Balasubramanian, "Amazon Web Services (AWS) Launches HealthScribe, a Generative AI Powered Clinical Documentation Tool," *Forbes*, July 26, 2023, https://www.forbes.com/sites/saibala/2023/07/26/its-official-amazon-web-services-aws-launches-healthscribe-a-generative-ai-powered-clinical-documentation-tool/?sh=7fc37073fd1b.

67. One Medical, "One Medical Announces Results for Fourth Quarter and Full Year 2022," news release, February 21, 2023, https://www.globenewswire.com/news-release/2023/02/21/2612770/0/en/One-Medical-Announces-Results-for-Fourth-Quarter-and-Full-Year-2022.html.

68. "Amir Rubin Net Worth," Wallmine, February 24, 2023, https://wallmine.com/people/114575/amir-dan-rubin/.

69. Interview with Dr. Zachary Ortiz, One Medical–Gilbert, January 24, 2023.

70. Interview with Diana Vinh, office manager, One Medical–Gilbert, January 24, 2023.

71. Interview with Dr. Rakesh "Rocky" Patel, One Medical–Gilbert, January 24, 2023.

72. Interview with Jacob Coleman, market operations leader (now director of operations), One Medical Seniors–Glendale, Arizona, January 23, 2023.

73. Interview with Kurt Neely, market operations leader for the Phoenix metropolitan area, One Medical Seniors, January 23, 2023.

74. Interview with Chekena "Kena" Carter, One Medical Seniors–Glendale, January 23, 2023.

75. Interview with Josh Perkins, nurse practitioner, One Medical Seniors–Glendale, January 23, 2023.

76. Interview with Dr. Natasha Bhuyan, national medical director, One Medical, January 24, 2023.

77. "How Will Changes to Amazon's Healthcare Business Impact Patients?," Advisory Board Daily Briefing, March 7, 2024, https://www.advisory.com/daily-briefing/2024/03/07/amazon.

Chapter 7. The Role of Private Equity

1. "Private Equity vs. Venture Capital: What's the Difference?," Investopedia, updated September 26, 2023, https://www.investopedia.com/ask/answers/020415/what-difference-between-private-equity-and-venture-capital.asp#:~:text=Private%20equity%20is%20capital%20invested,potential%20for%20long%2Dterm%20growth/.

2. Alexander Borsa, Geronimo Bejarano, Moriah Ellen, and Joseph Dov Bruch, "Evaluating Trends in Private Equity Ownership and Impacts on Health Outcomes, Costs, and Quality: Systematic Review," *British Medical Journal* 382 (2023): e075244, https://www.bmj.com/content/382/bmj-2023-075244.

3. Jane M. Zhu and Zirui Song, "The Growth of Private Equity in US Health Care: Impact and Outlook," National Institute for Health Care Management, May 20, 2023, https://nihcm.org/assets/articles/NIHCM-ExpertVoices-052023.pdf.

4. Sneha Kannan, Joseph Dov Bruch, and Zirui Song, "Changes in Hospital Adverse Events and Patients Outcomes Associated with Private Equity Acquisition," *JAMA* 330 (2023): 2365–75, https://jamanetwork.com/journals/jama/fullarticle/2813379.

5. Christopher Cai and Zirui Song, "A Policy Framework for the Growing Influence of Private Equity in Health Care Delivery," *JAMA* 329, no. 18 (2023): 1545–46, https://jamanetwork.com/journals/jama/fullarticle/2804025.

6. Marcelo Cerullo, Kelly Kaili Yang, Ryan C. McDevitt, et al., "Research: What Happens When Private Equity Firms Buy Hospitals," *Harvard Business Review*, March 20, 2023, https://hbr.org/2023/03/research-what-happens-when-private-equity-firms-buy-hospitals/.

7. Maureen Tkacik, "Quackonomics," *American Prospect*, May 23, 2023, https://prospect.org/health/2023-05-23-quackonomics-medical-properties-trust/.

8. Bain & Company, *Global Healthcare Private Equity and M&A Report 2023* (Boston: Bain & Company, 2023), https://www.bain.com/globalassets/noindex/2023/bain_report_global_healthcare_private_equity_and_ma_2023.pdf.

9. Robert Pearl, "Private Equity and Monopolization of Medical Care," *Forbes*, February 20, 2023, https://www.forbes.com/sites/robertpearl/2023/02/20/private-equity-and-the-monopolization-of-medical-care/?sh=2c9661a82bad/.

10. Umar Ikram, Khin-Kyemon Aung, and Zirui Song, "Private Equity and Primary Care: Lessons from the Field," *New England Journal of Medicine Catalyst*, November 18, 2021, https://catalyst.nejm.org/doi/full/10.1056/CAT.21.0276.

11. Ola Abdelhadi, Brent Fulton, Laura Alexander, and Richard Scheffler, "Private Equity-Acquired Physician Practices and Market Penetration Increased Substantially, 2012–21," *Health Affairs* 43, no. 3 (2024): 354–62, https://www.healthaffairs.org/doi/10.1377/hlthaff.2023.00152?url_ver=Z39.88-2003&rfr_id=ori%3Arid%3Acrossref.org&rfr_dat=cr_pub++opubmed.

12. "Oak Street Health," Crunchbase, accessed November 11, 2024, https://www.crunchbase.com/organization/oak-street-health/company_financials/.

13. Heather Landi, "CVS Closes $10.6 Billion Acquisition of Oak Street Health to Expand Primary Care Footprint," Fierce Health Care, May 2, 2023, https://www.fiercehealthcare.com/providers/cvs-closes-106b-acquisition-oak-street-health-expand-primary-care-footprint/.

14. Erin Brodwin, "Cityblock Health Raises Another Mega-Round of Funding, Tipping Its Valuation over $5 Billion," Stat, September 3, 2021, https://www.statnews.com/2021/09/03/cityblock-health-series-d-valuation/.

15. "Clayton, Dubilier & Rice Forms agilon health, a New Services and Technology Company at the Forefront of Value-Based Healthcare," Clayton, Dubilier and Rice, October 4, 2016, https://www.cdr-inc.com/news/press-release/clayton-dubilier-rice-forms-agilon-health-new-services-and-technology-company/.

16. Aledade Investor Relations, "Aledade Secures $260 Million Series F Financing Round to Expand and Enhance Services for Its Nationwide Network of Primary Care Practices," press release, June 20, 2023, https://resources.aledade.com/press-releases/aledade-secures-series-f/#:~:text=The%20round%20was%20led%20by,and%20Fidelity%20Management%20%26%20Research%20Company/.

17. Interview with Ravi Sachdev, Clayton, Dubilier and Rice, September 23, 2022.

18. "agilon health Reports Second Quarter 2023 Results," agilon health, August 8, 2023, https://investors.agilonhealth.com/news/news-details/2023/agilon-health-Reports-Second-Quarter-2023-Results/default.aspx.

19. Interview with Dr. William Wulf, chief executive officer [retired in December 2022], Central Ohio Primary Care, August 18, 2022.

20. This generally is defined as actively participating in clinic-wide meetings, suggesting various means to improve clinical care, coming up with ideas to strengthen business operations, working to increase communications and interactions with other staff members, and finding ways to increase the group's social cohesion and engagement with COPC's initiatives and goals. See John Nelson, "Good Citizenship," The Hospitalist, November 2, 2011, https://www.the-hospitalist.org/hospitalist/article/124623/good-citizenship/.

21. "Use of Inpatient Hospital Services in Traditional Medicare," in "State Health Facts, Timeframe 2021," Kaiser Family Foundation, accessed November 11, 2024, https://www.kff.org/medicare/state-indicator/medicare-service-use-hospital-inpatient-services/?currentTimeframe=0&selectedDistributions=discharges-per-1000-traditional-medicare-part-a-enrollees--total-days-of-care-per-1000-traditional-medicare-part-a-enrollees&sortModel=%7B%22colId%22:%22Location%22,%22sort%22:%22asc%22%7D.

22. Interview with Dr. Maria Vaveris, Central Ohio Primary Care, August 18, 2022.

23. George Eliot, *Middlemarch: A Study of Provincial Life* (London: Arcturus Press, 2022; originally published in 1871–72 by William Blackwood & Sons), 94.

24. Interview with Dr. James Dorado, Central Ohio Primary Care, August 18, 2022.

25. Interview with Dr. Donald Deep, chief executive officer [as of January 1, 2023], Central Ohio Primary Care, August 18, 2022.

26. "Acute Patient PPS [Prospective Payment System]," Centers for Medicare and Medicaid Services, September 6, 2023, https://www.cms.gov/medicare/payment/prospective-payment-systems/acute-inpatient-pps.

27. Kevin O'Leary and Amanda DiTrolio, "Weekly Health Tech Reads: 3/3/24," Health Tech Nerds, March 3, 2024, https://www.healthtechnerds.com/p/htn-weekly-health-tech-reads-33.

28. "Aledade Secures $260 Million Series F Financing Round to Expand and Enhance Services for Its Nationwide Network of Primary Care Practices," Aledade, press release, June 20, 2023, https://resources.aledade.com/press-releases/aledade-secures-series-f/#:~:text=The%20round%20was%20led%20by,and%20Fidelity%20Management%20%26%20Research%20Company/.

29. Farzad Mostashari, "Why We Became a Public Benefit Corporation," Aledade, January 5, 2023, https://resources.aledade.com/home/public-benefit-corporation/.

30. "Aledade Has Saved More Than $1.2 Billion in Unnecessary Health Care Spending by Helping Physicians Deliver More Primary Care," Aledade, September 15, 2022, https://resources.aledade.com/home/aledade-has-saved-more-than-1-2-billion-in-unnecessary-health-care-spending/.

31. Interview with Jennifer Thelwell, administrator, Stone Creek Family Physicians, October 4, 2022.

32. Interview with Rachel Bittle, nursing supervisor, Stone Creek Family Physicians, October 4, 2022.

33. Interview with Dr. Ryan Knopp, Stone Creek Family Physicians, October 4, 2022.

34. James Dom Dera, "How to Succeed in Value-Based Care," *Family Practice Management* 28, no. 6 (2021): 25–31.

35. Interview with Dr. Amy Cunningham, Stone Creek Family Physicians, October 4, 2022.

36. Deborah Cohen, Kevin Grumbach, and Robert Phillips, "The Value of Funding a Primary Care Extension Program in the United States," *JAMA Health Forum* 4, no. 2 (2023): e225410.

37. Heather Landi, "Cityblock Restructures Operations, Cuts 12% of Workforce as It Plots Plans for Growth, Profitability," Fierce Healthcare, June 8, 2023, https://www.fiercehealthcare.com/providers/cityblock-restructures-operations-cuts-12-orkforce-it-plots-plans-growth-profitability/.

38. "We See You," in "Our Story," Cityblock, December 10, 2023, https://www.cityblock.com/about?source=post_page/.

39. Interview with Phyllis Pendleton, community health worker, Cityblock Health, Washington, DC, July 29, 2022.

40. Interview with Dorthya "Dodie" Robinson, executive director, North Carolina market, Cityblock Health, April 20, 2023.

41. Interview with Angel Jones, Cityblock Health, Greensboro, North Carolina, April 20, 2023.

42. Interview with Dr. Dhruva Kothari, medical director, Cityblock Health, Massachusetts, January 5, 2023.

43. Interview with Dr. Michael Tang, head of behavioral health, Cityblock Health, Massachusetts, July 25, 2022.

44. Interview with Dr. Kameron Matthews, chief medical officer, Cityblock Health, Massachusetts, August 23, 2022.

45. Heather Landi, "CVS Closes $10.6 Billion Acquisition of Oak Street Health to Expand Primary Care Footprint," Fierce Healthcare, May 2, 2023, https://www.fiercehealthcare.com/providers/cvs-closes-106b-acquisition-oak-street-health-expand-primary-care-footprint/.

46. "Oak Street Reports Full Year 2022 Results," Business Wire, February 28, 2023, https://finance.yahoo.com/news/oak-street-health-reports-full-210500159.html#:~:text=Full%20Year%202022%20Financial%20Highlights&text=Capitated%20revenue%20was%20%242.13%20billion,%24(414.6)%20million%20in%202021.

47. Interview with Dr. Julie Blankemeier, regional medical director, Oak Street Health, April 6, 2023.

48. Interview with Dr. Francina Peralta-Machado, regional medical supervisor, Oak Street Health, April 6, 2023.

49. Email with Dr. Ali Khan, chief medical officer, Oak Street Health, November 4, 2023.

50. Interview with Dr. Andrea Khosropour, Oak Street Health–Edgewater, April 7, 2023.

51. "Oak Street Reports Full Year 2022 Results."

Chapter 8. The Future of Primary Care

1. Thomas Piketty, *Capital in the Twenty-First Century*, trans. Arthur Goldhammer (Cambridge, MA: Harvard University Press, 2013).

2. Interview with Stephen Greene, chief administrative officer, ChenMed, December 12, 2022.

3. Gordon Chen and Chris Chen, "The Case for Transformative Care," *NEJM Catalyst*, October 5, 2023, https://catalyst.nejm.org/doi/full/10.1056/CAT.23.0115.

4. "The ChenMed Family Story," ChenMed, accessed December 10, 2023, https://www.chenmed.com/about-us/chen-family-story/.

5. Christopher Chen and Gordon Chen, *The Calling: A Memoir of Family, Faith, and the Future of Healthcare* (New York: Simon & Schuster, 2022).

6. Interview with Jamey Lutz, managing director of brand and service excellence, ChenMed, December 12, 2022.

7. Interview with Dr. Daniel McCarter, national director of primary care advancement, ChenMed, December 12, 2022.

8. Interview with Dr. Gordon Chen, chief medical officer, ChenMed, December 12, 2022.

9. Interview with Dr. Christopher Chen, chief executive officer, ChenMed, December 12, 2022.

10. Interview with Dr. Tameka Joseph, Chen Senior Medical Center–95th Street, December 12, 2022.

11. Interview with Dr. Gordon Chen, chief medical officer, ChenMed, December 12, 2022.

12. Interview with Matthew Kaminske, director, Chen Senior Medical Center—Hollywood, Florida, December 12, 2022.

13. Interview with Dr. Yahaida Rimola-Dejesus, Chen Senior Medical Center—Hollywood, Florida, December 12, 2022.

14. "The Updated APM Framework: Figures 1 & 4," Health Care Payment Learning and Action Network, accessed December 10, 2023, https://hcp-lan.org/workproducts/apm-figure-1-final.pdf.

15. Troyen A. Brennan, *The Transformation of American Health Insurance: On the Path to Medicare for All* (Baltimore: Johns Hopkins University Press, 2024).

16. Alan Condon, "Nearly 80% of Physicians Now Employed by Hospitals, Corporations: 5 Things to Know," Becker Hospital Review, April 11, 2024, https://www.beckershospitalreview.com/hospital-physician-relationships/nearly-80-physicians-now-employed-by-hospitals-corporations-report-finds.html#:~:text=More%20than%2077%25%20of%20U.S.,2.

17. Susanna Vogel, "Allina Health Doctors Unionize over Health Systems Objections," Health Care Dive, January 17, 2024, https://www.healthcaredive.com/news/allina-health-doctors-union/704751/#:~:text=It's%20another%20victory%20for%20Doctors,union%2C%20according%20to%20NLRB%20documents.

18. Interview with Dr. Danielle Fincher, June 16, 2024.

19. Interview with Dr. James Tracy, June 18, 2024.

20. Interview with Dr. Allison Rigel, June 19, 2024.

21. Interview with Dr. Natasha Khawaja, June 19, 2024.

22. Thomas Piketty, *Capital in the 21st Century* (Boston, MA: Harvard University Press, 2013).

23. "How Has Wealth Distribution in the United States Changed over Time," USA Facts, November 13, 2023, https://usafacts.org/articles/how-has-wealth-distribution-in-the-us-changed-over-time/#:~:text=Americans%20held%20roughly%20$137.6%20trillion,Population%20Profiles.

24. Troyen Brennan, "Concierge Care and the Future of General Internal Medicine," *Journal of General Internal Medicine* 20, no. 12 (2005): 1190, https://onlinelibrary.wiley.com/doi/full/10.1111/j.1525-1497.2005.00276.x.

25. Phil Galewitz, "Hospitals Cash In on a Private Equity-Backed Trend: Concierge Physician Care," KFF Health News, April 1, 2024, https://kffhealthnews.org/news/article/concierge-medicine-physician-practices-hospitals-private-equity/.

26. Mercer, *Worksite Health Centers: 2021 Survey Report* (Dallas: National Association of Worksite Health Centers, 2021), https://www.mercer.com/content/dam/mercer/attachments/north-america/us/us-2021-worksite-health-centers-survey-report.pdf.

27. "Direct Primary Care versus Advanced Primary Care: What Is the Difference?," Marathon Health, June 5, 2023, https://www.eversidehealth.com/blog/direct-primary-care-v-advanced-primary-care.

28. Brennan, *Transformation of American Health Insurance*.

29. Ann O'Malley, Rumin Sarwar, Cindy Alvarez, and Eugene Rich, "Why Primary Care Practitioners Are Not Joining Value-Based Payment Models: Reasons and Potential Solutions," Commonwealth Fund Brief, July 17, 2024, https://www.commonwealthfund.org/publications/issue-briefs/2024/jul/why-primary-care-practitioners-arent-joining-value-based-payment.

30. "Making Care Primary (MCP) Model," Center for Medicare and Medicaid Services, accessed November 13, 2024, https://www.cms.gov/priorities/innovation/innovation-models/making-care-primary.

31. Centers for Medicare and Medicaid Services, *Innovation Center Strategy Refresh: October 2021* (Washington, DC: CMS, 2021), https://www.cms.gov/priorities/innovation/strategic-direction-whitepaper.

32. Heather Landi, "CVS Closes $10.6 Billion Acquisition of Oak Street Health to Expand Primary Care Footprint," Fierce Health Care, May 2, 2023, https://www.fiercehealthcare.com/providers/cvs-closes-106b-acquisition-oak-street-health-expand-primary-care-footprint/.

33. Michelle F. Davis, "Walmart Explores Buying Majority Stake in ChenMed," Bloomberg, September 8, 2023, https://www.bloomberg.com/news/articles/2023-09-09/walmart-is-said-to-explore-buying-majority-stake-in-chenmed/.

34. Heather Land, "Walgreens to Close 60 VillageMD Clinics as Part of Aggressive Cost-Cutting Strategy," Fierce Health Care, October 12, 2023, https://www.fiercehealthcare.com/providers/walgreens-close-60-villagemd-clinics-part-aggressive-cost-cutting-strategy/.

35. Richard Gilfillan and Donald Berwick, "Medicare Advantage, Direct Contracting and the Medicare Money Machine, Part 1: The Risk Score Game," *Health Affairs Forefront*, September 29, 2021, https://www.healthaffairs.org/content/forefront/medicare-advantage-direct-contracting-and-medicare-money-machine-part-1-risk-score-game.

36. Brennan, *Transformation of American Health Insurance*.

37. Linda McCauley, Robert L. Phillips, Marc Meisnere, and Sarah K. Robinson, eds., *Implementing High-Quality Primary Care: Rebuilding the Foundation of Health Care* (Washington, DC: National Academies Press, May 2021).

38. Andrew Ryan, Jared Perkins, and David Meyers, "Are Changes to the Medicare Physician Fee Schedule Driving Value in the US Health Care?," *Health Affairs Forefront*, August 12, 2024, https://www.healthaffairs.org/content/forefront/changes-medicare-physician-fee-schedule-driving-value-us-health-care.

39. Andy Slavitt and Andie Steinberg, "Mainstreaming Value-Based Care," Town Hall Ventures, accessed November 13, 2024, https://www.townhallventures.com/news-feeder/mainstreaming-value-based-care.

40. Noam Scheiber, "Doctors Unionize at Big Health Care System," *New York Times*, October 13, 2023, https://www.nytimes.com/2023/10/13/business/economy/doctors-union.html.

41. Soleil Shah, Suhas Gondi, and Amol Navathe, "Paying More for Primary Care—A New Approach by Medicare," *JAMA*, December 12, 2024, https://jamanetwork.com/journals/jama/fullarticle/2827947.

42. "Teaching Health Center Graduate Medical Education (THCGME) Program," Health Resources and Services Administration, accessed November 13, 2024, https://bhw.hrsa.gov/funding/apply-grant/teaching-health-center-graduate-medical-education/.

43. Deborah Williams, Lisa M. Grabert, Brian J. Miller, Betty Rambur, and Gail R. Wilensky, "Reducing Hospital Costs without Hurting Patients," *Health Affairs Forefront*, October 20, 2023, https://www.healthaffairs.org/content/forefront/reducing-hospital-costs-without-hurting-patients/.

44. "Summary of the Bipartisan Primary Care and Health Workforce Act," website of US Senator Bernie Sanders, September 14, 2023, https://www.sanders.senate.gov/wp-content/uploads/Bipartisan-Primary-Care-and-Health-Workforce-Act-Summary_09.14.2023.pdf.

45. John Berger, *A Fortunate Man: The Story of a Country Doctor* (London: Vintage Books, 1997).

46. Berger, *Fortunate Man*, 53.

47. Berger, *Fortunate Man*, 168.

48. See, e.g., James Deming, John Beasley, and Christine Sinsky, "Giving Patients the Focused Attention They Deserve," *JAMA Internal Medicine* 184, no. 1 (2024): 5–6, https://jamanetwork.com/journals/jamainternalmedicine/article-abstract/2811332.

49. Jeffrey Harris, "An AI-Enhanced Electronic Health Record Could Boost Primary Care Productivity," *JAMA* 330, no. 9 (2023): 801–2, https://jamanetwork.com/journals/jama/fullarticle/2808295.

50. Discussion with Alan Hutchison, Ryan Foley, and Garrett Adams, primary care team, Epic Systems Corporation, June 12, 2023.

51. Aaron Tierney, Gregg Gayre, Brian Hoberman, et al., "Ambient Intelligence Scribes to Eliminate the Burden of Clinical Documentation," *NEJM Catalyst* 5, no. 3 (2024): https://catalyst.nejm.org/doi/pdf/10.1056/CAT.23.0404.

52. Urmimala Sarkar and David Bates, "Using Artificial Intelligence to Improve Primary Care," *JAMA Intern Med* 184, no. 4 (2024): 343–44, https://jamanetwork.com/journals/jamainternalmedicine/article-abstract/2814643.

53. Isabel Ostrer and Louise Aronson, "The Perils of Artificial Intelligence in a Clinical Landscape," *Archives of Internal Medicine* 184, no. 4 (2024): 351–52, https://jamanetwork.com/journals/jamainternalmedicine/article-abstract/2814651.

54. Ankur J. Goel, Emily R. Curran, and Kristen O'Brien, "CMS Finalized Risk Adjustment Model in 2024 Rate Announcement for Medicare Advantage and Part D," McDermott Will & Emery, April 5, 2023, https://www.mwe.com/insights/cms-finalizes-risk-adjustment-model-in-2024-rate-announcement-for-medicare-advantage-and-part-d/.

55. Victoria Bailey, "MedPAC Calls on Congress to Modify Medicare Advantage Payment Policies," Public Payers News, HealthPayer Intelligence, March 21, 2023, https://healthpayerintelligence.com/news/medpac-calls-on-congress-to-modify-medicare-advantage-payment-policies/.

56. Polly Morland, *A Fortunate Woman: A Country Doctor's Story* (London: Picador, 2022).

57. Morland, *Fortunate Woman*, 120.

INDEX

Abbott, Christopher, 54–55
Abelson, Reed, 21
academic medical centers, 2–3, 27, 110–11, 139, 277, 363, 392
accountable care organizations, 51, 78–80, 85, 108, 109, 123, 146–49, 153–54, 159, 163, 166–67, 172, 174, 175, 192–93, 194, 196–97, 248, 270, 283, 351, 385; hospital-associated, 112, 202, 355; under Medicaid and Medicare, 159–62, 172, 174, 314; as MSSP basis, 51, 107–9, 157; private equity–financed, 317, 318, 319, 321, 322–23
Accretive Health, 303
ACO PC Flex program, 386
ACO REACH program, 108, 266, 300, 304–5, 315
advanced practice providers, 67–68, 78, 93, 99, 111, 167, 248, 251, 262, 281, 310, 326, 334, 335–36, 339. *See also* nurse practitioners
Advisory Board, 21, 206
Aetna, 49, 89, 122, 232, 241, 244, 270, 299, 350
Affordable Care Act (ACA/Obamacare), 22, 73, 97, 104, 126, 159, 168, 173, 178, 179, 199, 204, 239
agilon health, 49–50, 53, 54, 297–301, 304, 307, 312, 314, 318–19, 341, 381, 391
Alaska Natives: SCF health services, 129–36, 364, 374, 380; Tribal Health Compact, 129; Tribal Health Consortium, 129, 135
Albrecht, Jamie, 58–60
Aledade, 179, 214, 297–98, 301, 314–15, 340, 381, 391; Stone Creek Family Physicians, 313–24; Sunflower Health Plan, 318
Allina Health Care, 366, 385
All-Inclusive Population-Based Payment System, 147
allopathic physicians, 36, 68, 69, 78, 95, 99, 137, 152

Alternative Quality Contract, 192–93
American Academy of Family Medicine, 94
American Academy of Family Physicians, ix, 10, 25, 63, 127, 288
American Academy of Family Practice, 321
American Academy of Nurse Practitioners, 65–66
American Board of Family Practice, 2
American College of Physicians, 63, 127
American Medical Association, 13–14, 82, 124–26, 139, 365. *See also* Relative Value Scale Update Committee
American Nurses Association, 65
American Osteopathic Association, 63
AppleCare Medical Group, 248, 255
artificial intelligence, 25, 56, 71, 103, 104, 226, 263–64, 289, 389–90
Ascension Health Care System, 26, 28
Ascension Via Christi Hospital, 316, 317, 321
Ash, Arlene, 196
Aspen Valley Hospital, 202–4
Association of American Medical Colleges, 92
athenahealth, EMS platform, 48, 49, 57, 71–72, 268, 273, 327, 375
Atrius Health, 39, 237, 244–45
attribution, ix, 15, 16–17, 31, 75–76, 161, 162, 172, 305, 378
Axelman, David, 4
Ayanian, John, 107

Baig, Mirza, 39–40
Balanced Budget Act, 66, 142
Bandak, Tania, 372
Banner–University Medical Center, 279, 281, 287–88
Barnett, Michael, 67
Barry, Tim, 274
Bass, Jeff, 370–72

Basu, Sanjay, xii, 135, 163
Batniji, Rajaie, 144
Baylor Scott & White, xxiii–xxvii, 47–48, 184
Bayshore Medical Group, 257
Behavioral Health, Inc., 80
behavioral health services, 56, 59, 63, 67, 97, 122, 132, 153, 158, 160–61, 168–70, 172, 175–76, 193, 208, 209, 210, 213, 221, 253, 268, 285, 309, 325–26, 331, 349, 374–75, 387; capitated payments, 164–65, 167, 331; of FQHCs, 80, 84, 85, 164–65, 168–70, 171, 180, 181, 208, 210, 213, 215; of private equity–financed practices, 307, 319, 325–26, 330–32
Berenson, Robert, 127, 128, 364, 385
Best, Lydia, xxv–xxvii
Beth Israel Lahey Health, 360
Bhuyan, Natasha, 287–88
billing practices, 19, 45, 82, 124–25, 293, 385; revenue cycle system, 27, 48, 50–51, 54, 120, 156–57, 236, 249, 255, 259, 273, 314, 327–28
Billings, Stephanie, 82–84, 89
Bingham, Robert, 4
Bipartisan Primary Care and Health Workforce Act, 98
Bitton, Asaf, 106
BJC HealthCare, 110–11, 119
Blankemeier, Julie, 336–37
Blue Cross Blue Shield, 27–28, 49, 89, 122, 145, 147, 162, 177, 190–97, 206, 270, 318; Association, 190, 191–92
Bodenheimer, Thomas, 86–87
Boebert, Lauren, 198, 206
Borys, Tom, 376
Boston Medical Center, 167; HealthNet Plan (WellSense), 159
Boyd, Jessica Henderson, 366
Brewer, Rosalind, 273–74
Brittle, Rachel, 315, 316
Brooks, Ross, 204, 205, 206–9, 211, 212
Buchholz, Ryan, 366
burnout, xiii, xv, xx, xxi, 32, 42–43, 53, 71, 84, 170, 181, 227, 228, 247, 262, 282, 287–88, 305, 312, 316, 334–35, 344, 362–63, 389
Burrell, Chet, 193–94
Bush, Christopher, 197

Cahaba Medical, 27
Cai, Christopher, 294–95

California Hospital, 246, 260, 262
Calling, The (Chen and Chen), 346, 352–53
Cambridge Health Alliance Center, 172
Caminiti, Kendahl, 183–84
Capital District Physicians' Health Plan, 195–97
capitation payment system, xiii, 13, 14–16, 37, 61–62, 82, 138, 147, 172, 175, 238, 270, 349; in CINs, 49, 50–52, 55, 57–58; CMS/CMMI strategy, 123; coding function in, 240–45; CPC+ and, 105–6; fee-for-service system comparison, 40, 101, 352; financial risk/risk adjustment in, viii–ix, 12–13, 122, 194–95, 240–45, 257, 328; in FQHCs, 74, 79–80, 81–82, 85, 183; health insurers' opposition to, 220; in HMOs, 238; in independent physicians' groups, 246, 303; in Medicaid, 14, 82, 142–43, 159, 160–61, 162–63, 166, 170; in Medicare Advantage, 52, 53, 55, 75–76, 240–41; non-visit-based care under, 103; percentage-of-premiums-based, 52, 238, 246, 249–50, 277, 304–5, 319, 348, 350, 361–62; percentage-of-total-revenues-based, 106; per-member, per-month payments, 12, 156, 179, 195, 196, 207, 318–19, 361; in private equity–financed practices, 319, 331, 334; states' promotion of, 162–63; as value-based primary care basis, viii–ix, 45, 162–63, 377–79
care coordination, x, xix, xvi, 10, 59, 63, 83, 85, 122, 167, 193–94, 200, 208, 213, 216–17, 228, 306, 318, 322, 327, 329, 339, 355, 359, 359, 360–61
care management, 56, 58–59, 67, 79, 84–85, 105, 114, 115, 121, 122, 130, 146, 159–60, 175, 188, 208, 213, 215, 218, 219, 223, 225, 226–27, 229–30, 251, 267–68, 282, 304, 335–36, 355, 360–61
Carter, Kena, 286
Casalino, Lawrence, 245, 246
case management, 83–84, 114, 130, 146, 150–51, 153, 205, 208, 210, 215, 219, 221, 284, 285, 356
Castlight Health, 300, 314
Catalyst Health, xxii–xxiii, 46–60, 62, 75, 85, 86, 88, 214, 260, 263, 327, 341, 342, 363; Stellus Rx pharmacy service, 50, 59; Village Health Partners, 47, 58–60
Centene, 270

Centers for Disease Control and Prevention, 314

Centers for Medicare and Medicaid Innovation, 22, 88, 104–8, 123, 376; CPC and CPC+ programs, 105–7, 200–201, 303

Centers for Medicare and Medicaid Services, xix, 76, 88, 104–5, 109, 126, 143, 154, 175, 187, 252–53, 361–62, 376, 379, 380; ACO PC Flex program, 386; ACO REACH program, 108, 266, 300; authority over RUC, 126–27, 384–85; Making Care Primary program, 107, 123, 138, 379–80; Medicare Advantage oversight and reform, 19, 239, 242, 391; Multi-Payer Advanced Primary Care Practice initiative, 146; Stars program, 27, 249, 251, 253, 259, 350

Central Ohio Primary Care, 298–313, 341, 342; Foundation, 310

Chari, Roopa, 170

charting, 33–34, 71, 83, 114, 117, 120, 184, 210, 212, 226, 256, 268, 269, 273, 280, 281, 309, 323, 339, 389

Chen, Candice, 96

Chen, Christopher, 346, 347, 352–53, 354–55

Chen, Gordon, 346, 352–54, 355, 357

Chen, Jen-Ling James, 270, 345–46

Chen, Jessica, 352, 353

Chen, Mary, 348

Chen, Nelson, 346

ChenMed primary care practices, 266, 270, 345–62, 363, 364, 390, 391; InTouch Health, 353; Senior Medical Care Center, 359–61

Cherry, Wendell, 264

Children's Health Insurance Program, 204–5

Chin, William, 252

chronic disease management, x, xxiv, 29, 34, 38, 57, 59, 62–63, 107, 112, 134, 144, 145–46, 148, 157, 162, 164–65, 193, 223, 271, 282, 343, 385

Chronic Illness and Disability Payment System, 162

Cigna, 122, 145, 147, 190, 232, 270, 308

Cityblock Health, 324–33, 340, 341, 381

Clayton, Dubilier and Rice, 270–71, 297–98, 299–300, 303–4

clinically integrated networks, 51–60, 61, 218–19. *See also* Catalyst Health; Monument Health; USMD; WellMed

Coastal Medical, 156–58

Cochran, Susan, 4, 5

coding and documentation, 10–11, 13, 23, 50, 135, 157, 163, 179–80, 182, 227, 243, 249, 259, 289, 313, 339, 390–92; as administrative responsibility, 253; AI-based, 276, 278; in behavioral health care, 169–70; burden-of-illness tools, 304; CMS-HCC model, 240; code weight changes, 240–41, 243, 391; CPT codes, 124–26, 127–28; diagnosis-related groups, 311; for financial risk/risk adjustment, 162, 240–44, 269, 369, 391; G2211 code, 127; HCPCS, 124–25; inappropriate or fraudulent practices, xix, 75, 76, 241–44, 252–53, 309, 350, 364, 391–92; in Medicaid, 241; in Medicare Advantage, 75, 76, 240–44, 309, 350, 390–92; in private equity–financed practices, 319; reforms, 243–44, 385; as revenue driver, 252–53, 257; team-based, 285

Cohen, Mandy, 314

Cohen, Stuart, 28–30, 31, 35–36

Coleman, Jacob, 284, 285, 286

Colorado: Community Health Network, 206; Health Services Corps, 206, 213; Medicaid program, 198–99, 207–8, 220–21. *See also* Rocky Mountain Health Plan

commercial (private) health insurers, 16, 37, 47, 49–50, 89, 127–28, 146, 154–58, 232; CPT/HCPCS-based billing, 125; fee-for-service payments, 135; FQHC patient coverage, 204–5; hospital payment rates, 61; integrated delivery systems and, 16; preference for fee-for-service contracts, 49–50; primary care expenditures, 154–58, 174–75; private equity–financed, 310, 318; in privatized health care, 74–75; profit motive, 189–90; relationship with Medicaid, 143–44; relationship with Medicare Advantage, 54–55; replacement by government-sponsored health insurance, 393; in single-payer systems, 11, 41, 234–35; state-based oversight, 140, 186; support for value-based care, xx, 113, 138, 380

Commonwealth Care Alliance, 329

community-based approach, xxiv–xxvii, 133–34, 135, 145–46, 200–201

Community Care Cooperative, 78–80, 85, 163, 166–67, 172

Community Health Center Fund, 73

community health centers. *See* federally qualified health centers
Community Health Systems, 119–20
community health workers, xxv, 67, 87, 149, 181, 326, 327, 328, 330, 331–32, 336, 387, 388
Community Resource Network, 209
comprehensive care organizations, 12
concierge care, 41, 234, 276–77, 279, 369–73, 378. *See also* One Medical
Congressional Budget Office, 98, 105, 109
Conkling, Donna, 4, 5–6
Connors, Lisa, 84–85
Consolidated Appropriations Act, 94–95
consumerism, 23, 24, 40–41, 46
contracts, with health insurers, 49, 61; with ACOs, 108–9; capitated, 49, 57–58; with CINs, 48, 49–50, 51; dual eligible beneficiaries-focused, 329–30; fee-for-service, 49–50, 52, 61, 101; financial risk-based, 317, 318, 345, 384–85; full-risk, 345, 378; with integrated delivery systems, 57–58; with Medicare Advantage, 51–53; percentage-of-premium, 52, 238, 246, 249–50, 277, 304–5, 319, 334, 346, 348, 350–51; population health-focused, 122; with private equity–financed practices, 310, 318; subscription-type, 49; value-based, 48, 49–50, 51, 113, 122, 319, 386
convenor/facilitator services, 297, 314, 341
Conviva, 265–70
Coodley, Gregg, 234
coordinated care organizations, 174–76, 178
Corbett, Verlyn, 133–34
corporatization, of health care, 14–15, 40–41, 189–90, 365
costs, of health care, xii, xix, 13, 61, 134, 188, 377–78; under Blue Cross Blue Shield plans, 194, 195; cost control, viii, 16, 161, 173–74, 193, 236–37, 290; cost-effectiveness, viii, 12, 16, 45, 166, 173, 222–23, 229, 244, 300, 344, 352–53; CPT codes and, 124; effect of private equity firms on, 293–94; health care expenditures, xiii, xiv, 98, 106, 147, 154–55, 174–76, 234, 239–40, 343–44, 393; health insurers' role, 232; of hospitals, 202; of integrated delivery networks, 48; under Medicare Advantage, 241; under PCMHs, 194; per capita, 198

Council of Primary Care Nurse Practitioners, 65
COVID-19 pandemic, 42, 79, 114, 115, 150, 165, 167, 169, 195, 205, 212–13, 225, 228, 251, 254, 259, 307, 316, 321, 367
cross-coverage, 283
Crow, Christopher, xxii, 46–49, 53, 55, 58, 59, 244
Crowley, Athena, 102
Cunningham, Amy, 322–24
Cutting for Stone (Verghese), 10
CVS Health, xv, 223, 245, 271, 272, 275, 280, 341; Oak Street Health, 297, 333–40, 341, 358, 362, 381

Dartmouth Atlas of Health Care, 220
Dartmouth Hitchcock Medical Center, 147, 151, 153
Dartmouth Medical School, 4, 108
data analytics, 29, 58, 106, 175, 235–36, 304, 330, 331, 338, 374, 389–90, 391
Davidson, Harley, 181–84
DaVita dialysis clinic chain, 247, 252, 261
Deaconess health care system, 116
Dean Clinic, 110
Decker, Wyatt, 237, 245
Deep, Donald, 310–12
delivery system reform incentive payments, 159–60
Democratic party, 73, 109, 142, 145, 159
Denstad, Tyler, 248–49, 253
Desai, Amar, 237, 245, 347
Desert Samaritan Medical Center, 283
digital medicine, 249, 261, 263–64, 276, 277, 280, 289, 353
Dignity Health, 262, 279–80
Dimock Community Health Center, 331
direct primary care, 41, 234, 276–77, 279, 369–75; Direct Primary Care Coalition, 370
Discipline and Punish (Foucault), 11
Doctoring . . . (Cassell), 15–16
Doctor's Council, 365, 366, 367
documentation. *See* coding and documentation
Doing Better and Feeling Worse (Knowles), 1500
Dorado, James, 308–10
Dorney, Ann, 4–7, 14, 42–43
Dougé, Geronie, 260, 261, 262

Doyle, John, 314
Drago, Ozzie, 357, 358

Eby, Doug, 130, 134, 135
Echeverria, Luis, Jr., 156–57
eHealth, 216
electronic medical record systems, 6, 10–11, 23–25, 31, 32, 33–34, 38–39, 69, 86, 200, 222, 223, 224, 226, 227, 229–30, 234, 255, 256, 266, 268, 285, 286, 347, 360, 388, 389; AI integration into, 71, 104; Allscripts, 256; application programming interfaces, 280; athena, 48, 49, 57, 71–72, 268, 273, 327, 375; Canopy, 334, 336, 338, 339; Cerner, 29, 132, 287; CHIRP, 286, 287; of CINs, 48, 54, 57; Curity, 354–55, 358; eClinicalWorks, 219, 268, 316, 318; Elation, 268; electronic reminders, 306; federal funding, 23–24, 56; Greenway, 334, 338–39; HIEs and, 216; interconnectivity issue, 70, 330; KLAS ranking, 71–72; MEDITECH0, 151; NextGen, 179, 209, 279; 1Life, 280–81; as quality-of-care information source, 302, 318; regulatory oversight, 70; social support information in, 209
electronic messaging, xv, xxiii, 70, 71, 103, 226, 227, 228, 323, 229, 230, 256, 289, 338–39, 372, 389
Elevance Health, 191, 270–71
Ellis, Randall, 196
emergency department utilization, x, xii, 28, 56, 105, 119–20, 133, 150, 162, 175, 179, 185–86, 193–94, 196, 210, 212, 218, 265, 268, 293, 361; for pediatric patients, 185–86; private equity approach, 293, 298, 299, 302, 307, 309, 311, 315, 318, 319, 322, 331, 334
empanelment, 86, 130, 132, 134, 179, 209, 215, 273
Employee Retirement Security Act, 18, 140, 143–44, 145, 155
employers: health care reform role, 91, 203–4; on-site primary care services for, 373–75; of physicians, 237, 365
employer-sponsored health insurance, 17–18, 26, 127–28, 265, 277–78, 375; self-insured, 49–50, 140, 143–44, 158, 203, 373–75
Ensrude, Jayceen, 122
Enthoven, Alain, 12, 13

entrepreneurial primary care practices, 45–46, 51, 118–23, 205, 266, 292, 296–98, 333–34, 375
Epic (EMR system), 39, 57, 69–72, 79, 81, 83, 101, 104, 111–12, 114, 117, 120, 153, 163, 166–67, 185, 219, 224, 307, 354–55; Care Everywhere program, 167, 216; Chat GPT in, 389; Kaiser Permanente's adoption of, 223, 224, 228; MyChart patient portal, 71, 83, 103, 114, 179, 225, 409n41; population health management applications, 181
EpicCare, 11
Erickson, John, 266
Esparza, Alejandro, 77–81
Essa Health, 112, 303
Everside, 373, 374
Evolent Health, 297

Faherty, Brian, 168–70
Fallon, John, 99–100
Fallon, Michael, 99–100
Fallon Health, 159
family medicine: development, 1–4; as specialty, 21; training in, xxviii, 2, 27, 28, 36, 46, 53, 69–70, 94, 95, 100, 111, 118, 165, 166, 184, 227, 256, 336, 351
Faulkner, Judith, 11
federal government, influence on value-based primary care, 42, 87–88, 91–139, 344; Biden administration, 75, 94–95, 105, 144; Bush administration (George H. W.), xix, 22, 72; Bush administration (George W.), 22, 73, 104; Clinton administration, 11–12, 14, 15–16, 60–61; Ford administration, 72; health care expenditures, 383; Johnson administration, 72; labor laws, 139; Nixon administration, 14, 72; Obama administration, 104, 198, 214, 217; organizational restructuring focus, 92, 104–10; population health services, 129–36; primary care clinician training support, 92–104, 137–38, 386–87; Reagan administration, 72; Trump administrations, 73, 95, 104, 105, 144, 369, 383
federally qualified health centers, 22, 25, 69, 98, 135–36, 137, 147–48, 187, 261, 378, 380; Aledade's contracts with, 314–15; Cahaba Health, 27; capitation payment system, 85, 185; clinician training role, 72–73, 98;

Index   441

federally qualified health centers (*cont.*) collective bargaining units, 366–68; in Colorado, 197–222, 203; diagnostic coding practices, 243; EMR systems, 79, 81; financial risk, 163–64; funding, 72–74, 97, 163–64, 182; government funding, 72–74, 97, 163–64, 182, 376; in Massachusetts, 76–85, 159; MCOs' relationship with, 159; Medicaid funding, 178, 270; Medicaid patients, 74, 159, 204, 230, 243, 376; in New Hampshire, 149; NHSC's role, 82, 84, 97; in Oregon, 69–70, 138, 176–86, 315; performance quality, 164, 187; private equity affiliations, 317; Section 330 grants, 72, 73; uninsured patients, 165, 167, 178, 230, 376; unionization initiatives, 366–68; in Vermont, 147–48, 149. *See also* Holyoke Health Center; Lynn Community Health Center; Mountain Family Health Centers; One Community Health

Federal Tort Claims Act, 183

Federal Trade Commission, 236

fee-for-service payment system, vii, viii, 13, 21, 25, 27, 36–37, 38, 50–51, 86, 143, 219–20, 343, 363–64; adverse effects on health care system, xii–xiii, 8–9, 13, 23, 40, 44, 46–47, 61, 68, 91–92, 188, 305, 323–24, 343–44, 362; under Blue Cross Blue Shield, 190–91, 192; under employer-sponsored health insurance, 17; HCPLAN recommendations, 361–62; health insurers' attitudes toward, 89; hospitals' support for, 90, 124, 136, 220, 375, 377; of integrated delivery systems, 16, 49; of IPAs, 218, 220; managed care versus, 11–12, 13–17; of Medicaid, 143; of Medicare, 51, 52–53, 143; organized medicine's support for, 13–14; in population-based health care, 135; in private equity–financed practices, 294, 295, 305, 306, 308–9, 310, 312, 315–16, 318–19, 320–21, 323; proposed reforms, 383–86; RVUs-based, 158; SDOHs services and, 331; specialists' support for, 126–27, 375, 377; in transition to value-based care, 135–36, 345, 378–80; UAB Medicine case study, 25–38, 50, 86, 90, 114, 363; in underserved populations, 187

Fenn, David, 132

Fernandez, Art, 205, 206–7

Fernandopulle, Rushika, 277, 278

Fields, Clive, 272

financial risk and risk adjustment, 12–13, 60, 113, 117–18, 176, 186, 223, 254, 269, 300, 313, 328, 345, 348, 350, 361, 362, 381, 384–85; in ACOs, 107–8, 147, 159, 162, 173–74, 194, 196–97; in advanced primary care, 345; as basis for health care cost-effectiveness, 300; in Blue Cross Blue Shield plans, 194–95; category 3B level, 176; of CINs, 61, 218–19; CMS-HCC model, 240; codes, 314; downside, 159, 192, 201, 299, 318, 350; in FQHCs, 74, 163–64; for gaps in care, 350; of global capitation, 265, 270; health promotion teams and, 56; of IPA contracts, 265; of limited liability partnerships, 317, 318; in Medicaid, 143, 161–62, 163, 173–74, 201, 218–19, 240; in Medicare, 107, 161, 217, 240, 251, 257, 270, 312; in Medicare Advantage, xix, 51–52, 53, 55, 75, 76, 113, 122, 218–19, 242–43, 264–65, 275, 277, 290; in Medicare Shared Savings Programs, 314; partial, 122; in PCMH programs, 194–95; in PPOs, 17–18; in private equity–financed health care, 297, 299, 300–301, 303–4, 306, 318–19; in retail health clinic sector, 271, 272–73; Risk Adjustment Data Validation rule, 242; risk-bearing entities, 304; stop loss limits, 55; in 3PC program, 194–95; upside, 159, 192, 201, 299, 318; in value-based care, 113, 122, 265, 378

financial waste, vii, 13, 18, 40, 44, 45, 51–52, 61–62, 74, 88, 110, 138, 244, 291, 305, 375, 377, 383, 409n42

Fincher, Danielle, 366–67

Firtch, Grace, 224, 229

Fischer, Elliott, 108, 109

Fodor, Kim, 152

Ford, Loretta, 65

for-profit health care companies, xvii, 14–15, 232–35, 232–91, 340–42, 350, 382; health care reform advocacy, 89; Medicare Advantage focus, 290–91; retail health clinics, xv, 271–75, 290–91, 297; role in value-based primary care, 88, 233–34, 344, 380–83

Fortunate Man, A (Berger), 388

front office staff, 282, 359

gainsharing, 47, 48, 112, 208

Garg, Vivek, 265

gatekeeper role, of primary care physicians, x, 11, 15, 16, 17, 21, 24, 55–56
Gawande, Atul, 198, 199, 214, 217, 220
general medicine, relation to primary care, 1–3, 38, 86
Gettinger, Dave, 32–34, 390–91
Gitomer, Richard, 230
Goldman, Anna, 67
Goldman, Lee, 33
Gordon, Patrick, 201, 203, 220–22, 379
Graduate Medical Education program, 20, 93–95, 96–97, 137–38, 386–87
Grand River Health, 203
Greater Lawrence Community Health Center, 165, 166
Great Recession, 73, 205
Greene, Stephen, 348, 349, 351
Griffin, Ryan, 172–73
Group Health Research Institute, 62
Gruman, Alan, 34–35, 36
Grumbach, Kevin, 234–35
Grundy, Paul, 63
Guern, Candy, 116–17
Gurwitz, Jerry, 268

Haims, Rachel, 372
Harris, Andrea, xxv
Harvard Community Health Plan, COSTAR program, 11
Harvard University, 5, 171; Medical School, Ariadne Labs, 106; School of Public Health, 125
Hawaii Medical Services Association, 162, 193, 194–95, 197
Hayes, Steve, 169
Healthcare Associates of Texas, 237
Healthcare Effectiveness Data and Information Set scores, 11, 110, 132, 151, 196, 216, 263–64, 265, 285, 317
health care exchanges, 22, 203, 206, 221
Health Care Financing Administration, 19–20, 163–64; Healthcare Common Procedural Coding System, 124–25
health care navigators, 284
HealthCare Partners, 303; Downtown Los Angeles, 251, 260–64; Southern California, 247–60
Health Care Payment Learning and Action Network, 176, 361–62

health coaches, 67, 68, 277, 284, 285, 286, 287, 374–75
health exchanges, 22, 203, 206–7
health information exchanges, 209, 210, 215–17, 281
Health Information Technology for Economic and Clinical Health, 23–24
health insurance: deductibles, 206; disparities in coverage, 37–38; out-of-pocket costs, xxii, xxvii, 13, 18, 41, 241, 260, 317, 369, 370; purchasing cooperatives, 12; stop-loss policies, 350. *See also* premiums
health insurers: financial risk, 26; negative effects on primary care, 40; negotiations with primary care groups, 302, 303; primary care advocacy, xv, 89, 188; primary care expenditures, 154–55; of private equity–financed practices, 318
Health Maintenance Organization Act, 14
health maintenance organizations, viii, 12, 14, 60, 99–100, 142, 192–93, 238, 246, 258, 308, 349–50. *See also* Kaiser Permanente
health policy commissions, 174
Health Resources and Services Administration, 65, 66, 72–73, 80, 84, 92, 94–95, 97–98, 164, 182, 183; 340B drug-pricing program, 73–74, 73–75, 78, 80, 180; as FQHC funding source, 72–74, 182, 183; Health Workforce Strategic Plan, 98; National Health Services Corps, 82, 84, 168, 205–6, 266, 300–301, 366; primary care workforce shortage predictions, 92. *See also* Graduate Medical Education Program; National Health Service Corps
health savings accounts, 235–36
Heckert, Anneliese, 211–13
Heirs of General Practice (McPhee), 3–7, 10–11
Hemingway, Jenna, 51
Heritage of Northridge, 263
Herndon, Jay, 30–32, 36, 37
Hess, Lindsay, 258–60
hierarchical condition categories, 240–41
HIV/AIDS, 97, 243
Hoff, Timothy, xx, 2, 17, 40; *Searching for the Family Doctor: Primary Care on the Brink*, 234, 271
Holyoke Health Center, 76–85, 86, 163, 164
home care/visits, 236, 243–44, 258, 268, 270, 288, 306, 311–12, 326, 328, 329, 330

homeless populations, 77, 81, 133, 171, 260–61
Hospital Corporation of America, 182, 264, 269, 272, 294
hospitalists, 33, 39, 112, 156, 256, 262–63, 267, 302, 303, 310–11, 339, 356, 366
hospitals: acquisition by physicians' groups, 246; acquisition of primary care practices, 25, 42, 47, 111–12, 116, 119–20, 156, 201, 246; as critical access facilities, 119–20, 149, 202, 214; discharge policies, 33, 216, 267, 287, 318, 327; fee-for-service basis, 90, 136, 344, 377–78; financial risk, 267; hospital-physician organizations, 15–16, 57–58; hospital privileges, 1–2; hospital rounds, 5, 29–30, 33, 35, 70, 280, 283, 310, 311, 323, 356, 360, 409n41; independent, 78; Kaiser Permanente chain, 222; Medicare Advantage contracts, 376; Medicare dependency, 376; mergers, 110–11; movement toward value-based care, 110–23; opposition to RUC re-platforming, 384; opposition to value-based primary care, 136–38; private equity ownership, 293–95; relationships with FQHCs, 207; rural, 378; safety net, 159, 167; Sisters of Charity facilities, 110, 115–16, 202, 217; site-based reviews, 254; specialist-generated income, 20, 126–27, 136, 364; teaching hospitals, 25–38, 93, 115, 137; utilization, 56, 105, 133, 150, 179, 253–54, 259, 265, 267, 269, 307, 319, 328, 339, 350, 356, 357
How to Win Friends and Influence People (Carnegie), 120
Hsiao, William, 125
Hubbard, Kristen, 157–58
Huber, Trevor, xxii–xxiii
Humana, 89, 216, 232, 290, 341, 350–51, 382; CenterWell clinics, 265–66; Conviva subsidiary, 265–70; Medicare Advantage program, 264–70

IBM, 63, 127–28
immigrants, 38, 68, 164, 165–66, 172–73, 198, 205, 367
independent practice associations, 52, 219, 253, 256, 265–70, 283, 345; Mesa City, 217–18; Mesa County, 198, 199, 216, 217, 219; Optum Health / HealthCare Partners–associated, 248, 249, 252, 253, 257, 259, 263

independent primary care practices, 116, 148, 203, 207, 214, 218, 246–47, 265, 266–67, 296–97, 316, 320, 341, 380
Indian Health Service, 129, 134, 135
Indian Self-Determination and Education Assistance Act, 129
individual primary care practices, xvii, 322–23
inequities, in health care, xiv–xv, 37–38, 143, 160, 161, 165–66, 174, 175–76, 234, 344, 369–70, 378, 380, 393
Institute of Medicine, 62
integrated delivery systems, 3, 15–19, 20, 47–48, 52, 57–58, 61, 107, 108, 194, 197, 201, 215–16, 259, 270–71, 363
Intermountain Health, 121, 202
internal medicine, 2–3, 20, 25, 29–30, 36, 65, 92, 248–49, 251, 301, 310, 311
international medical school graduates, 36, 68–69, 95–96, 99
Iora Health, 277–78, 284, 333
Iora Primary Care / One Medical Seniors, 278, 284–88, 286, 289
IPAs. *See* independent practice associations
Iris Healthcare, 319

Janasik, Max, 177–78, 181
Jehnsen, Jennifer, 184–86
Johns Hopkins University, 9; School of Medicine, 266, 269–70
Johnson administration, 72
Johnston, Rona, 133
Jones, Angel, 329
Jones, David, Sr., 264
Joseph, Tameka, 357–58

Kaiser, Laura, 121
Kaiser Permanente, viii, 12, 14, 15, 35, 60, 142, 197–98, 222–31, 237, 238, 249, 259, 349, 362; NorCal division, 224–30
Kaminske, Matthew, 359–60
KanCare (Kansas Medicaid program), 318
Katakam, Kalyan, 110, 114–15, 122
Katz, Lauren, 102
Keckley, Paul, xvi–xvii, xx, 345
Kelsey-Seybold Clinic, 237
Kendall, Matt, 314
key performance indicators, 117, 121
Khan, Ali, 337–38
Khawaja, Natasha, 368

Khosropour, Andrea, 338–39
King, Deborah, 247–48
Kirk, Michael, 118–22
Kitzman, Harriet, 65
Kitzman, Heather, xxv
Knaus, Gery, 199–201, 203
Knopp, Ryan, 314, 315, 317, 318–22, 323
Koller, Christopher, 154
Kothari, Dhruva, 329–31
Krechetoff, Irene, 151–52
Ku, Leighton, 98
Kyle, April, 133, 134

Landon, Bruce, 106, 230
Lassaux, Marc, 216
Lawrence Community Health Center, xxviii, 164, 167, 171
Le, Baonhan, 227–28
Lee, Tom, 276–77, 278, 289
Leff, Bruce, 269–70
Lessens, David, 134
Levine, Stuart, 303
Lewis, Charles, 65
Liao, Monica, 81–82
Lifespan hospital group, 156, 157
Lin, Helen, 228–29
Liu, Cathy, 250
Loafman, Mark, 166
Locke, Kelli, 102
Locks, Jaye, 28
Lofberg, Per, 223
Lombard, Matthew, 255–56
Los Angeles Medical Center, 82, 255
low-income and underserved populations: primary care, xiv–xv; private equity–financed primary care, 271, 297, 324–41, 358, 375, 381, 391; social-impact investments, 351. *See also* inequities, in health care; Medicaid
Lumeris, 303
Lutz, Jamey, 347–48
Lynbaugh, Joan, 65
Lynn Community Health Center, xxviii–xxix, 163, 164–73, 360

MacColl Center for Health Care Innovation, 62
Magaziner, Ira, 12
Mahaniah, Kiame, 164–65
Maine Medical Center, 300

Making Care Primary program, 107, 123, 138, 379
malpractice, viii, 15, 118–19, 183
managed care, viii, 14, 15–16, 21, 49, 52, 54, 60–61, 99–100, 104, 134, 163, 290; backlash against, 198–99, 207, 220, 223, 252, 378; Medicaid programs, 142–43, 144, 198–99; relation to primary care, 14–16, 37, 41–42
managed care organizations, 17–18, 159, 161, 175, 178, 179, 182. *See also* health maintenance organizations; preferred provider organizations
management services organization, 345
Marathon Health, 373–75
Margolis, Robert, 246–47, 251, 252, 260
Markus, Jerry, 132–33
Marquez, Amy, 183–84
Marshall, Roger, 98
Martinez, Beth, 51
Massachusetts: Executive Office of Health and Human Services, 164; Health Policy Commission, 174; Health Safety Net Program, 167; uninsured population, 159, 165
Massachusetts Coalition for the Homeless, 171
Massachusetts General Brigham Hospital, 166, 170, 171, 371–72
Massachusetts General Hospital, 240–41, 370–71; Institute of Health Professionals, 172
MassHealth (Medicaid program), 82, 85, 88–89, 141–42, 144, 159–73; capitated payment program, 162–63, 166, 167, 170; Community Partners, 160; DSRIPs, 159–60; Flexible Services Program, 160; at FQHCs, 164–73; risk-adjustment strategies, 161–62; waivers, 159–61, 163
Matthews, Kameron, 332
Mayo model, of health care, 99
McCallister, Michael, 264
McCarter, Daniel, 351–52
McCauley, Lindsay, 3
McClellan, Mark, 108, 109
McKown, Christopher, 277
McMahon, Laurence, 23–24, 128–29
McPhedran, Alex, 4
MDVIP, 370
Medforth, 96

Medicaid, 37, 45, 65, 74, 115, 119, 141, 142, 147, 246, 263, 318; acute care coverage, 325; all-payer programs, 143–44; alternative payment model, 361–62; beneficiaries' medical practice acceptance rate, 74, 143; beneficiaries' turnover rate, 144; capitation-based payments, 14, 83, 142–43, 144, 149, 159, 160–61, 207–8, 221, 361–62, 383; continuous coverage issue, 176; CPT/HCPCS-based billing, 124–25; dual eligible beneficiaries, 330–31; eligibility, 206–7, 330–31; expansion under ACA, 22, 73, 173, 179, 204; federal funding, 141–42, 144; fee-for-service basis, 135, 143, 198–99, 207; financial risk payments, 163–64, 201; as FQHCs' funding source, 72, 73, 78, 163–64, 168, 178, 204–5, 207–8; as GME funding source, 94; as HIE funding source, 216; managed care contracts, 142–43; mandatory and optional services, 141–42; physician reimbursement under, 126, 135, 393; primary care expenditures, 154, 174–76; quality of care, 79–80, 392; states' role in, 141–45, 173, 186–87; waiver programs, 88, 142, 143–44, 145–48, 159–60, 159–61, 163, 165, 173, 175–76
Medicaid PRIME, 207–8, 213
Medi-Cal (California Medicaid program), 250
medical assistants, 30, 39, 67, 68, 80, 84, 113, 130, 135–36, 153, 157, 180, 205, 251, 256, 259, 261, 268, 285, 310, 312, 315, 316, 335–36, 338, 355, 359, 367–68, 374–75
Medical Expenditure Panel Survey, 154
medical loss ratio, 237–38
Medical Properties Trust, 295
medical schools/education, 42, 138; allopathic, 36, 69, 137; federal funding, 98, 302, 386–87; NHSC scholarships, 82, 84, 97, 98, 168, 184, 205–6, 266, 300–301, 366; off-shore/non-US, 36, 68–69, 77, 81, 96, 137, 386–87; osteopathic, xxii, 36, 69, 96, 99, 137, 151, 211, 322, 386–87; students' attitudes toward primary care careers, xiii, xv, 21, 64–65, 95–96, 98, 128, 288–89, 358. *See also* residents and residency programs
medical scribes, 71, 103, 114, 117, 120, 158, 273, 307, 309, 323, 334, 335–36
Medicare (traditional), 37, 65, 141, 147, 268, 300, 382–83; ACOs, 314; alternative payment model, 361–62; annual wellness visits, 113, 117, 121, 157, 273, 317, 319; beneficiary turnover rate, 144; CPT/HCPCS-based billing, 124–25; dual eligible beneficiaries, 330, 359; expenditures per beneficiary, 154; fee-for-service payments, 135, 239, 285; as FQHCs' funding source, 72, 73, 78, 204–5; as GME funding source, 93–97; hospital reimbursement program changes, 33; Humana's focus on, 264; Medicare Physician Fee Schedule (2025), 385; Payment Advisory Group, 126; per—member, per–month payments, 179, 361; Physician Group Practice demonstration projects, 107–8; physician reimbursement under, 19, 124–27, 127–28, 135, 136; primary care expenditures, 154; primary care reimbursement under, 19, 386; prospective payment system, 33; quality of care, 239–40; risk-adjustment, 240–41, 251, 257; specialists' reimbursements under, 127; as transition to single-payer system, 75, 382–83
Medicare Act, 1
Medicare Advantage, xix, 26, 29, 74–76, 109–10, 122, 218, 244, 382, 383; capitated payments, xix, 89, 240–45, 313, 360, 361; care management in, 114; chart review process, 309; CINs' arrangements with, 51–53, 218–19; comparison with traditional Medicare, 238–40, 242, 243, 244; dual eligible beneficiaries, 330; favorable selection bias, 241; financial risk/risk-adjustment, xix, 51–52, 75, 76, 163, 242, 244, 275, 290; FQHCs and, 179–80, 182, 261; home visits program, 243–44, 258, 268; patient panel size, 31, 251; patient steerage practice, 255; PPO orientation, 349–50; primary care expenditures, 174, 384; in private equity–financed practices, 290–91, 308–9, 333; prospective payment system, 88, 308–9; quality of care, 57, 239–40; reimbursement changes, xix, 376; reimbursement overpayments, 239–44, 290–91, 382; specific plans, 121, 122, 222, 238–39, 249–50, 252, 255, 264–70, 272, 275, 277–78, 284–85, 287, 290, 299, 300, 313, 346, 355–56, 359; Star Measures, 27, 50, 59, 249, 251, 253; venture capital–based contracts, 304; virtual-assisted care, 277–78

Medicare Advantage beneficiaries, 107, 114, 309; as percentage of all Medicare beneficiaries, 53, 75, 239
Medicare Modernization Act, 75, 104, 264
Medicare Part A, 265, 311
Medicare Part B, 75, 265
Medicare Part D, 265
Medicare Payment Advisory Commission, 93, 241–42, 243, 391
Medicare Shared Savings Program, 51, 107–9, 108, 123, 138, 157, 187, 215, 283, 314, 318; ACO PC Flex program, 386
Mehta, Minesh, 256–58
membership fee-based primary care, 276–77, 370; concierge care, 41, 234, 276–77, 279, 369–73; One Medical / One Medical Seniors, 276–88, 289, 333, 341; per-employee, per-month fees, 373–74
Memorial Healthcare System, 360
mental health care, 162, 164, 169, 172–73, 185–86, 282, 322, 326, 330, 331, 367. *See also* behavioral health services
mentoring, 102, 131, 281, 339, 352
Merrick, Melissa, 131
MetroWest Medical Center, 77
Mid-Columbia Medical Center, 70, 183, 184
Middlemarch (Eliot), 267, 306
migrant farm workers, 177–78, 184, 198
Milbank Memorial Fund, xiii–xiv, 22
Minnesota, Medicaid-based health reform, 144–45
mixed-compensation payment systems, 128–29
Molina, 270
Monarch HealthCare, 248, 255
Mongan, James, 223
Monument Health, 213–22; Clinical Effectiveness Committee, 218
moral hazard, 13
Mosaic Health, 270–71
Mostashari, Farzad, 314, 315
Mountain Family Health Centers, 203, 204–13; Social Health Advocates program, 208
MSSP. *See* Medicare Shared Savings Program
Myers, Griffin, 333–34
Myrter, Thomas, 151–52

National Academies of Science, Engineering, and Medicine, xiv, 7, 10, 66, 67, 94, 123–24, 384; *Implementing High-Quality Primary Care*, xi, 106–7, 126–27
national commercial health insurers, 189, 232–291; relationship with primary care, 232–35; support for value-based health care, 380. *See also* Humana; Optum Health
National Committee for Quality Assurance, 11, 58, 63, 200, 302–3. *See also* Healthcare Effectiveness Data and Information Set scores
national health care system, 233
National Health Service (UK), 1
National Health Service Corps, 82, 84, 97, 98, 168, 184, 205–6, 213, 266, 300–301, 366; Teaching Health Center Program, 97–98
National Institute for Health Care Management, 294
National Institutes of Health, xiv, 246
National Labor Relations Act, 365
National Labor Relations Board, 367
Neeley, Kurt, 286
Nelson, Steve, 346
net operating income, 121
Newell, Laura, 148–49
Nicholls, Brooke, 69–70, 180–81
Nieslanik, Maddie, 209–11
North American Medical Management, 248, 255
Northeastern Vermont Regional Hospital, 148–51; Kingdom Internal Medicine affiliation, 151–52
Northern Counties Health Care, 149
NPs. *See* nurse practitioners
Nurse Corps, 97
nurse practitioners, 3, 10, 30, 36, 39, 66, 78, 101, 102, 111, 115, 117, 151, 152, 208, 219, 226, 262, 271, 286–87, 289, 308, 343, 374–75; e-consult approach, 102–3; interactions with specialists, 118; NP:physician ratio, 209; patient panel size, 103, 117, 180, 212, 286; patient volume, 308; pediatric, 211; as percentage of primary care workforce, 65–67, 98–99, 100, 137; physician oversight, 65, 66–67, 113, 281; salaries, 103; training, 78, 102–3, 117, 138, 180, 219, 281, 286, 387; workforce increase, 65–67, 98–99, 100, 137
nurses, 36, 65, 66, 80, 84, 180, 205, 208, 228, 315; anesthetists, 65; licensed practical, 39; registered, 39, 66, 180, 182–83; training, 387

nurses' aides, 67
nursing homes/skilled nursing facilities, 293–94, 318

Oak Street Health, 271, 297, 333–41, 358, 362, 375, 381, 391
Obamacare. *See* Affordable Care Act
Office of the National Coordinator for Health Information Technology, 70, 266
OhioHealth, 301, 307, 355
Ohio State University, Wexner Medical Center, 301, 307
O'Leary, Kevin, xvi–xvii, xx
Omnibus Budget Reconciliation Act, 125
One Community Health Center, 69–70, 138, 176–86
One Medical, 276–84, 290, 297, 333, 341, 370; One Medical Seniors/Iora Primary Care, 278, 284–88, 286, 289; PeakMed, 288
Optum, 52, 100, 157, 235–37, 290; Optum Insight, 236; Optum One, 259; Optum Rx, 236
Optum Health, 39, 236, 237–39, 257–58, 269, 277, 286, 341, 347, 364; Medicare Advantage plans, 238–39, 249–50, 255. *See also* Atrius Health; HealthCare Partners; Reliant Medical Group
Oregon, value-based primary care initiatives, xx, 88–89, 173–86; CCOs, 174–76; Medicaid-based, 144, 173–74, 175, 179; Oregon Health Authority, 173; primary care payment reform, 173–76; statewide, payer-wide compact, 173–74, 176; Sustainable Health Care Growth Target Implementation Committees, 176
Oregon Health and Sciences University, 178, 179, 184, 185
organizational restructuring, of primary care, 64, 76, 129, 175, 263–64, 315–16; federal government's advocacy for, 92, 104–10
Orr, Robert, 94
Ortiz, Zachary, 279–82
osteopathic physicians, xxii, 36, 63, 68, 69, 78, 95, 96, 99, 137, 151, 152, 211, 322–24, 386–87
outpatient care, 28, 94, 202, 222, 265
overhead, 36–37, 57, 119, 233, 320, 321
Owens, Venita, xxiv

Pacificare, 52
Pacific Source Community Solutions-Columbian Gorge, 175, 179, 182
palliative care, 311, 329
parsimonious health care approach, 12, 31, 55–56, 109, 162, 176, 210, 212, 222, 223, 237, 242, 267
Partners HealthCare System, 223
Patel, Rakesh "Rocky," 283–84
Patel, Viresh, 272–74
patient-centered medical homes, 47, 50–51, 62–64, 86, 127–28, 146, 148, 155–56, 174–75, 178–79, 193–94, 215, 302–3; accreditation/certification, 58, 63, 64, 78–79, 174, 200, 302–3; Blue Cross Blue Shield support for, 193–95; FQHCs as, 78–79, 178–79; health outcomes, 64; pediatric, 62
patient panel size, 39, 41, 70, 87, 112, 121, 134, 152, 219, 227, 228, 229, 251, 262, 283, 285, 286, 288, 346. 355, 361, 371; at adult medicine clinics, 151, 152; of APPs, 167, 334; bonuses and compensation based on, 82, 101, 112, 121, 153, 157–58, 230, 255–56; at CINs, 54, 219; in concierge care, 41, 276–77, 371; financial risk-based stratification, 113; at FQHCs, 82, 83, 84, 167, 182, 185; gender inequity issue, 230; of hospital-affiliated practices, 112, 113, 114, 120, 157; impact of EMRs on, 33–34; Medicare Advantage beneficiaries-based, 31, 121, 251, 255–56, 262, 285; of NPs, 103, 117, 180, 212, 286; patient wait times and, 92–93; of physician assistants, 210; physician-patient relationship and, 83; at private equity–financed practices, 307, 316, 321, 336; at Veterans Health Administration, 286
patient portals, 24, 71, 83, 103, 114, 179, 225, 338–39, 389, 409n41
Patient Priority, The (Larsson, Clawson, and Kellar), 44–45
patients, as health services customer-owners, 132, 133
patient satisfaction, xi, 101, 130, 194, 196, 252, 265, 268, 281, 285, 302, 347, 350; net promoter score, 268, 281, 289, 348
patient visits, 183, 285, 369; appointment "no shows," 366; duration and frequency, 276–77, 285, 350, 353; group visits, 282; visit targets, 8–9; wait times, 31, 84, 92–93, 182, 347

patient volume, 31, 40, 83, 87, 119, 120, 152, 167, 210, 212, 213, 219, 225, 256, 273, 279, 281, 308, 316, 321, 323, 360, 364–65, 366, 371
Payments for Primary Care program, 194–95
PCMHs. *See* patient-centered medical homes
Pearl, Robert, 295
Pechinsky, Geoffrey, 165–66
Peralta-Machado, Francina, 337–38
Percy, Matt, 211–13
performance measures, 175–76, 194–95, 251, 259, 268–69, 285, 320, 357
Perkins, Joshua, 286–87
Permanente Medical Group, 222, 295
PersonalMD, 372–73
pharmacy chains, primary care clinics, xv, 271–75, 297, 381. *See also* CVS Health; Walgreens
pharmacy services, 50–51, 52, 56, 59, 67, 68, 74, 78, 80, 152, 157, 164, 167, 180, 200, 205, 236, 239, 268, 275, 281–82, 355; pharmacy benefits management, 235–36, 274; pharmacy support centers, 258. *See also* prescription medications
Philippe, Marc Todd, 224–26
physician assistants, 3, 36, 98, 100, 104, 111, 137, 209–10, 289, 315, 329, 343
Physician Group Practice demonstration projects, 107–8
physician-patient relationship, ix, 4–5, 6–8, 9, 15, 17, 21, 23, 24, 32, 34, 39–40, 86–87, 90, 225, 344, 348, 352, 355–56, 393–95
Physicians Medical Group of San Jose, 248
Pieninck, Brian, 194
Population-based Payments for Primary Care program, 194–95
population health management, 47, 49, 58, 105, 117–18, 121, 122, 152, 157, 200, 283, 328; accountability, 110; bonuses and compensation based on, 112–13, 116–17; employers' support for, 203; federal government's support for, 88, 104–10, 105, 107, 129–36, 144, 201; financial risk/risk adjustment, 49, 385; at FQHCs, 74, 78–79, 84, 85, 181; health insurers' support for, 89; in hospital systems, 112; integration into EMR systems, 70–71, 102, 114, 181; of Medicaid populations, 201; revenue level threshold, 135–36; team approach, 283
Poverty, by America (Desmond), 37–38

preferred provider organizations, 17–18, 23, 50, 193, 258, 259–60, 349–50
premiums, 13, 18, 118–19, 158, 202, 203, 204, 206, 238; flywheel effect, 272
prescription medications, xxii, 59, 121, 157, 185, 205, 258, 289; HRSA's 340B drug pricing program, 73–74, 78, 80, 180, 212; medication reconciliation, 122, 157; overmedication, 268; patient adherence, 50, 59, 258, 265, 329, 330; prior authorization requirement, 184–85, 272; "test-to-treat" programs, 183
preventive medicine, x, 9–10, 21, 41–42, 45, 63, 83, 179, 251, 317, 343, 345, 346, 378
Price, Geoff, 333
primary care: advanced, 345, 373–75; comprehensiveness, 3, 6, 8, 10, 32; continuity, x, xxiii, 3, 10, 16, 33, 41–42, 70, 87, 167, 363–64, 378, 392; coordination in, 10, 14, 16, 55–56, 87; definition, ix; enhanced, 196–97; extension model, 324; as foundation of health care system, xi–xxii; fundamental changes, 10–17; funding sources, 22; goals and mission, 3, 9–10; ideal components, 9–11, 86–87; proactive versus reactive, 179; recent history, 1–25; sustainability, xix–xx, 8, 120, 176, 187, 288, 394; traditional, 345; transformational, 345
Primary Care 1.0, 2.0, and 3.0, xix, xvi–xvii, xx, 9, 345, 379
Primary Care Collaborative, 65
Primary Care . . . (Starfield), xi–xii, 7–8, 9–11, 14, 16, 20–21, 34, 87
Primary Care Partners, 214
Primary Care Payment Reform Collaborative, 174
primary care practices: elements of, 36–37; self-assessment tool, 62
prior authorization, 13, 24, 35, 52, 143, 184–85, 228, 232, 239, 241, 272, 316
private equity–financed health care, xv–xvi, 40, 41, 42, 89–90, 235, 269, 292–342, 381; Aledade, 179, 201, 214, 297–98, 313–24; Central Ohio Primary Care, 298–313; Cityblock Health, 324–33; initial public offerings, 292–93, 296, 297; Oak Street Health, 333–40; proposed reforms, 294–96; quality of care, xx, 294, 297, 300, 305, 313, 319, 324–25, 351, 354; relationship with

private equity–financed health care (*cont.*) commercial health insurers, 293, 310; state oversight of, 295; Stone Creek Family Physicians, 313–24
privatization, of health care, 74–75
prospective payment system, ix, viii, xvi, 33, 40, 45, 72, 73, 75, 87, 88, 104, 221, 304–5, 308–9, 368
public health, xxiv, 21, 145, 378; Public Health Service Act, Titles VII and VIII, 72–73
Pykosz, Michael, 333–34, 336–37

Quality Health Network, 209, 210, 215–17, 218
quality of care/quality-of-care measures, xi, 11, 23, 58–59, 95, 99, 132–33, 188, 229, 251, 343, 382, 395; of AQC, 192–93; as bonuses and compensation basis, 50, 57, 101, 107, 109, 113, 132, 153, 194–95, 196, 197, 249, 255, 350; as CCPL basis, 349; CMS measures, 29; CPC+ measures, 105; effect of PCMHs on, 64; of FQHCs, 82; HEDIS scores, 11, 110, 132, 151. 196, 216, 263–64, 285, 317; KPIs, 117, 121; Malcolm Baldridge National Quality Award, 130; in private equity/venture capital–financed practices, xx, 294, 297, 300–301, 302, 305, 307, 313, 314, 317, 319, 320, 324–25, 328, 339, 351, 354; for specialists, 349
Qualtrix, 347
Quinn, Elizabeth, xxviii–xxix, 171–72
Quorum, 120

radiology services, 119, 184–85, 193, 212, 315, 355
Ramos, Jaime, 260–61, 262
Rapier, George, 52, 61
rationing, of health care, viii, x, 173
Rawle, Reija, 152–53
Recovery Act, 73
recruitment and retention, of primary care clinicians, 80, 100–102, 103–4, 112, 116, 131, 153, 158, 206, 208, 211, 213, 228, 248–49, 253, 254, 259, 263, 282, 286, 288–89, 319, 334, 349, 351–52, 358; APPs, nurses, and NPs, 205, 248; behavioral health specialists, 153, 158, 169; case managers, 205; in concierge care, 371
Redwood City Medical Center, 224
referrals, to specialists, 31, 55–56, 120, 135, 151, 193, 215, 219, 226, 229, 255, 339, 359, 375

Reicks, Gregory, 217–20, 233–34
reimbursement, for primary care, 3, 19, 27–28, 40, 66, 154–58, 232; under affordability standards, 154–56; alternative payment models, 361–62; AMA's initiatives, 124; in concierge care, 374; contracts-based increase, 48; disparity with specialty care, xiv, xiv–xv, 19–21, 65, 91–92, 126, 137; effect of contracts on, 48; for for-profit companies, 290; at FQHCs, 82; gainsharing in, 47, 48, 112, 208; in hospital systems, 112–13, 154–55; in integrated delivery systems, 19, 47, 48, 51; under Medicaid, 158; under Medicare, 19, 386; under Medicare Advantage, 290; in membership fee-based care, 374; in national health care system, 233; population-based, 361–62; proposed reforms, 364; reconciliation-based, 112; risk-based, 45–46; RVU-based, 153, 157, 272–73; traditional approach, 36–37; value-based care-based, 112–13. *See also* salaries, income, and compensation
Relative Value Scale Update Committee, 19, 100–101, 112, 125–27, 128, 137, 385; proposed re-platforming, 384–85, 386; specialty focus, 100–101, 126, 137, 364
relative value units, 37, 112, 115, 123, 125–26, 157–58, 180, 185, 197, 201, 222–23, 360; adverse effect on primary care, 87, 352, 384–86; as bonus and compensation basis, 82, 131–32, 153; as fee-for-service reimbursement basis, 158; at FQHCs, 82; recommendations for reform, 364, 384–86
Reliant Medical Group, 99–103, 244–45, 249, 258, 327; Fallon Clinic, 99–101
Republican party, 75, 109–10, 198
residents and residency programs, xiii, xiii–xiv, 2–3, 20, 26, 27, 28, 29–30, 33, 59–60, 69–70, 94, 96, 97, 103–4, 184, 227, 302, 368; for APPs and NPs, 28. 67, 67, 69–70, 102, 138, 180; expansion, 94–96, 97, 99, 137; federal funding and oversight, 92, 93–95, 96–97, 97–98, 102, 137–38, 386–87; FQCH-affiliated, 78; as hospital revenue source, 20; for NPs, 28, 67, 69–70, 102, 138, 180, 387; recruitment from, 253; in rural health, 180; unionization, 365
Resident Shortage Reduction Act, 95
Resnick, Barbara, 65

resource-based relative value scale, 19, 125–26
Ressler, Dave, 202–4
retail chain-associated health care, xv, xviii–xix, 271–75, 364, 376, 381–82
Rhode Island, health policy reforms, 88–89, 143, 144, 145, 154–58, 173, 174, 182–83, 186
Rigel, Alison, 368
Rimola-Dejesus, Yahaida, 359–61
Riverside Methodist Hospital, 301, 302, 306, 310
Robertson, Cynthia, 4
Robinson, Dorthya "Dodie," 327–28
Robinson, James, xiii, 128, 245, 246
Rocky Mountain Health Plan, 197–204, 208, 216; Medicaid plan, 198–99, 201, 203, 215, 218–19, 220–21; partnerships, 203–20
Rogers, Sean, 251–55
Rosenbaum, Sara, 98
Rosenstein, Lisa, 230
Rousse, Michael, 149, 150–51
Rubin, Amir Dan, 277, 278
Rubio, Nicole, 260, 261, 262
RUC. *See* Relative Value Scale Update Committee
rural health care, 3, 4, 67, 69–70, 74, 76, 94, 96, 99, 115–17, 116, 119–20, 129–36, 138, 149, 176–86, 178, 181, 243, 322–23, 351, 363, 377, 388; training programs, 42, 94, 96, 97, 98, 180, 386
Russell, William, 266–70
Ryan, Chelsea, 133

Sachdev, Ravi, 299, 300–301, 303–4, 332–33
St. Louis University Hospital, 110, 115
St. Mary's Hospital (CO), 115–16, 202, 214, 216, 218
salaries, income, and compensation, of primary care clinicians, xiii, 111, 123, 131–32, 151, 166, 205–6, 219, 222–23, 249, 255, 282, 307, 358, 361, 364–65; bonuses, 50, 57, 82, 96, 102, 105, 108, 108, 112, 131–32, 194–95, 196, 218, 219, 222–23, 249, 255–56, 269, 281, 304–5, 321, 350, 358, of care managers, 150–51; in concierge care, 372; CPT codes and, 128; disparities in primary care physicians versus specialists, 19–21; fee-for-service-based, 123; at FQHCs, 80, 82, 168; gender gap, 230; at HMOs, 308; initial, 102, 103, 111, 168, 219; low or inadequate, xiii, xiv–xv, 139, 168, 205–6, 362; of medical assistants, 205; of NPs, 103; number of patient visits-based, 31; as overhead, 320, 361; patient panel size-based, 82, 101, 112, 121, 153, 157–57, 230, 255–56, 336; patient satisfaction-based, 101; population health measures-based, 112; at private equity–financed practices, 307, 322; quality measures-based, 157; RVU-based, 157–58, 185, 201; in specialty care, 21

SalesForce Health, 268
Salsberg, Edward, 96
Sanders, Bernie, 98, 145
Schneeweiss, John, 100–102, 409n42
SCL Health, 217–20
selection bias, 241, 269
Serra, Connie, 177–80
Shalala, Donna, 73
Shrank, William, 144
Shumlin, Peter, 145–46
Sia, Calvin, 62
Silver, Henry, 65
Sinaiko, Anna, 64
single-payer system, 41, 49, 75, 83, 89, 145, 146, 148, 150, 172, 234–35, 239, 380–81
Sinsky, Christine, 388–89
Skowhegan Family Medicine, 4–8, 10, 14, 21, 29, 33, 35, 36, 42–43, 87
Slavitt, Andy, 385
social determinants of health focus, 115, 132, 134, 153, 161, 162, 170, 171, 171, 174, 175–76, 200, 201, 208, 209, 211, 213, 216–17, 220, 226–27, 251, 263, 310, 328, 331, 356, 361, 368, 378, 388
socialized medicine, 58
Social Security Act, Section 1115, 142
social workers, 56, 114, 200, 209, 219, 306, 322, 326, 336
SoftBank, 297, 324
Solomon, Martin, 370–71
Song, Zirui, 128–29, 294–96
SouthCentral Foundation, 129–36, 177, 364, 374, 380
Southwestern Vermont Medical Center, 152, 153
specialists and specialty care, 1, 2, 28, 105, 115, 122, 228, 238, 250, 254, 262, 304, 349, 367; adverse effects on healthcare system, 44,

private equity–financed health care (*cont.*) 343; anesthesiology, 65, 294; cardiology, 20, 21, 118, 226, 240–41, 283, 284, 352–53, 365; in ChenMed system, 349; in CINs, 55–56, 59, 215; in concierge care, 371; curbsiding consultations, 212, 281; demand and competition for, 18, 20; dentistry, 206, 250, 274, 365; dermatology, xxii, 28, 293; endocrinology, 185, 213, 262; fee-for-service payments, vii, 50, 126–27, 375; FQHCs's access to, 181, 185, 212; gastroenterology, 21, 101, 293, 296; geriatric medicine, 262, 267–68; as hospital income source, 20, 126–27, 136, 293; income, 19–20; in integrated delivery systems, 18, 48–49; interactions with hospitalists, 310–11; interactions with NPs, 118; interactions with primary care physicians, 229, 279–80, 283; internal medicine, 2–3, 20, 25, 29–30, 36, 65, 92, 248–49, 251, 301, 310, 311; multispecialty practices, 14–15, 60, 99–103; nephrology, 196, 247; obstetrics and gynecology, 2, 7, 8, 20, 171, 180–81, 250; opposition to RUC re-platforming, 384; opposition to value-based primary care, 136–37, 364; optometry/ophthalmology, 262, 274; orthopedics, 20, 21, 28, 58, 262; participation in hospital rounds, 280; pediatrics, 21, 62, 250, 328; at primary care groups, 303; private equity and, 293–94, 295, 296; psychiatry, 94–95; as RUC members, 100–101, 126; specialty deserts, 262; subcapitation contracts, 250, 254; surgical care, 20, 126, 127, 236; uninsured populations' access to, 212, 213, 233, 367, 392–93; virtual consultations, 338, 339
SSM Health, 110–23
state-based health insurers / health plans, 188–231, 380; comparison with commercial health insurers, 188–90; regulatory oversight, 188–89
states: insurance commissioners, 190; primary care expenditures, xiii; role in Medicaid, 91, 141–45; support for value-based primary care, xx, 87–89, 344, 380
Steinberg, Andie, 385
Steward Health Care, 295
Stone Creek Family Physicians, 313–24, 335
Stormont Vail Health, 316

Strohl, Robert, 309
substance abuse disorders, xxvi–xxvii, 132, 133, 146, 149, 153, 167, 171, 172–73, 184, 325
Sussman, Andrew, 96

Tang, Michael, 331–32
Teaching Health Center Program, 97–98
team-based approach, x, xxiii, 9, 10, 28, 36, 39, 57, 67–68, 86, 100, 101, 115, 156, 225, 228–29, 251, 259, 281, 283, 288, 289, 355, 356, 357, 358, 360–61, 375, 378, 388–89; in behavioral health, 169, 170; in CINs, 219; in clinician training, 121; in coding, 285; data analytics in, 389–90; in FQHCs, 84, 167, 170, 179, 208–9, 211; in population health management, 283; in private equity–financed practices, 306, 316, 322, 327, 335–36, 338; training in, 121, 130, 131, 138, 170, 389; workspace arrangements for, 130–31, 151
telemedicine, 182–83, 225, 254, 262–63, 385
Tenet hospital chain, 272
Tester, Shawn, 149–51
Texas, Medicaid program, 141–42
Texas Health Resources, 47
Thelwell, Jennifer, 315–16, 320
Thiry, Kent, 247
Thurow, Ashley, 214–15, 217, 376
Tierney, Steve, 132
Tinetti, Mary, 267–68
Tracy, James, 367–68
training, of primary care clinicians, 72–73, 80, 102, 104, 131, 137–38, 165, 166, 248, 349, 351–52; in family medicine, xxviii, 27, 28, 36, 46, 53, 69–70, 78, 94, 95, 100, 102–3, 111, 118, 137, 165, 166, 184, 227, 256, 336, 351; federal funding, 92–104, 137–38, 386–87; rural health care, 42, 94, 96, 97, 98, 180, 386; team-based 121, 130, 131, 138, 387
transfer pricing, 237–38
triage system, 84, 158, 228, 287, 289, 316
Tufts Health Plan, 159
Tufts Medical Center, 6

uninsured populations, 37, 45, 119, 383; of FQHCs, 74, 165, 204–5, 206–7, 212, 380–81; limited hospital care access, 212
unionization, xx–xxi, 41, 139, 365–68

UnitedHealthcare, 52, 54, 122, 145, 147, 190, 232, 235, 255, 346, 355, 381; Medicare Advantage plans, 218–19, 221, 255, 275; public resentment toward, 236–37, 383; Rocky Mountain Health Plan, 197–98, 199, 208, 221

UnitedHealth Group, 52, 89, 100, 197–98, 235–36, 264, 290, 382; Ingenix, 235–36; Prescription Solutions, 235–36. *See also* Optum; WellMed

US Department of Agriculture, 177, 324

US Department of Health and Human Services, 72, 123, 147

US Department of Veterans Affairs, Veterans Health Administration, 28, 138, 286, 332

Unity Health, 366–68

universal health care, 145, 159, 173, 233, 234

University of Alabama at Birmingham Medical Center, 25–38, 50, 86, 90, 114, 363, 390–91; Prime Care, 28–36, 37; Viva Health, 26–27, 28, 29, 31, 37, 50

University of Chicago, NORC, 154

University of Michigan, 23, 24, 25, 69, 184; Medical Center, 24

University of Pennsylvania, 162, 194, 195

University of Vermont Medical Center, 146–49, 153–54

University of Virginia, 351, 352

urgent care services, 32, 134, 160, 180, 236, 238, 261, 271, 273, 284, 286, 303, 309, 311, 315, 357

USMD, 52–53

utilization, of health care, vii, xiii, 13, 17, 23, 29, 61, 107, 196, 216, 251, 255, 304, 309, 328, 346, 349, 358, 373; under AQC program, 193; under Blue Cross Blue Shield programs, 162, 192; as bonuses and compensation basis, 196, 249, 285, 307, 350; under CPC+ program, 105, 106; in FQHCs, 179, 198, 216, 218, 219–20; health insurers' attitudes/policies, 216, 219–20, 232, 233–34; in hospitals, 133, 179, 253, 254, 269, 350; in IPAs, 198, 253, 254; under Medicare Advantage, 241, 251, 334, 346; in PCMHs, 47, 193–94, 195; in PPOs, 17, 23; under private equity, 294

Valley Health Alliance, 201–4
Valley View Hospital, 201–2, 203, 207, 212i

value-based primary health care, vii–xi, xv–xvi, xvii–xx, xxix, 1, 9, 12, 23, 24, 44–45, 87; as anticipatory care, 86, 136, 363–64, 368, 378, 380, 385; in CINs, 26–27, 55–56, 58–59; CMMI's support for, 105–7; as fee-for-service system alternative, 8–9, 27, 40, 41–42, 87, 363–64, 383–86; health insurers' approach to, 52; in hospital systems, 15, 110–23

value-based primary health care, issues affecting the future of, xxii–xxiii, xxix, 9, 38–43, 41–42, 46–60, 86–90, 343–95; capitated payments, 61–62, 377–79; clinician training, 386–87; demographic factors, xviii, 369; documentation and coding, 390–92; federal government's role, 42, 87–88; for-profit sectors' role, 233–34, 380–83; health care system's role, 379–80; health insurers' role, 87–88; inequities in health care, 392–93; patient focus, 17, 41–42; physician-patient relationship, 393–95; private equity's role, 42, 380–83; states' roles, 42; team-based care, 388–89; unionization, xx–xxi, 41, 139, 365–68, 385–86; value-based contracts, 48, 49–50, 51, 122, 319, 386; wealth distribution inequality, 369–70, 372–73, 378

Van Den Berghe, Clark, 166–69

VanGundy, Jason, 111–16

Varveris, Maria, 305–8, 309

venture capital–financed primary care, xx, 270–71, 292, 295–96, 297–99, 300–301, 303–4, 306, 315, 340–41, 344, 376, 381; differentiated from private equity, 292–93, 296, 340–4

Vera Whole Health, 299–300

Vermont, health policy reforms, 88–89, 144, 145–54, 186; All-Payer Accountable Care Organization Model, 146–47; Blue Cross's participation, 190; Blueprint for Health program, 146–47, 148, 149, 153; Comprehensive Payment Reform, 147–48; Green Mountain Care Board, 146–47, 148, 150; Green Mountain Health Care program, 145; Medicaid, 88–89, 145–48, 149, 150; Medicare, 144, 146–47–248, 150, 154; OneCare, 147–49, 153–54; Vermont Health and Human Services, 147

vertical integration, 17, 236, 237–38, 263, 341, 381, 382, 383
Vetter, Nicole, 117–18
Vickers, Selwyn, 27
Village Health Partners, 47, 58–60
VillageMD, 271–75
Vinh, Diana, 282
virtual health care, 223, 226, 229, 249, 262–63, 276–77, 280, 289, 338, 339

Wachter, Robert, 33
Wagner, Edward, 62
Walgreens, 271–74, 364, 381
Walmart, xviii–xix, xx, 275, 364, 381

WellMed, 51, 52–53, 61–62, 236
WellPoint Health Networks, 270
Wells, Jeff, 373, 375
Wentworth, Tim, 274
Western ACO, 202
Western Healthcare Alliance, 202
Weyenberg, Matt, 53–54
Williams, Ron, 299
Wood, Eileen, 197
workforce shortage, of primary care clinicians, xii, xiii–xiv, 64–65, 72–73, 91, 92–93, 99, 100–101, 111, 128, 137, 158, 362–63, 368–69, 384, 386–87
Wulf, William, 301–5, 306, 310, 311, 312–13, 376

Browse more books from HOPKINS PRESS

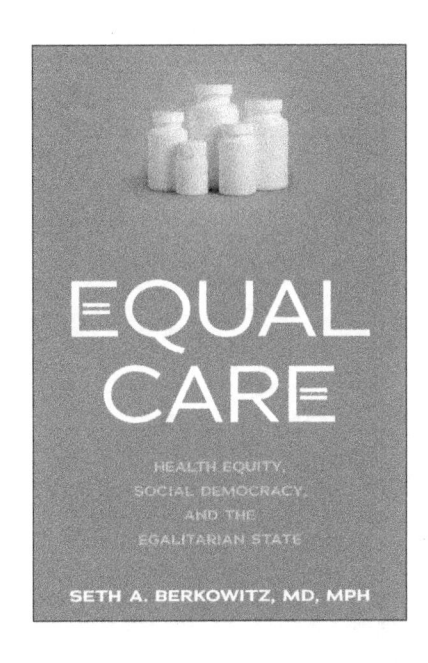

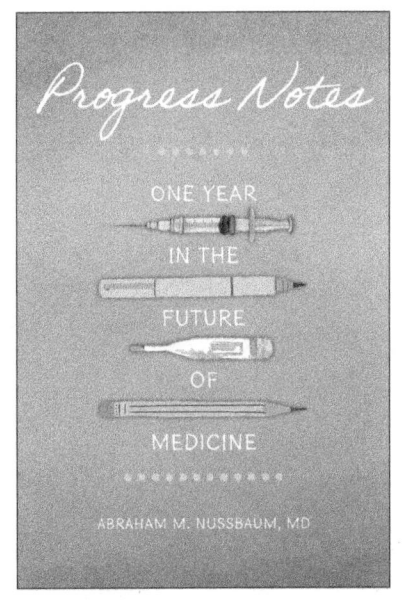

THE TRANSFORMATION OF AMERICAN HEALTH INSURANCE
ON THE PATH TO MEDICARE FOR ALL
TROYEN A. BRENNAN

EQUAL CARE
HEALTH EQUITY, SOCIAL DEMOCRACY, AND THE EGALITARIAN STATE
SETH A. BERKOWITZ, MD, MPH

BUILDING A UNIFIED AMERICAN HEALTH CARE SYSTEM
A BLUEPRINT FOR COMPREHENSIVE REFORM
GILEAD I LANCASTER, MD
FOREWORD BY CONGRESSMAN JIM HIMES
FOREWORD BY DAVID L. KATZ, MD, MPH

Progress Notes
ONE YEAR IN THE FUTURE OF MEDICINE
ABRAHAM M. NUSSBAUM, MD

JOHNS HOPKINS UNIVERSITY PRESS | PRESS.JHU.EDU